EMAIL

SEARCHING

& THE WORLD WIDE WEB

INTERNET TODAY!

Franklin, Beedle & Associates, Inc.
8536 SW St. Helens Drive, Suite D
Wilsonville, OR 97070
503/682–7668
http://www.fbeedle.com

Ernest Ackermann
Mary Washington College

Karen Hartman
Mary Washington College

President and Publisher	Jim Leisy (jimleisy@fbeedle.com)
Manuscript Editor	Sheryl Rose
Production	Susan Skarzynski
Illustrations	Steve Klinetobe
	Stephanie Welch
Cover Design	Tom Sumner
Marketing Group	Cary Crossland
	Jason Smith
	Marc Chambers
	Stacia Houston
Order Processing	Chris Alarid
	Lois Allison
	Krista Hall

Manufactured by Von Hoffmann Press, Inc.

Rights and Permissions
Franklin, Beedle & Associates Incorporated
8536 SW St. Helens Drive, Suite D
Wilsonville, OR 97070

Library of Congress Cataloging-in-Publication Data

Ackermann, Ernest C.
    Internet today : email, searching & the World Wide Web / Ernest Ackermann, Karen Hartman.
        p.   cm.
    ISBN 1–887902–43–0
    1. Internet (Computer network) 2. World Wide Web (Information retrieval system)   I. Hartman, Karen.   II. Title.
TK5105.875.I57A24   1999
004.67'8--dc21
                                                                                        98-55746
                                                                                        CIP

To the members of my family—Lynn, Karl, and Oliver—for their encouragement and support

—E. A.

To Jack, Tracy, and Hilary

—K. H.

CONTENTS

CONTENTS

CONTENTS

CONTENTS

CONTENTS

CONTENTS

CONTENTS

CONTENTS

Internet Today! is for people who want to learn to use the Internet and the World Wide Web effectively and efficiently. This book helps readers get the most from resources and services available online. Step-by-step instructions emphasize effective use of the Internet and the Web, and no prior online experience is assumed. This text is appropriate for a college-level introductory course serving students in liberal arts, humanities, and physical sciences. It covers a range of topics including services on the Internet and the Web, ways to find and evaluate online information, tips for writing Web pages, and the legal, ethical, and social issues related to the Internet.

This book is based on the best elements of our successful textbooks *Learning to Use the World Wide Web* and *Searching & Researching on the Internet & the World Wide Web*. We've updated and expanded on topics that best address the needs of students today. Thanks to the production staff at Franklin, Beedle & Associates, we've presented the material in an attractive format that is especially effective in the exercises. More important than the presentation, however, are the examples and exercises themselves, which are a result of our years of experience in teaching classes and workshops and using the Internet and Web.

We assume that readers of this book know the basics of using a personal computer, have a connection to the Internet, and have access to email and a Web browser. We use Netscape Navigator and Communicator to demonstrate skills and concepts, but other email programs or Web browsers can be used. We chose Netscape's collection of software because it works well on a variety of computer systems and can handle email, Usenet newsgroups, and interactive elements on the Web, such as JavaScript, Java applets, and inline plug-ins. Also, the Web provides a great body of support for and information about using Netscape. We've developed the text, examples, and exercises using a personal computer with Microsoft Windows. Readers will notice differences if they are using a Macintosh or Unix computer system or a Web browser other than Netscape, but the basics are the same. Our intent is to present the concepts and develop the skills that will best prepare the reader to work with a variety of Internet software.

Organization

Internet Today! introduces students to the important aspects of using the Internet and World Wide Web. The book is organized as follows:

Introduction to the Internet and the World Wide Web and instructions for using a Web browser	Chapters 1 and 2
Communication on the Internet through electronic mail	Chapter 3
Searching for and evaluating information on the Web and formulating search strategies	Chapters 4 and 5
Writing Web pages	Chapter 6
Telnet, FTP, and Gopher	Chapter 7
Legal issues, ethical issues, privacy, and security	Chapter 8

The first two chapters in the book are designed to quickly get the student started using the Internet and the World Wide Web. Chapter 1 explains basic terms and concepts, the history of the Internet, and some issues related to using the Internet; Chapter 2 covers the details of using a Web browser. Chapter 3 focuses on using electronic mail for communicating on the Internet. The examples demonstrate how to work with email in Netscape Messenger, the email program that's part of Netscape Communicator, but other email programs would work just as well here. Retrieving and working with information on the Internet—searching for and evaluating information and developing search expressions and strategies—are covered in Chapters 4 and 5. Chapter 4 introduces types of search tools: directories, search engines, virtual libraries, and other resources. Chapter 5 focuses on search strategies. Chapter 6 addresses the concepts, methods, and details of writing a Web page and getting

it noticed on the World Wide Web. Chapter 7 introduces several Internet services such as Telnet, FTP, and Gopher. Some of the important ethical, legal, privacy, and security issues surrounding the use of the Internet and the World Wide Web are covered in Chapter 8. The book concludes with a glossary of key terms. The diskette included contains additional material about using email discussion groups and Usenet news.

All of the chapters (except Chapter 8) contain step-by-step examples to demonstrate using the tools, services, and resources discussed in the text. Performing the steps provides the reader with hands-on experience. Because of the dynamic nature of the Internet and Web, providing step-by-step instructions is a risk. The Web is constantly evolving, and when you work through these examples you may see differences in the way information is displayed. Don't let this deter you. Be persistent and use your skills to adapt to a changing environment. One of the exciting things

about the Internet is its constant evolution toward becoming more and more useful.

The exercises at the end of each chapter provide further practice with the tools and techniques introduced. Doing is an important part of learning, as only practice and experience can help you master the skills necessary to use the Internet effectively. The wide variety of topics in the exercises expose the reader to many of the kinds of resources that make up the Internet.

Supplemental Materials

For adopters of this book, an instructor's guide is available on disk from the publisher. The author-maintained Web site to accompany the book, with the URL **http://www.mwc.edu/ernie/internet-today.html**, has individual Web pages for each chapter and the glossary. These pages contain current links to all the Web resources mentioned in the text. The links are periodically updated to keep the exercises and other material current.

Since Web sites often change, the updates will provide access to the most recent versions of information on the Web.

Acknowledgments

This book and all our projects wouldn't be possible without the support of our families. Ernie's wife, Lynn, and children, Karl and Oliver, and Karen's husband, Jack, and children, Tracy and Hilary, deserve special thanks and recognition. They, more than anyone else, give us the encouragement, support, love, and help that allow us to put our ideas and experiences into print.

We also want to thank the students, colleagues, and friends in Fredericksburg, Virginia, Mary Washington College, and elsewhere who have given us their encouragement and support. They've worked with us in preparing classes and workshops, listened patiently to our ideas and opinions, and (in the case of our students) shown us new ways to teach and learn. Special thanks to Steve Griffin who let us use images of his painting "Fleeing from Flamingos" in Figures 6.25 and 6.26.

Franklin, Beedle & Associates has played an important and supportive role in this project. We especially want to thank Susan Skarzynski for formatting this book, and Jim Leisy for moving the project forward. The other folks we've worked with on this project include Tom, Stephanie, Sue, Cary, Jason, Marc, Stacia, Chris, Lois, and Krista.

The reviewers listed below critiqued portions of prior manuscripts or the complete manuscript for this book. Their input has been invaluable and has greatly improved the quality of our effort.

David Bullock, Portland State University

Kris Chandler, Pikes Peak Community College
Lois Davis, Casper College
Kathy Finney, Central Oregon Community College
John McLain, University of Indianapolis
Bill O'Connor, Western Montana College
Tim Sylvester, Glendale Community College
Jane Turk, LaSalle University
Tom Wiggen, University of North Dakota
Mimi Will, Foothill College

We hope you like *Internet Today!* and find it useful. Feel free to send us email to share your opinions, suggestions, or comments about our work. When you have time visit our home pages at **http://www.mwc.edu/ernie** and **http://www.library.mwc.edu/~khartman** and leave a note in our online guestbooks.

Peace.

Ernest Ackermann
Department of Computer Science
Mary Washington College
ernie@mwc.edu
http://www.mwc.edu/ernie

Karen Hartman
Simpson Library
Mary Washington College
khartman@mwc.edu
http://www.library.mwc.edu/~khartman

chapter 1

INTRODUCTION TO THE INTERNET AND THE WORLD WIDE WEB

Millions of people around the world use the Internet to search for and retrieve information on all sorts of topics in a wide variety of areas including the arts, business, government, humanities, news, politics, recreation, and the sciences. People use the Internet to communicate through electronic mail. They share information and make commercial and business transactions. All this activity is possible because tens of thousands of networks are connected to the Internet and exchange information in the same basic ways.

The *World Wide Web* (**WWW**) is a part of the Internet, but it's not a collection of networks. Rather, it is information that is connected or linked together like a web. You access this information through one interface or tool, called a Web browser. The number of resources and services that are part of the World Wide Web is growing at an astounding rate. There are over 100 million people online, connected to the Internet, throughout the world. By using a computer (hardware) connected to the Internet and a browser program (software) to retrieve information on the World Wide Web, Internet users have access to a wide variety of services, tools, information, and opportunities.

This book is about learning to use the Internet in a way that allows you to take advantage of the resources and services that the Internet makes available. Prior experience with the Internet isn't necessary, but it will help you move through some of the material more quickly. The text, examples, and exercises will take you through the basics of accessing and using the Internet and the World Wide Web. You'll learn how to tap the virtual cornucopia of information on the WWW and find the resources you want. You'll also learn how to create documents (called Web pages) so you can put your own information on the Web.

We'll cover how to use a variety of Internet services such as email, FTP, Telnet, and others. You'll also learn a little bit about how the Internet and the Web work. To take advantage of the benefits of the Internet and the WWW, you need to become familiar with the services and tools available and know about some of the major information sources.

Several exercises appear after each chapter summary. These exercises will help you practice using the Internet and will reinforce the concepts in the chapter.

This chapter contains detailed examples of using a Web

The concept behind the World Wide Web is the development of a **hypertext networked information system.** One of the goals was to give a uniform means of accessing all the different types of information on the Internet.

browser to access information on the World Wide Web. These and other examples in the book demonstrate concepts and techniques. As you read the examples and follow along, you'll get step-by-step instructions for working with the World Wide Web. Remember, though, these examples reflect the Internet and World Wide Web at the time of writing. Because things change frequently on the Web, the search returns and screens may not appear on your screen as they do in this book. The World Wide Web and the Internet are constantly changing, but don't let that hold you back. Be persistent and use your skills to work in this important environment. Change is one of the things that makes the Internet and the World Wide Web exciting, vigorous, and useful.

This book deals with using the Internet and the Web in the Microsoft Windows operation system. We'll be using the phrase *click on* regularly. This means you use a mouse to point to something and then click or press the mouse button. If your mouse has two buttons, press or click on the left button. If you're working in another windowed environment you'll find most of the instructions are the same.

Now, let's get started!

The World Wide Web

Whether you've worked on the Internet before or not, you'll be pleased with how easy accessing the Internet is through the Web. It's also enticing. There are thousands of Web sites on the Internet, and you can access virtually any Internet service or resource through the programs you use to work with the WWW.

You can think of the World Wide Web as a large collection of information that's accessible through the Internet. You use hypertext and multimedia techniques to browse the Web, to find information in various forms, and when you're ready, to contribute to the Web.

The concept behind the World Wide Web is the development of a hypertext networked information system. One of the goals was to give a uniform means of accessing all the different types of information on the Internet. Since you only need to know one way to get information, you concentrate on what you want, not how to get it. Instead of having to contact and know the addresses of many different Internet sites and having to know all the details of using different Internet services (Telnet, FTP, or Gopher, to name a few), you start a program

called a Web browser that lets you access a WWW site. From there you can go to other locations on the Internet connected through the WWW to search for, browse, and retrieve information in a variety of forms. You'll be able to select items by choosing them and clicking with a mouse. The items you choose from are images, icons, or text. The text is either underlined, in bold, or highlighted. The information you retrieve or view can be text, programs, graphics, images, digitized video, or digitized sound. Using a Web browser is a relatively easy way to work with information on the WWW. You need to know different ways of using other services on the Internet, but with the WWW you have just one type of interface or way of working with the Internet.

How the WWW Works

The concept of the WWW was developed by Tim Berners-Lee at CERN, the European Laboratory for Particle Physics in Geneva, Switzerland. The Web was started to provide a single means of access to the wealth of services and resources on the Internet. You access the WWW by using a program called a *Web browser*. There are several browsers available; the first popular browser was Mosaic, and the current most popular ones are Netscape Navigator and Microsoft Internet Explorer. Mosaic was developed by Marc Andreessen, Eric Bina, and others at the National Center for Supercomputing Applications (NCSA) at the University of Illinois, Urbana-Champaign. Andreessen and others left NCSA to form a company called Netscape Communications Corporation, which (at the time of writing) continues to develop and market Netscape Navigator.

Each browser provides a graphical interface. You move from place to place and item to item on the Web by using a mouse to select and click on a portion of text, icon, or region of a map or image. These items are called *hyperlinks* or *links* for short. Each link you select represents a document, an image, a video clip, or an audio clip somewhere on the Internet. You don't need to know where it is or even the way your browser follows the link. What is important is what you want, not necessarily how to get it or where it is. In order for this to work, there are standard ways of specifying the links and creating documents that can be displayed as part of the Web. Items accessible through the Web give hypertext access to the Internet, so you don't have to know any other techniques except how to select a title, phrase, word, or icon.

What Is Available on the Web

All sorts of things are available on the Web in many different formats such as data, documents, images, programs, and sound files. Essentially, if something can be put into digital format and stored in a computer, then it's available on the Web. Tim Berners-Lee (who started the WWW project at CERN) wrote in the document *About The World Wide Web*, "The World Wide Web (known as 'WWW', 'Web' or 'W3') is the universe of network-accessible information, the embodiment of human knowledge." (By the way, that document is available on the WWW by using the URL **http://www.w3.org/WWW**—we'll say more about URLs a little later.) That's a strong statement, but it's certainly true. You'll find items on all kinds of topics on the WWW. There's a wide range of materials available on subjects such as art, science, humanities, politics, law, business, education, and government information. You can find scientific and technical papers, financial data, stock market reports, government reports, advertisements, and publicity and news about movies and other forms of entertainment. Through the WWW you can find information about many types of products, infor-

mation about health and environmental issues, government documents, and tips and advice on recreational activities such as camping, cooking, gardening, and traveling. You can also conduct commercial transactions on the Web; you can make purchases, go shopping, or retrieve information about something that you are thinking of buying. You can tour museums, plan a trip, make reservations, visit gardens throughout the world, and so on. Just a little bit of exploring will show you the wide range and types of information available.

When you find a document or information you want, you can save it to a file on your computer, print it, or send it by *email* to

Be flexible.

Remember that the Web is always changing and that your results may differ from those shown in the examples in this book. Don't let this confuse you. The examples demonstrate fundamental skills that don't change, even though the results obtained or the actual screens may look different. ◆

any Internet address. Instructions for saving and printing files when you're using Netscape Navigator are given right after the end of Example 1.1. Email is covered in detail in Chapter 3. You can also make your own information available on the WWW. See Chapter 6 for information about that.

To put our discussion in context, we'll start with an example of what you're likely to see when you use Netscape Navigator to access the WWW.

EXAMPLE 1.1
A First Look at Netscape Navigator and the World Wide Web

Netscape Navigator is one of the most popular programs used for accessing information or browsing the World Wide Web. Here we're assuming the program is on your computer and you have a connection (either by a network cord or modem) to the Internet.

In going through the steps of this example, we'll start the browser, explain some of the items you'll see on your screen, and then look at one of the many directories available that give easy access to a lot of information on the WWW. We'll follow these steps:

1. Start Netscape Navigator.

2. Browse or explore a popular directory.

3. Explore the WWW.

4. Exit Netscape Navigator.

Looking at Netscape Navigator will set a context for some of the concepts and terms in this and other chapters. As you work through this and other examples, ✚ indicates something for you to do.

◆ Start Netscape Navigator.

You start Netscape Navigator by either clicking on an icon labeled **Netscape** or choosing **Netscape** from a menu. In some cases you may have to select a program group from the list of programs you can run, or you may have a shortcut to Netscape on your desktop. Suppose the Netscape icon is on your desktop.

✚ Double-click on the **Netscape** icon. The icon may appear as one of the following:

This will start Netscape Navigator, and a window similar to the one in Figure 1.1 will appear on your screen. (In some cases your computer may go through the steps necessary to connect to the Internet. If you use a modem to connect to the Internet, the program to use the modem will start and the modem will dial the number used to connect to the Internet.) The image or text you see in the window may be different from Figure 1.1; it depends on how Netscape Navigator has been set up or configured. (Setting preferences and configuration options for the browser program is covered in Chapter 2.)

The first document you see is called the ***home page***. When you're browsing the Web, the home page is your starting point. The term home page also has another meaning. When individuals, organizations, or companies want to have a presence on the WWW or want to make information available on the WWW, they create a home page. In that sense the home page acts as a contact point or starting point for the connection between that individual, organization, or company and the rest of the World Wide Web. We'll discuss creating home pages and other Web pages in Chapter 6. The one in Figure 1.1 is the home page for Netscape Netcenter.

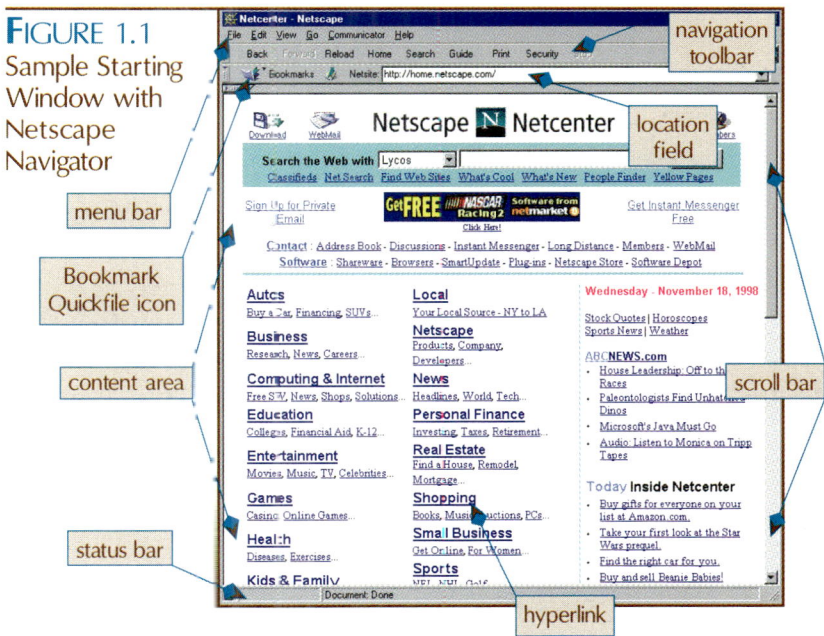

FIGURE 1.1
Sample Starting Window with Netscape Navigator

menu bar

Bookmark Quickfile icon

content area

status bar

navigation toolbar

location field

scroll bar

hyperlink

If you're familiar with a Windows environment, you should feel very comfortable using a Web browser. You work with many of the items in this window in the same way as any other window. You can resize the window or switch between the window and an icon representing the window. The menu commands are across the top row:

<u>F</u>ile   <u>E</u>dit   <u>V</u>iew   <u>G</u>o   <u>C</u>ommunicator   <u>H</u>elp

The commands contain the items (such as **File**, **Edit**, and **Help**) that are common to several Windows applications. Each command represents a pull-down menu. Click on it and a menu will appear.

One of the items in the navigation toolbar pointed out in Figure 1.1 will be used in this example. You select an item with your mouse and click on it (using the left button if your mouse has more than one button). That causes an action; sometimes the current page is replaced by another (as in the case of pressing on the **Search** button). You can get back to a previous page by clicking on **Back** in the navigation toolbar. There are at least two ways to access online help—use the pull-down menu item **Help** or press the function key **F1**. A detailed explanation of the menu bar, navigation toolbar, and location toolbar is in Chapter 2.

Most of the window is taken up by the view of the current Web page. There are several hyperlinks (we've pointed out one in Figure 1.1) on that page. The hyperlinks are part of the document, usually marked in some way so they stand out; they are either underlined, in bold, or a different color. They represent other documents or locations on the WWW. You use a mouse to move the pointer to a hyperlink. Click on a hyperlink and the browser tries to get the information associated with the hyperlink. Then the current document is replaced. As you move the cursor with the mouse through a Web page, the cursor turns into a hand when it's on a hyperlink. Text, icons, or images can represent hyperlinks.

▶ Browse or explore a popular directory.

There's lots of information on the WWW and it's just about impossible to keep track of it all. To help, some hyperlinks are arranged into categories to create directories. One popular, large, and well-designed directory is named Yahoo!. You can get to that directory by clicking on the button in the navigation toolbar labeled **Search** or by typing the directory's URL in the location field. In this example, we'll click on **Search**.

✛ Use the mouse to point to **Search** in the navigation toolbar and click the (left) mouse button.

Clicking on **Search** causes Netscape Navigator to activate a hyperlink to a Web page that contains hyperlinks to the Yahoo! directory and a few others. Another document will replace the one in Figure 1.1. A portion of it is shown in Figure 1.2. If the Yahoo! directory doesn't appear at first, you can get to it by clicking on **Yahoo!** in the longer list further down the page.

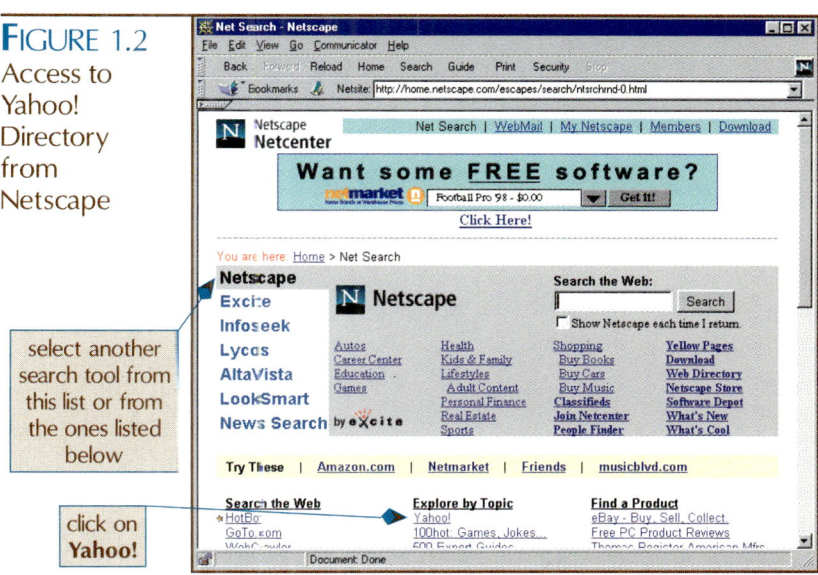

FIGURE 1.2
Access to
Yahoo!
Directory
from
Netscape

select another
search tool from
this list or from
the ones listed
below

click on
Yahoo!

🔷 **Explore the WWW.**

✛ Use the mouse to point
to the hyperlink **Science**
and click on the (left)
mouse button.

To explore the WWW using a directory, all you have to do is follow
hyperlinks. First we'll get the home page of the directory. Click on
Yahoo! as shown in Figure 1.2. That brings up the home page for
Yahoo!, as shown in Figure 1.3.

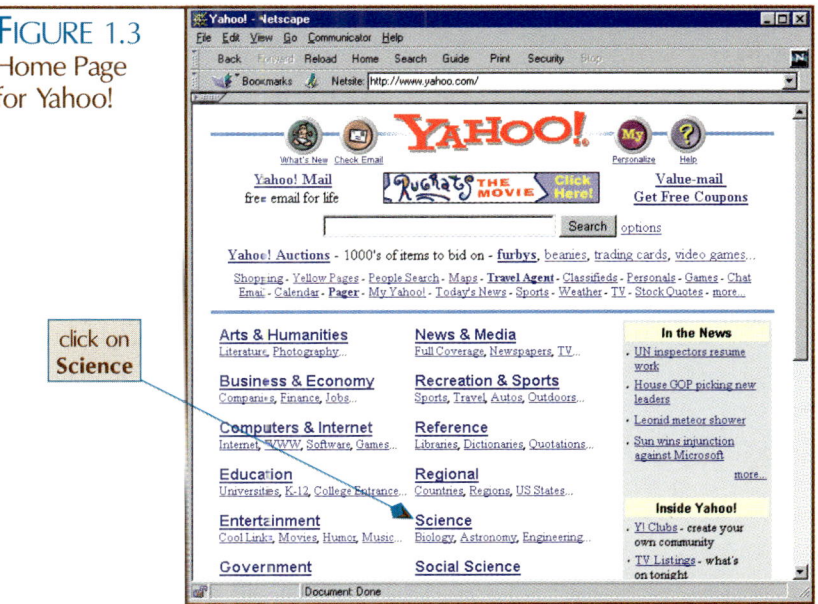

FIGURE 1.3
Home Page
for Yahoo!

click on
Science

There's plenty of exploring to do. To be specific, click on the
link **Science** as indicated in Figure 1.3. That will take you to a screen
like the one shown in Figure 1.4.

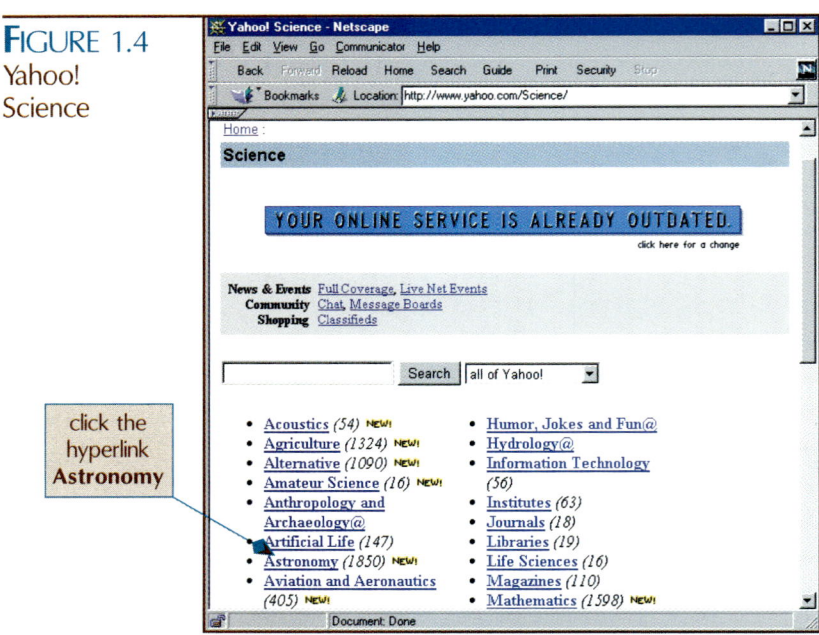

FIGURE 1.4
Yahoo!
Science

You can see there are still many topics to explore. Again, to be definite, select the hyperlink labeled **Astronomy**.

Use the mouse to point to the hyperlink **Astronomy** and click once with the (left) mouse button.

Figure 1.5 shows a portion of the document under the heading **Astronomy**. There are several items you might like to peruse.

FIGURE 1.5
Yahoo!
Astronomy

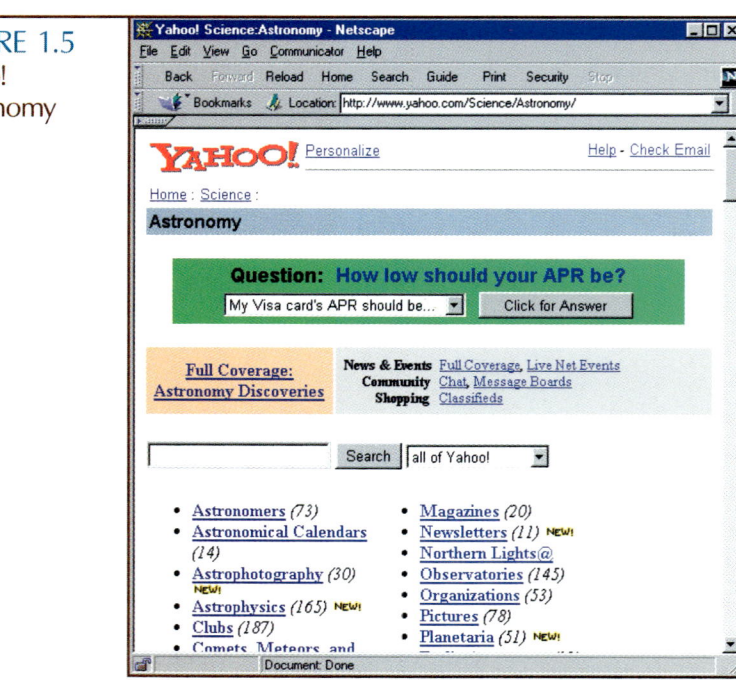

There are lots of links to follow here, and you can follow these or any links to explore the WWW. You'll find you can move from page to page easily with a little practice. Remember to press **Back** in the navigation toolbar to go back through previous pages. Spend some time exploring these topics or others. When you're ready, go on to the next step.

④ Exit Netscape Navigator.

✛ Click on **File** in the menu bar and then click on **Exit**.

The window will close and you will have ended this session with Netscape Navigator. If you're using dialup networking (using a modem with a SLIP/PPP connection) and you're paying by the minute or hour for the connection, then be sure your connection is terminated if you're done working with the Internet for now.

Of course, you can exit Netscape Navigator in the same way you exit most other Windows applications. Click on **File** in the menu bar and select **Exit** or press Alt+F and then **X**, or double-click on the button in the upper-left corner of the window.

End of Example 1.1

Once you've been browsing on the Web you'll probably find lots of information you'd like to save or print.

To save a document in a file while you're using Netscape, choose **File** from the menu bar, and then choose **Save As**. A dialog box will open. You can type in the name of the file and it will be saved as a *Web page*. We'll explain how to save it as text in the next chapter.

To print a document while you're using Netscape, click on **Print** in the navigation toolbar and a dialog box will pop up on the screen. Click on the **OK** button to print, and that's all there is to it, provided your printer is set up to print from any Windows application.

Key Terms and Concepts

Now that you've had a little experience with the World Wide Web, it's a good time to mention a few key terms and concepts.

✦ Hypertext, hypermedia, hyperlinks.

When you use the WWW, you work in a hypertext or hypermedia environment. That means you move from item to item and back again without having to follow a predefined path. You follow hyperlinks according to your needs and interests. Sometimes the items you select are part of other sentences or paragraphs; the links to other Internet resources are presented in context. The links can also be represented by icons or images, or you can select regions from a map or display.

✦ Web browser, graphical user interface, bookmark list.

A program that lets you contact a WWW site is called a *Web browser* or *browser* for short. The WWW doesn't require you to always use the same browser. Microsoft Internet Explorer and Netscape Navigator work with a graphical user interface (GUI). They let you interact with the Internet and the information on the WWW in a multimedia setting. As you use a Web browser you'll be able to save the locations of information or sites you find interesting so that you'll be able to return to them anytime you use your Web browser. If you're using Netscape, they're saved in a bookmark list.

✦ URL, Uniform Resource Locator.

The hyperlinks are represented in a specific format called a *URL* or *Uniform Resource Locator*. The portion of the Netscape window labeled **Location:** holds the URL of the document in the window. Each Web page has a URL as its address. For example, the URL for the first of several Web pages to accompany this book is **http://www.mwc .edu/ernie/internet-today .html**.

✦ Protocols, HTTP.

The documents or Web pages are passed from a server to a client according to specific rules for exchanging information called *protocols*. Other services on the Internet operate according to specific protocols. The WWW protocol is named *HTTP*, which stands for *hypertext transfer protocol* because the documents, pages, or files passed from one computer to another are in hypertext form.

✦ HTML.

The rules for creating or writing a Web page are all specified as *HTML—hypertext markup language*. This language provides the formal rules for marking text, which govern how it is displayed as part of a Web page. It would be used, for example, to mark text so it appears in boldface or italic. In order for text or an icon to represent a hyperlink, it has to be marked as a link in HTML, and the actual link itself is written as a URL. Each hyperlink on a Web page is represented by a URL. Chapter 6 covers HTML in more detail.

✦ Client, server.

Netscape Navigator is an example of a program called *client* software. While it's running it communicates with a computer known as a *server*, communicating your commands and receiving information. You work with the client and it communicates with the server. The documents or pages you see on the screen are passed to your computer (the client) from another computer (the server). You don't have to know all the technical details to use the programs.

Hypertext and Hypermedia

The term *hypertext* is used to describe text that contains links to other text. When the text and links are from a variety of media (text, video, sound), as is the case in the WWW, we use the term *hypermedia*. When you're working with a screen or page, you see items in bold, underlined, or in a different color. Each one represents a link to another part of the current document, screen, page, file, image, or other Internet resource. Selecting one of these links allows you to follow or jump to the information the link represents. Also, you can return to a previous link. There's a definite starting point, but the path you take after that is your choice. It's not constrained by having to go in some sort of line; you can think of being able to go up, down, right, or left from any link. The term hypertext was originally coined by Ted Nelson in the mid-1960s to talk about moving through text in a nonlinear manner. Web browsers allow the links to be represented by text, images, or digitized sound.

As an example, we'll take a look at an excerpt from a hypertext glossary. The definitions and explanations in the glossary are connected through hypertext. The excerpt here is taken from a glossary of Internet terms to accompany this book, and it's available on the Web in hypertext form. To see it, use the URL **http://www.mwc.edu/ernie/InternetToday/glossary.html**.

Web Page The information available and displayed by a <u>Web browser</u> as the result of opening a local file or opening a location (<u>URL</u>). The contents and format of the Web page are specified using <u>HTML</u>.

If you used your mouse to select one of the underlined words or phrases and clicked on it, you'd be taken to another part of the glossary. For example, choosing **URL** takes you to a definition of URL. From there you could browse the glossary following other links or return to the entry for **Web Page**. You could always follow the links back to return to where you started from. The information in the glossary wouldn't change, but the way you access it and the order in which you do it would.

Many of the resources, sites, and services you access as part of the Web are accessible through several paths. The WWW allows you to browse and select those resources by letting you choose your own path within the context of Web pages and hyperlinks on those pages or screens.

Uniform Resource Locator—URL

Each of the links on the World Wide Web uses a Uniform Resource Locator, or URL. The URL gives a Web browser the location and the means to get to a specific resource on the Internet. You need to know about URLs if you want to access something that doesn't have a link to it on the Web page you're working with or if you want to go directly to that page, bypassing many pages. When someone writes about a Web page or service, they will usually give you the URL. There are references to Web pages or URLs in lots of documents you'll see on the World Wide Web, and also in other media like newspapers, magazines, television, and radio. You've seen some examples of URLs in the figures in Example 1.1, such as **http://home.netscape.com** in Figure 1.1, and **http://www.yahoo.com/Science** in Figure 1.4.

The URLs that point to Web pages all start with **http://**. That's because those are all transmitted according to HTTP (hypertext transfer protocol). You'll see something different for URLs that are used to access information through other Internet services or protocols. Gopher (discussed in Chapter 7) once was a popular Internet ser-

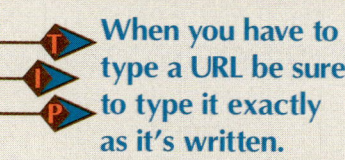

When you have to type a URL be sure to type it exactly as it's written.

The URLs for most sites are case-sensitive—upper- and lowercase characters are treated as different characters. For example, Wells Fargo Bank provides a newsletter titled "Foreign Exchange Commentary and Economic Review" on the WWW through the URL **http://wellsfargo.com/inatl/newsletters/forexreview**. If you use **http://wellsfargo.com/INATL/newsletters/forexreview**, you won't get anything except an error message saying the Web page couldn't be found. So be careful when typing. Pay attention to letter case and punctuation. ◆

vice. To access the Gopher menu you would use a URL that starts with **gopher://**. For example, the Library of Congress makes information available through Gopher and the WWW. To access the information it makes available as a Gopher menu, use the URL **gopher://gopher.loc.gov**. The URL for the Library of Congress' home page is **http://www.loc.gov**.

You can **go directly to a Web page** without having to follow hyperlinks. You may want to do this if you find out about a URL but don't have it as part of some other Web page.

You'll find it helpful to think of a URL as being

```
how-to-get-there://where-to-go/what-to-get
```

Its general form is

```
service://domain-name-of-site-supplying-service/full-path-name-of-item
```

The term *service* refers to an Internet service or protocol such as FTP, Telnet, or HTTP. Essentially, this is like a sign pointing to something on the Internet. Starting at the left, the portion of the URL before the colon (:) tells the type of Internet service or protocol to use, such as FTP, Gopher, or HTTP. The Internet domain name or address of the site supplying the information comes after the characters ://. After the first single slash is the full path name of the item. All slashes go in the same direction.

You can view files on your computer through Netscape Navigator, Internet Explorer, or any Web browser. To do that, use a URL of the form

```
file:///DRIVE¦/name-of-file
```

Substitute the name of the disk drive that holds the file for *DRIVE¦* and the file name for *name-of-file*. For example, the URL for the file **goodnews.htm** on Drive C is **file:///C¦/ goodnews.htm**. Remember to use the full file name and that all slashes look like /. For example, if the file **goodnews.htm** were in the directory **A:\mystuff \webpages**, its URL would be **file:///A¦/mystuff/ webpages/goodnews.htm**.

Sometimes you will want to go directly to a Web page without having to follow hyperlinks. You may want to do this if you find out about a URL, but don't have it as part of some other Web page. In this case you'll want to type in the URL and have the Web browser follow the URL. One way is by typing the URL in the location field. There are other ways to give the browser a URL to use as a hyperlink, but entering the URL in the location field is the quickest way. The different ways depend on which browser you're using.

Regardless of which method you use, you're explicitly giving the Web browser a hyperlink to follow. We'll provide more details about using URLs in Chapter 2, and a list of the different types of URLs in Chapter 6. For now we'll look at an example of using Netscape Navigator and going directly to a Web page by typing in a URL.

EXAMPLE 1.2

Going to a Web Page by Typing in a URL and Getting Information About a City

When you're working on the WWW you may want to visit a Web page that isn't listed as a hyperlink in the document you're browsing. To do that you type the URL in the location field of the browser's window and press **Enter**, rather than select a hyperlink. That's what we'll do in this example.

Suppose that you'll be taking a trip to Rio de Janeiro, Brazil. A friend has told you that you can find information about cities around the world by looking them up on the World Wide Web through something called City.Net, whose URL is **http://www.city.net**. To test it you've got to start your Web browser and get it to use the URL. That means getting the browser to go to the Web page whose URL is **http://www.city.net**. Then you can follow hyperlinks to get information about Brazil and Rio de Janeiro. In addition to going through the steps to go to or retrieve a Web page, we'll follow a hyperlink that's part of a map by using the mouse to point to a region of a map and click. Here are the steps to follow in this example:

1. Start Netscape Navigator.

2. Go to a Web page by typing a URL.

3. Use the hyperlinks on the map to get information about Brazil.

4. Follow a hyperlink to get to information about Rio de Janeiro.

5. Exit Netscape Navigator.

❶ **Start Netscape Navigator.**	Click on an icon labeled **Netscape** or **Netscape Navigator**. We saw how to do that in Example 1.1.
✚ Double-click the **Netscape** icon.	This will start Netscape Navigator with the home page as it's set for your version of Netscape. Figure 1.1 showed the home page for Netscape Netcenter. The image or text you see in the window may be different.
❷ **Go to a Web page by typing a URL.**	Here we'll go directly to the home page for City.Net by typing its URL in the location field (also called the *location box*) of the browser window and then pressing the **Enter** key. The location field is shown in Figure 1.1. It should hold the URL of the current Web page. The field is labeled either **Location:** or **NetSite:**.
✚ Place the mouse over the location field and click once.	Use the mouse so that the pointer is on top of the location field and click once. The location field will change color.
✚ Type **http://www.city .net** and press **Enter**.	Type the URL you want to open or follow. That will replace the URL that was present in the location field. Press **Enter**. The location field should look as it does in Figure 1.6.

FIGURE 1.6
URL Typed
in Location
Field

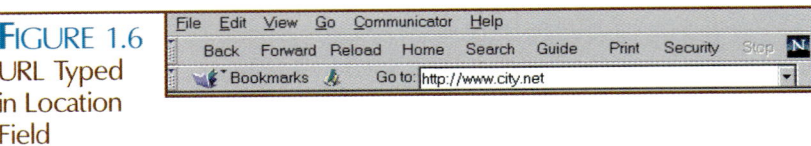

You should see some changes around the large **N** in the upper right of the window. It looks like the **N** is in the middle of a star or meteor shower while Netscape is contacting the WWW server at City.Net and retrieving the information indicated by the URL. You should see the City.Net home page (Figure 1.7) after a short while. If things are taking too long (more than a few minutes), click on **Stop** in the navigation toolbar to stop Netscape from trying to get information from City.Net.

You don't have to type the complete URL in the location field when you're using Netscape Navigator version 2 or later. Omitting the leading **http://www.**, you can just type **city.net** in the location field. The browser will retrieve the page whose full URL is **http://www.city.net**.

FIGURE 1.7
Home Page
for City.Net

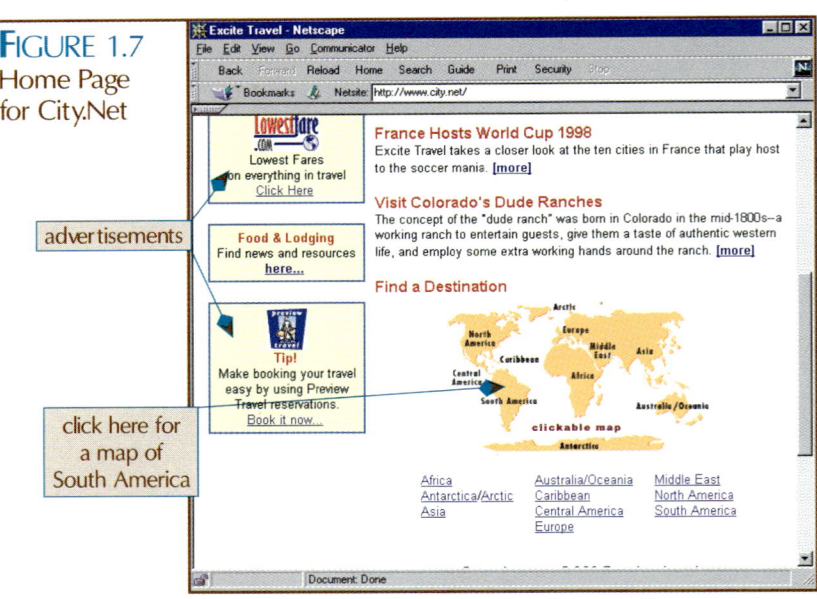

⑤ Use the hyperlinks on the map to get information about Brazil.

The home page for City.Net includes a map of the world. We will follow two more hyperlinks to get to a map of Brazil and links to information about its cities.

➕ Click on the region of the map labeled South America.

That takes you to the Web page shown in Figure 1.8, a map of South America with links to its countries. There's only one more link to follow to a map of Brazil.

FIGURE 1.8
Map of
South America

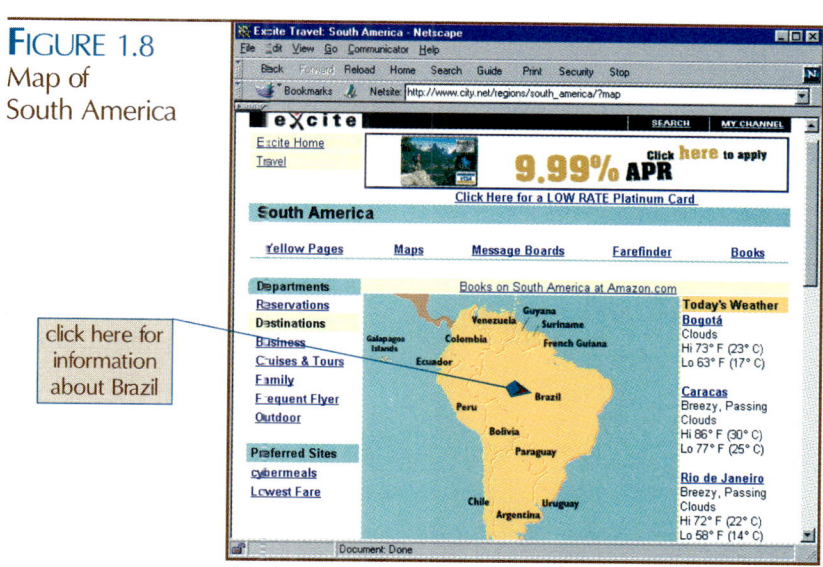

Now move to some Web pages with further information about Brazil and Rio de Janeiro.

Click anywhere on the portion of the map within the borders of Brazil, as shown in Figure 1.8.

After clicking on Brazil on the map another document will appear with hyperlinks to cities in Brazil as shown in Figure 1.9.

FIGURE 1.9
Excite Travel
Web Page
for Brazil

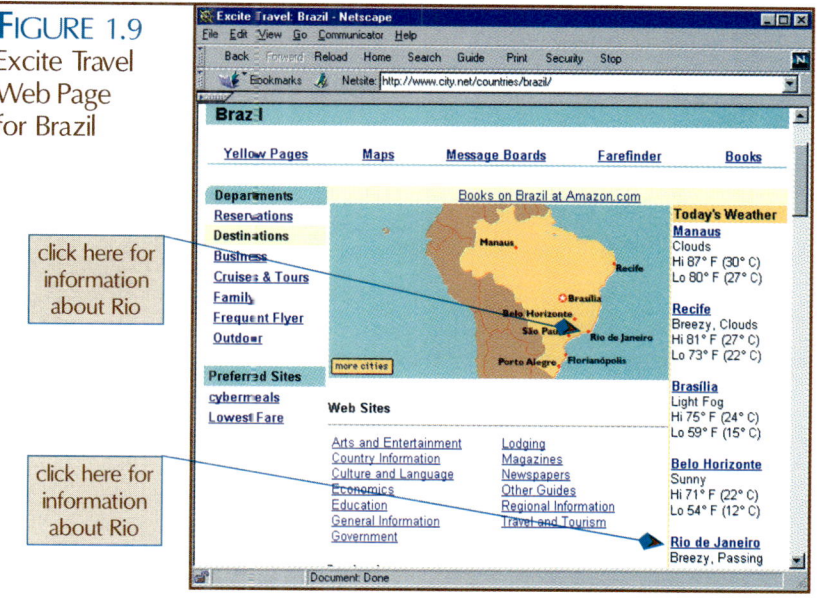

Follow a hyperlink to get to information about Rio de Janeiro.

✦ Click on the hyperlink **Rio de Janeiro**.

You can click on the hyperlink **Rio de Janeiro** to retrieve a Web page about Rio. One is shown in Figure 1.10.

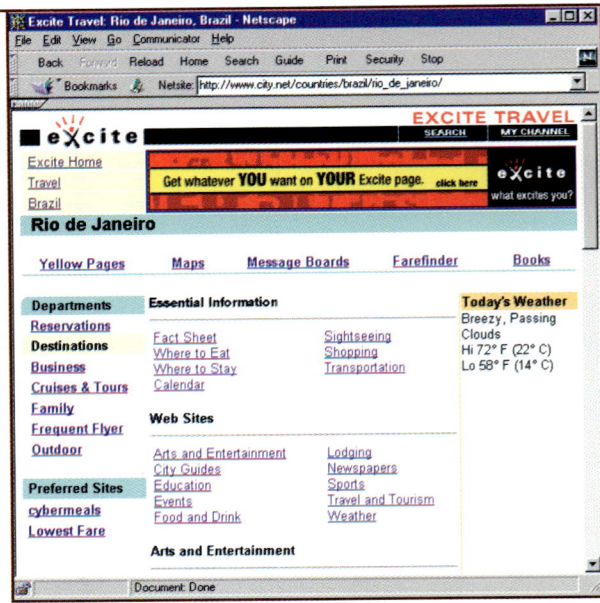

FIGURE 1.10
Excite Travel
Web Page for
Rio de Janeiro

You're on your own now. Follow any of the hyperlinks on this or other Web pages to get some information about Rio de Janeiro or other places.

▶ Exit Netscape Navigator.

✦ Click on the **File** pull-down menu, then click on **Exit**.

End of Example 1.2

Other chapters in this book give more details about using the World Wide Web to find specific information. We've concentrated on getting a Web browser started and then browsing the WWW.

Now on to information about the Internet!

The Internet

This section contains basic information and concepts about the Internet. The topics include:

✦ A Description of the Internet

✦ Explanation of Internet Domain Names and Addresses

✦ Your Internet Connection

✦ Proper Network Etiquette

✦ How the Internet Developed

A Description of the Internet

There are several ways to describe the Internet:

- **From a practical, recreational, or commercial point of view.**

The *Internet* is a vast collection of information that can be searched and retrieved electronically. This includes advice on all sorts of topics, data, electronic texts, government information and data, images, museum exhibits, scholarly papers, software, and access to commercial activities. Tapping into these resources requires knowing the tools and services to use and how to use them.

- **From a technical point of view.**

The Internet is a network of over one hundred thousand computer networks. The networks consist of over 30 million computer systems. These computers and networks communicate with each other by exchanging data according to the same rules, even though the individual networks and computer systems use different technologies.

- **From a social point of view.**

Millions of people throughout the world have access to the Internet. They use it to communicate with each other; they send and receive messages. An individual on the Internet can communicate with anyone else on the Internet. Since its beginnings, the Internet has been a place where people can communicate with others no matter where they are, what their status, or how great their expertise. What's important is the quality of the communication, not where or who it comes from. It's not a place where people only read or see what others have done; two-way communication is welcomed, expected, and encouraged.

Many people on the Internet form personal or group relationships or keep in touch with friends. Electronic mail doesn't give the opportunity to see someone and talk face-to-face, and you might think it's impersonal. Yet there is something very personal about writing to someone through email. You type a message at the keyboard with an image in your mind of the person who'll receive the message. Not all communications are personal; there's also a spirit and an expectation of sharing resources and information. It's satisfying knowing there are people around to answer questions and give help on almost any topic. It's also satisfying being able to share information you have. In some ways it's not surprising that there is so much communication and sharing on the Internet. At its technical basis the Internet is a network, and networks are created to share resources.

People communicate on the Internet in a variety of ways:

- **Electronic mail (email).**

This is a basic Internet service that allows individuals to communicate. It's the foundation for the ways discussion or interest groups operate, and it can be used for access to other Internet services.

- **Discussions carried on in a group setting using email.**

Some names for these groups are interest groups, discussion groups, Listserv, and mailing lists. Internet users join, contribute to, and read messages to the entire group through email. Several thousand different groups exist; they're used to share opinions and experiences, ask and answer questions, or post information about a specific topic or interest.

- **Group discussions, asking questions, and sharing information through Usenet (also called Internet News).**

The messages are called *articles* and are grouped into categories called *newsgroups*. Individuals can post articles to specific groups, reply to an article so the reply is posted to the newsgroup or sent only to the original author, or read articles. The communication here is from one computer system to another; it's available to individuals but isn't carried through their email. Usenet existed before the Internet was in the form it is today, but the *news* (as it's called) is often carried from site to site on the Internet.

There is no organization or agency controlling activity on the Internet. Control is in the hands of individuals and local organizations, schools, or businesses. This allows for the formation of discussions, the exchange of ideas, and the spread of information in a free and open manner. The users come from a variety of countries and cultures, and this diversity, along with this open two-way communication, contributes to the Internet's utility and vigor. Some people describe the Internet as a form of anarchy, mainly because there isn't any central control. However, a number of laws apply to communications and activities on the Internet, local and regional network policies govern its use, and Internet-wide rules of etiquette and rules for acceptable behavior exist. The laws of one country or rules for one network can't be applied to everything that happens on the Internet. But, because the communications often travel across several networks going from their source to their destination, local policies and laws can apply. Individuals have been arrested, sued for libel, or otherwise censured because of messages sent on the Internet. The people using the Internet have a say in the way it's used. Inappropriate messages and practices are often met with a large number of complaints and protests, and sometimes result in the offenders losing access to the Internet. Some of these issues are discussed in detail in Chapter 8.

The number of people gaining access to the Internet is growing at an astounding rate. If the number of users increases at the same rate as in 1998, every person on Earth could have Internet access by 2003! This isn't technologically possible, and there are a few countries the Internet doesn't touch. However, the Internet is a growing, vigorous, and valuable means for communication and interaction.

FROM A PRACTICAL, RECREATIONAL, OR COMMERCIAL POINT OF VIEW. The Internet offers a staggering amount of information on a wide variety of topics. Some of it is practical; it can be used for business, research, study, or technical purposes, including access to the services and information provided by professional organizations: documents, government information, data, online bibliographic searches, articles, publications, and software. You can also use the Internet for commercial applications. This includes researching and using financial and economic data, marketing and buying items of all types, and making services available for a fee. Additionally, you can use your access to the Internet for personal and recreational purposes: finding information related to your interests and hobbies, getting software and other items you'll find personally useful, and even getting advice. Other types of information include travel recommendations and news, medical and health information, weather reports, entertainment listings, library holdings, museum exhibits, and sports news. You'll be able to find people interested in and information about almost any topic. You can tap into university and other libraries throughout the world, museums, commercial publications, archives of software for many different types of computer systems, and databases of information dealing with topics such as art history, extragalactic data, literature, and molecular biology, to name a few.

Sharing information and resources is at the very heart of the Internet, so most things are available free of charge other than what you pay to access the Internet. However, some information such as articles from magazines, newspapers, and periodicals do carry an extra charge. Carrying on secure business transactions on the Internet is becoming more commonplace.

It's easy to see how, as Internet use becomes more commonplace, one of the fastest growing sectors is in the area of commercial applications. Some are concerned that this will ultimately restrict the free-flowing sharing of information. On the other hand, a large involvement by the commercial sector will likely speed up the development of faster and more secure means of transferring information on the Internet.

You access the information or communicate with others on the Internet by using a collection of tools and services that connect you to people, information, and resources. There are three basic services:

✦ Electronic mail (email).

An efficient and convenient means of user-to-user communication.

✦ Telnet.

Allows you to connect to and log into a remote computer. It appears as if there is a direct connection between your computer or terminal and the one at the remote site. You can then access any of the public services or tools at the remote site. Telnet can be used to access libraries, databases, and other Internet services.

✦ FTP (file transfer protocol).

Transfers files from one computer on the Internet to another. Many systems on the Internet make archives or collections of files available to anyone on the Internet through anonymous FTP.

Newer tools and programs provide a common method to access almost everything on the Internet. Having a single way to access all the Internet services means more than having one super-duper program or exceptional tool. You need that, but you also need a standard, Internet-wide way to indicate which service to use, which site to contact, and what to do at that site. That's the idea behind the World Wide Web—provide a single means of access to virtually everything available through the Internet: services, resources, tools, and information.

FROM A TECHNICAL POINT OF VIEW. The Internet is a network connecting thousands of other computer networks. Each network on the Internet has a unique address, and the computer systems making up the network have an address based on the network's address. At a basic level the addresses are numeric, a sequence of four numbers separated by periods. An example is **192.65.245.76**. You don't need to memorize numeric addresses; often they can also be specified as names, such as **www.mwc .edu**. Each piece of information passed around the Internet contains the sender's address and the delivery address. As information is passed around the Internet, each of the networks decides whether to accept it or pass it on. Once information is accepted within a network, it's the network's job to get it to a specific computer system.

The Internet is designed so the computer systems within one network can exchange information with computers on other networks. The rules that govern this form of communication are called protocols. Using the same protocols allows different types of networks and computer systems to communicate with each other. Each needs to have the software and hardware in place so it can deal with information in the form specified by the pro-

tocols. This means a computer system or network has to be able to transform information from its own form into the form(s) designated by the protocol, transform information from the protocol's form to its own form, and send and receive information in that form. Two protocols are *Internet protocol* (*IP*) and *transmission control protocol* (*TCP*). You'll often see these mentioned together as TCP/IP when dealing with the software needed to make an Internet connection.

Packets of characters (bytes), like envelopes holding messages, carry information on the Internet. Using IP, a message consisting of at most 1,500 bytes or characters is put into a packet. Each packet has the address of the sender and the address of the destination. These addresses, mentioned above, are called *IP addresses*. You can think of a packet in the same way you think of a letter sent by a postal service. Using TCP, a single large message is divided into a sequence of packets, and each is put into an IP packet. The packets are passed from one network to another until they reach their destination. There, the TCP software reassembles the packets into a complete message. If packets are lost or damaged, a request is sent out to resend them. It isn't necessary for all the packets in a single message to take the same route through the Internet, or for the same message to take the same route each time it's sent. This notion of a message naturally applies to email, but it's extended to apply to many of the other services on the Internet.

The Internet is actually a packet-switched network. The emphasis is on transmitting and receiving packets, rather than on connecting computer systems to each other. When Telnet, for example, is used it appears as if there is a direct connection between two computers on different parts of the Internet. However, it's a virtual connection; the two systems aren't directly connected to each other, it just appears that way. In reality, packets are being passed from one system to another. Passing information and implementing the Internet services with packets, instead of one long steady stream of bytes, keeps one system from tying up the networks with a connection dedicated to one program.

Most Internet services operate according to a scheme called client/server. A user on one computer system starts a program that contacts another remote computer system. The client is the program the user is running, and the server is running on the remote system. The user gives commands to the client, which passes them on to the server. The server interprets those commands and returns information to the client, which passes information to the user. Web browsers operate on the same principle. When you use Netscape or another Web browser, you start a program that acts as the client, and it contacts a computer system running a Web server. The information you see is passed from the server to the client. The commands you give are either used by the client to

work with information on your system or passed from the client to the server, since any server can deal with several clients. So a single WWW server can handle requests from many client programs. A server simply responds to individual requests from clients, and the clients take care of presenting the information to the user. All of this information is passed as packets between the server and the client.

The networks on the Internet use hardware or a device called a *router* to communicate with other networks. The router on a network accepts packets addressed to it and passes on packets addressed to other networks. It's up to the individual computer systems to take care of sending and receiving packets. Each computer system with a direct connection to the Internet has to have the hardware and/or software to allow it to work with packets. This usually means either a network card with TCP/IP software is in the computer you use, or you get a dialup connection by using *PPP* (*point-to-point protocol*) or *SLIP* (*serial line Internet protocol*) software and a modem. If you're using a modem, but not using PPP or SLIP, then you probably don't have a direct connection to the Internet, but you're contacting a computer that does.

Not all computer networks are part of the Internet; some use a different technology for their network operations. These can, however, exchange information with the Internet. This is done through a gateway, which allows different networks to communicate with each other. Systems connected through gateways can usually exchange electronic mail, but other Internet services may not be available.

Explanation of Internet Domain Names and Addresses

Networks and computer systems on the Internet exchange data and communicate with each other. An address is assigned to each network, and each computer in a network has an address based on the network's address. These addresses are made up of a sequence of four numbers separated by periods, such as **192.65.245.76**. Each of the numbers is in the range of 0 through 255. Starting from the left, the numbers in the address identify a network, and the number or numbers on the right identify a specific host or computer system. For example, the network portion of the address **192.65.245.76** is **192.65.245** and the host portion is **76**. On networks with more hosts, the last two or three numbers are used. An address in numeric form is called an IP address. Information sent from one site on the Internet to another is divided into packets, and each packet has the IP address of the sender and the IP address of the destination.

This numeric scheme of IP addresses works well for computer systems, but it's difficult (close to impossible) for people to remember, and type correctly, a sequence of four numbers for every Internet site they need to contact. Therefore, many Internet sites also have names; for example, **jupiter.research** **.wonder.com** or **cs.greatu.edu**. The name is called a *domain name*. Like the numeric address, domain names are a sequence of words separated by periods. How many words? There are at least two, with three and four being more common, but there could be more. The most specific information, usually the name of a computer system or host, is on the left and you get more general information as you move to the right. This is the opposite of the arrangement of a numeric address.

The collection of networks making up the Internet is divided into groups called *domains*. The domains represent either a type of organization or a geographical location. For example, a site in the domain **edu** would be an educational institution, and a site in the domain **tx.us** would be in Texas in the United States. Each IP address (numeric address) is associated with one or more domain names. An address specified as a domain name is automatically converted to the IP address. The name of a specific computer system or host on a network is called a *fully qualified domain name*. Here's a dissected example.

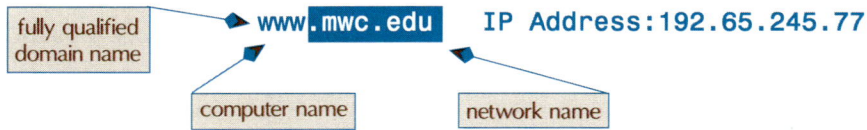

Table 1.1 lists domains by type of organization.

TABLE 1.1

Top-Level Domains

Domain	Type of Organization	Example Name	Example IP Address
com	commercial organizations	www.fbeedle.com	199.2.194.43
edu	educational institutions	www.eas.asu.edu	129.219.30.21
gov	government (U.S.)	csab.larc.nasa.gov	128.155.26.10
mil	military (U.S.)	nic.ddn.mil	192.112.36.5
net	networks	www.laze.net	199.231.129.59
org	nonprofit organizations	ftp.eff.org	204.253.162.4

The geographical names representing a country or state are two letters long. Here's an example:

```
Fully qualified domain name:    askhp.ask.uni-karlsruhe.de
Two-letter domain code:         de
Country:                        Germany
```

Since there are hundreds of countries throughout the world, we can't list them all here. *FAQ: International Email accessibility*, compiled by Olivier M.J. Crepin-Leblond, contains a list of two-letter country codes. The document is available on the Web by using the URL **http://www .nsrch.org/codes/country-codes.html**. (In case you're wondering, FAQ stands for frequently asked questions. It's a common term on the Internet used to describe a collection of common questions about a topic. Don't worry, a FAQ contains answers as well.)

A domain name can tell you something about the site or computer system you'll be contacting. If the domain name is geographical, you can tell the country and maybe more information about the locality. Let's look at the fully qualified domain name **www.physics.utoronto .ca**. Starting from the left, **www** indicates this system is probably a WWW server, **physics** means this system is probably connected with the physics department, and **utoronto.ca** places the site at the University of Toronto, Canada. Except for knowing that Canada corresponds to **ca**, all of this was guesswork. There are no hard-and-fast rules for local names. However, you'd be making a good guess if you got mail from **somebody@lib.umich.edu** and

speculated that the person was connected with the library at the University of Michigan.

Your Internet Connection

You're using a computer or a computer terminal to access the Internet. You know how to turn it on and get things set up so you can tap into the Internet. That's great! The details about doing these things vary depending on the type of computer and software you're using and a number of other things. This book focuses on accessing the resources and services on the Internet and the World Wide Web after you're connected. If you need some help getting started or connected, find a local expert, get in touch with the company or organization that's providing you with Internet access, or start reading the manuals. A number of good books explain the hardware and software issues of getting connected, and there's lots of good advice about that on the Internet.

In order to use a graphical Web browser—such as Netscape Navigator—you need a computer system that can deal with graphics easily, such as one that can run Microsoft Windows, X Windows (Unix), or a Macintosh. Also, you're going to

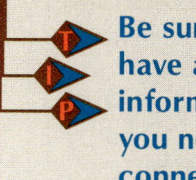

Be sure you have all the information you need to connect to the Internet.

You have to have an IP address to communicate on the Internet. The IP address can be static (never changing) or dynamic and is generally assigned to you by the host or server system when you make a connection to the Internet. You'll also need to know your domain name, the IP address of the router or gateway (the system that communicates the information between the network and the Internet), the IP address of the domain name server (the system that handles translating IP addresses into numeric addresses), and the IP address or the fully qualified domain name of the servers that will provide you with email (the mail or SMTP server) and Usenet news. These have to be set when you first connect to the Internet. Be sure to get all the information listed above from your Internet service provider.

If you want to provide information from your system to the Internet, such as a home page on the Web, then you'll need an IP address that doesn't change. This means you'll need a fully qualified domain name, and the computer you'll be using has to be running all the time. In that case, you may want a direct IP connection to the Internet. An alternative is to prepare your Web pages on one computer and then have them stored on another computer that is a server to the WWW. Check to see what the service provider's policies are toward the amount of email you can receive and how much you can store. Finally, be sure you know the charges associated with use. For many personal dialup IP connections, the user pays a flat monthly fee for a fixed number of hours and extra hours are charged at a separate rate. For example, one commercial service recently quoted charges of $15.00 per month for four hours per day access, and it charges extra hours at the rate of $1.95 per hour.

need software to enable you to use the Internet protocols (TCP/IP), and you need to have a connection to the Internet. Contacting the Internet occurs in one of two ways: connecting directly to a network from your computer by having a network card with TCP/IP software, or using a dialup connection where your computer uses a modem and software for SLIP or PPP to connect to a network.

Your computer is directly connected to a network.

It has the hardware (usually called a *network card* and a cable connecting you to a network) and the software (TCP/IP) to allow it to send and receive packets with other computers on the Internet. In this case, we say you've got a direct IP connection to the Internet.

You use a modem to call and connect to a network.

Your computer and the network you reach through the phone lines communicate with each other by using software called PPP (point-to-point protocol) or SLIP (serial line Internet protocol). Both of these allow your computer to send and receive packets just as if there were a direct and dedicated connection to a network.

This is called a dialup IP connection to the Internet.

With either of these types of connections you'll have to have some software and hardware installed on your computer. You'll have access to all the services and resources on the Internet and be able to take advantage of graphical interfaces to use the Internet, as well as sometimes only text.

Proper Network Etiquette

The Internet connects networks throughout the world and there isn't any one agency controlling it. People from many different countries, cultures, and backgrounds use it in an effective way. All this diversity, along with no central control, could lead to disorganized anarchy, a lack of concern for the effects of using resources at other computer systems, and an indifference to the feelings, opinions, and concerns of individuals. Any of these effects would be intolerable and would detract from the utility, richness, and vigor of the Internet. It may seem too good to be true, but the users of the Internet generally behave in a way that protects individuals, fosters the sharing of information, and preserves Internet resources. This is because users realize the benefits both to individuals and to the group of maintaining the manner in which the Internet has developed and continues to grow.

Over the years organizations have developed policies, rules, and codes for acceptable behavior. We'll list a few issues here that you'll want to consider as you use the Internet:

✦ Resources and services.

The services and resources on the Internet are generally offered in a spirit of cooperation or sharing. They need to be used in the same manner. In many cases you'll be a guest, accessing resources on a remote computer system. Be a good guest and show respect for the needs and wishes of the host. This can mean limiting the amount of time you spend using a remote system, limiting the amount of disk space or other resources you might use on a remote system, and limiting your access to nonpeak times.

✦ Individuals.

There is strong support for individual rights, feelings, and opinions on the Internet. The users represent a wide range of opinions and values. Some folks may express opinions that aren't to your liking; some things may be offensive to you. Before mak-

ing an immediate reply or taking instantaneous action, take some time to consider your response. Treat others with respect and concern.

✦ Copyrights.

Copyright laws or treaties generally protect material on the Internet. Because something can be copied electronically and is easy to obtain, doesn't mean it can be distributed without permission. Some of the information contains a copyright statement indicating that it can be distributed electronically and used for noncommercial purposes. This applies to text, images, and other types of information.

✦ Commercial activities.

For a relatively long time in terms of the history of the Internet, commercial activity wasn't allowed. That's not the case now, but the Internet is still not wide open to marketing or commercial announcements. It's technologically possible to send an email promotion of a product or service to thousands of people on the Internet. That type of activity is usually met with many protests, wastes resources, and generally does more harm than good. Take time getting to know the culture and expectations of Internet users before attempting commercial activities.

✦ The law.

Generally, laws governing espionage, fraud, harassment, libel, pornography, and theft apply to messages and other activities carried on electronic networks. Several laws have been passed in the U.S. and other countries that apply specifically to electronic communications. There is a lot of freedom and openness on the Internet, but that doesn't mean it's beyond the rule of law.

✦ Contributions to the Internet.

The Internet connects networks, and networks are created to share resources. When you have the opportunity to make something available to others on the Internet, do so. This includes helping others with questions, collecting and organizing information, or sharing your resources.

How the Internet Developed

In the late 1960s the United States Department of Defense, through its Advanced Research Projects Agency (ARPA), funded research into the establishment of a decentralized computer network. From the beginning, some of the developers and researchers saw the advantages of a network in which computer systems of differing types could communicate. They also foresaw the development of a community among the users of this network. The network, named *ARPANET*, linked researchers at universities, research laboratories, and some military labs. The 1970s saw the further development of the ARPANET and the establishment of networks in other countries. There were less than 100 computer systems on these networks. In the early 1980s other networks around the world were established. The widespread acceptance and implementation of the basic Internet protocols (IP, TCP, FTP) were crucial to the growth and development of what came to be called the Internet.

In the late 1980s the United States National Science Foundation funded the development of a network to connect supercomputer centers in the U.S. Many colleges and universities were encouraged to connect to this network, which was named *NSFNET*. The number of sites increased at an astounding rate; there were over ten thousand sites in 1987 and over one hundred thousand in 1989. Similar activity, although not on such a large scale, was taking place in other countries as well.

Usenet, the User's Network, originated in 1979 and allowed people to share information in the form of articles arranged by topic into newsgroups. Usenet was developed completely separate from the Internet, but programs and protocols for distributing Usenet articles on the Internet became readily available. A number of commercial networks started in the 1970s and 1980s weren't adapted to Internet protocols. Public access to the Internet was always an issue during its development. The Cleveland Free-Net, a community-based network, was also developed in the late 1980s to give Internet access to anyone with a computer and modem.

The government funded the development and operation of ARPANET, NSFNET, and several other networks throughout the world. These networks established acceptable use policies, which gave rules for their use and stated what types of activities were allowed on these publicly supported networks. The policies prohibited any purely commercial activities and set the tone for a developing code of network ethics or etiquette. Commercial networks were also being developed, although they could not, under the acceptable use policies, use transmission links of public networks. So, for some time, commercial activity on the major

portion of the Internet was prohibited in the United States. In 1988, several commercial networks reached an agreement with NSFNET to allow their email to be carried through NSFNET.

In 1990 ARPANET ceased to exist as an administrative entity, and the public network in the United States was turned over to NSFNET. The Internet was growing at a remarkable rate and clearly becoming bigger than the public institutions wanted to manage or support. It also became clear that the Internet would become an important part of the world's information infrastructure, supporting research, education, and commercial activity. In the early 1990s commercial networks with their own Internet exchanges or gateways were allowed to conduct business on the Internet, and in 1993 the NSF created *InterNIC* (the *Internet Network Information Center*) to provide services, such as registration of domain names, directories and databases, and information about Internet services to the online community. These services were contracted to the private sector.

The 1990s also saw the development of other protocols and software designed to make it easier to access and use the Internet. These include Archie for finding files available through FTP, Hytelnet for contacting sites available through Telnet, WAIS (Wide Area Information Service) for searching and retrieving items from databases on the Internet, Gopher for giving access to information and services on the Internet in a menu-oriented system, and, most notably, the World Wide Web.

The concept of the WWW is credited to Tim Berners-Lee. The Web was started to provide a single means of access to the wealth of services and resources on the Internet. What made the Web and Internet extremely popular was the ability to access the WWW by using a program called a Web browser. The first popular browser was Mosaic (1993) and it had a significant impact on the growth of the Web and the Internet. Mosaic was the first to have a graphical, easy-to-use interface to the Web.

Internet traffic directly related to the WWW increased at a rate of several hundred thousand percent, and this was accompanied by extraordinary growth in the number of commercial sites connecting to the Internet and the number of Internet service providers. Marc Andreessen, Eric Bina, and others developed Mosaic at the National Center for Supercomputing Applications (the NCSA) at the University of Illinois, Urbana-Champaign. Andreessen and others left the NCSA to form a company called Netscape Communications Corporation, which (at the time of writing) continues to develop and market Netscape Navigator and Netscape Communicator. Microsoft Corporation, likely sensing a huge market developing, eventually developed and distributed another popular Web browser, called Microsoft Internet Explorer.

The explosive growth on the Internet and the inclusion of commercial networks and services has been accompanied by an astounding increase in the population of Internet users, including users who are not part of the academic or research community. The Internet is reaching the size and importance of an infrastructure, a necessary underpinning of society. In approximately 30 years the Internet has grown rapidly from a research project into something that involves millions of people worldwide.

Want to read more about the history and development of the Internet? Take a look at these sites:

- ✦ "A Brief History of the Internet"
  **http://www
  .isoc.org/
  internet-history/
  brief.html**

- ✦ "History of the Internet"
  **http://w3.aces.uiuc
  .edu/AIM/scale/
  nethistory.html**

- ✦ "Hobbes' Internet Timeline"
  **http://info.isoc.org/
  zakon/Internet/
  History/HIT.html**

Summary

The Internet is used by millions of people around the world for communication, research, and business, as a source of all sorts of information, and for recreation. One of the most popular and effective ways to tap into its resources is through the World Wide Web (WWW). The WWW is a vast collection of information that's connected like a web. There is no beginning or end; the information is accessible in a non-linear fashion through connections called hyperlinks. You view the resources on the WWW by using a program called a Web browser. This book focuses on the Netscape Navigator browser. You navigate through the WWW by pointing to hyperlinks (underlined or boldfaced words, icons, or images) and clicking once with the mouse. To use the WWW and the Internet effectively, you need to know how to use some of the services, tools, and programs that give access to their resources, as well as some of the sources of information.

It's possible to link information in almost any digital form on the World Wide Web. Text files, programs, charts, images, graphics files, digitized video, and sound files are all available. Not only do you find things from a variety of media, but you also get a great deal of information in many categories or topics.

When using the WWW you work in a hypertext or hypermedia environment. Items, services, and resources are specified by a Uniform Resource Locator or URL. These are used by Web browsers to specify the type of Internet service or protocol to use and the location of the item. The URL for the Library of Congress' Internet resources about Abraham Lincoln, for example, is

```
http://lcweb2.loc.gov/ammem/alhtml/alrel.html
```

The protocol or service in this case is **http**, or hypertext transfer protocol, and a Web browser using it would contact the Internet site **lcweb2.loc.gov** and access a document with the full path of **ammem/alhtml/alrel.html**. Hypertext documents are exchanged according to a protocol called HTTP (hypertext transfer protocol). The documents on the WWW are called Web pages. These are written and constructed using a language or rules called hypertext markup language (HTML).

The Internet can be described in a variety of ways. It can be viewed in terms of the people who use it and the ways they communicate with each other to share information and ideas. It's also reasonable to look at it as a vast information system on all sorts of topics. From a technical point of view, the Internet is a network of thousands of computer networks comprised of over a million computer systems. These networks and computers communicate with each other according to certain rules or protocols. The ones mentioned most frequently are the Internet protocol (IP) and the transmission control protocol (TCP). You'll often see them referred to together as TCP/IP.

There are a variety of tools and services used to access the Internet. Three basic services form the foundation for other Internet services:

✦ Electronic mail enables users to exchange messages electronically.

✦ Telnet allows users on one computer to log into and access services on another (remote) computer on the Internet.

✦ *FTP (file transfer protocol)* allows users to copy files between computer systems on the Internet.

Users can communicate with individuals using email, but there are also facilities for group discussions:

✦ Interest groups, Listserv, or mailing lists make it possible for users to engage in discussions focused on a specific topic by using email.

✦ Usenet or Internet News is a system for exchanging messages called articles arranged according to specific categories called newsgroups. Here the messages are passed from one system to another, not between individuals.

There are several other resources and services, and using a Web browser allows you to access all of them. Using a Web browser also means that you generally don't have to learn different ways of doing things as you go from one type of service or protocol to another.

Each site on the Internet has a unique numeric address

called its IP address and usually a corresponding name called the domain name. Information is passed around the Internet in packets. Each packet contains information, the address of the sender, and the address of the destination. The packets can take different paths through the Internet. It's up to the software at the destination to receive the packets and reassemble them. The emphasis is placed on the packets, not on the connections between systems. Users generally access sites by giving a domain name; the hardware and software convert a domain name to an IP address.

Many of the services available operate according to a client/server model. A program called the client is started on one system and contacts a program called the server at another computer on the Internet. The commands typed or given by a user are sent to the server by the client. The server sends a reply to the client, and the client presents the information to the user.

You can access the Internet by having a direct connection from your computer to a network. In that case, you'd be using TCP/IP. Another way is by using a modem to call an Internet service provider and gaining access through a PPP (point-to-point protocol) or SLIP (serial line Internet protocol).

The Internet developed through projects sponsored by governments in the United States and elsewhere to allow researchers to communicate with each other and share results. The initial work began in the late 1960s. There has been a tremendous growth both in the number of networks communicating according to the Internet protocols and the number of users accessing the Internet during the 1980s and 1990s. Now the Internet connects commercial, research, academic, and government networks throughout the world.

There is no central controlling agency that governs the activities on the Internet. However, a number of local laws, acceptable use policies, and codes of ethics adopted by most users help to make the Internet productive, useful, and exciting.

To use the Internet effectively you have to learn to use the services and tools described in this and the following chapters. You need to remember you're sharing a resource that's spread throughout the world. There will be times when everything doesn't work perfectly. You'll need to practice using the Internet. In any case, be persistent and be ready to learn new things. You won't break or damage the Internet. It's a dynamic and vigorous place to learn, work, and enjoy yourself! ✦

Selected Terms in This Chapter

ARPANET
client
email
file transfer protocol (FTP)
home page
hyperlink
hypermedia
hypertext
hypertext markup language
(HTML)

hypertext transfer protocol
(HTTP)
Internet
Internet protocol (IP)
InterNIC (the Internet Network Information Center)
NSFNET
point-to-point protocol
(PPP)
protocol

serial line Internet protocol
(SLIP)
server
transmission control protocol
(TCP)
Uniform Resource Locator
(URL)
Web browser
Web page
World Wide Web (WWW)

Questions About Your Access to the Internet

1. What type of connection do you have to the Internet (TCP/IP, SLIP, PPP)? What are the charges for Internet access and who pays them?

2. Write down the steps you have to follow to access the Internet.

3. What is the domain name and IP address of the system you use to connect to the Internet?

4. What is your email address?

5. Is there a person or organization who is responsible for providing help with the network you use to connect to the Internet? If so, give the name, email address, and phone number of the person you may contact when you have problems or questions about using the Internet. Is there someone else you contact when you have a problem or question? If so, what are your reasons for not always asking the person or organization responsible for providing network help?

6. Does your organization, school, or network provider have rules regarding proper use and behavior on the Internet or on the network you use to access the Internet? Where are they located? State the three that, in your opinion, are the most important.

7. What's the name of the World Wide Web browser that you use (Netscape Navigator, Internet Explorer, or perhaps a different one)?

Getting Information About the WWW

For this group of exercises you're going to have to get to the home page for the World Wide Web Consortium. Regardless of what browser you're using, you can get there by opening the location whose URL is **http://www.w3.org**. Click on the location field, type the URL, and press **Enter**, as we did in Example 1.2.

8.   What are the four major hyperlinks on the home page for the World Wide Web Consortium? Follow one and describe what you find.

9.   Select the hyperlink **About the W3C** from the home page. What are some of the items listed? What does this Web page tell you about the history of the W3C?

10. Follow the hyperlink **People of the W3C**. Who is each of the following: Tim Berners-Lee, Irène Vatton, Henrik Frystyk Nielsen, and Judy Brewer?

11. We mentioned three histories of the Internet in this chapter:
     + "A Brief History of the Internet" by Barry M. Leiner, Vinton G. Cerf, David D. Clark, Robert E. Kahn, Leonard Kleinrock, Daniel C. Lynch, Jon Postel, Larry G. Roberts, and Stephen Wolff
     + "History of the Internet" by Bruce Sterling
     + "Hobbes' Internet Timeline" by Robert "Hobbes" Zakon

     Choose any two and write a comparison of them. Your comparison should contain
     + a brief description of each work.
     + an evaluation of each in terms of how useful it is to a person researching the history of the Internet.
     + a statement of your professional or personal opinion as to which of the two you would refer to in the future when you need to determine some information about the history of the Internet.

Browsing the WWW

12. Another way to get to the home page for the World Wide Web Consortium is to go to the home page for Yahoo!, **http://www.yahoo.com**, click on **Computers**, click on **World Wide Web**, and then click on **Organizations**. You'll see a hyperlink to the World Wide Web Consortium listed

among others. Pick out three other organizations in the category and for each write the URL of its home page and a brief description of the organization.

13. Go to the WWW Virtual Library home page, **http:// www.vlib.org**. Follow the hyperlink **Humanities** and then **Archaeology**. Describe what you find.

14. While in the Virtual Library, select an area that you find particularly interesting. Which is it? Describe what you found.

15. Go to Yahoo!, **http://www.yahoo.com**. Select the hyperlink **Entertainment**. By following hyperlinks, visit three different amusement parks from three different countries. Which ones did you choose? What did you find?

16. Go to Yahoo! and select a category that you would like to browse. Write down the hyperlinks of at least three documents that you find interesting. Save those three documents as files on your computer and print them.

USING A WEB BROWSER

By following the examples and exercises in Chapter 1, you know that with a little practice the basics of using a Web browser are relatively easy to learn. This chapter deals with the practical issues of using a Web browser and how to use the commands and tools to make effective use of the information and resources available on the World Wide Web.

When you start a Web browser or follow a hyperlink, the browser (acting like a client) sends a request to a site on the Internet. That site (acting like a server) returns a file that the browser then has to display. In order for you to see or hear what's in the file, the browser has to be able to interpret its contents. This differs depending on the type of file; text, graphics, and/or images may be displayed. If the file is written using hypertext markup language (HTML), the browser interprets the file so that graphics and images are displayed along with the text. Depending on the HTML code in the file, the text is displayed in different sizes and styles and hyperlinks are represented on the page.

What to Expect from a Web Browser

Before we get involved in the details, let's discuss what to expect from a Web browser. Of course, you can expect to use a Web browser to look at Web pages throughout the Internet or to connect to various sites to access information, explore resources, and have fun. The Web browser will enable you to follow the hyperlinks on a Web page and also to type in a URL for it to follow. You expect the browser to have a number of other commands readily available through menus, toolbars, and buttons. And what about the times you need help? Your browser ought to include an easy way to get online help as well as built-in links to other resources on the Web that can give you help or answers to your questions.

You'll definitely want a way to save links to sites you've visited on the Web so you can get back to them during other sessions. Web browsers take care of those in two ways: through a history list, which keeps a record of some of the Web pages you've come across in the current session, and a bookmark list, which you use to keep a list of Web pages you want to access any time you use your browser. The title of the page and its URL are kept in these lists. The bookmark list is particularly important and the browser will contain tools to manage and arrange it.

The Web browser will include the means for you to **search for information** on the current page as well as search the WWW itself. Web browsers also give you access to email.

The Web browser will include the means for you to search for information on the current page as well as search the WWW itself. You'll be able to save a Web page in a file on your computer, print a Web page, and send the contents of a Web page by email to others on the Internet. Web browsers also give you access to email. Netscape Navigator has all these features, and starting with version 2, also includes the software for you to handle sending and receiving your email.

Web pages can contain text and images, as well as hyperlinks to digital audio, digital video, or other types of information. Your Web browser is probably equipped to handle many of these data types. But whether you can access something also depends on the software and hardware on your computer. If you don't have the programs and the hardware to play a sound file (a sound card and speakers), then your Web browser will be unable to handle sound files.

Web browsers do let you add to the list of software they use to display or play different media, however. If you come across a file or hyperlink to something the Web browser isn't configured to handle, you can add *helper applications* or *plug-ins*. These programs allow you to work with certain types of files. You do this by setting preferences for your browser. In setting preferences, you can choose the font and colors used for displaying text, set your email address, and select other items. We'll go over setting preferences and working with helpers when appropriate in this chapter.

For more complete and detailed information, look at:

+ The section "The Preference Panels" of online help. (Press F1, click on **About Navigator**, and then click on **The Preference Panels**.)

+ Appendix B of *Learning to Use the World Wide Web: Academic Edition* by Ernest Ackermann.

Quick Review and Some Tips

In this chapter we'll cover the details of using a Web browser. Before getting started, here are some terms that were introduced in the last chapter and are worth reviewing.

+ **Home page.**

When you start a Web browser, the first page or document you see is called the *home page* for the browser. It's where you start on the WWW, and it's one of the preferences you can set. The term is also used another way. Individuals, corporations, institutions, and organizations often have a page or document on the WWW that gives information about them. This is also called a home page. For example, the URL for the home page for MTV is **http://www.mtv.com**, the URL for the home page for the Smithsonian Institution is **http://www.si.edu**, and the authors' home pages are **http://www.mwc.edu/ernie** and **http://www.library.mwc.edu/~khartman**.

+ **URL, Uniform Resource Locator.**

A *URL* is the World Wide Web address of a page or location. For example, **http://cirrus.sprl.umich.edu/wxnet/servers.html** is the URL to use to get to a long list of sites on the WWW that give weather information. Interested in finding subway routes in any of several cities throughout the world? Use the URL **http://metro.ratp.fr:10001/bin/cities/english**. Want the instructions in French? Use **http://metro.ratp.fr:10001/bin/cities/french**. The first part of the URL indicates the protocol to use to contact a remote site. The ones that use hypertext transfer protocol, which is used to transmit Web pages across the Internet, all start with **http://**.

+ **Page, location, document.**

The terms *location*, *Web page*, and *document* are used interchangeably. Each of these terms refers to the information you get from one World Wide Web address. Sometimes the information fits in just one window, but when a document is more than one window long, you can scroll through it using the scroll bars on the window or keyboard commands. You use the browser to go from one page to another, from one location to another, or from one document to another.

You access Netscape online help by pressing **F1** or clicking on **Help** in the menu bar and selecting **Help Contents**.

Starting and Stopping the Web Browser

A Web browser is a computer program, or software, which is run on your computer. Just like other programs, it has to be started before you can use it. When you're finished browsing the Web, you'll want to end the Web session by stopping the browser or exiting the program.

Starting the Web Browser

Before you can start the browser, you need access to the Internet. If your computer is directly connected to a network, you have access to the Internet. If you gain access to the Internet by using a modem, you likely have SLIP or PPP access to the Internet. SLIP (serial line Internet protocol) and PPP (point-to-point protocol) are standards for transmitting information on the Internet over serial lines. A modem is a serial device, meaning that information is transmitted one bit at a time. To activate your connection, it may be enough to start Netscape Communicator or Navigator. This will start a program that dials the correct number and then prompts you for a login name and password. If you have a network card in your computer and you connect to your local network or the Internet through a cable, then different protocols are used. There are other variations, so it's a good idea to check with the folks who provide your Internet connection for the exact details.

If you're using Communicator, you may have to set up or select a user profile before you access Navigator. The first time you set up a user profile, you'll need to supply your name and email address, so be sure you know an email address to use

Point and click.

Although the appearances and the details of using Web browsers are different, they're all used essentially the same way:

You use a mouse to move a hand or pointer to an icon, menu item, button, or underlined portion of the window and click the mouse button (the left one if your mouse has more than one button). If you've clicked on a link in the document, the browser follows that link and the current document is replaced or another window pops up. Clicking on text or icons in the border of a window pops up a menu from which you can choose an action. Clicking on an icon or button in the border may cause an action without your having to choose from a menu or dialog box. +

before you start. You'll also be asked for the Internet address of the SMTP gateway (the computer that sends your email out) and the Internet address of your POP or IMAP server (the computer that receives and sends

This chapter contains the important details about the menus and options available with a Web browser, but we won't go into all the details. There are too many to list in the space we have here, some are likely to change, and most browsers give you easy access to an online handbook and online help. If you get into the habit of looking at the help available online, you'll know how to help yourself. Also, you'll know where to get up-to-date information. Where it seems appropriate, we will refer you to the online handbook for further details or explanations. ✦

email to your computer). SMTP? POP server? This may seem confusing, but don't worry! Just be sure to get that information from your Internet service provider (ISP) or the people who support your computer system.

To start a Netscape session, double-click on the **Netscape** icon. Look for an icon that looks like one of the following:

Ending a Session on the WWW; Stopping the Browser

Ending a session on the WWW means stopping or leaving the browser program. You may also have to terminate your connection to the Internet.

You stop the Web browser program in the same way that you end almost any other Windows program or application. Here are some ways to do that:

✦ Double-click on the upper-left corner.

✦ Click on the ✖ in the upper-right corner.

✦ Click on **File** in the menu bar, and then click on **Exit**.

✦ Press **Alt**+**F**, and then press **X**.

Here are some ways to end the modem session, in case that doesn't happen automatically when Netscape ends:

✦ Click on the button **Disconnect** in the dialog box or window that represents your dialup networking connection.

✦ Select a command from a pull-down menu that hangs up the phone (modem).

Just remember to terminate the connection so that you or someone else doesn't get an expen-

sive bill from the company that provides your Internet services.

If there is more than one open window with a connection to the Internet, such as another browser window or an email window, then you can close the current window without disconnecting from the Web or Internet. Follow any of the first three steps above for stopping a Web browser program, or press **Alt**+**F**, and then press **Q**.

Exploring the Web Browser's Window

When you start a Web browser, a window opens on your screen. It's the Web browser's job to retrieve and display a file inside the window. What is in the window will change as you go from site to site, but each window has the same format. The items that help you work with the Web document in the window include the scroll bar, the menu bar, and the toolbar, which are the same every time you use the browser. The major components of a Web browser's window are labeled in Figure 2.1. They include the following:

✦ **Title.**

The title of the Web page is created when the page is written. A page's title is not the same as its URL, just as a book's title is different from its library call number.

 Menu bar.

The *menu bar* near the top of the window includes the following pull-down menus:

File   Edit   View   Go   Communicator   Help

You choose any of these by moving the mouse pointer to the word and clicking on it. You can also activate one of these choices by using the [Alt] key along with the underlined letter. For example, to display the menu associated with **File**, use [Alt]+**F**.

Selecting an item from the menu bar brings forth a pull-down menu with several options. For example, if you click on **File**, you see the menu shown to the right.

Select any item in that menu either by clicking on it with the mouse or by pressing the underlined character in its name. To print the current Web page, you can click on **Print** in this menu or you can press **P** (upper- or lowercase). Some items on the menu are followed by [Ctrl]+ a letter, such as the following:

Save As...   [Ctrl]+S

This means that to select the command from the menu, you can either click on **Save As** or use the keyboard shortcut of

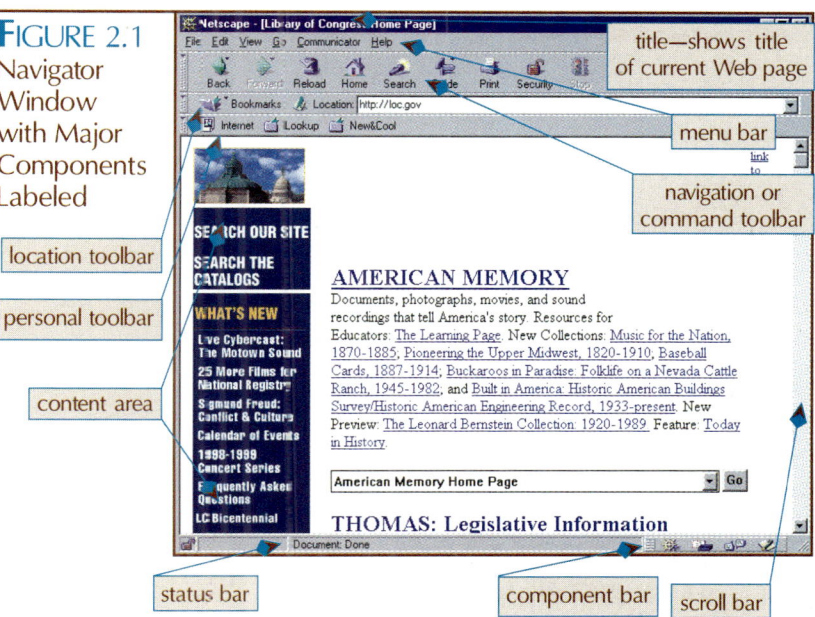

FIGURE 2.1
Navigator Window with Major Components Labeled

[Ctrl]+**S**. With this particular command, you save a copy of the Web page in a file on your computer.

When you select an item that's followed by **...**, as in **Save As...**, it brings up a dialog box. The box will request more information or will ask you to select additional options. If, for example, you select **Save As...**, you will then need to type in or select a file name. When you select an item that's followed by an arrow, as with **New**, it brings up another menu.

Here are some details about the options for each of the pull-down menus:

 File.

Using the commands in the **File** menu, you can open a new

browser window, send an email message, or open a page in the Web editor (Composer) that's part of Netscape Communicator. You can also use this menu to *open* a page in the browser—either a Web page (which you would open by giving its URL) or a file on your computer. You

Giving commands using the keyboard: keyboard shortcuts.

You can access all the commands for using a Web browser by pointing and clicking on a word, icon, or portion of the window, but sometimes you may want to give a command using the keyboard. To do this, use the keys labeled **Ctrl** or **Alt**, along with another key. For example, to mail a document to an Internet address, you can select **Mail** from a menu or use **Ctrl**+**M**. Using **Ctrl**+**M** means holding down the key labeled **Ctrl**, pressing the key labeled **M**, and then releasing them both. As another example, using the keyboard shortcut **Alt**+**H** will display the **Help** menu from the menu bar. You hold down the key labeled **Alt**, press **H**, and then release them both. ✦

can go in "offline" mode, which means working with files or messages on your computer without being connected to the Internet. The menu options also allow you to print, mail, or save the current document into a file. One item related to printing lets you select a printer, and another lets you preview a document before it's printed. This menu has items that permit you to close the window, end the WWW session, or both. There are also menu items that let you work with frames if they're present.

✦ **Edit.**

Use the **Edit** menu to copy items from the current document to other applications, such as a word processor. You can also use **Copy** and **Paste** to copy URLs or email addresses from one window into the location field or address field of a message. In addition, the menu contains the item **Find**, which presents a dialog box that lets you search the current document for a word or phrase. **Search Internet** and **Search Directory** are used to search for items on the Internet or to search for email addresses or phone book information. **Preferences** brings up a screen through which you set preferences; these determine how the Web browser operates, what items appear in the window, and how a document looks. For example, you can set the programs that will be run to view images and play sound or video as part of a Web page. You can control what's shown on the screen and how Netscape works with your network and computer system. There's a separate item for the preferences that you must set to use email and Usenet news. These include the domain names or IP (Internet protocol) addresses of the mail and news servers.

✦ **View.**

The items on the **View** menu change what you see and your view of those items. You can use this menu to hide any of the toolbars (or to show them if they're not in view) or to change the font size (the size of the letters in the Web page). You also use the **View** menu to reload a copy of the current document; this is useful if there have been changes to the source page since it was originally loaded or if the images in the document were not loaded automatically. The menu includes options to stop the current page from loading or to stop animations. The item **Page Source** lets you view the source version of the current page so you can see which HTML commands were used to create it. Selecting **Page Info** shows information about the current document, such as when it was last modified and whether it's a secure document (used for commercial or private transactions).

✦ **Go.**

Items in the **Go** menu allow you to return to different documents or pages that you have viewed during the current Netscape session. Netscape keeps a list of the pages (the history list) you've traveled through to reach the current document. You can choose **Back** to return to the previous page or **Forward** to move to a page from which you've just come back. You can also go to the home page for that session or to any of the recent pages on the history list.

✦ Communicator.

An important use of the **Communicator** menu is to access the bookmark list. With that list, you can look up names of URLs that you've put in the list, add new items, and otherwise manage the bookmark list. The complete history list is available from this menu. You can also use this menu to reach the other components of Netscape Communicator, including the email system (Messenger Mailbox), Usenet newsreader (Collabra Discussion Groups), the Web page editor

(Composer), Address Book, and others. Selecting **Security Info** gives information about the current Web page, including whether it was sent in a secure (encrypted) mode and the name of the Web server from which it was sent.

✦ Help.

Choose the **Help** menu to obtain information about using the Web browser. This menu includes a link to online help, product information and support (which itself has links to lots of helpful information), and information about netiquette, plugins or helpers, and other items.

Toolbars

Web browsers, like other Windows software, have one or more rows of icons called *toolbars* just below the menu bar. Each icon works like a button. When you press it with the mouse, some operation or action takes place.

In some cases, a dialog box pops up. For example, if you click on the icon to print the current document, you can select a printer and specify whether you want to print the whole document or just a part of it. The icons give you a visual clue to the operation or action they represent. The commands they represent are all available through the items on the menu bar, but the icons give a direct path, or shortcut, to the commands. There are three toolbars in Netscape Navigator 4: the navigation toolbar (also called the command toolbar), the location toolbar, and the personal toolbar. You can hide each toolbar by clicking on its left edge, making it disappear from the browser window. Click on the edge again to make it reappear.

NAVIGATION TOOLBAR. Table 2.1 explains all the icons in the navigation toolbar, which is also called the command toolbar.

TABLE 2.1

Items in the Navigation Toolbar

Name	Icon	Explanation
Back, Forward	Back Forward	These two buttons with directional arrows move between documents or Web pages that you've already seen. **Back** takes you to the previous page, and **Forward** can only be used if you've previously used **Back**. To obtain a list of sites to go back to or forward to, put the mouse pointer on either of these icons and click the *right* mouse button.

Reload		This button reloads the current Web page from the source. If the page didn't load completely, if the loading process was disturbed in some way, or if the source has changed since you last accessed it, you may want to reload the Web page.
Home		This button takes you to your home page, the one you first saw when you started the browser.
Search		This button takes you to a Web page where you select a service to search the WWW. This is a good guide to different search services.
Images		This button appears only if Netscape Navigator has *not* been set to automatically display images while loading a Web page. With that setting, Web pages load more quickly. To load the images, click on this button. To set a preference for automatically or not automatically loading images, select **Preferences** from **Edit** in the menu bar, then select **Advanced**, and finally click on the box next to **Automatically load images**.
Guide		This button represents a menu of several guides to Web or Internet resources and a hyperlink to the Netscape Web guide to sites, news, and events on the Internet. Click with the mouse button to bring up the menu. The entries are as follows: **The Internet,** a guide to sites, news, and events on the Internet; **People**, a guide to white pages services for finding email and street addresses; **Yellow Pages**, a guide to businesses on the Web; and **What's New & What's Cool**, a guide to new and noteworthy Web sites. All of these options are available through the directory button in earlier versions of Netscape Navigator. Click with the left mouse button to go to Netscape's guide to the Internet.
Print		This button allows you to print the current document. You can specify whether you want to print all or some of the pages, as well as other printing options.
Security		This button displays the page dealing with security information. It brings up the same page you would see if you selected **Security Info** from the **Communicator** menu in the menu bar. You can use this option to check security, obtain encryption information about the current Web page, set a Netscape password for yourself, and perform other security-related tasks.

| Stop | | **This button stops a current Web page from loading. This is useful if it's taking a long time to contact a site or load a page.** |

LOCATION TOOLBAR. The location toolbar includes the Bookmark Quickfile icon, which serves as a link to the bookmark list; the Page Proxy icon, which lets you add sites to the bookmark list, personal toolbar, or the desktop; and the location field, which holds the URL for the current Web page. We'll discuss the essential features of each.

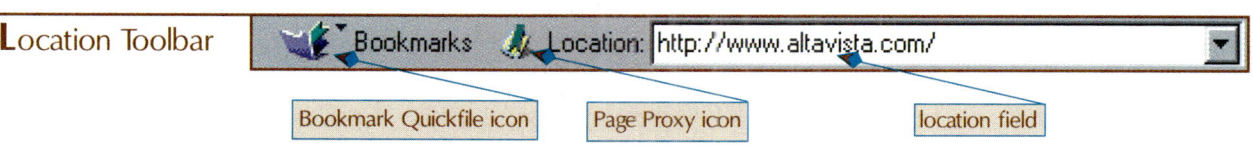

The Bookmark Quickfile icon labeled **Bookmarks** is used to bring up a menu of items:

- The first item, **Add Bookmark**, lets you add the URL and title of the current Web page to the bookmark list. The title is what you see when you look through the list. Once something is in the bookmark list, you can access the Web page in one or two clicks. The bookmark list is therefore very useful when you're doing research.

- The second item, **File Bookmark**, is used to highlight a folder in the list. It's used with the Page Proxy icon to the right of the Bookmark Quickfile icon.

- The last item, **Edit Bookmarks**, lets you arrange bookmarks into folders, rename items, delete items, and otherwise manage the list.

You use the Page Proxy icon, or Page icon for short, to copy the URL of the current Web page. Move the mouse pointer over the icon and hold down the left mouse button. Then drag it to the desktop to make a shortcut to the Web page. Click on the shortcut and you'll go directly to the Web page. Alternately, drag it to the personal toolbar where it is added as an icon. As a third option, drag it to the Bookmark Quickfile icon and add it to the bookmark list, or click on **File Bookmark** and select the folder to which it will be added.

The location field holds the URL of the current Web page. In Example 1.2, we showed how you can go directly to a Web page by clicking on the lo-cation field, typing in the URL, and pressing **Enter**. Clicking on the arrow displays a list of URLs for Web pages you've visited recently. Click on any one to go directly to it.

PERSONAL TOOLBAR. The personal toolbar contains icons that represent Web pages. Clicking on an item takes you directly to that Web page. What you see the first time you use Netscape varies depending on what version you're using or whether someone else has used the browser. Figure 2.1 shows three icons in the personal toolbar. The one titled **Internet** is a hyperlink to the Netscape Internet guide. The others titled **Lookup** and **New&Cool** represent folders that contain several hyperlinks to Web sites.

There are two ways to put items in the personal toolbar. One way is to use the Page icon to place (drag and drop) an icon for the current Web page into the personal toolbar. In this way, the personal toolbar consists of hyperlinks to Web sites. Another way is to select a folder (a collection of bookmarks) in the bookmark list as the one that will be used for the personal toolbar entries. Check the online help for a way to do that, because it gives you quick access to a collection of bookmarks that might be useful when you're researching a topic.

CONTENT AREA OR DOCUMENT VIEW. The *content area* is the portion of the window that holds the document, page, or other resource as your browser presents it. It can contain text or images. Sometimes the content area is divided into or consists of several independent portions called *frames*. Each frame has its own scroll bar, and you can move through one frame while staying in the same place in others.

The content area holds the Web page you're viewing, which likely contains hyperlinks in text or graphic format. Clicking on a hyperlink with the *left* mouse button allows you to follow the link. Clicking with the *right* mouse button (or holding down the mouse button without clicking if your mouse has only one button) brings up a menu that gives you options for working with a hyperlink. We discuss using the right mouse button in a later section.

SCROLL BAR. Netscape has horizontal and vertical *scroll bars*. The horizontal one is at the bottom of the window, and the vertical one is at the right of the window. These scroll bars and their associated arrows help you move through the document. The scroll bars work the same way as those in common Microsoft Windows applications.

STATUS BAR. When you are retrieving a document, opening a location, or following a hyperlink, the bar along the bottom of the window (the *status bar*) holds the URL that's being used. It also lets you know whether a site is being contacted, if it's responding, and how the transmission is progressing. The bar on the left, called the *progress bar*, gives a graphical view of how much of the complete page has been received.

The icon on the left that looks like a lock is the Security icon. Clicking on it brings up the same window as clicking on the Security icon in the command toolbar. If it looks like the lock is open, then the document you're viewing has not passed through secure channels. If the lock is closed, then some security has been put in place during the transmission of the Web page or document.

Information available on the World Wide Web passes across the Internet. That means that any site on the path of the transmission can intercept the packets that make up the document or Web page. Thus, it's difficult to guarantee the security or privacy of information (such as a credit card number) exchanged on the WWW. We all face that same problem whenever we use a portable wireless telephone.

Netscape Communications Corporation and others provide the means to guarantee secure transmissions. If the document you're working with is secure, the lock will be closed. It's not a good idea to send sensitive or valuable information through the WWW if the lock isn't closed, but that's always up to you.

COMPONENT BAR. Netscape Communicator consists of several software tools for working on the Web and the Internet. The component bar gives quick access to some of these: Navigator for browsing the Web, Mailbox for working with email, Discussion Groups for working with Usenet news, and Composer for writing Web pages. Clicking on any of these takes you to them. If mail arrives while you're using Netscape, a green arrow appears as part of the mail icon.

Using the Right Mouse Button

Most of what we've said about using the mouse relates to using the *left* mouse button, but the browser takes advantage of the *right* mouse button as well. If your mouse has only one button, then holding it down is usually equivalent to pressing the right button on a mouse with two or more buttons.

Here are some of the ways to use the right mouse button:

◆ If the mouse pointer is on the item **Back** or **Forward**, clicking the right mouse button brings up a list of sites; you can go backward or forward to these. Select one from the list and click on it.

◆ You can use the right mouse button to copy and paste information from a Web page, email, or other windowed source. Say that you're working with email or are in the content area

of a Web page and are *not on a hyperlink*. Using the mouse, move the cursor or pointer to the beginning of the text you want to copy. Hold down the left mouse button, use the mouse to highlight the text, then click the right mouse button and select **Copy**. Now move the mouse pointer to where you want to paste the text—maybe you've copied a URL and want to put it in the location field. Press the right mouse button and select **Paste**. If you are pasting a URL into the location field or some other field in a form, be sure to click on the location field with the left mouse button first to highlight the text you want to replace.

◆ If the mouse pointer is in the content area but *not on a hyperlink*, clicking the right mouse button brings up a menu with several useful items, many of which appear as part of other menus or toolbars. These include items to go **Back** or **Forward** to a Web page and to **Re-**

load or **Stop** loading the current Web page. You can set the background image as wallpaper for your desktop, save the image in a file, add the current page to the bookmark list, create a desktop shortcut to the page, or send the Web page via email.

◆ If the mouse pointer is *on an image*, then you have the same choices as when it's in the content area and not on a hyperlink. In addition, you can view the image in a separate window, save the image in a file, or copy the URL for the image (in case you want to include it in a Web page you're constructing).

◆ If the mouse pointer is *on a hyperlink* (remember, when it's over a hyperlink, the pointer changes to a hand) and you click the right mouse button, then a menu appears with all the same items as when the pointer isn't on a hyperlink. In addition, the menu includes items to open the link in a new, separate window or to open it in Netscape

When you start a Web browser, you see a portion of a page or document in the window. Many **pages contain more information than is immediately displayed**, so you need to know how to move through a document.

FIGURE 2.2
Find Box

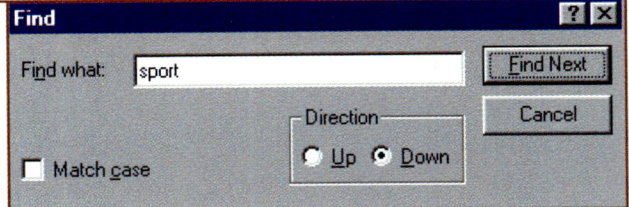

Composer. You can also save the Web page represented by the link to a file, or you can copy the link, which means copying the URL for later use with the paste operation.

Getting Around a Page and World Wide Web

You've probably spent some time browsing the World Wide Web and some of the resources and information it has to offer. In this section, we'll go over how to move around within a page and how to go from one page or location to another. Knowing this, you'll be able to get around the WWW effectively.

Moving Through a Page

When you start a Web browser, you see a portion of a page or document in the window. As you may remember, the starting page is called the home page. Many of these pages con-

tain more information than is immediately displayed, so you need to know how to move through a document. You can do this by using the scroll bars, using the keyboard, or searching for a specific word or phrase.

USING THE SCROLL BARS. You can move around or through a document by using the vertical and horizontal scroll bars on the right and bottom of the window. The scroll bars on a Netscape Navigator window are used the same way as on any other window.

USING THE KEYBOARD. Pressing the up or down arrow will move you up or down one line. Pressing the **PgUp** key moves up one window length, and pressing **PgDn** moves down one window length. Pressing **Ctrl**+**Home** takes you to the beginning of the document, and pressing **Ctrl**+**End** takes you to its end.

FINDING TEXT OR SEARCHING A PAGE. You can search a document for a word, portion

of a word, phrase, or any string of characters. To find a string, you first have to bring up the dialog box labeled **Find**, as shown in Figure 2.2. There are two ways to do this—either by selecting **Edit** from the menu bar and choosing **Find in Page...**, or pressing **Ctrl**+**F** on the keyboard.

Once the **Find** dialog box is up, type in a string (words or characters) and press **Enter** or click on the **Find Next** button. You can cancel a search by clicking on the **Cancel** button. You can search in one of two directions. **Down** searches from your current position to the end of the document. **Up** searches from the current position to the beginning of the document. Mark the **Match case** box if you want to match the capitalization in the string exactly.

Moving Between Pages

As you work with and browse the World Wide Web, you'll often go from one page to another. Much of the time, you do this by clicking on hyperlinks, but you can also go directly to a Web page, document, or location by typing its URL and then letting the browser retrieve it for you. To move between pages you've already visited during a session, you can use the **Back** or **For-**

ward arrow icons on the toolbar. Web browsers also let you save URLs and titles of the pages you've visited in one session so that you can access them easily during that or any other session. This information is saved in the *history list* (a list of all sites visited during recent sessions) and in the *bookmark list* (a list of hyperlinks to sites you have explicitly saved from one session to the next).

GOING DIRECTLY TO A WEB PAGE.

We'll describe two ways to go directly to a Web page, document, or location. In both cases, you type the URL and press **Enter**. The browser tries to make the connection, and if it can retrieve the page, it will bring the page up in its window.

If the browser can't retrieve the page, check your typing to make sure you have the URL right. There could be other problems as well. If the page is not available to the public, you'll see the message "403 Forbidden" in the window. If the page doesn't exist, you'll get the message "404 Not Found." It could also be that the site is out of service or too busy to handle your request.

One way to go directly to a Web page is to click on the location field. After the pane changes color, type the URL

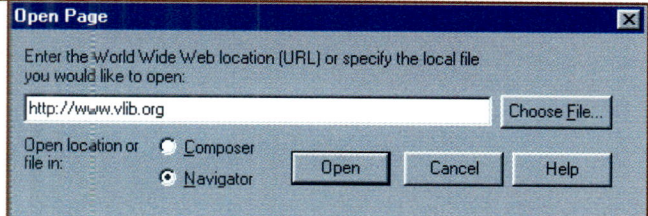

FIGURE 2.3
Dialog Box to Open a Page

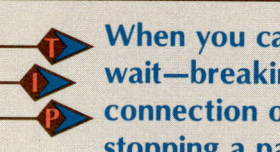

and press **Enter**. We did that in Example 1.2.

Another way to go directly to a Web page is to click on **File** in the menu bar and then to select **Open Page** (the keyboard shortcut is **Ctrl**+**O**). A dialog box labeled **Open Page** pops up on the screen, as shown in Figure 2.3. Type the URL of the site you want to go to, be sure you've selected **Navigator** as the way you want the page opened, and click on the button labeled **Open**. (Figure 2.3 shows the dialog box filled in with the URL for the World Wide Web Virtual Library, **http://www.vlib.org**. Why not try it and browse the library?) The Web browser then attempts to make the connection, and the page you've requested replaces the current one in the window. You can also use this method to view a local file—one that's on a disk drive on your computer or local network.

USING BACK AND FORWARD.

You can go to a previous Web page by clicking on either of the items. You can

When you can't wait—breaking a connection or stopping a page.

Press the key labeled **Esc** or click on the **Stop** icon to stop a page from being loaded into your browser or to stop the browser from trying to connect to a site. When you want to follow a link or go after a document, click on hypertext or an icon. Watch the status bar to see if the remote site holding the information has been contacted and if it's responding. Your Web browser will try for a certain amount of time (a minute or so) to contact the remote site. If you don't want to wait that long or you don't want to wait for the browser to display a complete page, press the **Esc** key or the **Stop** icon. This doesn't close the browser; it just interrupts the transmission or attempted connection. ✦

FIGURE 2.4
History List

lighted item to the bookmark list. You will want to add the name of a Web page (and its URL) to the bookmark list when you want to be able to return to it in another session on the WWW. As you can see from Figure 2.4, there's lots of information in the history list about the sites visited through Navigator.

KEEPING TRACK—THE BOOK-MARK LIST. The bookmark list is a collection of hyperlinks to Web pages that you want to save from session to session. They could be your favorite sites, ones you find useful, or ones you've looked at briefly but want to return to in the future (particularly good when you're starting to research a topic). Each item on the bookmark list is a Web page title, and each entry is a hyperlink. The browser includes a program to let you manage and arrange the list.

To use the bookmark list to go from the current Web page to another, first view the list onscreen by clicking on the **Bookmarks** icon in the location toolbar and move the mouse over the entries. When you've highlighted the one you want, click it with the left mouse button.

Another way to bring up the list is to select **Bookmarks** from the **Communicator** menu

---

Be flexible.

Remember that the Web is always changing and that your results may differ from those shown here. Don't let this confuse you. The examples demonstrate fundamental skills that don't change, even though the results obtained or the actual screens may look different.

---

also go back or forward by selecting either option from the **Go** menu in the menu bar. The keyboard shortcuts are **Alt**+← to move backward and **Alt**+→ to go forward. You can also move in these directions by pressing the right mouse button (while the pointer is on a Web page) and then selecting **Back** or **Forward** from the menu that pops up on the screen.

KEEPING TRACK—THE HIS-TORY LIST. The Web browser keeps a record of the path you've taken to get to the current location. To see the path and select a site from it, click on **Go** in the menu bar. The browser keeps track of all the Web pages visited recently in the history list. The number of days an item may be kept on the list is set in the **Preferences** panel category titled **Navigator**. To get to the spot where you can set it, click on **Edit** in the menu bar, select **Preferences**, and then click on **Navigator**. You can use this list to go directly to a Web page without having to go through all the pages in between.

To bring up the history list: use the keyboard shortcut **Ctrl**+**H** or click on **Communicator** from the menu bar and select **History** from that menu.

Figure 2.4 illustrates a portion of a history list. You can select and highlight any item by using the up or down arrow on the keyboard or by using the mouse. Once you've highlighted the location you want, double-click on the highlighted item. If you click on the right mouse button, a menu pops up that allows you to go directly to the Web page or to add the name and URL of the high-

48

in the menu bar. Pressing **Ctrl**+**B** from the keyboard produces the list in editing mode. In that mode, you can not only highlight and select an item but also manipulate the entries on the list. Figure 2.5 shows a portion of a bookmark list with folders.

Now we'll take a break from our detailed description of how to use a Web browser and we'll go through an example. The example provides practice with using commands to browse a section of the WWW.

FIGURE 2.5
Portion of a Bookmark List

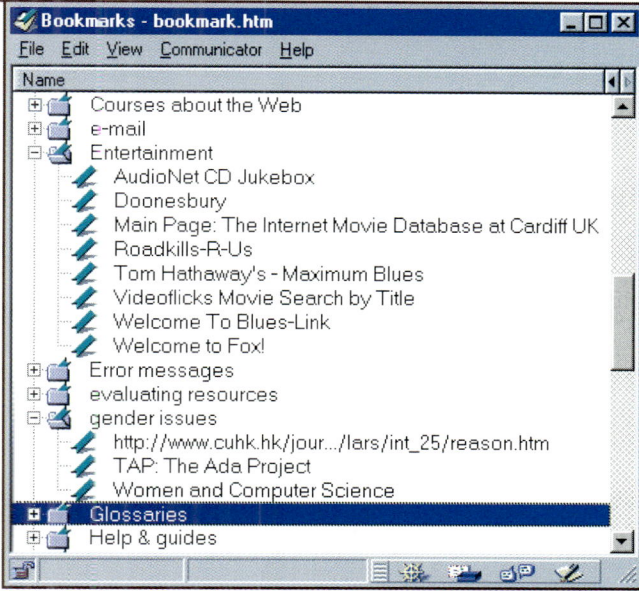

EXAMPLE 2.1

Browsing the WWW Virtual Library—Sports

This example takes us to the WWW Virtual Library, which is arranged by subject. It's a good place to keep in your bookmark file because it contains hyperlinks to information on lots of subjects, from Aboriginal Studies to Zoos. Going from site to site is sometimes referred to as *browsing* or *surfing the Internet*. That means going from location to location finding interesting, entertaining, or useful sites and resources, regardless of the type of information you're dealing with. Just to show how easy it is to visit a number of sites, regardless of where they are located, we will look in the subject area Sport in the WWW Virtual Library for information about (water) surfing (pardon the Net pun!), take a trip to Virtually Hawaii, and then check on some information about golf.

Although this example mainly focuses on the topic of sports, you will also see hyperlinks that could easily take you to different topics if/when you choose to follow them. It's this interconnection of sites and topics that makes the term World Wide Web appropriate. Even though some of the steps can be followed by using commands from the keyboard, we'll use the mouse to point and click on the appropriate hyperlinks or items from the menu bar or toolbar. As you work through this and other examples, indicates something for you to do. Here are the steps we'll follow:

1. Start Netscape.

2. Go to the home page for the World Wide Web Virtual Library (WWW VL) arranged by subject.

3. Go to the WWW VL section titled Sport.

4. Search the Sport section for items about surfing.

5. Select the hyperlink to the "La Jolla Surfing" page.

6. Browse the "La Jolla Surfing" site for pictures of La Jolla and weather information.

7. Take a (virtual) field trip to Hawaii.

8. Use the history list to go back to the Sport home page.

9. Get information about golf (explore the links!).

10. End the session.

While you're going through the steps in this example, practice using **Back** and **Forward** in the navigation toolbar. As long as you click on **Forward** as many times as you click on **Back**, you won't lose your place.

▶ **Start Netscape.**

The way you start Netscape Navigator depends on how it's installed on your system and the type of networking you use. You may have to start your Internet connection first—especially if you're using dialup networking. Then you need to select and double-click on the program icon for Netscape Navigator. It may be in a folder on your desktop or in the program list. If you've installed it yourself then you probably know where it is, otherwise you need to ask for some help or search your system for a program file whose name is Netscape.

▶ **Go to the home page for the World Wide Web Virtual Library (WWW VL) arranged by subject.**

When you start your Web browser, your home page will appear on the screen. There just might be a hyperlink to the WWW Virtual Library on that page. Browse through your home page by either pointing to the vertical scroll bar and moving it down, by pressing the down arrow or spacebar, or by pressing the **PgDn** key. If you don't find a hyperlink to the Virtual Library then follow these instructions:

➕ Click on the location field, type **http://www.vlib.org**, and then press ⎡Enter⎤.

➕ The home page for WWW VL is shown in Figure 2.6.

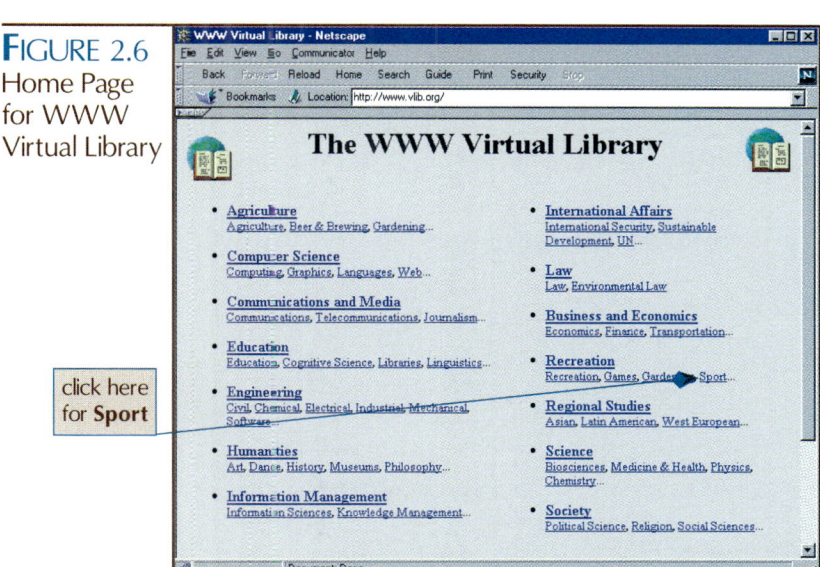

FIGURE 2.6
Home Page for WWW Virtual Library

❺ Go to the WWW VL section titled Sport.

The home page for the WWW Virtual Library lists several categories and subcategories. We see there is one labeled **Sport**, as shown in Figure 2.6.

➕ Click on the hyperlink **Sport** on the home page for WWW VL.

In a few seconds you should see the Web page for the section Sport in the WWW VL as shown in Figure 2.7.

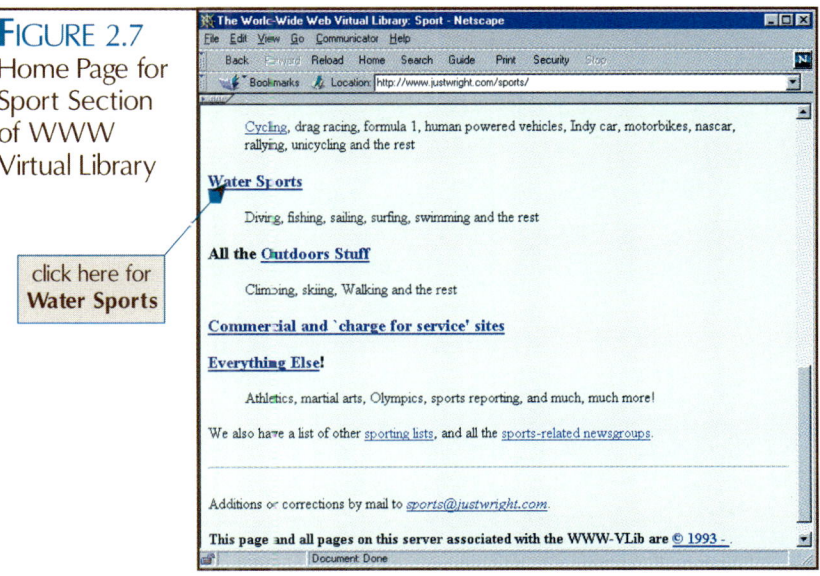

FIGURE 2.7
Home Page for Sport Section of WWW Virtual Library

❹ Search the Sport section for items about surfing.

We'll follow some hyperlinks to get to the water surfing section.

✛ Using the scroll bar, **PgDn** key, or down-arrow keys, scroll down the page until you see the hyperlink **Water Sports**. Click on it.

The Water Sports page will appear as shown in Figure 2.8.

FIGURE 2.8
Web Page for Water Sports

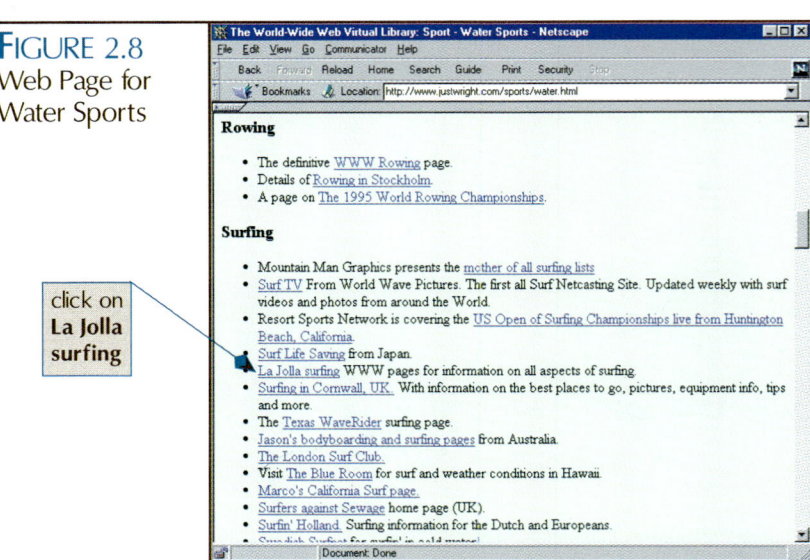

click on
La Jolla surfing

✛ Scroll down the Water Sports page until you see the heading **Surfing**.

There are several hyperlinks here for surfing. We're going to follow the one for La Jolla surfing. If that's not present in the list you see or there is some other problem, try another.

5 Select the hyperlink to the "La Jolla Surfing" page.

FIGURE 2.9
Web Page "La Jolla Surfing"

✛ Click on the hyperlink **La Jolla surfing**.

✛ The Web page titled "La Jolla Surfing" appears. It's shown in Figure 2.9.

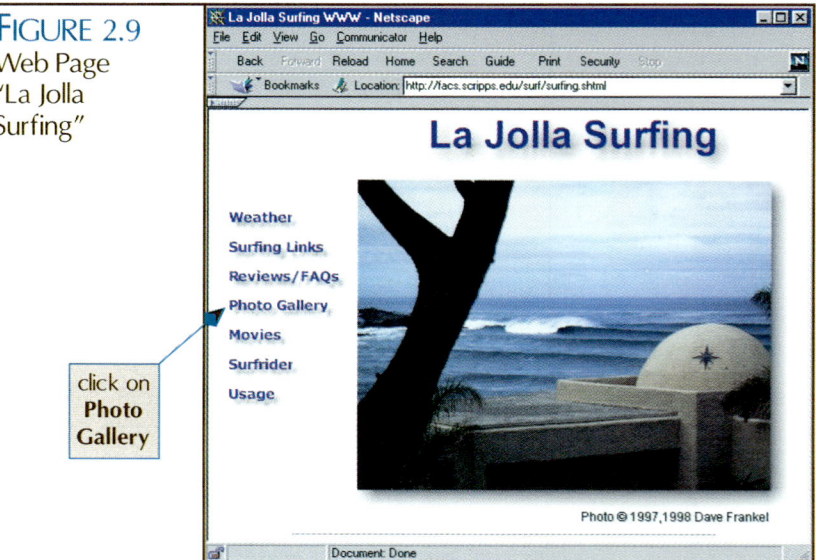

click on
Photo Gallery

6 Browse the "La Jolla Surfing" site for pictures of La Jolla and weather information.

This is a very nice Web site and has won some awards. We'll spend a little time looking at pictures of La Jolla and checking the weather information.

➕ Click on the hyperlink **Photo Gallery**.

This takes you to a Web page with several photos and lots of links to other photographs. We could spend hours here! Take a look around some and then check out the weather.

➕ Click **Back** on the navigation toolbar until you return to the "La Jolla Surfing" home page.

We show the weather page in Figure 2.10.

➕ Click on the hyperlink **Weather** on the "La Jolla Surfing" home page.

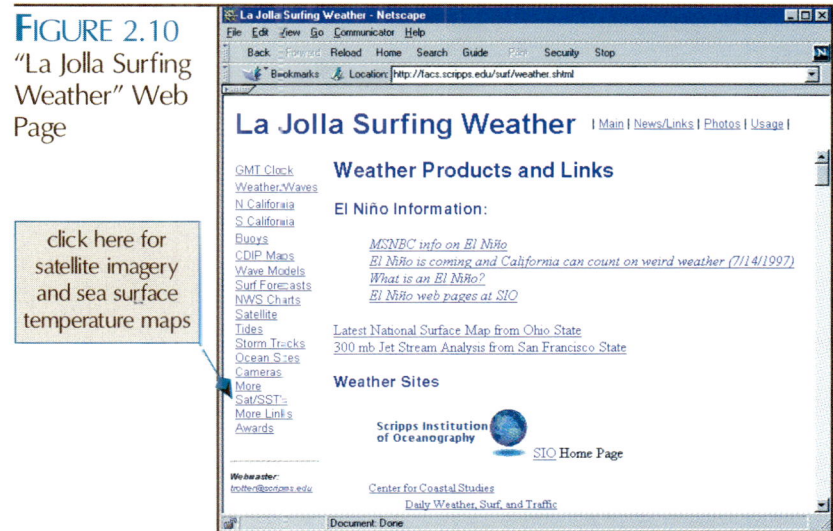

FIGURE 2.10 "La Jolla Surfing Weather" Web Page

Now we're going to look at some maps and images from satellite photos and imaging.

➕ Click on the hyperlink **Satellite** on the "La Jolla Surfing Weather" page.

The Web page for SOEST is shown in Figure 2.11.

➕ Click on the hyperlink **SOEST - School of Ocean & Earth Science & Technology, SOEST SatLab (U Hawaii)**.

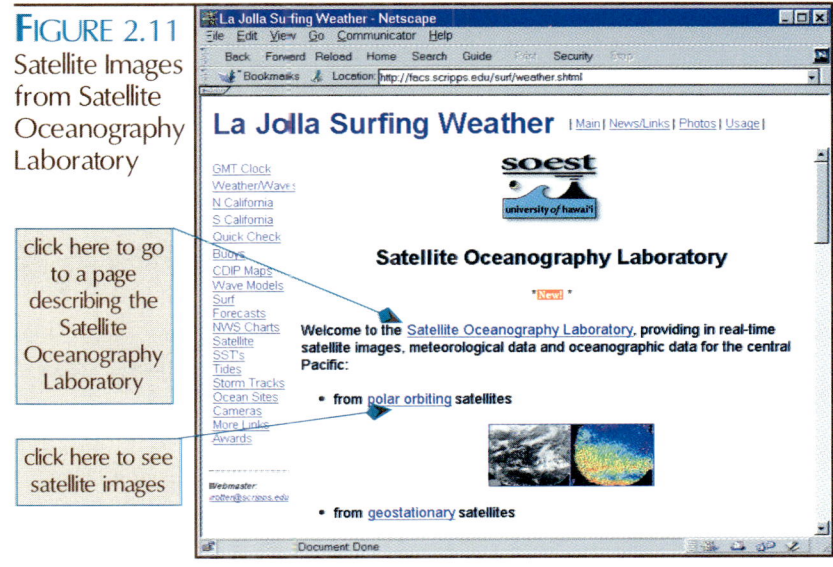

FIGURE 2.11 Satellite Images from Satellite Oceanography Laboratory

We've pointed out one hyperlink to follow for images in Figure 2.11. There are lots of others to visit. For now we're going to move on to a field trip to Hawaii. If you've followed a hyperlink to some images click on **Satellite** in the menu on the left and then select **SOEST** again.

7 Take a (virtual) field trip to Hawaii.

Now for a trip to Hawaii! It will be a virtual trip, but sure to be enjoyable nonetheless. Follow these steps to get to the Web site "Virtually Hawaii."

✈ Return to the "SOEST Satellite Oceanography Laboratory" Web page.

FIGURE 2.12
Virtually Hawaii

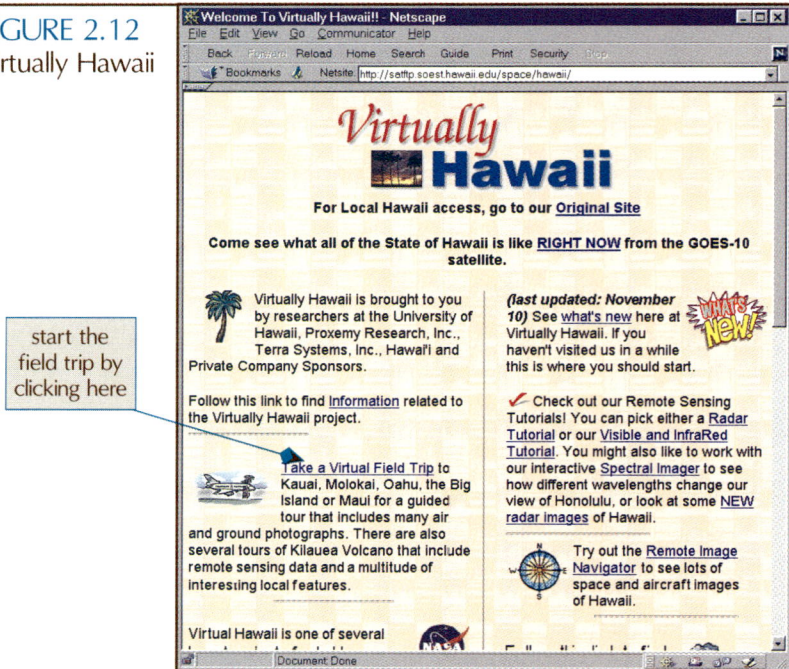

✈ Use the scroll bar or keyboard shortcut **Ctrl** + **End** to get to the end of the Web page.

✈ Click on the hyperlink **HTTP**, which gives access to the SOEST data directory.

✈ Click on the hyperlink **./space/hawaii/** for Virtually Hawaii, which is comprised of satellite images and virtual field trips.

We hope you've made it here without much trouble. Figure 2.12 shows the home page for Virtually Hawaii. Its URL is **http://satftp.soest.hawaii.edu/space/hawaii**.

Now for the field trip.

✈ Click on **Take a Virtual Field Trip** to explore Virtually Hawaii.

Take your time, look around for a while. We're going to leave here eventually (you decide when) and look at some other sports-related Web pages.

8 Use the history list to go back to the Sport home page.

We've traveled through several pages and now would like to get back to the home page for Sport in the WWW Virtual Library. Certainly one way to do that is by clicking on **Back** in the navigation toolbar until the proper page appears. But then we'd have to go through all the intervening pages. It's quicker to select the site from the history list. You can get to the list with **Ctrl**+**H** from the keyboard.

🔸 Press **Ctrl**+**H** from the keyboard.

This displays the history list as shown in Figure 2.13.

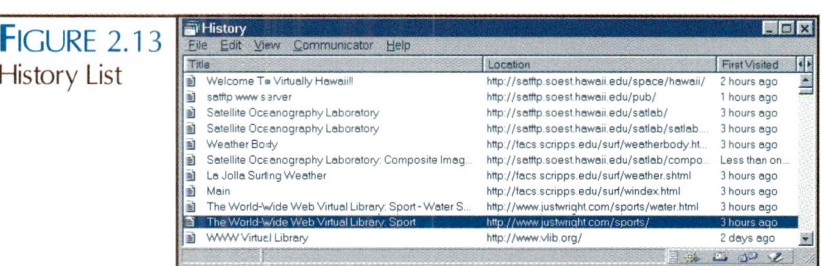

FIGURE 2.13
History List

🔸 Return to the Virtual Library Sport page by double-clicking on the (most recent) URL **http://www .justwright.com/ sports**—the one labeled **The World-Wide Web Virtual Library: Sport**.

Once the Sport page appears, you may want to close the history list. Do it the same way you'd close any window.

🔹 Get information about golf (explore the links!).

Now you are at the Sport home page. We'll follow some (hyper)links for information about golf.

🔸 Click on the hyperlink **Ball Sports**.

We're going to use the browser feature Find in Page.

🔸 Click on **Edit** in the menu bar, select **Find in Page**, type **golf** in the dialog box and press **Enter**.

Figure 2.14 shows the **Find** dialog box with the keyword **golf** typed in.

FIGURE 2.14
Using Find to Search for Keyword "golf"

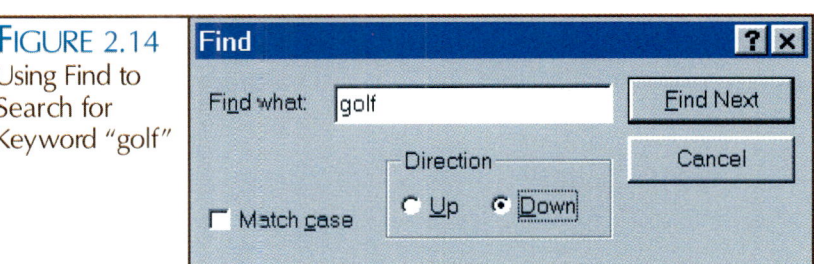

When you get to the section labeled **Golf**, click on **Cancel** to close the **Find** box.

There's lots to see here and the choice is yours. Two items with links to lots of other information about golf are GolfWeb and The Virtual Golfer.

Explore the links!

End the session.

You knew when we started that this had to end sometime. Now's the time.

Click on **File** on the menu bar.

Select **Exit** from the menu.

That's it!

End of Example 2.1

Getting Help

There are several ways to get help with using Netscape Navigator. Online help is available while you're using Netscape. There is a list of frequently asked questions (FAQ) with answers about using Netscape. Several Usenet newsgroups are dedicated to discussions about using a Web browser.

Online Help

To receive online help while using Netscape Navigator, click on **Help** on the menu bar. This pulls down a menu from which you can select one of several types of information, including **Help Contents**. You can also activate this option by pressing the function key F1. Online help starts in a separate window. It contains information that you may need while using Navigator or other parts of Communicator. Another useful item is **Product Information and Support**. Clicking on that takes you to a Web page supported by Netscape Communications. That Web page has many useful links for getting answers for your questions about using Netscape products.

Frequently Asked Questions (FAQ)

Frequently asked questions or *FAQ* is a traditional way to collect common questions and provide their answers on the Internet. As you browse the Internet, you'll see FAQs on all sorts of topics.

Here's a list of some useful FAQ sites that deal with using a browser and the World Wide Web:

- "Frequently-Asked Questions," published by Netscape.
  http://help.netscape.com/faqs

- "The Netscape Unofficial FAQ," maintained by Netscape employees and regular contributors to Netscape newsgroups.
  http://www.ufaq.org

- "WWW FAQ," by Tom Boutell. This hasn't been updated since 1996, but it still contains lots of useful information.
  http://raq002.aa.net/faq/oldfaq

Usenet Newsgroups

There are several (at least 15) Usenet newsgroups that host discussions about the WWW, and each maintains its own FAQ. A list of Usenet newsgroups about the WWW is available through the World Wide Web FAQ mentioned above.

One direct link to the list of newsgroups is found at **http://raq002.aa.net/faq/oldfaq/ngroups.htm**. You ought to check this URL because it has the names and descriptions of the groups.

You may want to read the following Usenet newsgroups:

+ **comp.infosystems .www.browsers.ms-windows**

    For discussion of Web browsers used with Microsoft Windows and NT operating systems.

+ **comp.infosystems .www.announce**

    Used to announce new Web pages.

The disk included with this book contains general information about Usenet newsgroups and instructions for getting your browser set for Usenet newsgroups. To read it, place the disk in Drive A and start your browser if it isn't already started. Click on **File** in the menu bar and select **Open Page**. Type

A:\Usenet.htm in the pane of the window that pops up and press **Enter**.

Saving, Printing, and Mailing Items from the WWW

Suppose you're working on the WWW and you come across a document, data, program, picture, sound or video clip, or anything you'd like to save. Or maybe you want to email one of those items to someone else or get a printed copy of it. A Web browser comes with tools and commands to let you do these things. Commands are available through the pull-down menu under **File** in the menu bar, through some of the icons in the command toolbar, and through keyboard shortcuts.

Remember, just because something is available on the WWW doesn't necessarily mean you may make a copy of it. In many cases, the material—text, images, sound—can't be used for commercial purposes without written permission.

Saving Web Pages in a File

You can save any Web page in a file on your computer. When a page is saved, you get the text portion along with the HTML

code for the page. Images, audio, and other types of elements in the page are not included because these things exist in files other than the one that holds the text you see on the screen. You may want to save a Web page in a file on your computer so you can access it in the future without connecting to the Internet. If the Web page has frames, click on the frame you want to save before following these steps.

To save a page, click on **File** in the menu bar and select **Save As** from the menu. The keyboard shortcut is **Ctrl**+S. A dialog box opens in which you confirm or give the name of the file to hold the page.

By default, a page is saved in source format, which means that it includes the text along with the HTML commands or tags used to create the page. It's really useful to see how others have used HTML to create and make Web pages when you're thinking about translating your designs for Web pages into HTML. To save only the text without HTML, you need to be sure the file name ends with **.txt** and that the file type selected is **Plain Text**. Figure 2.15 shows this.

Saving Items on a Web Page into a File

Almost anything that has a hyperlink to it can be saved in a

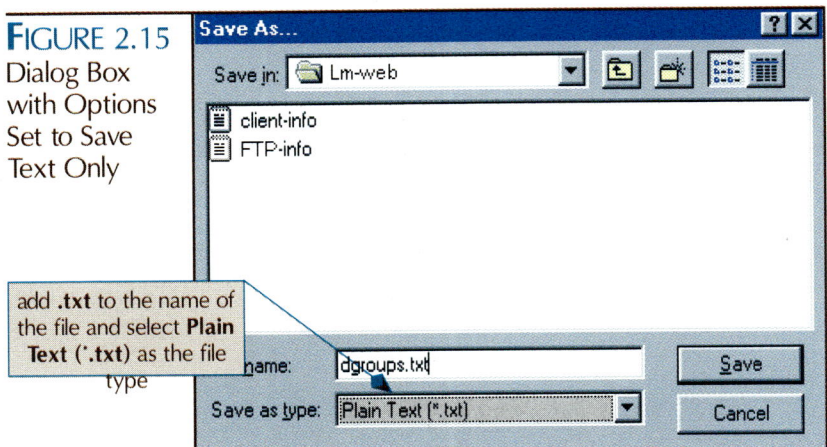

FIGURE 2.15
Dialog Box
with Options
Set to Save
Text Only

add **.txt** to the name of the file and select **Plain Text ('.txt)** as the file type

file. You can save items after you receive them—like saving a Web page to a file once the page is on the screen—or you can save them without seeing or hearing them beforehand. All the items are saved as files. Often, you're able to tell the type of information in a file by looking at the extension of the file name, such as **.doc** for a Microsoft Word file, **.gif** for an image, or **.wav** for an audio file. Saving a file from the Internet is called *downloading* the file.

To save whatever is on the other end of a hyperlink without viewing it first, move the mouse pointer to the hyperlink and click the *right* mouse button. When a shortcut menu pops up, select **Save Link As**. Another way to do this is to move the mouse pointer over the hyperlink, to hold down the Shift key, and to click the (left) mouse button.

The link can point to anything on the World Wide Web—

another Web page, a document in special format (such as a document prepared with a word processor or spreadsheet), an image, a compressed archive of files, a video file, an audio file, or even other possibilities. (Who knows what you'll find on the WWW?)

You can save an image in the browser window to a file by moving the mouse pointer over the image, clicking the *right* mouse button, and selecting **Save Image As** from the shortcut menu.

Whenever you save a file from the Internet, either directly or through a hyperlink, there's a possibility that the file will contain a computer virus or other software that may damage or erase your files. After you download a file, be sure to check it with antivirus software, which is a program that checks a file for viruses. A good source for information about com-

puter viruses is the PC Webopedia entry for the term *virus*, **http://webopedia .internet.com/TERM/v/ virus.html**.

Printing a Web Page

You can print whatever you see in your browser window with a printer that's connected to your computer. When a Web page is printed, everything you see in the window—text, graphics, images—is passed on to the printer.

Giving the command to print brings up a dialog box in which you can select the printer, determine the number of copies, and indicate which pages of the Web page you want to print. The phrase "pages of the Web page" may seem strange, but remember that a Web page isn't a physical page. The Web page, in fact, exists only in electronic form. You can preview the printing by picking the preview option. This will give you an idea of the printed Web page's physical layout.

Mailing a Web Page

The text on a Web page can be mailed to any Internet address. Mailing a page means sending only the text on the page or sending the source. The source is the text, as well as all the

HTML statements that specify hyperlinks, control the page format, and identify the source of the images and graphics on a page. In this sense, mailing a Web page is similar to saving a Web page in a file.

To mail a Web page, click on **File** in the menu bar and select **Mail Document**. A window pops up in which you indicate where you want to send the email, the subject, and anything else you'd like to write or include. The URL for the current Web page is automatically included in the message. You can send the page (either text or source) as an attachment to the email, or you can send it quoted (as text) in the body of the message. If you find something on a page that you want to share with someone else, it might be appropriate to mail them the URL. If they don't have access to a Web browser, then it would be better to attach or quote the Web page. If you quote or copy the Web page text in the body of your message, you can edit the text and send only a portion of the page.

Using a Web Browser with Local Files

You can use a Web browser to view files on a disk on your computer. You don't need the Internet to access these files,

called *local files*. It's really convenient to use your Web browser to look at local files—sometimes easier than opening another application or program to view a file. Once you view a file with the Web browser, you can work with it just like any Web page, including printing it or sending it by email. This is also a convenient way to check Web pages while they're being developed.

The local file has to be one with which your browser can work. You can't expect it to display a spreadsheet file without a program that lets you work with spreadsheets. On the other hand, you can expect it to work well with a text file or HTML file. The browser will let you view graphics or images if they're stored in GIF (file names end with **.gif**) or JPEG (file names end with **.jpg**) format.

These types of files work well, because your browser is already configured to work with such file types. For other types of files, you may have to set some options for helper applications in the Preferences section of your browser. When you want to view a file, the browser starts a program called a *viewer* that lets you look at the file's contents. For example, if it's a text file, it's displayed in the window just as it appears. If it's

a GIF file, then the browser starts a viewer that lets you look at images. If it's an HTML file, the browser displays it by following all the HTML commands. If there is no viewer for your file, Netscape lets you know and gives you a chance to name a viewer for the file. A viewer is more than a program that lets you look at a file. It can also be a program that lets you hear the sound encoded in an audio file.

To view a local file, choose **File** from the menu bar and then select **Open Page**. This will bring up a dialog box, as shown in Figure 2.3. When that happens, you can type in the file name. Alternately, you can browse through your files. Click on **Choose File** until you find the one you'd like to view. That opens another dialog box titled **Open**. You can look for files of a specific type or all files by making a choice in the item labeled **Files of type....**

If the browser can work either directly, through a plug-in, or through a helper application, it will. If not, a dialog box will appear that lets you download the appropriate plug-in or associate a helper application with files of that type. If you know the helper application you want to use, fill it in. If not, you may have to ask someone for assistance.

Here are some places to check on the WWW for information about plug-ins and helper applications:

- "Browser Plug-ins," Netscape Communications Corporation, Inc., Mountain View, CA, **http://home .netscape.com/ plugins**

- "Windows Helper Applications," Netscape Communications Corporation, Inc., Mountain View, CA, **http://home .netscape.com/assist/ helper_apps/ windows_helpers.html**

- "WWW Browsers, MIME and Helper Applications," by Doug Tower, University of California, San Diego, CA, **http://ssdc.ucsd .edu/dt/helpers.html**

Using Bookmarks to Keep Track of Resources

You can save links to interesting and useful Web pages by adding hyperlinks to your bookmark list. The bookmark list is the name Netscape gives to the collection of hyperlinks you've saved; each one is like a bookmark into the World Wide Web. Whenever you're using the browser, you can call up your bookmarks and follow any of the links. You'll want to keep adding bookmarks to Web pages as you collect sources for research. Netscape and other Web browsers give you the tools to add, delete, annotate, and rename the bookmarks. You can also arrange them into folders, list them various ways, keep different files of bookmarks, and otherwise manage the collection. We will now go over some of the essential bookmark operations, and you'll see that sometimes there is more than one way to perform each one.

Adding a Bookmark

Adding a bookmark means placing the Web page on the bookmark list. The phrase *bookmark a Web page* also means the same thing. Here are various ways to add a bookmark:

- Use the keyboard shortcut **Ctrl**+**D**.

- Click the *right* mouse button when the mouse pointer is on the Web page, frame, or hyperlink, and select **Add Bookmark**.

- Click on the **Bookmarks** icon in the location toolbar and select **Add Bookmark** from the menu.

- Drag and drop: Move the mouse pointer to the Page Proxy icon in the location bar and hold down the left mouse button. Without letting go of the mouse button, drag the icon to the Bookmarks icon. A menu appears. Drag the Page Proxy icon to **Add Bookmark** on the menu and let go of the mouse button. The Web page is added to whatever folder is set to hold new bookmarks. To add a bookmark to any folder, drag the Page Proxy icon to the Bookmarks icon as before and choose **File Bookmarks** from the menu. That brings up a list of the folders in the bookmark list. After you drag the icon to a folder, "drop" it.

Displaying the Bookmark List

For the next few things we'll mention, you need to display the bookmark list either in a separate window or as a menu.

To display the bookmark list in a separate window, do one of the following:

- Use the keyboard shortcut **Ctrl**+**B**.

- Click on the **Bookmarks** icon in the location bar and select **Edit Bookmarks** from the menu. The bookmark list appears as a menu. You can display a folder or select an item in the list.

Jumping to an Item in the Bookmark List

Jumping to an item means going directly to the Web page that the item represents. First, display the bookmark list, then move the mouse to the bookmark you want to use and click on it. If the bookmarks are arranged in folders or categories, select a category and then a bookmark.

Deleting an Item from the Bookmark List

There will be times that you'll want to remove an entry from the bookmark list. To do that, display the bookmark list in a separate window, and click on the item to delete. Once you select an item in this way, you can delete it by doing one of the following:

- Press the **Delete** key.

- Press **Ctrl**+**X**.

- Click on **Edit** in the menu bar of the bookmark window and select **Cut** or **Delete**.

Searching the Bookmark List

If there are many entries in the bookmark list, you may want to search the list for an entry. First, open the bookmark list in a separate window. Click on **Edit** and then select **Find**. (You can also use the keyboard shortcut **Ctrl**+**F**.) When a dialog box appears, type the word or phrase and click on the button labeled **OK**.

The bookmark list has many useful features. You'll learn how to take advantage of some of them after gaining experience and feeling comfortable with the bookmark list. We'll go over a few features in the next example.

EXAMPLE 2.2

Working with the Bookmark List

In this example, we'll add items to the bookmark list. Then, we'll create a folder or category and add some items to it. Several other things can be done with the bookmark list and its entries, but to conserve space we won't demonstrate all of them here. When the bookmark list is displayed in its own window (see Figure 2.5), the commands for working with the list are all available through the window's menu bar. Here are a few things you can do from the pull-down menus:

- Insert a new bookmark, new folder, or new separator.

- Import a bookmark file.

- Save the current bookmark list to a file using **File** menu commands.

- Cut, copy, paste, delete, or find items in the list.

- Access **Properties** from the **Edit** menu.

◆ Sort the bookmarks.

◆ Set the selected folder as the personal toolbar.

◆ Set the selected folder that will be used to hold new bookmarks.

◆ Select **Update Bookmarks** from the **View** menu to have Netscape see whether any of the bookmarks have changed since they were last visited.

In this example, you'll see several different windows without a clear connection of how you get from one to the other. That's intentional. We want to concentrate on setting and using bookmarks. The windows that appear here could have come from one session or several sessions.

Suppose you've started your Web browser in the same way as in previous examples and you're browsing the home page for the World Wide Web Virtual Library. A URL for that site is **http://www.vlib.org**. You'll want to add this page to your bookmark list so you can return to it in the future without having to type in the URL or remember the path you took to get there.

▶ Add the current page to the bookmark list.

✚ Press **Ctrl**+**D** to add the current Web page to the bookmark list.

Suppose that while you're browsing the Virtual Library, you select the section **Humanities**, then **Archaeology**, and click on the hyperlink **Museums**. This takes you to the Web site "ArchNet: Museums on the Web," whose URL is **http://archnet.uconn.edu/museums**, as shown in Figure 2.16.

FIGURE 2.16
ArchNet: Museums and Research Facilities

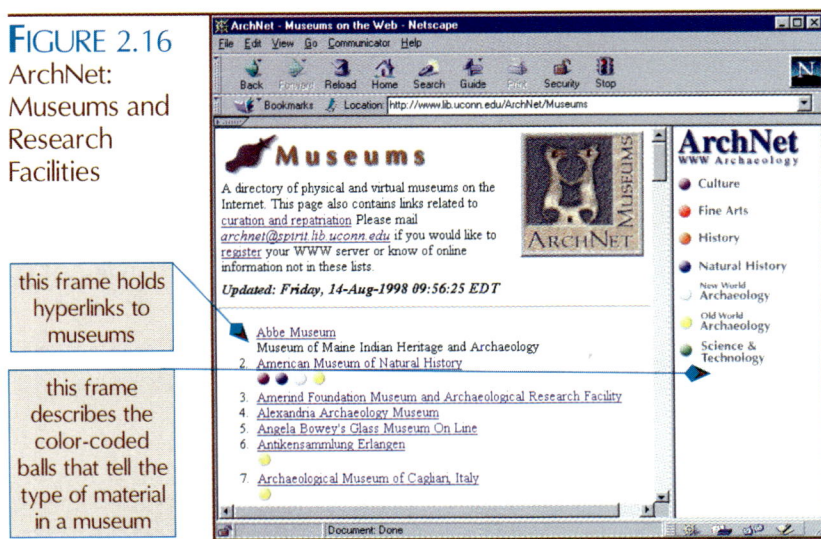

this frame holds hyperlinks to museums

this frame describes the color-coded balls that tell the type of material in a museum

From here, you visit several museums on the list and add some to the bookmark list. If the bookmark list was empty when we started or had no folders, then the bookmarks are added one after the other. If folders already exist, the new bookmarks are added to the folder that's labeled with a graphic image indicating it is the "new bookmarks" folder. For now, we'll assume that there weren't any folders in the bookmark list.

▶ View the bookmark list.

✈ To view the bookmark list, use the keyboard shortcut **Ctrl**+**B**.

In the section before this activity, we discussed other ways of viewing the bookmark list. You may want to try one of those methods instead.

Figure 2.17 shows the current bookmark list.

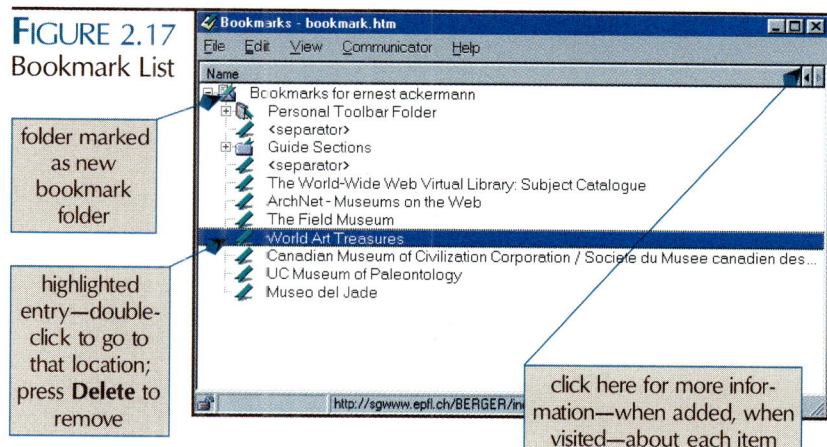

FIGURE 2.17
Bookmark List

folder marked as new bookmark folder

highlighted entry—double-click to go to that location; press **Delete** to remove

click here for more information—when added, when visited—about each item

♦ Clicking once on an entry highlights it. To jump to the location specified by the item, double-click on it.

♦ To change the name or other information about a bookmark item, select **Properties** from the View pull-down menu.

♦ To delete or remove an entry from the bookmark list, highlight it and press the **Delete** key or select **Cut** from the pull-down menu under **Edit**.

♦ Select or highlight several entries by highlighting one and holding down the **Ctrl** key as you click on others. You can delete a group in the same way as you delete one item.

♦ To sort the entries, highlight a group and choose one of the sort options—**By Name**, **By Location**, **By Created On**, or **By Last Visited**—from the menu under **View**.

✦ Close the bookmark window by pressing **Ctrl**+**W** or clicking on the ✕ in the upper-right corner. The window can stay open while you're doing other things on your computer or on the Internet.

You can add more items to your bookmark list at any time when you're browsing or working with information on the World Wide Web. At some point, you may want to arrange your bookmarks into categories. Starting with the bookmark list shown in Figure 2.17, we'll add one folder titled **Museums** and put all the museum sites in that folder. Once the bookmark window is open, you can create a folder.

╋ Click on **File** in the menu bar and select **New Folder**.

Clicking on **New Folder** brings up the window that appears in Figure 2.18, except that the first pane is called **New Folder** and the second larger one is empty.

▶ Name the new folder.

Figure 2.18 shows the new folder window with all the information entered. Netscape automatically fills in the date on which this new piece of data was added.

╋ Click on the top frame and type **Museums**. Click on the bottom frame and type **Interesting Museums on the World Wide Web**. Click **OK** when you're finished.

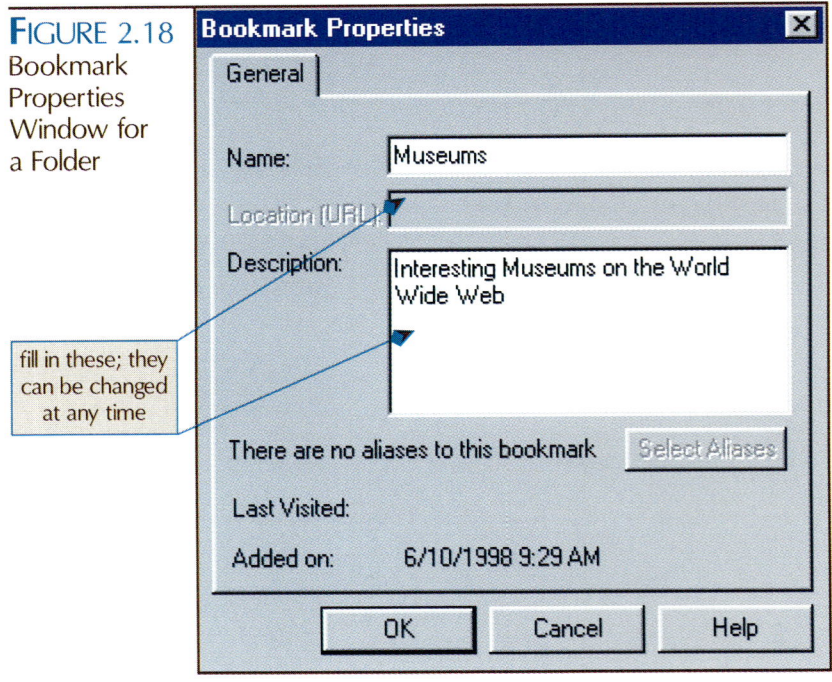

FIGURE 2.18 Bookmark Properties Window for a Folder

After you click **OK**, the folder is added to the bookmark list as shown in Figure 2.19.

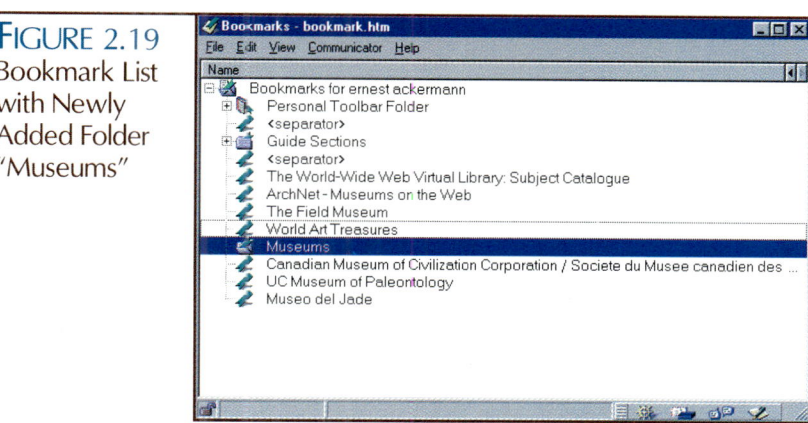

FIGURE 2.19
Bookmark List with Newly Added Folder "Museums"

You can insert each of the hyperlinks or entries that represent a museum into the new folder in the same way, by using the drag-and-drop technique we mentioned earlier. Here are the instructions to move the item **The Field Museum of Natural History** into the folder.

Another way to move an item to a folder is to highlight the item, select **Cut** from the **Edit** menu, highlight the folder, and select **Paste** from the **Edit** menu.

After all the entries for museums are placed in the folder, the bookmark list will look as shown in Figure 2.20.

❹ Edit the bookmark list.

✦ Click on **The Field Museum of Natural History** and hold down the left mouse button. Drag the highlighted entry to the folder called **Museums** and release the button.

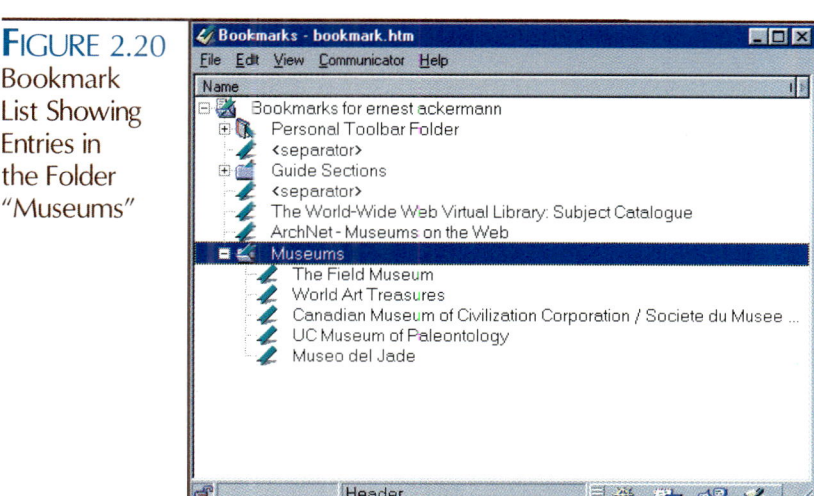

FIGURE 2.20
Bookmark List Showing Entries in the Folder "Museums"

As we said earlier, there are other things you can do when working with the bookmark list. Here are some things you may want to try:

◆ Double-click on the open folder to close it so that only the folder name appears in the list.

◆ Double-click again to open the folder.

◆ Move items that aren't in the open folder to the bottom of the list in the same way that you added items to the folder.

◆ Sort the items in the list by highlighting more than one and choosing one of the sort or list options from the **View** menu.

End of Example 2.2

Example 2.2 showed how to arrange bookmarks into a folder. Once you start collecting bookmarks, it's a good idea to think about organizing them. You'll also want to think about deleting or discarding bookmarks when you no longer need them.

Setting Preferences

Your Web browser lets you set several options and preferences. This allows you to customize the Web browser to meet your needs through the options you specify. The preferences let you set items that deal with the way Web pages are displayed, the way the browser's toolbars are displayed, and the way the browser works with other programs. Some of the things you can do are set the startup or home page, specify the way the Web browser displays pages and

images, determine how your browser will deal with email and Usenet newsgroups, and set other preferences for the way the browser will work with your computer system and network. Many of these preferences will be set for you the first time you use the browser, and we won't cover all the preferences here. When you have questions about some of the preferences, it's a good idea to ask someone about them, read the online manual included with your browser, or check some of the sections on the online help. Experimentation is good, but be sure to write down the current settings before you change anything. You don't want to create unnecessary problems for yourself or someone else.

To set options and preferences, click on **Edit** in the menu bar, and select **Preferences**. A new window pops up with a list of categories on the left. Each

one corresponds to a panel on the right. Select a category to examine or modify the current settings. Some options or preferences are easy to find. We'll look at setting the home page and how long an item stays in the history list in Example 2.3, below. Some preferences aren't so easy to find. If it's taking a long time for you to retrieve pages with images, you may want to set the browser so images aren't automatically loaded with every page. You can then choose to display images by clicking on **Images** (it's only there if you don't automatically load images) in the navigation toolbar. To set this preference you need to select **Advanced** from the list of categories and then click on the checkbox to the left of **Automatically load images**.

Example 2.3 shows how to set the home page and work with link styles.

EXAMPLE 2.3

Setting the Home Page and How Long an Item Stays in the History List

Netscape Navigator allows you to set several preferences for the browser. Most are preset so you don't need to set a lot of preferences before you use the browser. In this example we'll set preferences that name the home page for the browser and specify how long an item stays in the history list. Preferences are set by first clicking on **Edit** in the toolbar, selecting **Preferences**, then selecting a category or subcategory, and setting the options from there. Assuming that Netscape Navigator is already started we'll follow these steps:

1. Select **Edit** from the menu bar.

2. Select **Preferences**.

3. Select the category labeled **Navigator**.

4. Set the home page.

5. Modify the number of days an item stays in the history list.

6. Put the new settings into effect.

Now to go through it step by step:

▶ Select **Edit** from the menu bar.

A pull-down menu is displayed. Select **Preferences**.

✛ Click on **Edit** on the menu bar.

▶ Select **Preferences**.

This brings up another window with categories and subcategories listed on the left. You may want to take a little time to get familiar with the frame that appears on the right as you select a category. We're going to use the category labeled **Navigator**.

✛ On the pull-down menu, click **Preferences**.

▶ Select the category labeled **Navigator**.

The frame for the category **Navigator** may have come in view when you completed the previous step. If it didn't then bring it into view.

✛ Click on the tab labeled **Navigator**.

The **Navigator** frame will appear as shown in Figure 2.21.

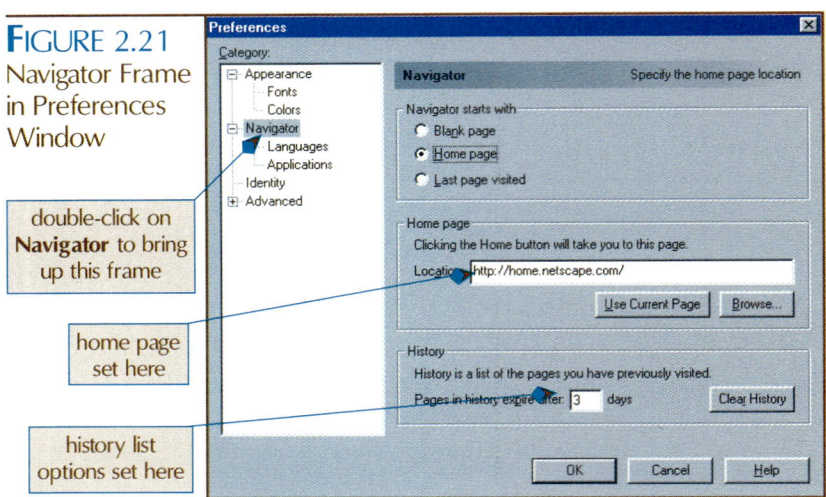

FIGURE 2.21
Navigator Frame
in Preferences
Window

double-click on
Navigator to bring
up this frame

home page
set here

history list
options set here

There are several preferences that can be set here. With the current settings, Navigator starts with a home page (the home page for Netscape) and items will stay in the history list for three days.

◆ **Set the home page.**

＋ Highlight the entry in the pane holding the URL of the home page by double-clicking on it.

We're going to set the home page to the home page of Franklin, Beedle & Associates. They're the folks who publish this book. Feel free to set yours to whatever you'd like. It's common to set it to your personal home page or the home page of your school, organization, or business.

＋ To replace the current URL, type **http:// www.fbeedle.com** and press Enter.

◆ **Modify the number of days an item stays in the history list.**

The current setting for how long items will stay in the history list is three days. It would be reasonable to change that if we didn't use the Web browser that frequently on this computer, or if we wanted to keep track of what we had been doing over a period of time longer than three days. How about we change it to seven days?

＋ Highlight the entry in the box just to the left of the word **days**.

The modified settings should look like the one in Figure 2.22.

＋ Type 7 and press Enter.

❻ Put the new settings into effect.

✛ Click on the button labeled **OK**.

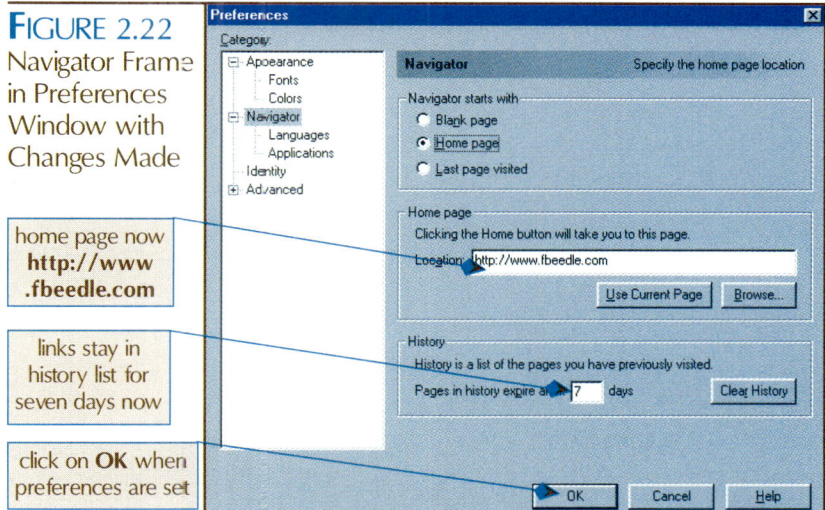

FIGURE 2.22 Navigator Frame in Preferences Window with Changes Made

home page now **http://www .fbeedle.com**

links stay in history list for seven days now

click on **OK** when preferences are set

✛ To see if the changes have taken effect, click on **Home** in the navigation toolbar.

End of Example 2.3

Summary

A Web browser is used to access the information and resources on the World Wide Web. Whenever you start the browser or access a hyperlink, the browser—which is a computer program—sends a request to have a file transferred to it. The browser then interprets the information in the file so it can be viewed in the browser's window, or in some cases, viewed through another program. For example, if a hyperlink points to a text file, then the file is displayed in the window as ordinary text. If the hyperlink points to a document written in hypertext markup language (HTML), then it's displayed by the browser, or if the file is a sound file or an animation, then a program different from the browser is started so the file can be heard or seen. Most of the facilities and capabilities are built into the browser, but in some cases your computer needs to have special equipment or programs. A good example of this is a hyperlink that points to a sound file. Your computer needs to have a sound card, speakers, and the appropriate software to play the sounds.

Starting a Web browser usually means first activating your connection to the Internet and then clicking on an icon or command to launch Netscape Navigator. If the cost of using the Internet access depends on how much time is spent being connected, then be sure to terminate the Internet connection when your session on the Web is over.

The commands you use to work with the Web browser are available through the menu bar, the toolbar, the directory buttons, and the keyboard. These, along with the scroll bars, stay the same regardless of what you're viewing or working with on the World Wide Web. The menu bar is a collection of pull-down menus that you can use for almost every operation or command. Click on **Edit** and select **Preferences** to set preferences for the Web browser. The preferences may be personal or depend on the computer or network. Another menu (**Help**) lets you select one of several ways to help yourself learn about Netscape, including an online manual. A number of items in the navigation toolbar give quick access to some of the commands in the pull-down menu. Several commands are also available as keyboard shortcuts, meaning that you can type them directly on the keyboard instead of using a mouse.

Once a page is in the browser's window, you can move around the page using the keyboard, scroll bars, or mouse. You can search for words in the page. Move the mouse to a hyperlink (the pointer turns to a hand) and click on it to follow it. A URL can be typed in the location bar or you can select a command to open a location. In any of these cases, the browser will follow the URL you've typed or represent the hyperlink to view another Web page.

The browser keeps track of the sites you've visited within a session. It does this so you can backtrack and return to sites during a session. The backtracking is restricted to traveling in a straight line. Suppose you start at site A, go to B, and then go to C. If you click on **Back** you'll be taken to B. Click on it again and you'll go to A. You can click on **Forward** and be taken to B (from A) and click on it again and you'll go to C. Now, suppose you go from a site called Base, then go to a site named Right, return to Base (by pressing **Back**), then go to a site named Left, and then return to Base again. If you click on **Forward** now, you'll be taken to Left. The browser keeps a list, called the history list, of the sites you've visited within a session that are accessible by **Back** and **Forward**. You can collect a set of hyperlinks in a list called the bookmark list. These will be available from one session to the next. The browser contains commands to let you maintain and manage your bookmark list.

Provided you're not breaking copyright laws or conventions, information found on the World Wide Web can be saved into a file, printed, or mailed to an Internet address. You can also use the browser to view local files without connecting to the Internet. When you're developing your own Web pages, you may want to use this to test them before making them available to anyone on the Internet.

There are a number of sites on the Internet from which you can retrieve the most recent copy of a Web browser; programs that work as plugins for the browser to display/view/play certain types of files; and useful information and help. The browser lets you access, retrieve, work with, and enjoy the information and resources that make up the World Wide Web. To coin a phrase—the browser is your window to the Web.

Selected Terms in This Chapter

bookmark list
content area
frame
frequently asked questions
   (FAQ)

helper application
history list
home page
menu bar
plug-in

scroll bar
status bar
toolbar
Uniform Resource Locator
   (URL)

These exercises are designed to help you become familiar with using your Web browser. They may also introduce you to some interesting sites on the WWW. As you do them, refer back to the material in this chapter and to the online manual included with Netscape.

1. Start your Web browser.
   a. Describe what's on the home page.
   b. Go to the bottom of the home page using the scroll bar.
   c. Go to the top of the home page using a keyboard short-cut.
   d. Follow a hyperlink from the home page, then follow a hyperlink from that page. Click on **Back**, then click on it again. Where are you? Click on **Forward**. Where are you now?

2. Go to the WWW Virtual Library arranged by subject, **http://www.vlib.org**.
   a. Add it to your bookmark list.
   b. Go to the section of the Virtual Library for the subject Music. First go to the section **Humanities** and then select **Music**. Who maintains this area of the library?
   c. What resources are available from the main Music page?
   d. Follow a few hyperlinks according to your interests. What's in your history list?
   e. Go to a location in the middle of your history list by selecting it from the list, and now return to the site at the top of the history list. What sites did you visit?

3. Spend a little time browsing through the **Medicine & Health** section of **Science** in the WWW Virtual Library. Add a few sites you find interesting to your bookmark list. What's in your bookmark list now?

4. Go to the section **Games**, in the category **Recreation** in the WWW VL arranged by subject. Work through this to find five bookmarks related to either one type of game or a

collection of games you're interested in. Add them to your bookmark list.

5. Go to a site on the WWW that holds the World Wide Web FAQ. (One place to start is **http://raq002.aa.net/faq/ oldfaq**.)

   a. List the URLs of four different sites that hold the WWW FAQ in four different countries on three different continents.

   b. Add the one that's closest to your bookmark list.

   c. Give a summary of the answers to these questions from the section titled "Introduction to the World Wide Web."

      What is the Web?

      What is a URL?

      Can I catch a virus from a Web page?

6. Open the location or go to the Web page for the Consumer Information Center using the URL **http:// www.pueblo.gsa.gov**. Select the section from the catalog dealing with employment. Follow the hyperlink to a pamphlet such as "Tips for Finding the Right Job" or "Resumes, Application Forms, Cover Letters, and Interviews."

   a. Save a copy of the article in a file on your computer.

   b. Print a copy of the article.

   c. Send a copy of the article by email to a friend who can use it.

7. For the file you saved in the previous exercise,

   a. view it as a local file using Netscape Navigator.

   b. copy it to a floppy disk or include a portion of it in a document you can prepare using a word processor on your computer.

8. If you've done the previous exercise, you've probably collected a number of entries in your bookmark list. Using the instructions in Example 2.2 and the online help, arrange

your bookmark list so the items are arranged into at least three categories (with at least three headers).

9. Go to the home page for National Public Radio (**http://www.npr.org/**). Follow the link **news now** and find a hyperlink labeled **Audio**.

   a. If a Real Audio player isn't present on your computer, go back to the NPR home page and follow the link **Real Audio**.

   b. Follow the instructions on the NPR Real Audio page to download the Real Audio player and set it as an application in your browser.

   c. Now go to the Web page "Showcase," **http://www.real.com/showcase/index.html**. What's there? Try viewing/listening to some of the items in the showcase. Which do you think makes a good use of the technology? Why?

10. There are several sites that track changes in Web browsers and have information about several specific ones.

   a. Take a look at the Web page whose URL is **http://www.browsers.com**. What are the latest versions available for the more popular Web browsers? What is Opera? What are some of the top plug-ins listed?

   b. What's available at the "BrowserWatch Home Page" at **http://browserwatch.internet.com**? Give a description and an example of what's available.

   c. Suppose you were interested in keeping up with changes in Web browsers. Which of these sites would be more useful to you? Why?

chapter 3

THE BASICS OF ELECTRONIC MAIL AND USING NETSCAPE EMAIL

This chapter focuses on the basics of email. All versions of Netscape Navigator have the capability to send email (we looked at that in Chapter 2), and Netscape version 2 or later includes the programs to both send and receive email. Some folks use other email programs, such as Eudora, cc:Mail, Mailx, Microsoft Office Express, or Pine. Regardless of which you use, you'll have to understand many of the following topics:

- **How Email Works**
- **Advantages and Limitations of Email**
- **Understanding Internet Email Addresses**
- **Dissecting a Piece of Email—Headers, Message, and Signature**
- **Finding Someone's Internet Email Address**
- **Email Etiquette**
- **Working with Nontext Files**
- **Working with Netscape Mail**

We'll demonstrate using email by working with the email system that comes with Netscape Communicator. Most email programs operate in basically the same way. The topics we'll cover here include:

- **Setting Options in Netscape to Let You Use Email**
- **Reading Email**
- **Saving, Deleting, and Printing Messages**
- **Composing and Sending Email**
- **Replying to a Message**
- **Working with an Address Book**

Electronic mail, or email, lets you communicate with other people on the Internet. Email is one of the basic Internet services, and by far the most popular. You can use it for any type of conversation; it's a way to keep in touch with friends, get information, start relationships, or express your opinion. Much of the time you'll be exchanging messages in plain text form (like the words on this page), but you can also exchange files in other formats such as spreadsheets, files for word processors, images, or programs. You can use email to join discussion groups and access other Internet services. You can send messages to anyone with an Internet address, and likewise, you can receive email from anywhere on the Internet. With over 100 million people having some sort of connection to the Internet, you've got the opportunity to communicate with people nearby and around the world in a relatively quick and efficient manner.

You use a mail program on your computer to compose, send, and read email. Once you compose (write) a message, it's sent in electronic form, usually passing through several other sites on the Internet. Email is held at its destination until the person to whom it's addressed reads it, saves it in a file, or deletes it. The recipient does not have to be logged in or using a computer for the email to be delivered. When she does use her computer and checks for email, it will be delivered to her.

Email is a very convenient way to communicate with people; it's personal, and it seems everybody likes to get mail. Because email is used so often, it's worth spending some time to learn about how it works and its capabilities.

How Email Works

Electronic mail lets you send and receive messages in electronic form. The person you communicate with could be any other user on the Internet, someone using the same computer system as you, or someone on a computer system thousands of miles away. The email is transmitted between computer systems, which exchange messages or pass them on to other sites according to certain Internet protocols or rules. You don't need to be concerned with many of the details; that's the computer's job. But you ought to know a little bit about the way email works.

Sending email is similar to sending something by a postal service. If you're sending a letter or a package to someone, you follow these steps:

1. Write the letter or make up the package.

2. Address it.

3. Put on the proper postage or pay the charges to send it.

4. Drop it off somewhere so it can be sent and eventually delivered.

You don't care much about which methods are used to deliver it or what route it takes. You prepare what you want to send, address it, and hand it to the postal service or delivery company. You expect them to take care of the details of delivering the letter or package. With email you follow similar steps:

1. Start an email program.

2. Give the address of where to send the email.

3. Compose a message using that email program.

4. Give a command to send the message.

You've probably noticed that we've left out the part about adding postage and paying charges. Individual users (usually) don't pay a per message fee for email. One email address is included with most Internet services' fees, with an extra charge for each additional address or mailbox.

You use an email program to address, compose, and send the message. Email programs are called *mail user agents* because they act on the user's behalf. The user agent lets you prepare and send messages and also work with the mail you've received. The email program acts as a go-between with you and computer systems, and the computer systems handle the details of delivering and receiving mail. Once again, you don't have anything to do with how the mail is delivered.

Messages are sent from one site to another on the Internet in this way. When you compose your message, it's all in one piece, but when it's sent out to the Internet, it's divided into several pieces called *packets*. The number of packets depends on the size of the message. Each of the packets contains, among other things:

- The email address of the person who sent the mail, the sender.

- The email address of the person to receive the mail, the recipient.

- Between 1 and 1,500 characters of the message.

The packets are sent to the destination, passing through several Internet sites. Thousands of networks and millions of computers make up the Internet, and packets are passed from system

to system. Each site accepts the packets addressed to it, but passes on the messages destined for another address. The packets can travel or arrive at their destination in any order, and they don't all have to take the same path. When you communicate with a remote site, you may think you have direct connection, but that's usually not the case. At the destination, the packets are collected and put in order, so the email appears to be in the same form it was sent. If there are errors in the packets or if some are lost, the destination sends a request back to the source asking for the message to be resent. All of this takes place according to *SMTP, simple mail transfer protocol*, the protocol the Internet commonly uses to transport message between computer systems. SMTP uses TCP, transmission control protocol, which provides a reliable means of communication.

To put it all in a nutshell: A message sent by email is divided into packets, and the packets are sent (possibly by different paths and passing through different sites) to the destination, where they are reassembled into the original message.

When you use a personal computer for email, your computer isn't turned on all the time. There has to be another computer system, called a *mail server*, that's (almost) always running and connected to the Internet and is able to receive mail for you at any time. That other system—perhaps the one at your Internet service provider or network center—holds the email addressed to you until you start an email pro-

gram on your system and check to see if you've received any new email. Your computer sends email to the email server by SMTP, and the server system exchanges email with the rest of the Internet. When you check to see if there's any new email, another protocol, either *post office protocol* (*POP*) or *Internet message access protocol* (*IMAP*), is used.

Once a message is sent, it's put out on the Internet and usually delivered in a short time—minutes or seconds. But a few things could cause problems:

◆ **There are delays.**

The computer system at the destination might not be accepting messages because it's down (not working) or too busy doing other things, or there is no path on the Internet to the destination—which usually means that some computer system or network is temporarily unavailable. If a message is delayed, the program handling mail will try to send it at another time.

> ✦ **The mail can't be delivered to the remote site.**

The system at the destination could be down for several days, or perhaps the address is wrong. Most programs handling email try to deliver a message for at least three days. If it can't be delivered at the end of that time, you'll probably receive email notifying you of the problem. If you type an address that doesn't exist, you'll be notified about that as well—usually pretty quickly.

> ✦ **The mail is delivered to the remote site but can't be delivered to the recipient.**

The local part of the address might be wrong; you'll get email back about that. The recipient might have no more space left in his mailbox; either a disk is full or a quota (set by the system administrator) was exceeded. In this case you, the sender, may not be notified. After all, the mail was delivered to the remote site and the address is correct.

> ✦ **Other problems.**

The person to whom you sent the message doesn't check to see if there is any email, doesn't read the email you sent, or accidentally deletes it.

You may never know if any of these things happens. The most you can expect from an email system is for it to notify the sender if there is some reason why the recipient could not receive the email.

When you read your email, once again you use a program (a mail user agent) that helps you work with the messages you have waiting for you. On many systems you're told if you have email when you log in, access the system you use to contact the Internet, or start your system. The email messages can arrive at any time. They're added to a file, your mailbox or inbox, which is part of a directory that holds all the email for the system. The packets making up an email message arrive at the email server, they're assembled, and then added to your mailbox. It holds all the messages on the server addressed to you, and only you or the system administrator can read your mail. If for some reason your mailbox gets scrambled, corrupted, or is changed so you can't read your mail, get in touch with the system administrator or call your Internet service provider. On many systems, all the users share

the space allocated for the directory that holds email. Usually there's enough space to hold a lot of messages, but it's important that you delete old email messages and messages you've read so there is space to hold everybody's email.

Advantages and Limitations of Email

Advantages

Email has a number of advantages over some other forms of communication. It's quick, convenient, and nonintrusive.

> ✦ You can communicate quickly with anyone on the Internet. Email usually reaches its destination within a matter of minutes or seconds.

> ✦ The cost of communication has nothing to do with distance, and in many cases, the cost doesn't depend on the size of the message.

> ✦ You can send letters, notes, files, data, or reports all using the same techniques. Once you learn how to use your email program, everything is sent the same way.

- You don't have to worry about interrupting someone when you send email. The email is sent and delivered by one computer system communicating with the Internet. Although it is put into someone's mailbox, the recipient isn't interrupted by the arrival of email.

- You can deal with your email at a convenient time. You don't have to be interrupted when email arrives, and you can read it or work with it when you have the time. Also, you can send it at a convenient time. It doesn't have to be written or sent at a time when you know the recipient will be available.

- You don't have to play phone tag or make an appointment to communicate with someone. Once again, the email is sent when it's convenient for you, and it can arrive even when the recipient isn't using her computer.

- You don't have to be shy about using email to communicate with anyone. Email isn't anonymous—each message carries the return address of the sender—but you can write to anyone with an Internet address. All the messages appear the same to the person who gets the email. The messages are generally judged on what's in them, not where they're from.

Limitations

- Email isn't necessarily private. Since messages are passed from one system to another, and sometimes through several systems or networks, there are many opportunities for someone to intercept or read email. Many types of computer systems have protections built in to stop users from reading others' email, but it's still possible for a system administrator to read the email on a system or for someone to bypass the security of a computer system. This is discussed in more detail in later.

- It may be difficult to express emotion using email. The recipient doesn't have the benefit of seeing your facial expressions or hearing your voice. You have to be careful with humor or sarcasm, since it's easy for someone to take your message the wrong way. Some folks use emoticons—icons that are meant to convey emotions, to help. For example, :-) or :) represents a smile. Put that after a line in a message if you're kidding. For more information on emoticons look at the Web page "What Is...an emoticon or a smiley (a definition)," **http://whatis.com/emoticon.htm**.

- You can receive too much email, and you have to take the time to deal with it. You'll probably have some limit on the amount of space your email can take up on the computer system you use. If you join a discussion group, it's possible that you'll be flooded with messages that may be of little value or even offensive, since you can receive "junk" email, called *spam*, in the same way you receive other types of junk mail. Some people see email as an

When you know someone's email address, you have an idea of their **login name and the name of the Internet site** they use. You should be able to send email to **postmaster** at any Internet site.

inexpensive way to market products or advertise. In any of these cases, you may have to take active steps to delete the email you receive and try to stop it from being sent to you in the first place.

➤ It's possible to forge email. This is not com-

mon, but it is possible to forge the address of the sender. You may want to take steps to confirm the source of some email you receive.

➤ Some email systems can send or receive text files only. Although you can send and receive images,

programs, files produced by word-processing programs, or multimedia messages, some folks may not be able to properly view your message.

Although there are some drawbacks to using email, it's still an effective and popular way to communicate.

Understanding Internet Email Addresses

An email address on the Internet usually has the form:

```
local-address@domain-name
```

The *local-address* part is often the user's login name, the name given to get in touch with the Internet server. That's followed by the character @, called the *at sign*. To its right is the domain name of the computer system

that handles the email for the user. Sometimes the *domain-name* portion is the name of a specific computer, such as **oregano.mwc.edu**. It could be more general, such as **mwc.edu**, and in this case the systems at the

site **mwc.edu** handle delivering mail to the appropriate computer. The portions or fields making up the domain name are separated by periods (the periods are called *dots*).

Here are two examples:

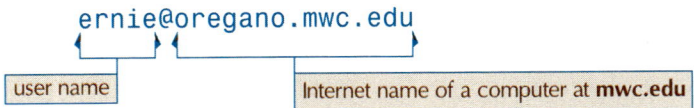
ernie@oregano.mwc.edu
user name · Internet name of a computer at **mwc.edu**

If you were going to tell someone the address, you would say "ernie at oregano dot mwc dot edu." (*ernie* and *oregano* are pronounced as words, but *mwc* [em double-u see] and *edu* [e dee you] are pronounced as individual letters.)

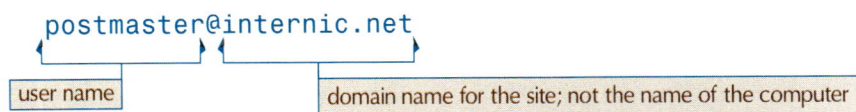
postmaster@internic.net
user name · domain name for the site; not the name of the computer

When you know someone's email address, you have an idea of their login name and the name of the Internet site they use. You should be able to send

email to **postmaster** at any Internet site. That's the address to use if you have questions about email to or from a specific host or site or general ques-

tions about a site. However, you may not get a quick response, since the person designated as postmaster usually has lots of other duties.

Dissecting Email—Headers, Message Body, and Signature

One piece of email has three main parts:

1. Headers

2. Message body

3. Signature

The headers are pieces of information that tell you and the email system several important things about a piece of email. Each header has a specific name and a specific purpose. You'll see some, but not necessarily all the headers each time you read a piece of email. They're all generated and put in the proper form by the email program you use, some with information from you, such as the address of the recipient, and some done automatically, such as the date.

When you read an email message, you're likely to see these headers. Here is a list of the most common headers. Figure 3.1 shows these as part of an email message.

Subject:	The subject of the email
Date:	When the email was sent
From:	The email address of the sender
To:	The email address of the recipient

The message body is the content of the email—what you send and what you receive. When you're sending email to a computer system where your message will be interpreted by a computer program, you will be given instructions to use specific words or phrases in the message body. One time you might have to follow instructions like this when you subscribe to a discussion group. Here's an example of what you might see:

```
TO SUBSCRIBE (UNSUBSCRIBE): Send email message to:
            Majordomo@world.std.com
The body of the message should read: Subscribe (unsubscribe) rocks-and-fossils
```

The *signature*, which is optional, isn't a signed name but a sequence of lines, usually giving some information about the person who sent the email. It is made up of anything the user wants to include. Usually a signature has the full name of the sender and some information about how to contact the person by email, phone, or fax. Some signatures also contain a favorite quotation or some graphics created by typing characters from the keyboard. Make sure it's not too long. The longer it is, the more bytes or characters have to be sent, and so the more traffic to be carried on the Internet. It's fun to be creative and come up with a clever signature, but try to limit it to five lines.

You don't have to type in the signature each time. Email programs will automatically append the contents of a specified file to each outgoing message. The name of the file depends on the program you're using for email. Some common names are **signature**, **sig.txt**, or **signature.pce** on computers that use Microsoft Windows as the operating sys-

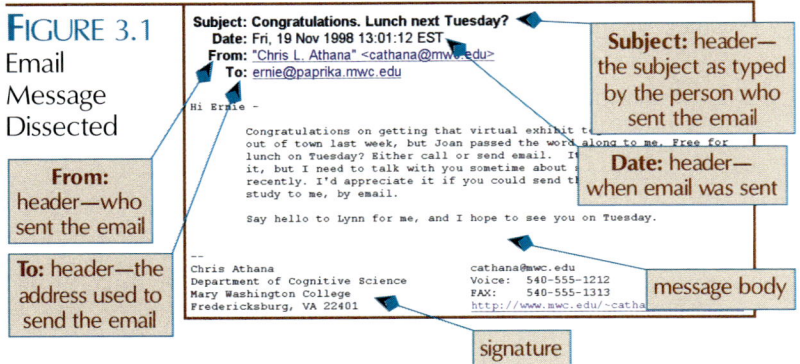

tem. On Unix systems the name **.sig** or **.signature** is often used. Most email programs allow you to specify what file to use as a signature, but you should check with a local expert about the precise name of the signature file. With Netscape, you set the name and location of the signature file in the **Mail & Groups** section of the **Preferences** pull-down menu.

Figure 3.1 shows an email message dissected into its parts: headers, body, and signature.

The email you receive may include other headers as well as those shown in Figure 3.1. We wanted to show the major ones.

Finding Someone's Internet Email Address

Once you get the bug of communicating by email, you'll probably start to wonder about the email addresses of your friends, and there may be other times you'll want to know someone's email address. Some methods and services exist to help find email addresses, but none of them are guaranteed to produce satisfactory results every time. A few of them will be covered in this chapter.

The problem with finding someone's email address is that there is no central directory. If you were looking for someone's phone number, you'd either look in a phone book or call an information service. That approach usually works; everyone with a phone number usually receives a bill to pay for phone services, and even though there are lots of phone companies, each has up-to-date and readily available records. The situation on the Internet is much different. Many users don't pay any direct fees, and there isn't any central agency that registers each user. Users are added and deleted by individual Internet sites; the decisions are made locally. It might be advantageous to have a directory of all Internet users and their email addresses, but such a directory just doesn't exist.

There are a few ways to find someone's email address. One way is to ask. You can call or write to ask for an email address. This is usually the easiest method. Another good idea is to check for an email address on a resume, business card, stationery, or Web page. If you have received email from the person whose address you seek, you can usually find the return address in the **From:**, **Return-Path:**, or **Reply-To:** email headers.

Use one of the online "white pages" services. These services let you search for email or street addresses. They're commercial services, but don't charge individuals for the service. You just have to put up with advertisements on their Web pages. Type in a person's name, where they're from, or some other information, and the service returns an email address, provided it can find a match in its database. One such service is Netscape People Finder with the URL **http://home.netscape .com/netcenter/whitepages .html**.

Consult some directories for collections or lists of email addresses or Web pages. Here are two Web pages with hyperlinks to lists of collections of white pages services:

- "CMC Information Sources CULTURE— People—Lists—directories, home pages" **http://www .december.com/cmc/ info/culture-people-lists.html**

- The section Reference : Phone Numbers and Addresses : Email Addresses : Individuals **http://dir.yahoo .com/Reference/ Phone_Numbers_and _Addresses/Email _Addresses/ Individuals**

Read and use "FAQ: How to Find People's Email Addresses," **http://www.qucis .queensu.ca/FAQs/email/ finding.html**, maintained by David Alex Lamb (**dalamb @qucis.queensu.ca**). It contains lots of resources and tips for finding email addresses.

Use the Usenet-addresses database. It's a database of the email addresses of people who've posted messages to Usenet maintained by a computer system at **rtfm.mit.edu**. You search the database by sending email to **mail-server@rtfm.mit.edu** with **send usenet-addresses/name** in the body of the message. For *name* substitute one or more words separated by spaces to represent the name of the person whose email address you are seeking. (For example, try the message **send usenet-address/ ernest ackermann**.) You will get a reply by email. How long you have to wait, an hour or two or longer, depends on the load on the system **rtfm.mit.edu**.

Email Etiquette

Writing to someone through email is communicating with another person. You need to remember that the recipient will read it without the benefit of being with you and seeing your expressions or getting your immediate and considerate reactions. You need to say what you mean in a clear, direct, and thoughtful way. Here is a list of rules you should follow when writing email:

- Choose the subject heading carefully. Make it brief, descriptive, and to the point. In many cases, it's the thing that will either get a reader's attention or make the reader ignore your message.

- Make your message as short as possible, but don't make it cryptic or unclear. Lots of users have to deal with storage quotas that limit the amount of email they can receive. Keep the body of the message succinct. Limit a message to one or two screens.

- It's a good idea to include parts—but not all—of the original message when you are writing a reply. Include only the portions pertinent to your reply. Many email programs allow you to annotate or include your remarks within the body of a message you've received. If you can't do that, summarize the original message and write a reply. For an example of this kind of correspondence, look ahead to Figure 3.15.

- Include a signature with all your email. This ought to include your full name and some information about how to contact you by telephone or traditional mail. Try to keep the signature to four or five lines.

- Check the address when you are composing a message or replying to a message you've received.

All mail systems can send and receive text (also called ASCII) files—ones that contain only plain characters. Many email programs can deal with messages encoded in Multipurpose Internet Mail Extensions (MIME). MIME is the standard way to work with nontext files as part of email or Usenet articles.

Be sure your message is going only to the person(s) who ought to receive it. If the original message was sent to a group of people such as a mailing list or discussion group, be sure of the address you use so the reply goes to an individual or the entire group as necessary. It's embarrassing when email is sent to a group but is meant for an individual.

◆ Take some time to consider what you will write. You can never be sure where the email you write will end up. Also, if someone writes something that upsets you, don't react immediately. Perhaps you've misinterpreted the original message. You'll find you can usually give a better response if you take some time to think about it.

◆ Be careful about spelling and punctuation. Try to follow the same rules you'd use if you were writing a letter or a memo. If you want to state something strongly, surround it with asterisks (*) or write it in uppercase, but don't take this too far. Some folks equate items in uppercase letters with SHOUTING.

◆ Be careful when using humor and sarcasm. The person reading the mail may misinterpret your remarks, and you won't be around to immediately clear up a misunderstanding.

◆ Don't assume the email is private. It's easy to forward email, so the message you send could be shared with others.

Working with Nontext Files

All mail systems can send and receive text, also called *ASCII* (*American Standard Code for Information Interchange*), files—ones that contain only plain characters. In fact, some are designed to do only that. Other types of information such as images, sound, video, programs in the machine language of a computer, spreadsheets, compressed files, or files produced by a word-processing program can't be sent or read unless the email program uses some scheme to handle these types of files. In general terms, before a nontext file is sent it has to be *encoded* into a form the email program can deal with. In order to read, view, or hear this encoded file, it has to be *decoded* into its original format. Many email programs, including the one with Netscape, can deal with messages encoded in *Multipurpose Internet Mail Extensions* (*MIME*). MIME is the standard way to work with nontext files as part of email or Usenet articles. But there are other programs or formats for encoding and decoding. *BinHex* has been used on Macintosh systems and with older versions of Eudora, a popular email program. The most common programs for this purpose on Unix systems (and many DOS systems) have been uuencode and uudecode. We'll be working with MIME later in this chapter along with other details of using the email portion of Netscape Communicator.

The programs *uuencode* and *uudecode* are commonly used to encode (before sending) and decode (after receiving) files. To send a nontext file, first encode it with a command similar to:

```
uuencode filename filename > filename.out
```

This takes the contents of the file named *filename* and puts it in a form that can be sent by any email program. The file *filename.out* has the original file in encoded form. The first line of the file *filename.out* will look something like:

```
begin 600 filename
M1G)O;2!N971W;W)K<RUR97%U97-T'9I<F=I;FEA+F5D=2!&<FD@3F]V(#$$X
```

The line **begin 600 filename** is a giveaway that this file was constructed with uuencode and that it can be decoded by using uudecode. You may see a number different from 600; the number depends on what has been encoded. If a file like this is received as part of an email message, first save it to a file, say **xyz**, and then decode it with the command:

```
uudecode xyz
```

That will create a file whose name is the same as the name in the first line of the encoded file. Files encoded according to MIME also have a specific format and boundary or tag lines so you know that MIME is involved and something about the format of the file that's been encoded.

Figure 3.2 is an excerpt from an email message encoded using MIME as it would appear to a mail program that doesn't recognize messages in that format.

```
This message is in MIME format. The first part should be
readable text, while the remaining parts are likely unreadable
without MIME-aware tools.


—1728402941-851401618-815583599:#1830
Content-Type: TEXT/PLAIN; charset=US-ASCII


Hi -


Here's that image you wanted. Let me know if it's appropriate
for the cover.


—1728402941-851401618-815583599:#1830
Content-Type: IMAGE/GIF; name="eagle.gif"
Content-Transfer-Encoding: BASE64
Content-ID: <Pine.3.89.951105C959.A1830@s850.mwc.edu>
Content-Description:


R0lGODlhgALgAff/AP///wD///8A/wAA//fv9+fn7+fG7+fn597e58bW5/fe
```

boundary lines marking different portions of the message

MIME headers giving context type and encoding methods

encoded image starts here

When you view a message that's in uuencode or MIME format using most modern email programs, the attached encoded file is either displayed in original form or the mail program gives

FIGURE 3.3

Netscape
Mail Window

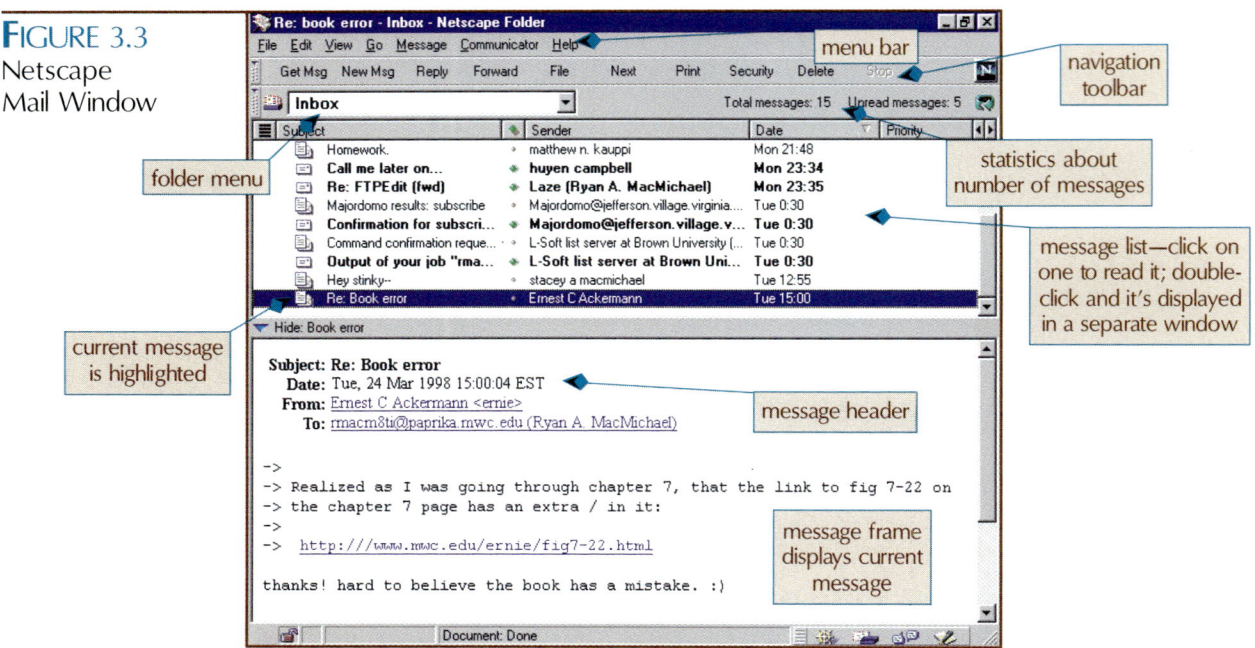

folder menu

current message
is highlighted

menu bar

navigation
toolbar

statistics about
number of messages

message list—click on
one to read it; double-
click and it's displayed
in a separate window

message header

message frame
displays current
message

you the option of saving the encoded information in a file. In the latter case, it is decoded and saved in its original format.

Working with Netscape Mail

In this section we'll look at using the email program (Netscape Messenger) that's included with Netscape Communicator. For the first few times you use it, you'll want to have the help window on the screen so you can refer to it quickly. When Netscape is started, press **F1** to activate the help window, select **About Messenger**, and then pick **Using Messenger**. You'll find that the commands and procedures for using Netscape Messenger are

similar, but not the same, as those used with other email programs.

Figure 3.3 shows a Netscape mail window that you'd use to read your email. To get to this window and to start to read your email, click on **Communicator** in the menu bar and then select **Messenger Mailbox** from the pull-down menu. Another way is to click on the mailbox icon in the component bar in the lower right of the window.

As in other Netscape windows, there is a menu bar with pull-down menus and a navigation toolbar. The top portion (called a *frame*) of the window tells about your messages. It holds a list of the messages in the current folder. The bottom frame holds the current message, the one highlighted in the

upper frame. Click on any message to read it. Click on the drop-down folder list to select another folder and get another list of messages. Once a message is open for reading you can print it, delete it, or save it to a different folder. You send a reply to the person who sent it to you by clicking on the button labeled **Reply**, or forward the message to another Internet address by clicking on the button **Forward**.

Figure 3.4 shows a window you'd use to compose a message. It too has a menu bar and a toolbar. You can get to this window by typing **Ctrl**+**M** anytime, clicking on the icon labeled **New Mail** from the Netscape mail window, or by clicking on **File** from the menu

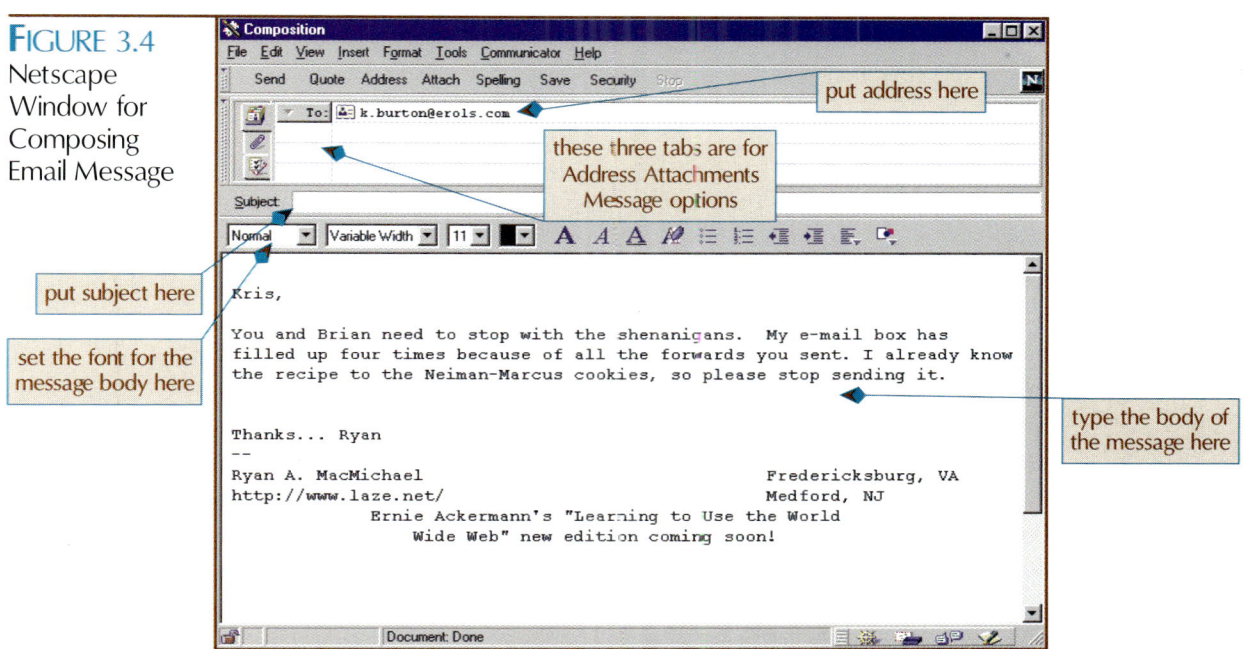

put address here

these three tabs are for
Address Attachments
Message options

put subject here

set the font for the
message body here

type the body of
the message here

bar of the Netscape browser window, selecting **New**, and then selecting **Message**. Once the window (called the Message Composition window) is active, you can compose or write a message. Position the cursor in the bottom frame with the mouse and start typing. Fill in the address (**To**) and **Subject**, and send it off when you're ready. Commands to fill in and modify the panes in the window are available through the pull-down menus in the menu bar or by clicking on the items in the navigation toolbar.

You can use the commands at any stage; they are available through the menus and icons. Online help is always available by clicking on **Help** in the menu bar. The email program also has MIME (Multipurpose Internet Mail Extensions), so the mail you read and send can contain information in text format as well as a range of other types.

The topics covered in this section include:

◆ Setting Crucial Mail Preferences in Netscape

◆ Getting Help

◆ Knowing When New Mail Has Arrived

◆ Opening and Closing the Mail Window

◆ The Netscape Mail Window

◆ Reading Email

◆ Saving, Printing, and Deleting Messages

◆ Setting Other Mail Preferences

◆ Composing and Sending Email

◆ Replying to a Message

◆ Forwarding Email

◆ Working with an Address Book

Setting Crucial Mail Preferences in Netscape

Before you can receive or send email some preferences need to be set. They're crucial in the sense that you won't be able to send or receive mail unless these are set properly. They are:

◆ **Identity**—your name and email address

◆ **Mail Server**—Internet names or addresses of

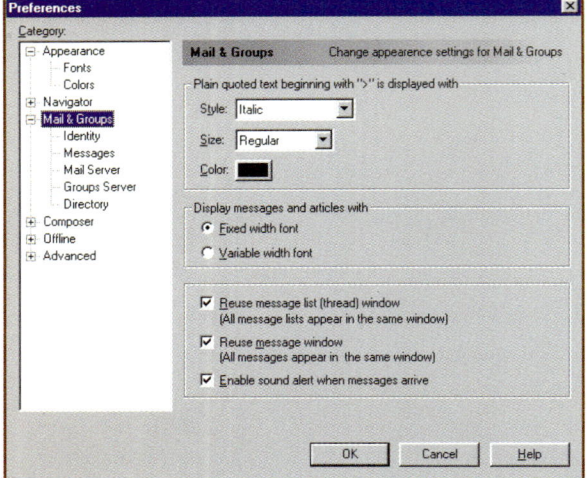

FIGURE 3.5

Preferences Panel for Mail and Usenet News (Groups)

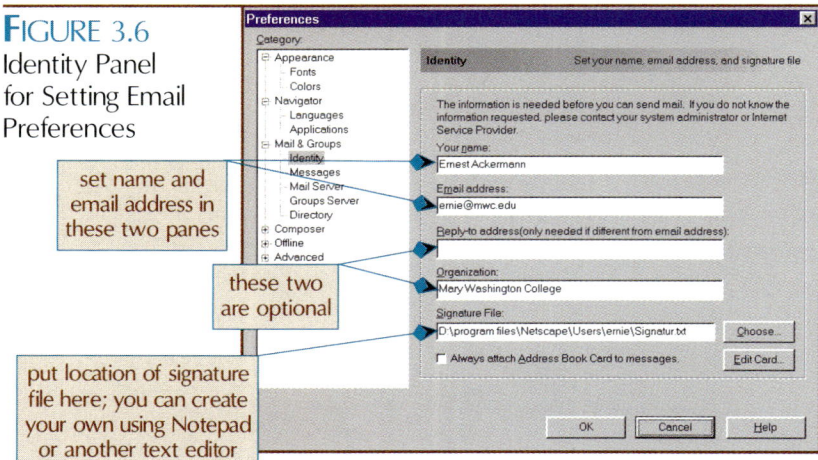

FIGURE 3.6

Identity Panel for Setting Email Preferences

set name and email address in these two panes

these two are optional

put location of signature file here; you can create your own using Notepad or another text editor

the SMTP server and the POP server

It's essential that you have the correct name of your SMTP and POP servers, otherwise email can't be sent or received. You get those names from a support person or group in your school or organization, your Internet service provider, or the resident email expert.

To set these preferences click on **Edit** in the menu bar and se-

lect **Preferences**. Select the category **Mail & Groups.** A panel like the one in Figure 3.5 appears.

Click on **Identity** to set the necessary preferences so you can send email. A panel similar to the one in Figure 3.6 appears.

The preferences are labeled and set as follows:

✦ **Your name.**

Type your name and press **Enter**. You can type any name

here, it's the name folks will see when they receive mail from you. Want people to think they have email from the Lone Ranger? Type **Lone Ranger** in here!

✦ **Email address.**

This is the address that will be filled in the From: header on messages you send.

✦ **Reply-to address.**

The address used when folks reply to your email. You only need to set this if it is different from the email address.

✦ **Organization.**

Type the name of your organization, school, or business.

✦ **Signature file.**

Type the location of your signature file or use the Browse button to select the file. It's not necessary to set this before sending email.

Other options may be set in this category. Click on the **Help** button for more information.

Click on **Mail Server** to set the necessary preferences for sending and receiving email. A panel similar to the one in Figure 3.7 appears. Most of this information will have to come from your Internet service provider (ISP) or the folks who administer the computer systems in your organization.

The preferences are labeled and set as follows:

◆ **Mail server user name.**

You'll have to supply a user name when you contact the computer system that holds your email as it arrives from the Internet.

◆ **Outgoing mail (SMTP) server.**

Electronic mail is sent according to a protocol named simple mail transfer protocol (SMTP). When you send a message from your PC it will be transmitted to another system that uses SMTP to pass the message to the Internet. You type the Internet domain name or IP address of that system here.

◆ **Incoming mail server.**

Mail is received from the Internet by a computer that's always running; one that's provided by your ISP or organization. You type the Internet domain name or IP address of that system here.

◆ **Mail server type.**

There are two choices here, POP3 or IMAP. Select the one your ISP or organization uses. In either case you can choose to leave the messages on the server after you've retrieved them to your PC or not. If the mail is left on the server, it may build up there and each time you check

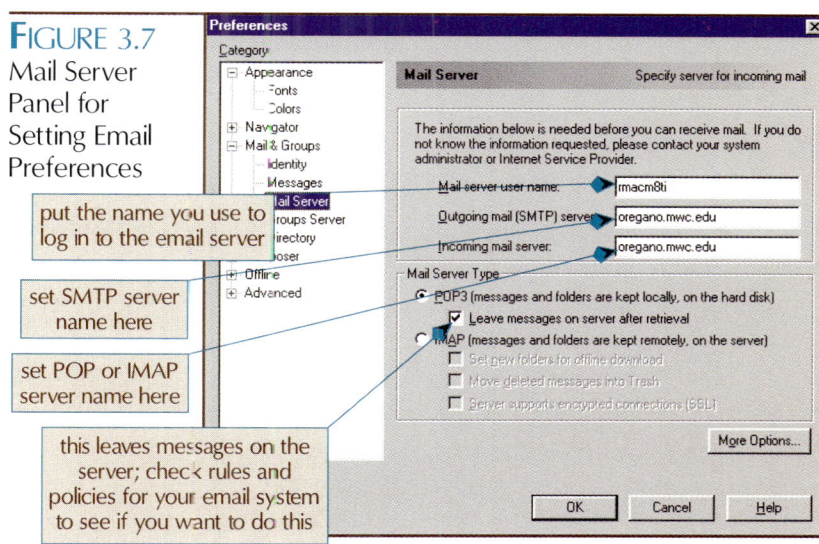

Figure 3.7
Mail Server Panel for Setting Email Preferences

put the name you use to log in to the email server

set SMTP server name here

set POP or IMAP server name here

this leaves messages on the server; check rules and policies for your email system to see if you want to do this

your email you'll get more than one copy of the same email. If you always use the same computer to check your email and you're allowed to keep files on it, then you'll probably want to *not* have messages left on the server. IMAP isn't universally available. If it is available you may want to choose that protocol; it allows you to manage the messages on the server before bringing them to your system.

Getting Help

Online help for using or setting up email is readily available. Press **F1** to bring up the Netscape help window, then select **About Messenger**, and then pick **Using Messenger**. For information about setting options in a specific preferences panel, click on the button labeled **Help** for each panel. Here's a list of resources

you may want to consult for help with email:

◆ "A Beginner's Guide to Effective Email" **http://www.webfoot .com/advice/ email.top.html**

◆ "Email Web Resources" **http://andrew2 .andrew.cmu.edu/ cyrus/email/ email.html**

◆ "Mary Houten-Kemp's Everything Email" **http:// everythingemail.net**

Knowing When New Mail Has Arrived

You can tell when new email has arrived for you by looking at the mailbox icon in the bottom right corner of the border of a Netscape window. When a green arrow appears alongside the icon, it means that new email has arrived.

Opening and Closing the Mail Window

In order to read your email, you have to open the mail window. Once Netscape Communicator is started, you click on the pull-down menu **Communicator** in the menu bar and then choose **Messenger Mailbox.** The first time you open the window you'll be prompted to enter your email password. That's the same password (usually) that you use to

access your Internet account or service. Figure 3.3 shows a sample mail window. This is where you work with your email. You can select messages to read, save to a folder, print, or delete. You can reply to messages and forward messages to other email addresses. After you are finished with your email, you close the window by pressing `Ctrl`+**W** on the keyboard or clicking on the **File** pull-down menu and then choosing **Close.** You can keep this window on your desktop so you can go to it quickly.

The Netscape Mail Window

We've taken a quick look at the Netscape mail window before. Figure 3.3 shows a sample window, and here we'll take a more detailed look at it. Here we'll discuss the menu bar, toolbar, and the mail window. Notice the window is divided into two frames—one for the messages list and one to display a message. Each of these can have its own scroll bar, and you can move through one independent of the other.

Menu Bar

| File | Edit | View | Go | Message | Communicator | Help |

Each entry in the menu bar represents a pull-down menu. Clicking on each shows the menu. Some of the items in a menu are listed with keyboard

shortcuts (keys to press that immediately start an action). The fifth one, **Message,** for example, has an item **Forward Ctrl+L.** You can forward the current mes-

sage to another Internet address by selecting this item or pressing `Ctrl`+**L** on the keyboard at any time, without selecting the menu.

File	Lets you check for new mail from the POP or IMAP server or deliver mail you've composed in case you've set email options so email isn't delivered immediately. It also contains items to let you work with your mail folders by opening a folder, creating a new folder, compressing a folder (which means removing the messages you've deleted), or emptying (deleting the messages from) the **Trash** folder. You can print the current message, the one that's displayed in the message frame. Finally, it contains items to close the mail window or exit. **Exit** means to end the Netscape Communicator session.
Edit	Use the items here to copy a selection from the message frame to the clipboard so it can be pasted into another application, delete a message or a folder, select a thread of messages (ones all on the same topic), or search for specific text within the current message. It also contains items to select if you want to *undo* a previous edit action. You can also use the items on this menu to select one or more messages and to search for a word or phrase in selected messages or in the entire mailbox. This also has a link

	for finding email addresses on the Internet. You may also set mail filters here. These are used to work automatically with incoming mail to do things such as put all email from a specific address or with a specific **Subject:** heading into a folder.
View	These options deal with how the list of messages in a folder and individual messages are displayed. You can use the item **Sort** to arrange your messages in order by date, subject, or sender. For the message you're currently viewing in the message frame, you can select an item so that all headers are shown. Otherwise you see only the **Subject:, Date:, From:,** and **To:** headers. These are the most important and showing only headers makes it easier for you to concentrate on the text of the message. You can specify whether attachments are to be displayed inline or shown as links to be activated by a mouse click.
Go	The items here take you to the next or previous message. You can also go to the next or previous unread or marked message, or to the next folder.
Message	This menu has a number of items that let you compose new messages (**New Mail Message**), reply to the current message, or forward the current message to another email address. You can reply to the sender of a message (**Reply**) or to everyone listed as a recipient (**Reply to All**). Use this to mark the current message or a list of messages and to move or copy messages to folders. Moving a message removes it from the current folder, and copying it makes a copy of it. You can also add the sender of the current message to the address book.

The remaining menu items have the same function as in the browser window so we won't repeat them here.

Toolbar

The toolbar is a sequence of labeled items that you click on to perform the indicated action. We'll discuss them by listing the labels.

Get Msg	Clicking on this causes Netscape to contact your POP or IMAP server to see if any new mail has arrived. If it has, it's delivered to your system.
New Msg	Use this to compose a new message.
Reply	Use this to reply to the sender of a message. Clicking on this pops up the window used for composing messages, but first you have to select whether you'll be replying to the sender or the sender and all recipients. The email is automatically given the correct address.
Forward	Clicking on this sends a copy or forwards the highlighted message in the message list to another Internet address. You get the window for composing a message with the **Subject:** header filled in. You need to give the address of

91

	where it's going to be sent. You can also modify the outgoing message. The original message is sent along as an attachment.
File	Click here to send the current message or selected messages to a another mailbox or file. This is good for organizing messages.
Next	This takes you to the next unread message.
Print	Click on this to print the message displayed in the message display area.
Security	This brings up another window that tells whether the current message was encrypted when sent and/or whether it has a digital signature. This is related to security issues we mentioned in Chapter 2.
Delete	This deletes the selected message or messages. A deleted message is moved to the folder titled "Trash." To remove a message from the computer you'll have to empty the Trash folder. Do that from the File menu in the menu bar.
Stop	This stops the transmission of one or more messages from the POP server to your computer.

FOLDERS, LIST OF MESSAGES, AND MESSAGE DISPLAY.

Folders.

The drop-down list of folders in the upper-left portion of the email window holds a list of folders or mailboxes. Select one by clicking on its name. Email messages are stored in the folders, so some folks call them mailboxes. You can create folders to save messages by clicking on **File** and selecting **New Folder**. This helps you organize the messages you've received if, for example, you get a number of messages on a topic or from someone. You can go through a folder replying to, deleting, printing, or forwarding the messages. Putting email in folders keeps you from having to deal with a hundred or more different messages that aren't organized in any way. Three

folders will usually be present: **Inbox**—messages you've received but haven't put into any other folder; **Sent**—copies of the messages you've sent; and **Trash**—copies of messages you've deleted.

Messages.

The messages frame shows a list of the email messages in the currently selected folder. The list is arranged either by date, subject, or sender. You specify the way the list is sorted by clicking on **View** in the menu bar of the mail window. The headings along the top of the panel are **Subject**, a dot, **Sender**, **Date**, a flag, **Status**, and **Size**. **Subject** shows the **Subject:** header of the message; the dot indicates whether the message has been read—a bright ball shows it hasn't been read yet; **Sender** shows the

name of the person who sent the email; **Date** shows the date the message was sent; the flag is used to mark or select messages; **Status** tells whether the message has been replied to; and **Size** gives the size of the message in bytes. Clicking on a message in the list displays it in the message display area. A selected message can be deleted, printed, or saved to a folder. To save it to a folder, click on **Message** in the menu bar, choose **File** or **Copy**, and then select the name of the folder. Clicking in the flag column marks or flags a message. You can mark a message as read or unread by clicking on the dot. Using the vertical scroll bar in this pane lets you scroll through the list. If all the headers don't show, or the listing seems cramped, change the size of the mail window.

✦ Message display area.

Email messages are displayed in the bottom pane of the mail window in the message display area. The current message is displayed here. To see another message, click on it in the message list or use the **Next** icon in the toolbar. A message is displayed with headers including **Subject:**, **Date:**, **From:**, and **To:**, followed by the body of the message. This pane has both a horizontal and vertical scroll bar to use to move through the message. You can also use the up or down arrow keys to move up or down through the message one line at a time. Netscape email displays any attachments if they're images that the browser can display. It displays anything, including attached Web pages that can be viewed by the browser. If an attachment can't be viewed this way, it's displayed as an icon. Clicking on the icon starts a program on your computer to view or play the file, provided it's of a type that's listed in the browser's helper applications.

Otherwise, the file is saved to your computer.

Reading Email

To read your email, you have to open the mail window. If this is the first time you've opened this window in this Netscape session, you'll be asked for the password for your mail system or POP server. Type it in the dialog box and press **Enter**. Then the mail user agent (Netscape in this case) contacts the system that delivers mail to you. If any messages have arrived at the server since you last checked, they'll be delivered now, and the oldest of the new messages will be displayed in the message display area of the window. In any case, when you open the mail window you'll be looking at the messages in the folder **Inbox**. This is where the computer delivers all incoming messages. You can, however, save email in other folders and use the mail system to manage and read these folders. The list of folders is available through a drop-down menu on the email page. You can read messages in any folder by

clicking on the name of the folder.

Clicking on an entry in the message list displays the corresponding message in the message display area. You move from message to message by either selecting a message from the message list and clicking on it with the mouse, clicking on the icon **Next** from the toolbar, or choosing an item from the **Go** pull-down menu that takes you to another message.

Be flexible.

The examples in this chapter demonstrate the steps to follow when you're working with email. You won't have the same messages and folders as those shown in the examples. Don't let this confuse you. The examples demonstrate fundamental skills. These skills don't change, even though the actual screens may look different. ✦

EXAMPLE 3.1

Opening the Mail Window, Reading a Message, and Closing

You open the mail window by selecting **Messenger Mailbox** from the **Communicator** pull-down menu in the menu bar. If necessary, give your email password; type it in the dialog box that appears on the screen. If there's email waiting for you on your mail server, it will be delivered to you, and a message will be displayed in the message display area or pane. If there is no new mail you can select one from the message list. We'll follow these steps:

1. Open the mail window.

2. Read the email.

3. Close the mail window.

▶ Open the mail window.

✚ Click on **Communicator** in the menu bar and then click on **Messenger Mailbox**.

FIGURE 3.8
Mail Window, Reading a Message

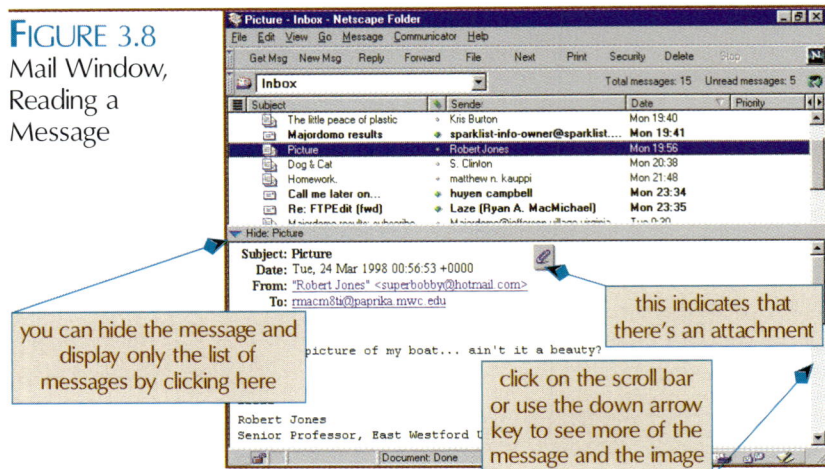

Opening the mail window checks for new mail, lists your messages, and displays a message. The current message is highlighted as shown in Figure 3.8. **Inbox** is the folder that's currently open. To see the messages in another folder, click on the drop-down menu and select the desired folder. (You'll see later how to save messages in folders.) The current message is displayed in the message display area. The message in Figure 3.8 includes text and an image. The image was sent as an attachment, but nothing extra had to be done to see it here. Netscape mail will automatically display images in uuencode, GIF, or JPEG sent as attachments. If a message contains a Web page in HTML format or anything in HTML as an attachment, then it's displayed just as if you were viewing it with the Netscape browser.

❷ Read the email.

Open the mail window and the message list pane holds a list of messages in your folder **Inbox**. The listing for each message includes the name of the sender, the subject, and the date it was sent. Messages that haven't been read are marked with a green dot. Messages can also be flagged or marked by clicking on the dot in the column headed by a red flag. Figure 3.8 shows three unread messages and two flagged messages.

- To read any message, click on its entry in the message list.

- To read the next message in the list, press the down arrow key (↓). To read the previous message in the list, press the up arrow key (↑).

When viewing or reading a message, it is displayed in the bottom pane, the message viewing area of the window. The message display area is like other windows in the sense that it has horizontal and vertical scroll bars and you can use the appropriate keys on the keyboard, for example, **PgUp** or **PgDn**, to move through the message.

While you're reading your messages, new messages might arrive for you. If they're not delivered immediately, you can check the POP or IMAP server for them by clicking on the icon labeled **Get Msg**. In this case Netscape contacts the server and checks for new mail. If there is any new email, it's delivered.

When you're done working with your mail, you may want to close the mail window.

Close the mail window.

- Press **Ctrl**+**W** or click on **File** in the menu bar and select **Close** to close the mail window.

End of Example 3.1

Saving Messages

You can save a message into a file or into a folder. To save an email message in a file, go to the message list and highlight the entry for the message you want to save by clicking on it. Then click on **File** on the menu bar and select **Save As**, or press **Ctrl**+**S**. A **Save As...** dialog box pops up, and you type in the name of the file to hold the message. If you pick a name that already exists, you'll be asked if you really want to replace it with the message you're going to save. Saving a message to a

file is useful if you're going to use the body of the message with some other program. Suppose, for example, your partner sends you a copy of a project she's working on that you'd like to include in a presentation. You might want to save it in a file and then import or copy it into the presentation.

Saving email in folders is a convenient way to organize your email. Since you create the folders, you may want to have some that deal with a specific topic or project and others that hold the email you've received from one person. You can go

through a folder replying to, deleting, printing, or forwarding the messages.

To create a folder, click on **File** on the menu bar and select the item **New Folder...**. A dialog box pops up and you type in the name of the folder. You can create the folder as a folder inside the current one, or at or above the same level of the current folder.

To save a message into a folder, go to the message list and highlight the message you want to save by clicking on it. More than one message can be saved into a folder by highlighting a

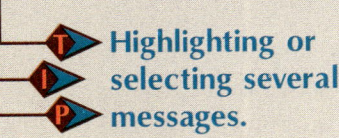
To select more than one message from the message list: first select one message by clicking on it, then move the mouse pointer to another message, but don't click yet. Press **Shift** and click (the left button if your mouse has more than one button) to select all the messages including the first one marked up to and including the message at the mouse pointer. Press **Ctrl** and click to select the message at the pointer in addition to the first message highlighted. If others are highlighted, the one at the mouse pointer will be added to the group once you click on it. ✦

group of messages. Now click on **Message** on the menu bar, and then choose either **File** or **Copy**. Choosing either one brings up a menu from which you choose the folder you want to hold the message(s). Moving means taking the email from one folder and putting it into another. Copying means making a copy of the message and putting it into the folder you choose. (You would have two copies of the message.)

Printing Messages

To print a message, select it by clicking on its entry in the message list and then click on the **Print** icon. Printing is allowed only if one entry is highlighted. A window pops up, the same one you would see for printing anything from the browser program. You can select a printer, set options (if necessary), and

finally click on the **OK** or **Cancel** button.

Deleting Messages

Deleting messages is easy and necessary to keep the amount of email in the **Inbox** and other folders under control. Highlight the entries in the message list and press the icon labeled **Delete** or press the **Delete** key on the keyboard. Deleting a message sends it to the folder **Trash**. You could go into that folder to reclaim a message, in case you delete one by mistake. Deleting a message from the folder **Trash** removes it permanently.

You can delete messages from the **Inbox** or any other folder. You probably face some limit on the amount of space you're allowed so think about deleting messages regularly. Do a little more than think about it—delete some messages.

EXAMPLE 3.2

Creating a Folder; Saving and Deleting Email

In this example we'll save email into a new folder and then delete three messages. We'll follow these steps after starting Netscape Communicator:

1. Open the mail window.

2. Create a new folder.

3. Move several messages to the new folder.

4. Delete several messages.

5. Close the mail window.

❶ Open the mail window.

✚ Click on the **Communicator** menu in the menu bar and choose **Messenger Mailbox**.

Suppose that after we open the mail window and check for new email we see the message list as shown in Figure 3.9.

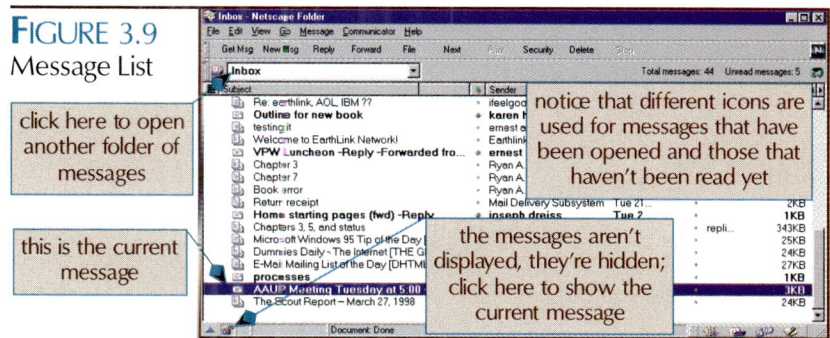

FIGURE 3.9
Message List

click here to open another folder of messages

this is the current message

notice that different icons are used for messages that have been opened and those that haven't been read yet

the messages aren't displayed, they're hidden; click here to show the current message

❷ Create a new folder.

✚ Click on **File** in the menu bar and choose **New Folder…**.

✚ Type **ryan** and click on the **OK** button.

We've got several messages from Ryan MacMichael and we're going to save them into a folder named **ryan**.

A dialog box pops up in which you type the name of the folder.

A folder named **ryan** is created. If after we put messages in the folder we want to read the messages we can click on the drop-down menu of folders to read what's there.

❸ Move several messages to the new folder.

✚ Click on the entry for the first message from Ryan MacMichael in the message list.

✚ Move the mouse pointer to the second entry from Ryan MacMichael in the message list, press [Ctrl], and press the mouse button (the left one if your mouse has two buttons).

Now that the folder is created we can mark several messages from Ryan and move them into the folder.

Continue this process until all messages from Ryan are highlighted. Figure 3.10 shows the messages highlighted.

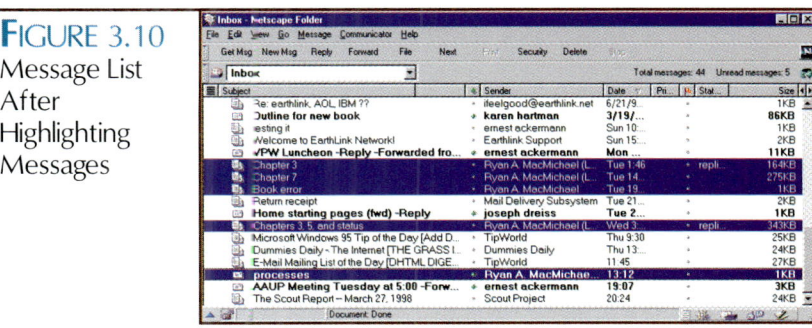

FIGURE 3.10
Message List After Highlighting Messages

Now we're ready to move the selected messages to the folder named **ryan**. This will take them out of **Inbox**. We can save other messages from Ryan, if he ever writes to us again, in the same folder.

✚ Click on **Message** on the toolbar and then choose **File**.

Another menu appears listing the names of the folders.

✚ Click on **ryan**.

The messages will be removed from the **Inbox** folder and copied to the folder named **ryan**.

◆ Delete several messages.

To demonstrate how to mark a range of messages and delete messages, we'll delete three messages from **Inbox**. We show the messages marked in Figure 3.11.

✚ Click on the fifth entry from the bottom in the message list.

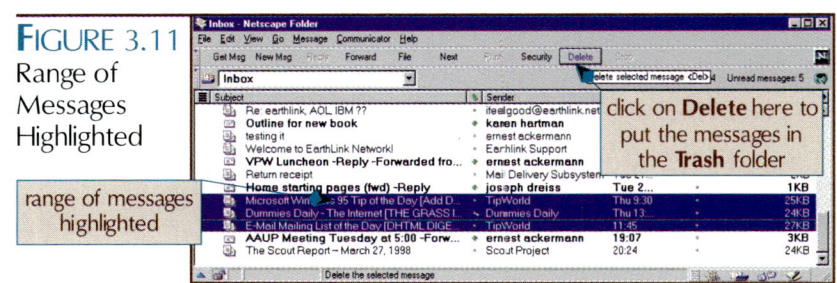

FIGURE 3.11
Range of Messages Highlighted

range of messages highlighted

✚ Move the mouse pointer down two messages, but don't click.

✚ Press **Shift** on the keyboard and click the left mouse button.

Figure 3.11 shows the messages highlighted. To delete them we need to click on **Delete**.

✚ Click on **Delete** in the navigation toolbar.

This moves them to the folder **Trash**. At some point you'll want to delete them from **Trash** as well. You do that by clicking on **File** in the menu bar and selecting **Empty Trash Folder**.

◆ Close the mail window.

Closing the window ends the email session, but doesn't end the Netscape Communicator session. To end the Netscape session, click on **File** on the menu bar and then choose **Exit**.

✚ Press **Ctrl**+**W**.

End of Example 3.2

Setting Other Mail Preferences

We talked about setting crucial options for email earlier. In this section we'll cover setting pref-

erences that control the way email is displayed, the way it's sorted, how nontext email is encoded and handled, and what file to use as your signature file.

To set these preferences, click on **Edit** in the menu bar and select **Preferences**. Then select **Mail & Groups**. (You go through the same steps to configure Usenet news.) This brings up a window similar to the one shown in Figure 3.5. You set options for any of the categories below by clicking on the tab by that name and then filling in the forms or clicking on the buttons indicated.

MAIN PANEL. Here you set options that deal with the way the text within messages is displayed. You can use this to customize the fonts that are used. You can also select whether to use the same message list and message window when you change from one folder to another. You can also set an option so your computer generates a sound when a new message arrives.

MESSAGES. Click on the tab **Messages** to bring up the window dealing with the properties of outgoing messages.

In the first group of options you set whether to automatically send messages in HTML format. That lets you send some nice looking email, but you have to be sure the person who is going to receive it has an email program that interprets HTML. You also set an option about quoting messages when you write a reply and the maximum line length.

The second group deals with keeping copies of outgoing messages. Some folks like to keep copies of everything they do (they're the ones with lots of disk

FIGURE 3.12
Setting Options for Copies of Outgoing Email

copies of messages are saved in a folder named **Sent**. check it if you're looking for a copy of a message you sent to someone. to conserve space on your computer, delete some of the messages from the **Sent** folder

when you reply to a message, the original is included

space!), while others keep a copy until they know a message has been received. The next set of options deals with whether copies of outgoing messages are sent to some address on the Internet or saved on your computer. You may want to do this to keep copies of the email you write so you know what you've said. However, you'll occasionally want to delete some of these since they do take up space on your disk or network. You can have copies of all messages (and articles when you're using Usenet news) automatically sent to a specific email address. Fill in the address in the appropriate panes. Also, you can have copies automatically saved on your system. Figure 3.12 shows a portion of the category **Messages** set so a copy of each email message is saved in the folder **Sent**. (Before putting an address in the **Other address:** pane, make sure you have the per-

mission of the person who'll be receiving the email.)

More Options takes you to a panel where you set whether nicknames from your address book are used for addresses, how to deal with messages being sent to addresses that are unable to properly display messages in HTML, and the encoding method for sending messages. Choose either **allow 8-bit** or **MIME**. Both allow for including nontext files. You select **allow 8-bit** if you're including characters that aren't in the English alphabet or lines that are longer than 70 characters. A rule of thumb is to select **MIME**, and if there are problems with some characters not being transmitted, then try composing and sending messages using **allow 8-bit**.

MAIL SERVER. We looked at this before when we discussed setting crucial prefer-

There are several options you can use to choose different headers, include files, use an address book, etc. Other sending options include whether to use encryption and/or a digital signature with the message, the type of MIME encoding, and whether to request a return receipt.

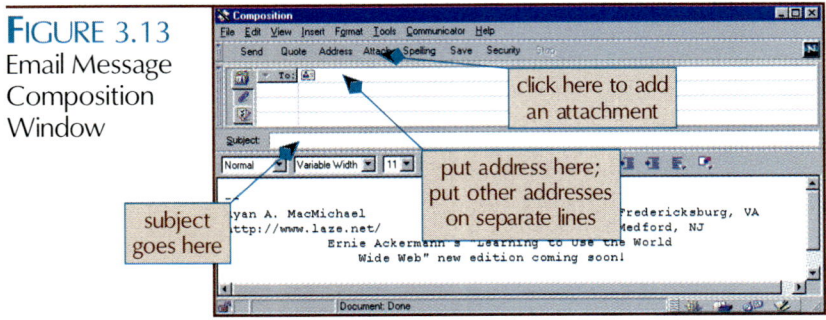

FIGURE 3.13
Email Message Composition Window

click here to add an attachment

put address here; put other addresses on separate lines

subject goes here

ences and options. In addition to the options we discussed then, you can also set whether Netscape will remember your email password for you. If this option isn't selected, you'll have to enter your email password (usually the same as the password you need to access the Internet) the first time you check your email during a Netscape Communicator session. It's more convenient to have the password remembered, but if someone else is using your computer and the save password option is set, then they'll have access to your email. Additionally, here is where you set the local mail directory and how often to check for email.

Composing and Sending Email

You can send a new email message from any part of Netscape, whether you're using the browser or working in the mail window or the news window. To send an email message, press **Ctrl**+**M** or click on **File** on the menu bar and choose **New** and then **Mail Msg**. If you're work-

ing in the mail window, click on the icon labeled **New Mail**. In any case, a window similar to Figure 3.13 will pop up.

Use the mouse to click on any of the panes or portions of the mail composition window.

The window has places for you to fill in the headers (**To**: address(es) of primary receivers; **Subject**: a brief description of what the message is about) and tabs (**Attachment**: name(s) of files to attach to the message and email sending options). You can also move from header to header by pressing the **Tab** key. You can separate multiple addresses with commas or spaces if you're sending the same email to several people. Use **Attach** from the navigation toolbar to include files (text or nontext) with the message. You'll want to be sure the receiver can handle working with nontext files sent this way. The receiver's email program has to include MIME (Multipurpose Internet Mail Extensions). Type the name of the file to include or browse through your folders to find the file to

attach; Netscape email attaches the file to the message.

There are several options you can use to choose different headers, include files, use an address book, etc. Other sending options include whether to use encryption and/or a digital signature with the message, the type of MIME encoding, and whether to request a return receipt. Some of these options are discussed in this chapter and you can read about them all in the online Netscape help. To get a message off in a straightforward manner you need to follow these steps:

1. Open the Compose Message window (**Ctrl**+**M**).

2. Fill in the address in the pane or block next to the button **To:**.

3. Compose/type the message body.

4. Send it off by clicking on the icon labeled **Send**.

Figure 3.14 shows a message ready to send. It's addressed to several people—the different addresses are on separate lines. The header **Cc:** is used to send a copy of the message to an Internet address. In this case the message is sent to four addresses. Three are listed in the **To:** header and one in the **Cc:** header. The text in the message body was typed directly into the message using the keyboard. The sections below discuss composing a message and attaching files.

✦ Composing the message body.

Type your message into the message body or compose the message using tools or programs with which you're comfortable. You can copy text from another Windows application or Web page. Any text on the clipboard can be pasted into the mail message. To copy/paste between applications click on **Edit** on the menu bar and select the appropriate action. Whether you type your message, include something from another application, or a combination of these, the email program will take care of formatting the text. Type or copy the message and press Enter at the end of a paragraph. The email program will handle adjusting the length of a line. You can only send plain text—no underlining, boldface, or italics—in the message body.

✦ Including attachments.

Anything that's not in plain text format has to be an *attachment* if it's sent by email. (Text files can be sent as attachments too.) Click on the icon labeled **Attachment** to attach a file to the message. A dialog box pops up. You select whether the attachment is a Web page or a file. If you choose to attach a Web page, then type in

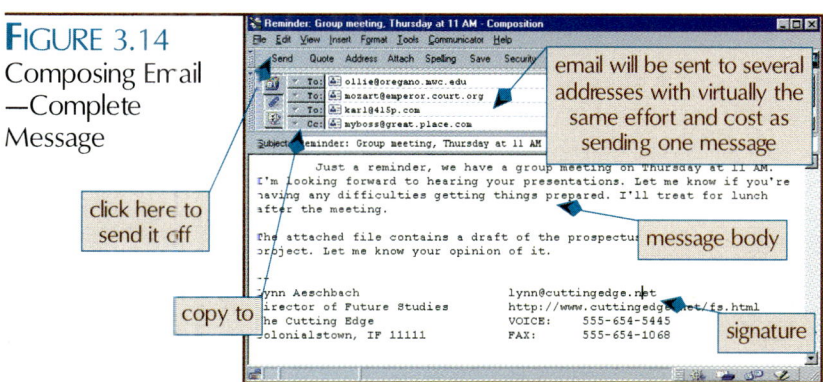

FIGURE 3.14
Composing Email
—Complete
Message

its URL. If you're going to attach a file, click on **Attach File**. Another window appears from which you select the file to attach or type in its name. Press the button labeled **Open** when you've got the file you want. You can include several files and URLs as attachments.

✦ Including a Web page.

Suppose you're viewing a Web page that contains some interesting information and you want to send a copy of it by email to a friend. To send the Web page, either in HTML or text format, click on **File** on the menu bar, and then choose **Send Page...**. The Message Composition window pops up and the URL of the current Web page is automatically included in the body of the message. You can also include the Web page as an attachment or include the text of the page in the body of the message. Here's an example. You're planning to visit the Mount Wilson Observatory near Pasadena, California,

on your next trip to California but need directions to get there, and you also want to send a copy of the directions to some friends who will meet you there. You make your way to the home page for the observatory, **http://www.mtwilson.edu**, follow the link labeled **General Information**, and then **Directions and Hours of Operations, http://www.mtwilson.edu/General/directions.html**. It's just what you were hoping to find. You send copies of the page to your friends—and yourself to be sure you have a copy—by pressing **Ctrl**+M, filling in the email addresses in the **Send To** block, and then clicking on **File** and choosing **Include Original Text**. The text of the Web page becomes part of the body of the message.

Replying to a Message

You reply to the current message by clicking on the icon labeled **Reply**. You do this while you're reading a message or after click-

Be sure you don't send something to a group that you'd like to send to an individual. This can be embarrassing, especially if the reply is personal. In many situations, it's a good idea to **include at least a portion of the original message** so your reply can be read in context.

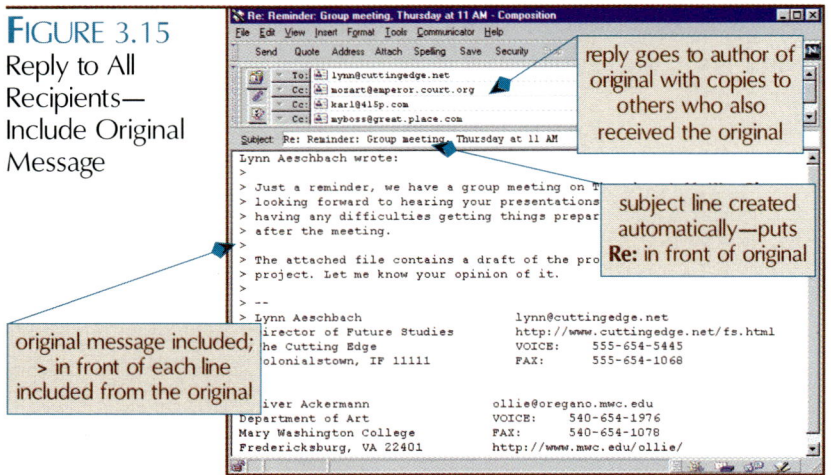

FIGURE 3.15
Reply to All
Recipients—
Include Original
Message

ing on its entry in the message list. Clicking on the **Reply** icon brings up a mail composition window just like the one for a new message (Figure 3.13), except that the **To:** address is automatically filled in so the reply goes to the Internet address taken from the original message. The **Subject:** will be set to **Re:** followed by the subject of the original message. If the address list in the original one includes several people you can send a reply to everyone on the **To:** or **Cc:** list by pressing the icon labeled **Reply All**. It's your choice; just be sure you don't send something to a group that you'd like to send to an individual. This can be embarrassing, especially if the reply is personal. In many situations, it's a good idea to include at least a portion of the original message so your reply can be read in context. This is particularly true if you're replying to a message that was sent to a group. Be

sure to include only the relevant parts. To include the original message, click on **File** and then select **Include Original Text**. You'll have to edit the message to include the important parts.

Figure 3.15 shows what a person would see if he started a reply to everyone who received the email in Figure 3.14.

At this point, you type/compose your reply, deleting lines from the original and including your own as you see fit. Use the arrow keys or the mouse to move the cursor to wherever you want to type. Use the mouse to highlight a portion of the text and then the items in the **Edit** menu to copy, cut, or paste a portion of the message. When it's complete, you can send it off by clicking on the icon labeled **Send**.

Forwarding Email

Forwarding email means passing the email you've received on to

another address. You can do this by highlighting one or more entries in the message list and then clicking on the icon labeled **Forward**.

When you select messages to be forwarded, a message composition window pops up like the one in Figure 3.13. The **Subject:** is filled in with **[Fwd: Subject of original message]** and the message or messages being forwarded are included as attachments. Any attachments to the original message are included with the forwarded message. You can include anything you'd like in the body of the forwarded email. If you're forwarding one message, you can also include the text of the original message in the same way as including it in a reply to an email message.

Working with an Address Book

Netscape email includes an address book that's an integrated part of the email program. You can add addresses by typing them in or having the program take them directly from a message. You give each address a nickname or short form so you can use it when you're composing or replying to a message. When you're using the mail composition window, clicking on the icon labeled **Address** opens a copy of the address book so you can select an address for the **To:**, **Cc:**, or **Bcc:**

header. (**Bcc:** is like **Cc:**. A copy of the message is sent, but none of the recipients—except for the one(s) listed under **Bcc:**—know a copy is being sent.) Furthermore, several addresses can be grouped together so you can send email to all members of a group or organization. It's a good idea to keep frequently used addresses in the address book. That way you don't have to remember people's addresses. Also, you won't have to save a message just because you need someone's address.

ADDING ADDRESSES. There are essentially two ways to add an address to the address book: take it from the current message, or type it into the address book.

To take an address from the current message, click on **Message** on the menu bar and then choose **Add to Address Book**. Netscape fills in the name and email address by taking them from the appropriate headers in the message. You need to add a nickname for the address book. You can add a description or other information to the entry in the address book. Figure 3.16 shows a filled-in entry.

To add an address manually, click on **Communicator** on the menu bar and select **Address Book**. Once the address book is open click on **New Card** from

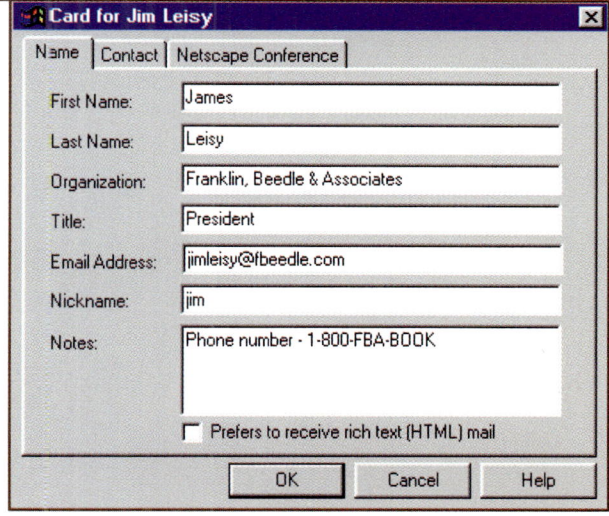

FIGURE 3.16
Completed Entry in Email Address Book

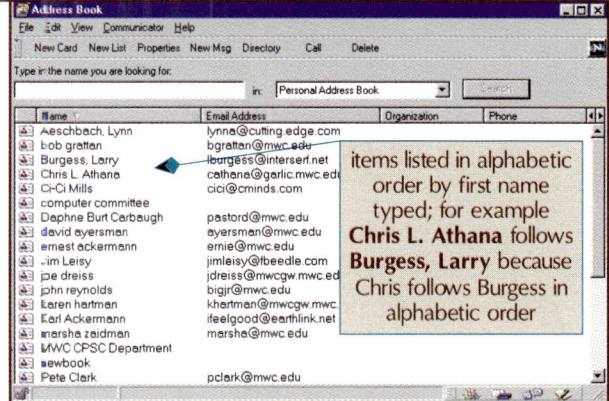

FIGURE 3.17
Address Book

its toolbar. A window similar to the one shown in Figure 3.16 will pop up. You fill in all the blanks.

After you've added the necessary information in the properties window, click on the **OK** button to save it in the address book. You can change the information for an entry at any time by opening the address book, clicking once on the entry in the list, and then choosing **Properties** from the **Edit** entry in the menu bar. Figure 3.17 shows an address book.

WORKING WITH A DISTRIBUTION LIST OR GROUP ADDRESS. You can also create a distribution list, a list of addresses associated with a single nickname. That lets you send one email message to a group. It's particularly useful if you regularly need to send or share email with several people. To create a distribution list, first go to the address book (click on **Communicator** on the menu bar and select **Address Book**), click on the **File** menu, and choose **New List**. A

FIGURE 3.18
Completed Entry for Group Address

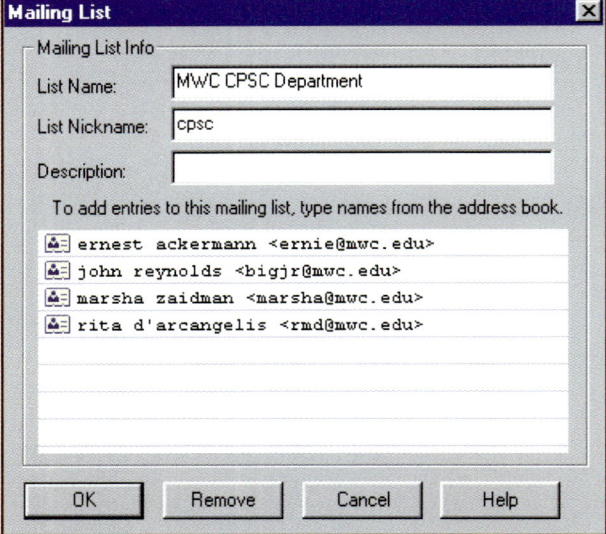

Mailing List

Mailing List Info

List Name: MWC CPSC Department

List Nickname: cpsc

Description:

To add entries to this mailing list, type names from the address book.

ernest ackermann <ernie@mwc.edu>
john reynolds <bigjr@mwc.edu>
marsha zaidman <marsha@mwc.edu>
rita d'arcangelis <rmd@mwc.edu>

OK   Remove   Cancel   Help

window pops up, similar to the one for adding an address. You type in the nickname, and in the block labeled **List Name** type a name for this list. You can type a description of the list in the pane labeled **Description**. (To change any of this information later, click on the folder in the address book, click on **Item** in the menu bar, and select **Properties....**) Figure 3.18 shows a completed entry for a group address. After you fill in the information, an icon—with the name you typed for it—will appear in the address book. Names can be added to the list only from the group of users already in the address book. To add them, first go through the steps to add a user. Then click on the name once in the address book list, hold down the mouse button, and drag the name to the entry for the list you've added.

DELETING ADDRESSES. Addresses can be deleted from the address book by first opening the address book, then highlighting an address (clicking on it once), and finally pressing the ⏎Delete⏎ key. Addresses used in distribution lists are aliases or copies of addresses from the list of individuals. Deleting one that's part of a list removes only that copy of it. Deleting a name from the list of individuals removes the name completely from the book, including all lists in which it appears.

USING ADDRESSES. You use the nickname you've assigned to an address for sending, replying to, or forwarding email. Suppose, for example, we've given the list MWC CPSC Department the nickname **cpsc** as shown in Figure 3.18. To send email to this address, just type **cpsc** in the **To:** field of a message you're composing. The address will be looked up in the address book. The email program fills in the Internet address(es) associated with the nickname. Nicknames are useful with names you'll be using frequently. You don't have to remember them. Whenever you're composing a message, click on the icon labeled **Address** to display the address book on the screen. Then double-click on the one you want to use.

Summary

Electronic mail allows users on the Internet to communicate with each other electronically. Using an email program, you can compose messages or write and then send them to any other Internet address. You can read the messages you've received, save them to a file, print them, or delete them. You can also reply to a message or forward one to another Internet address.

An email message consists of three main parts—the headers, which contain information about the address of the sender, the address of the recipient, when the message was sent, and other items; the message body, which holds the text portion of the email; and an optional signature, which can hold information about the sender such as full name, mailing address, phone number, etc. The signature ought to be limited to four or five lines, and it's put into a file so it's automatically included with each message.

In order to send email, you give the Internet address of the recipient, compose or write the message, and then give a command to send it on its way. The message is broken up into packets, each containing the address of the sender and the address of the recipient, and the packets are routed through several sites on the Internet to the destination. The computer systems on the Internet handle the transmission and delivery of the email. Once email arrives at a site, it's put into a system mailbox for an individual user. She can read her mail from the system program by using an email program like Netscape Messenger.

Email is a convenient and efficient means of communication. However, most communication is by the text of the message, so you have to be considerate and careful to communicate effectively, without misunderstandings. Since most users have a limited amount of space for their email, be sure to get rid of unwanted or unnecessary email and also be sure to send concise, appropriate messages to others. Email isn't necessarily private. Because it's transmitted electronically, there are several opportunities for someone to read your messages. It's relatively easy to forward copies of email so a message sent to one person can be easily transmitted to others.

Email or Internet addresses usually have the form of **local-name@domain-name**. *local-name* is often the login or user name of the email recipient, and *domain-name* is the Internet name of the site or computer system receiving the messages. You can send email to addresses on networks not on the Internet. You must know the proper form of an address to communicate with users on these networks.

Finding someone's email address isn't always easy. There is no central directory keeping a list of email addresses for everyone on the Internet. If you want to find someone's address, one of the best things to do is to call or write that person and ask for the email address. There are a number of automated services for searching for an email address. You can query a database of addresses of people who've posted articles to Usenet, and several Web servers provide directories for finding addresses.

The email program for Netscape Communicator was discussed in this chapter. It's a full-featured email program. You need to set some preferences before using it. Messages can be saved into folders, and can include text and other types of items (images, sound, programs, spreadsheets, word-processed documents, Web pages, etc.) as part of the message or as attachments. The email program includes an address book. Reading and managing email is carried on in the Netscape mail window, and you compose email in a message composition window. Online help is available. ✦

Selected Terms in This Chapter

American Standard Code for Information Interchange (ASCII)
attachment
BinHex
decoded
encoded
Internet message access protocol (IMAP)
mail user agent
Multipurpose Internet Mail Extensions (MIME)
post office protocol (POP)
signature
simple mail transfer protocol (SMTP)
uudecode
uuencode

Questions About Your Email

1. What is your email address? What is the email address of someone at your site to contact if you have questions or problems?

2. What is the name of the SMTP server for your email account? Do you use a POP or IMAP server? What's its Internet address or name?

3. Is there a quota or limit on your email? What is it?

Using Email

4. Send email to yourself with a reminder about something you need to do in the next few days.

5. Read your email. Reply to at least one message. Delete two messages and forward one message.

6. Send a message, using multiple addresses, to at least three other people.

7. Using your email program, save a message to a file and print the same message.

8. Create a signature for yourself and test it by sending yourself a short message.

Finding Email Addresses

9. Use Internet Address Finder, **http://www.iaf.net**, or Info-Space, **http://www.infospace.com**, to search for email addresses for the authors of this book. Search for your own email address or email addresses of people with the same last name as yours. Search for the email address of a friend.

10. Send email to **mail-server@rtfm.mit.edu** with **send usenet-addresses/name** in the body of the message to try to find the email address of a friend. How long did it take before you received a reply?

chapter 4

FINDING INFORMATION ON THE WEB

All types of digital information are on the World Wide Web. You can find everything from government statistics, fast-breaking news stories, up-to-the-minute weather reports, sales catalogs, and business information to radio programs, movies, and virtual art galleries and museums. In addition to this immense collection of valuable information generated by entities such as educational institutions, corporations, associations, and government agencies, there are hundreds of thousands of individuals all over the world who are contributing to this vast accumulation of resources every day by adding their home pages to the Web.

Finding these resources can be a challenge. This is why evaluating your information needs effectively and learning database search techniques are some of the most important skills you can acquire. In this chapter, we'll focus on search tools that are evolving to meet the needs of many types of users and show you, with examples, how to use the major types of search tools. All of the resources covered have their advantages and disadvantages; depending on what kind of information you're looking for and how experienced a user you are, each resource can be useful. The topics we'll cover in this chapter are:

- ✦ The First Step: Evaluate Your Information Needs

- ✦ The Best Search Tool to Start With

- ✦ Directories

- ✦ Virtual Libraries

- ✦ Search Engines and Meta-Search Tools

- ✦ Intelligent Agents

There is a wealth of information on the Web. Without a well-defined search plan, it would be virtually impossible to locate specific information, even if that information were available on the Web. This chapter considers different search tools and strategies for finding information online.

The First Step: Evaluating Your Information Needs

Before you get online and start your search for information, think about what types of material you're looking for. Are you interested in finding supporting arguments, authoritative opinions, statistics, evaluative reports, or descriptions of events, images, or movie reviews? Do you need current information or facts about an event that occurred 20 years ago? When are you sure that the Web is a smart place to start? Sometimes information is on the Web, but it is difficult to find. A reference book in your library may have the information you need, and you'll find the information more quickly there. Don't think that just because you can't locate the material you need on the Web it doesn't exist. It may seem that the Web would contain all the information that you'd need, but this is not always the case.

Types of Information Most Likely to Be Found on the Internet and World Wide Web

- Current information. Many newspapers and popular magazines provide Web versions of their publications and news updates throughout the day. Up-to-the-minute financial and weather information is also easily accessible.

- U.S. government information. Most federal, state, and local government agencies provide statistics and other information freely and in a timely manner.

- Popular culture. It's easy to find information on the latest movie or best-selling book.

- Full-text versions of books and other materials that are not under copyright restriction; for example, Shakespeare's plays, *The Bible*, *The Canterbury Tales*, and hundreds of other full-text literary resources are available. Several of these texts have been made into searchable databases that have enhanced scholarly research in the humanities.

- Business and company information. Many companies provide their Web pages and annual reports, and there are also several databases that contain in-depth financial and other company information.

- Consumer information. The Internet is a virtual gold mine of information for people who are interested in buying a particular item and want opinions from people about that item. By reading reviews on the Web and Usenet newsgroup articles, consumers can find out about almost any item before they buy it.

- Medical information. In addition to several excellent sources provided by hospitals, pharmaceutical companies, and non-profit organizations, the National Library of Medicine has provided the Medline database to the public for free since late 1997.

- Unique archival sites. For example, the Library of Congress' American Memory Collection.

Some Reasons Why the World Wide Web Won't Have Everything You Are Looking For

- Publishing companies and authors who make money by creating and providing information will choose to use the traditional publishing marketplace and will not provide the information for free via the Internet.

- Scholars most often choose to publish their research in reputable scholarly journals and books from university presses rather than use the Web to distribute their research. More academic journals are becoming Web-based, but electronic journals may cost as much money as print-based periodicals.

- Several organizations and institutions would like to publish valuable information on the Web but are unable because of a lack of staff or funding.

- The Web tends to include information that

is in demand to a large portion of the public, but can't be relied upon consistently for historical information. For example, if you needed today's weather data for Minneapolis, Minnesota, the Web would certainly have it; however, if you wanted Minneapolis climatic data for November of 1976, you might not find it on the Web.

You'll find that by evaluating your information needs before you start your research, you sometimes won't need to get online at all. You may find out that your library has an excellent CD-ROM database that provides all the information you need. Perhaps your library will have a better source in paper form. Don't be shy about asking a reference librarian to help you determine whether the Internet or some other resource will have the most appropriate material to choose from on the topic you are researching.

Choosing the Best Tool to Start With

Once you've decided that the Web is likely to have the information you're seeking, you'll need to choose an appropriate search tool. Table 4.1 shows the major types of search tools available on the World Wide Web and their major characteristics.

TABLE 4.1

Major Search Tools and Their Characteristics

Type of Search Tool	Major Characteristics
Directories and Virtual Libraries	◆ Hierarchically arrange topical lists of selected resources ◆ May rate and review Web resources ◆ Are meant to be browsed, but can also be searched by keyword ◆ Are most dependent upon user input for selection and control of the included resources ◆ Are usually used for broad topics ◆ Are updated less frequently than search engine databases ◆ Tend to be small databases ◆ Contain links to subject guides and specialized databases
Search Engines	◆ Claim to index most of the World Wide Web ◆ Most are full-text databases ◆ Require knowledge of search techniques to guarantee good results ◆ Create their databases with computer programs called spiders or robots ◆ Are most often used for multifaceted topics and obscure subjects ◆ Search very large databases that are updated frequently
Meta-Search Tools	◆ Some allow you to search several search engines simultaneously ◆ Some supply lists of databases that can be searched directly from their pages ◆ Provide a good way to keep up with new search engines

	✦ May not contain features that are included in individual search tools, so you must keep your searches simple
Intelligent Agents	✦ Are software entities that perform tasks on your behalf
	✦ Some can send the information requested on a schedule that you define
	✦ Are sometimes referred to as bots or robots
	✦ Work with some degree of autonomy

Selecting a Tool Wisely: Knowing the Difference Between a Directory and a Search Engine

As you can see from the list, there are several types of search tools. How do you choose the best one to start with? Knowing the difference between a search engine and a directory is crucial to your success. Browsing *directories* can be a very effective way to find general information you're looking for. If you need specific information, however, you'll want to use a search engine. The reason is that directories do not index all of the Web pages in the World Wide Web, nor do they index all of the words that appear in the Web pages they catalog. Search engine databases, however, aim to cover the entire Web, and most index every word in every Web page. Directories depend on humans to create and maintain their collections; of this group, virtual libraries are the most dependent on people for their creation.

Here's an example that illustrates the difference between search engines and directories.

Let's say we want to find information on a multifaceted topic, such as the regulation of food safety. We may find something by browsing in a directory, but we'd have to be sure of the category that included that topic. Would we look under science, health, or government? We could search the directory using the keywords **food**, **safety**, and **government**, but if these words didn't appear in the categories, Web page titles, or annotations, there would be no results. In a search engine database, by contrast, all we would need to do is type **"food safety"** (as a phrase) **AND government** in a search form.

THERE ARE ALWAYS EXCEPTIONS. Sometimes specific information is more easily found in a directory than in a search engine. For instance, let's say you want to know the name of the first prime minister of independent India. If you typed in the search expression **"prime minister" AND India**, you'd probably get thousands of hits and perhaps many of them would be about the current

prime minister and not the one you were looking for. A directory might be the best place to go for this information. There may be a site that focuses on India's history and politics and contains a detailed listing of past leadership and other statistics.

Virtual Libraries: Directories with a Difference

Virtual libraries are similar to traditional libraries. Information specialists who manage virtual libraries select and catalog the Web pages included in their directories in the same way that traditional librarians select and catalog materials included in their libraries. Virtual libraries are the best directories to go to for subject guides, reference works, and specialized databases. To return to an earlier example, if you're looking for the state of Minnesota's climatic statistics for November 1976, you'll want to find a site that collects authoritative weather data. You may want to start out by using a *virtual library* to find hyperlinks to a meteorological database.

Directories and virtual libraries are most useful when

- you're beginning your research.

- you are searching for an overview of a topic.

- you want evaluated resources.

- you are searching for facts (for example, population statistics or country information).

- you need to find a specialized database for specific information.

Search engines should be consulted when

- your topic has many facets.

- you're looking for a person's name.

- you want very recent information on a topic.

- you want to limit your search to a certain period of time.

- you are seeking obscure information.

Meta-search tools help you
- save time by searching several tools simultaneously.

- locate obscure topics.

Intelligent agents are useful when

- you regularly search for the same type of information.

- you want a program to repeat a search over and over again.

- you want the program to perform a particular task with the information it finds (for example, comparing prices of certain items).

Now that you have an idea of what types of search tools are available, the next section will cover each in detail. For the most common types of tools—directories, virtual libraries, and search engines—we've supplied hands-on activities to give you practical experience in how to use them. The exercises at the end of the chapter will give you an opportunity to try meta-search tools.

Directories and Virtual Libraries

Directories, sometimes referred to as subject catalogs, are topical lists of selected Web resources arranged in a hierarchical way. By hierarchical, we mean that the *subject categories* are arranged from broadest to most specific. For example, the following is a *hierarchy*:

business
    management
        human resources
            wages and benefits

In this example, *management* is a subcategory of *business, human resources* is a subcategory of *management*, and *wages and benefits* is a subcategory of *human resources*. In a hypertext environment like the World Wide Web, moving from a broad subject to a more detailed part of that subject is quite simple. You click on **business**, which is the *top-level category* or heading, and the computer screen fills with a list of subject categories that are narrower than the business category; in our case, management. By clicking on **management**, the screen fills with even more subject categories and we choose the subject we want, which is **human resources**. Then we click on yet another subcategory: **wages and benefits**. After choosing each subcategory, the screen fills with lists of subcategories and Web pages that you can choose by clicking on their titles.

Table 4.2 lists the most well-known directories on the World Wide Web along with their URLs:

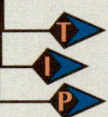

The Web has information on directories.

- "Searching by Means of Subject Directories" http://www .monash.com/ spidap1.html #directories

- "Comparing the Subject Directories" http://www .notess.com/ search/dir/

- "Searching the Internet Part II: Subject Catalogs, Annotated Directories, and Subject Guides" http://rs .internic.net/ nic-support/ nicnews/oct96/ enduser.html

Many of the major search tools contain a directory and a search engine. This way you can try both methods in one service. The directory part of the search tool is usually a subset of the entire search engine database, and the sites listed in a directory are often evaluated,

TABLE 4.2

Major Directories on the World Wide Web

Directory	URL
Galaxy	http://galaxy.einet.net/
Infoseek	http://infoseek.go.com
LookSmart	http://www.looksmart.com
Lycos Top 5%	http://point.lycos.com/categories
Magellan Web Guide	http://magellan.excite.com
NetGuide: Your Guide to the Net	http://www.netguide.com
WebCrawler Channels	http://webcrawler.com/
Yahoo!	http://www.yahoo.com

summarized, and rated. For example, Magellan is a search engine database that indexes most of the World Wide Web; its directory, Magellan Web Reviews, includes rated and reviewed Web pages and covers a small portion of the resources available in the search engine database.

Characteristics of Directories

While all directories rely on people to select, maintain, and update their resource lists, the level of quality control involved in the management of each directory differs.

For example, some directories have very little control over their collections and rely on Web page submitters to provide annotations and decisions about where their resource should be placed in the directory's hierarchy. Other di-

rectories are much more selective about not only which resources are included, but also where those resources will be located in the subject hierarchy. Such directories write detailed page annotations, which can be evaluative, descriptive, or both. The annotated directories rate Web resources using criteria that vary from one directory to another. What is an inherent strength of a directory can sometimes be a weakness, and vice versa. We'll examine some of the strengths and weaknesses of directories here.

STRENGTHS OF DIRECTORIES.

- Directories contain fewer resources than search engine databases.

- Many directories rate or evaluate chosen resources.

114

- Directories increase the probability of retrieving relevant results.

Since directories are maintained by people, they contain fewer resources than search engine databases. This can be a plus, especially when you are looking for information on a general topic. In addition, many directories rate, annotate, analyze, or evaluate the resources that are included, so you can quickly access useful resources of high quality.

With thousands of resources appearing on the Web each day, it is important that there are people determining which sites and Web pages on the World Wide Web have the highest quality. For example, if we want to find some of the best Web resources that provide translation information, we could try Magellan's directory. Magellan's Web Guide is a directory that rates selected sites. Figure 4.1 shows the top-level categories of Magellan. For our current search, we would click on **Reference** first.

After choosing **Reference**, your browser window would show subcategories that you could then choose from. A logical choice would be to click on **Reference Desk**. From there, you would select **Dictionaries**. After choosing **Dictionaries**,

FIGURE 4.1
Magellan Web Reviews Directory

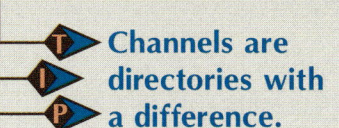

Reference is a top-level category

you'd have more choices that would lead you to the results you want. After choosing **Translation**, you would get a list of resources that you could then look through. If you scrolled down the list, you'd find several Web sites that focus on translation. The first two are recommended and have reviews attached, as shown in Figure 4.2.

WEAKNESSES OF DIRECTORIES.

- Resources in directories may be assigned to arbitrary hierarchical arrangements.

- Directories are infrequently updated.

- The various rating systems and annotations are subjective.

Channels are directories with a difference.

Some tools bring together different types of resources (chat groups, statistics, Web pages, and other types of information) into subject categorizations called modules, channels, or sections, depending on the tool that provides the service. The following are some examples:

- "My Yahoo!"
  http://my .yahoo.com

- "Excite"
  http://www .excite.com

- "WebCrawler"
  http://www .webcrawler.com

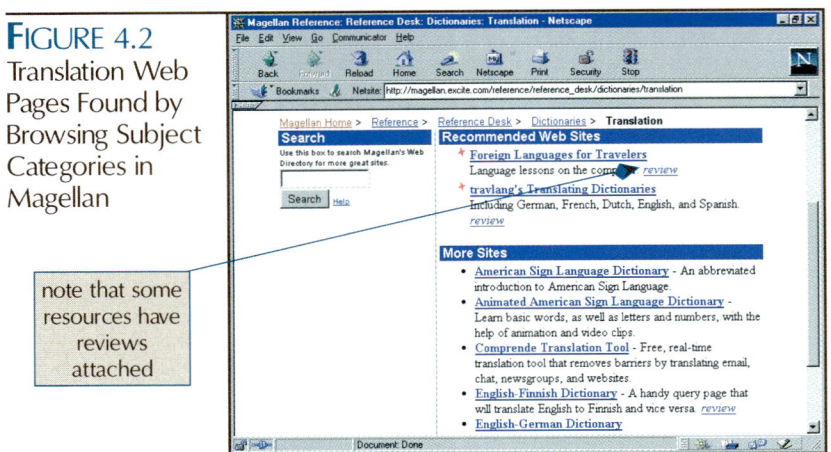

FIGURE 4.2
Translation Web Pages Found by Browsing Subject Categories in Magellan

note that some resources have reviews attached

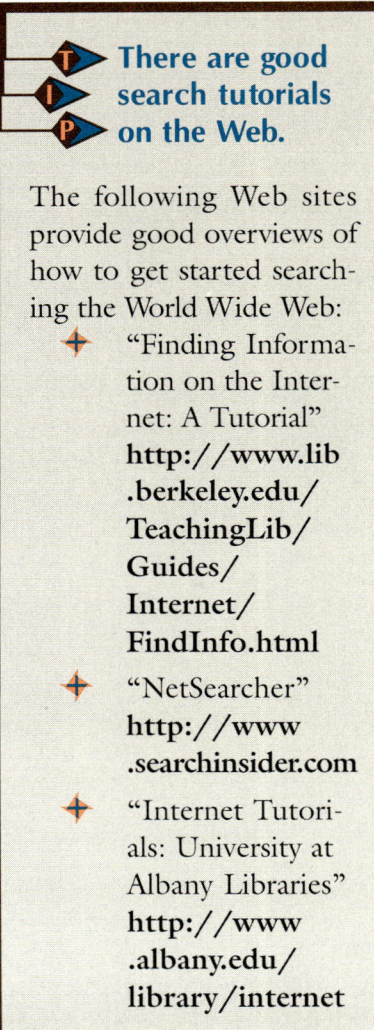

There are good search tutorials on the Web.

The following Web sites provide good overviews of how to get started searching the World Wide Web:

- "Finding Information on the Internet: A Tutorial" **http://www.lib.berkeley.edu/TeachingLib/Guides/Internet/FindInfo.html**

- "NetSearcher" **http://www.searchinsider.com**

- "Internet Tutorials: University at Albany Libraries" **http://www.albany.edu/library/internet**

It may be helpful to think of browsing a directory by subject as similar to going through subjects in a card catalog. You may find exactly what you are looking for by browsing through many pages or cards filled with information; then again, you may miss some related information because your subject may appear in many different categories. For example, resources on translation appeared in the Reference category in Magellan, but this information may be in the Business category too, since business people often need translation information. Browsing a directory requires that you think categorically about the subject you are looking for. Keyword searching was created to help you find information when you don't know which category the information may be in. Many directories have simple keyword searching ability for just this reason. A well-

designed directory with keyword searching ability can help alleviate the problem of arbitrary hierarchical arrangements.

Since people, not machines, maintain directories, directories are not updated as quickly as search engine databases that rely on computer programs to add new Web pages automatically. Keep this in mind when you are looking for very recent information.

Another drawback concerns directories that rate and review resources. The fact that an individual has selected, rated, and possibly reviewed the resource makes the directory subjective and restricts your choices. You may not agree with the selections or ratings that the directory administrators have made. What seems to be a good resource to one person may not seem that way to the next. This is why it's important that the directory has well-stated criteria for the selection and rating of resources that it includes in its database.

Now that we've discussed the major characteristics of directories, let's try an example in Yahoo!, currently the most popular and most comprehensive directory on the Web. You can browse Yahoo! by subject category or search it by keyword. If you do a keyword search and the keyword isn't found in the Yahoo! database, Yahoo! automatically sends your search request to a full-text search engine. In the following example, we'll browse Yahoo! for our topic and then we'll search the database by typing in a keyword.

EXAMPLE 4.1

Using a Directory to Find Information

In this example, we'll go to the directory Yahoo! and browse its subject categories for information on international refugees. We're looking for authoritative information, including statistics. We'll find information on this topic by first browsing the subject categories, and then by searching using a keyword. We'll compare the results from browsing by subject and searching by keyword and show you the difference between the two modes. We'll follow these steps:

1. Go to Yahoo!'s home page. (We'll assume that the Web browser is started.)

2. Browse Yahoo! for information on refugees.

3. Search Yahoo! by typing **refugees** in the search form.

4. Bookmark the most promising Web page.

1 ▶ Go to Yahoo!'s home page.

╋ Point to the location field and click. This highlights the URL of the current Web page. Now you can type in Yahoo!'s URL.

╋ Type **http://www .yahoo.com** and press Enter.

2 ▶ Browse Yahoo! for information on refugees.

Browsing a directory requires that you make guesses about what your topic's hierarchical arrangement will be. In this example, we'll

✛ Click on **Society & Culture**, as shown in Figure 4.3.

start with the top-level category **Society & Culture**, since our topic has to do with the movement of people.

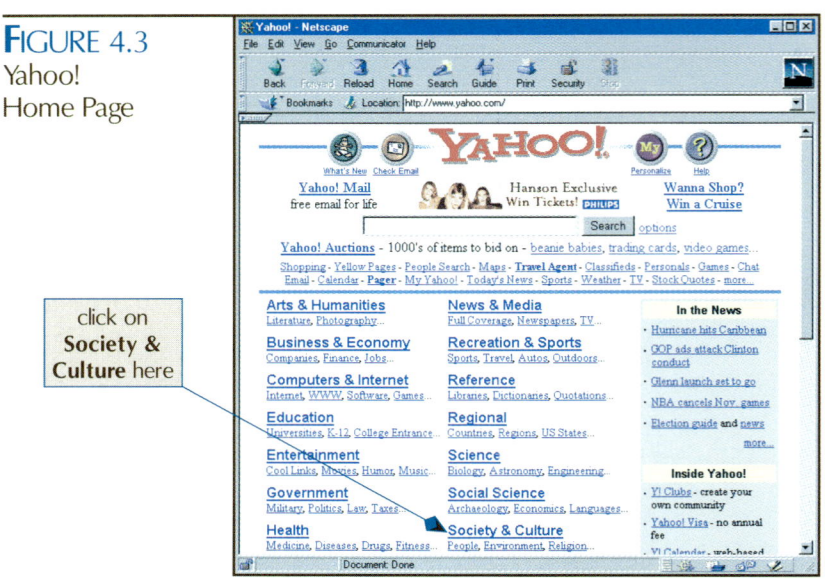

FIGURE 4.3
Yahoo!
Home Page

Figure 4.4 shows the categories under **Society & Culture**. There are a few categories that may provide you with connections to information about refugees. The **Issues and Causes** category seems to be the best category to choose. From there, we'll explore the **Human Rights** subcategory. A lot has been written about the international refugee situation as a human rights cause.

✛ Click on **Issues and Causes**, as shown in Figure 4.4.

✛ From the resulting categories, click on **Human Rights**.

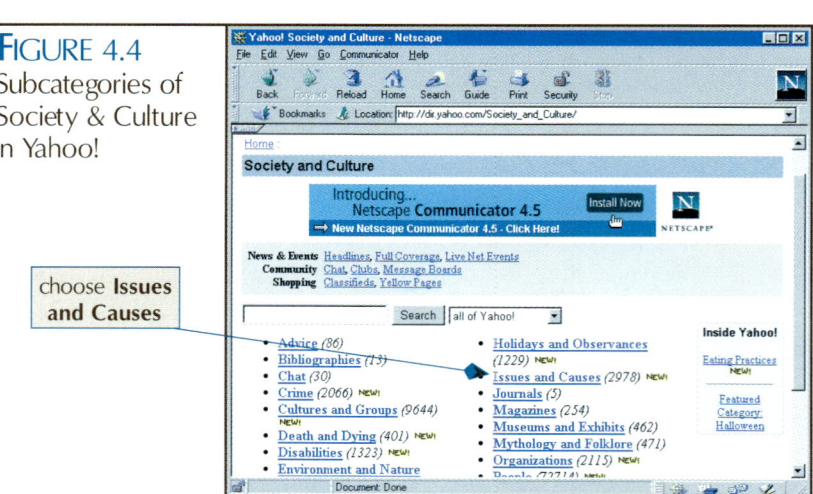

FIGURE 4.4
Subcategories of
Society & Culture
in Yahoo!

Note in Figure 4.5 that **Refugees** appears as a subcategory. Go ahead and click on it.

✛ Click on **Refugees**, as shown in Figure 4.5.

FIGURE 4.5
Subcategories of Human Rights in Yahoo!

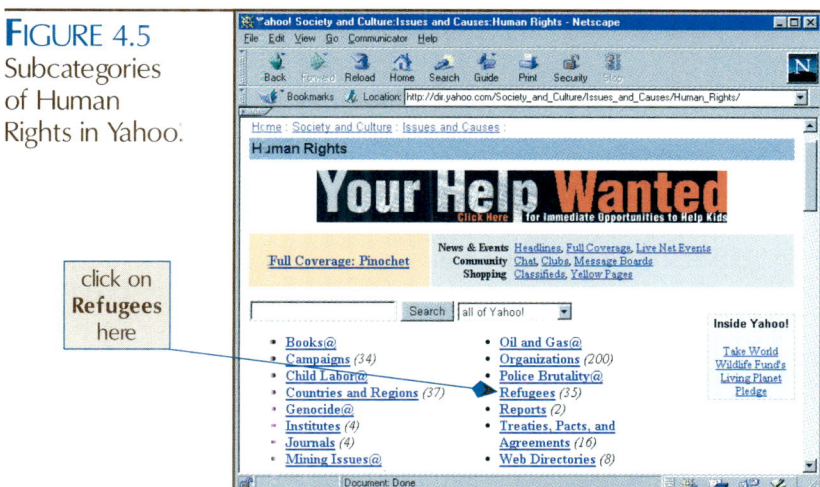

Any one or more of the Web pages retrieved (shown in Figure 4.6) may be useful. It's a good idea to also do a keyword search to check for listings in other categories. To do that, type a keyword in the search form, select whether to search the whole database or just this category, and click on **Search**.

❺ Search Yahoo! by typing **refugees** in the search form.

✛ Type **refugees** in the search form provided, as shown in Figure 4.6. Make sure that **all of Yahoo!** is selected, and click on **Search**.

FIGURE 4.6
Results of Structured Browse and Initiation of Keyword Search

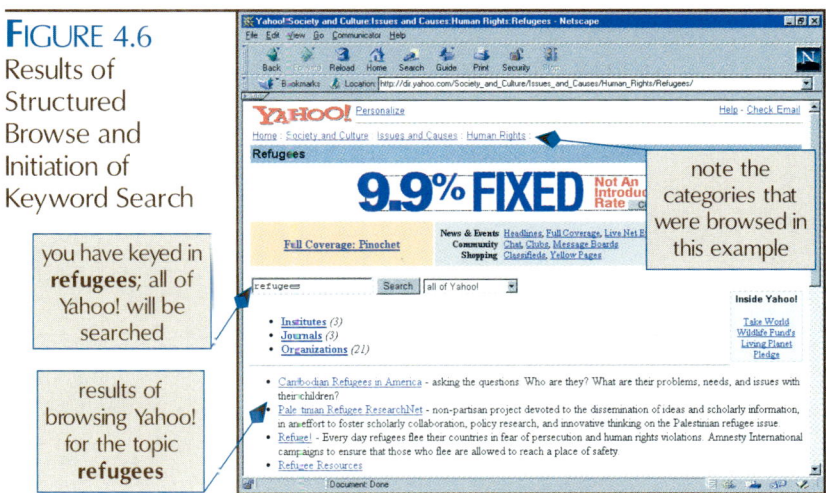

Figure 4.7 shows the results of this keyword search. Note that the second category match is from a category that we didn't browse. It is a subcategory of Government: International Organizations: United Nations: Programs and is called United Nations High Commissioner for Refugees. This category looks extremely promising because it is information provided by the United Nations, which may have the authoritative data we need.

✛ Click on the link **Government: International Organizations: United Nations: Programs: United Nations High Commissioner for Refugees**, as shown in Figure 4.7.

✛ Click on **United Nations High Commissioner for Refugees (UNHCR)**.

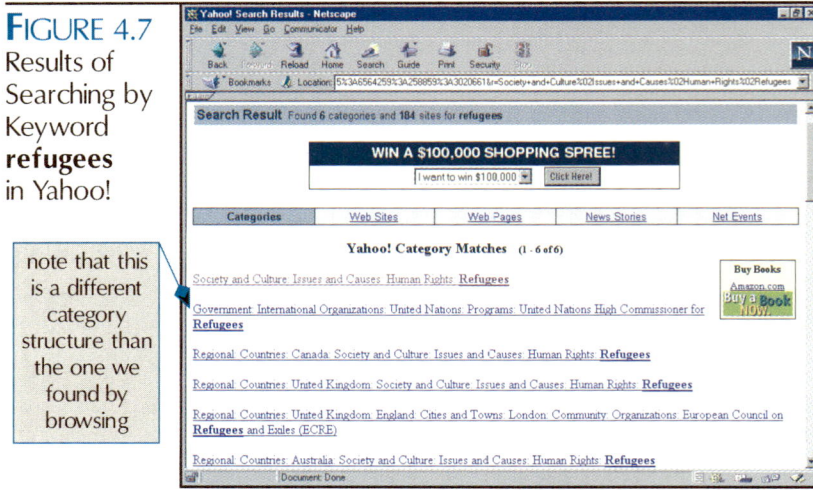

FIGURE 4.7 Results of Searching by Keyword **refugees** in Yahoo!

note that this is a different category structure than the one we found by browsing

◆ Bookmark the most promising Web page.

This Web page is exactly what we are looking for. The United Nations is a reliable source, and it keeps annual worldwide demographic statistics. After exploring this site's links and discovering that it lists the numbers and types of refugees in all the countries of the world, we decide to bookmark it so that we can come back to it later.

✛ Click on **Bookmarks** in the location toolbar. Point your mouse to **Add bookmark** and click.

The title of the Web page is added automatically to your bookmark list. You can access this Web page later by clicking its title in your list.

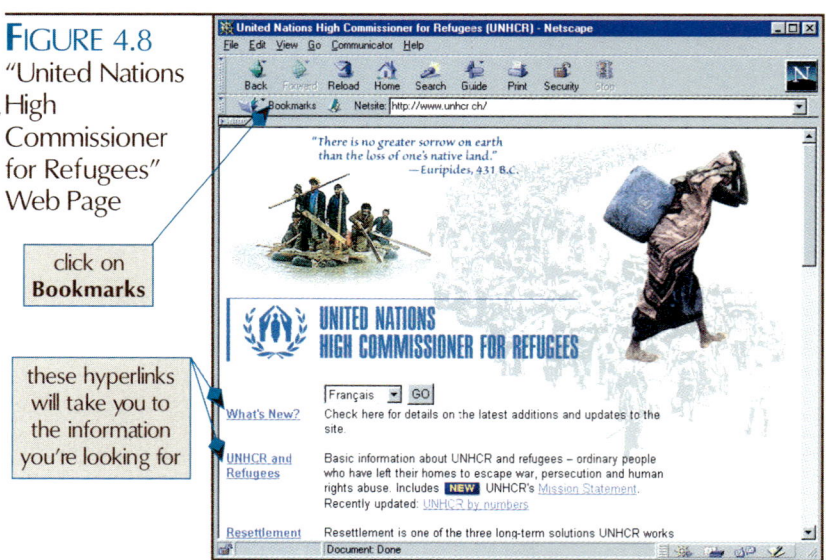

FIGURE 4.8 "United Nations High Commissioner for Refugees" Web Page

click on **Bookmarks**

these hyperlinks will take you to the information you're looking for

End of Example 4.1

Keyword searching helps us find information quickly on the Web, in the same way that computerized library catalogs help us find books quickly. If you know specifically what you are looking for and you don't want to take the time to browse categories in a directory, you may want to search the directory by keyword. You may want to do both. It is a good idea to use different tactics when looking for something on the Web.

Virtual Libraries

Virtual libraries are directories that contain collections of resources that librarians and information specialists have carefully chosen and organized in a logical way. The Web pages included in a subject category are usually evaluated by someone knowledgeable in that particular field. Virtual libraries typically provide an organizational hierarchy with subject categories to facilitate browsing. Most include query interfaces in order to perform simple searches. Virtual libraries are great places to begin your research. The following is a list of a few of the most well-known virtual libraries on the Web:

TABLE 4.3

Virtual Libraries

Virtual Library	URL
Argus Clearinghouse	http://www.clearinghouse.net
INFOMINE	http://lib-www.ucr.edu
Internet Public Library	http://www.ipl.org
Librarians' Index to the Internet	http://sunsite.berkeley.edu/internetindex
World Wide Web Virtual Library	http://www.w3.org/vl

The main difference between virtual libraries and directories is that virtual libraries are much smaller since the resources included are very carefully selected. The people who organize virtual libraries are usually on the lookout for three types of information: subject guides, reference works, and specialized databases.

Subject Guides

A *subject guide* is a World Wide Web resource that is devoted to including hyperlinks for most, if not all, of the Web pages on that particular subject. For example, the resource devoted to listing Web pages on environmental ethics pictured in Figure 4.9 is a subject guide. Some people refer to subject guides as metapages; in Yahoo!, they are called indices.

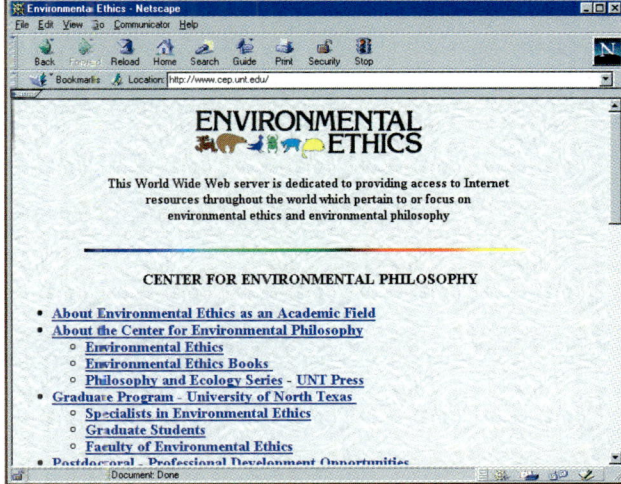

FIGURE 4.9
Environmental Ethics Subject Guide

World Factbook is a handbook published by the U.S. Central Intelligence Agency

FIGURE 4.11
PubMed: The
National Library
of Medicine's
Service that
Includes the
Medline
Database

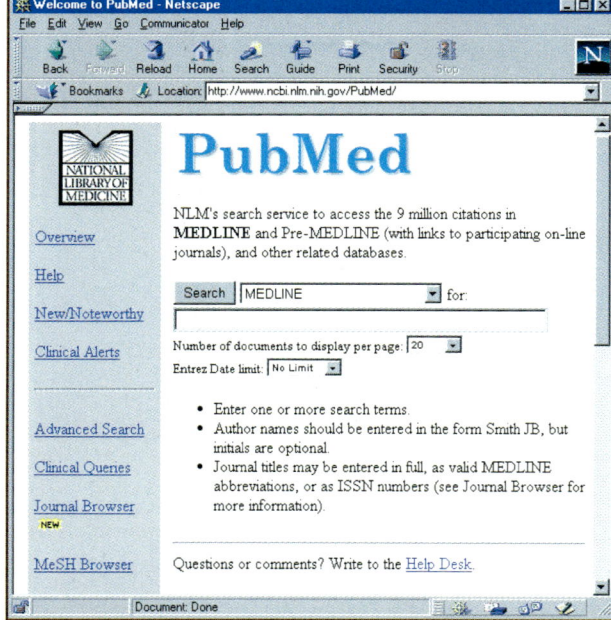

Reference Works

Another common type of resource that is collected by virtual libraries is a reference work. A *reference work* is a full-text document, and may be self-contained. In other words, it doesn't necessarily contain hyperlinks to other resources. A reference work on the World Wide Web is very similar to its print counterpart. A dictionary on the Web looks very much like a dictionary on a library reference shelf. The only difference is that the Web version of a reference work may allow you to move around the document using hyperlinks, instead of turning pages and looking in the index for related topics. There are encyclopedias, handbooks, dictionaries, directories, and many other types of reference works on the World Wide Web. The work pictured in Figure 4.10, the World Factbook from 1997, is a reference work.

Specialized Databases

Virtual libraries are useful for finding specialized databases as well. A *specialized database* is an index that catalogs specific material like patent literature, journal article citations, company financial data, court decisions, and so forth. Specialized databases can usually be searched by keyword and often support sophisticated search features and capabilities. Figure 4.11 shows the home page for PubMed, the National Library of Medicine's search service that includes Medline, a database of article citations and abstracts from premier medical journals. Medline covers more than 3,500 international journal titles.

Let's do a brief example to see how useful a virtual library can be.

EXAMPLE 4.2

In this example, we are going to look for information on the country Azerbaijan. We hope to find a reference work, perhaps an encyclopedia-type publication that includes history, statistics, and other general information about the country. A virtual library is an excellent place to start looking for information like this. We'll use the Librarians' Index to the Internet, developed by librarians at the public library in Berkeley, California.

We'll follow these steps:

1. Go to the home page for the Librarians' Index to the Internet.

2. Browse the subject categories for country information.

3. Access the Web page for Country Studies/Area Handbooks.

4. Choose **Azerbaijan**.

5. Explore the country study for Azerbaijan by searching it by keyword.

◆▶ **Go to the home page for the Librarians' Index to the Internet.**

✛ Point to the location field and click. Now you can type in the URL for the Librarians' Index to the Internet.

✛ Type **http://sunsite .b e r k e l e y . e d u / internetindex/** and press [**Enter**].

The home page is shown in Figure 4.12. Note that it looks very similar to Yahoo!, with the alphabetical list of top-level subject categories and the search form at the top.

❷▶ **Browse the subject categories for country information.**

Once again we have to make an educated guess about where to find our topic when browsing subject categories in a directory. In this case, the choice is pretty straightforward. We'll need to choose **Cultures (World)**.

✛ Click on **Cultures (World)**, as shown in Figure 4.12.

FIGURE 4.12 Librarians' Index to the Internet Home Page

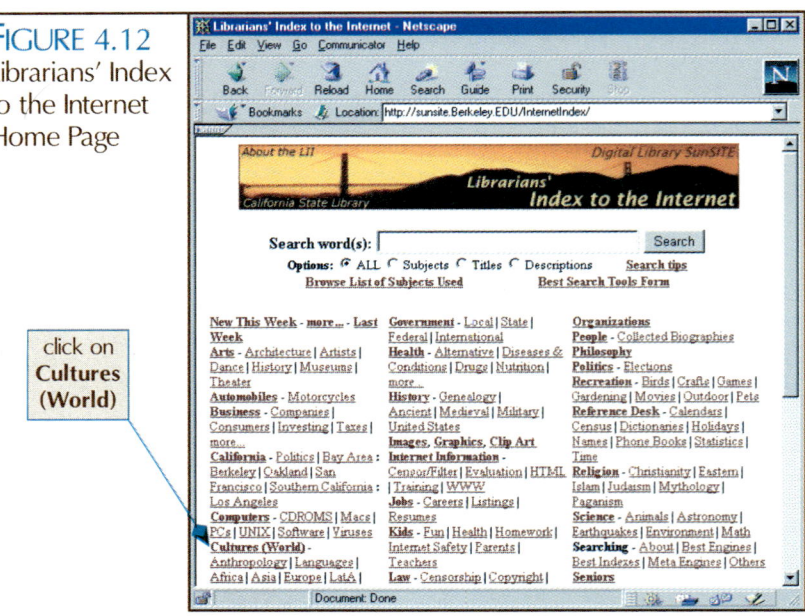

click on **Cultures (World)**

⑤ Access the Web page for Country Studies/Area Handbooks.

The first hyperlink in the list of results is for the **Country Studies/Area Handbooks** Web page. The annotation indicates that this is a series of books that have been translated into HTML format and put on the Web by the Library of Congress and the Department of the Army. Let's see if Azerbaijan has been included.

✛ Click on **Country Studies/Area Handbooks**, as shown in Figure 4.13.

FIGURE 4.13 Web Pages in Cultures (World) Category

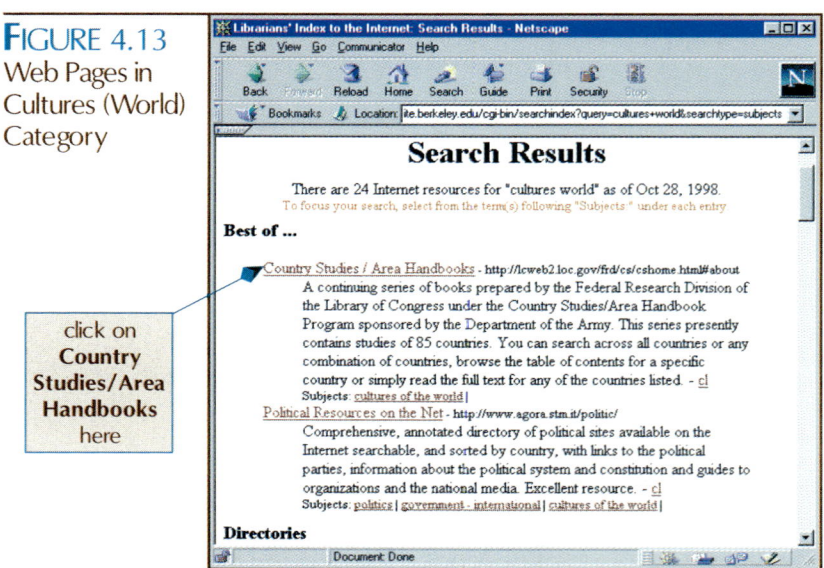

click on **Country Studies/Area Handbooks** here

④ Choose **Azerbaijan**.

Figure 4.14 shows a list of the country studies included in this series. Note that Azerbaijan is listed.

✈ Click on **Azerbaijan**.

FIGURE 4.14
List of Country Studies Available

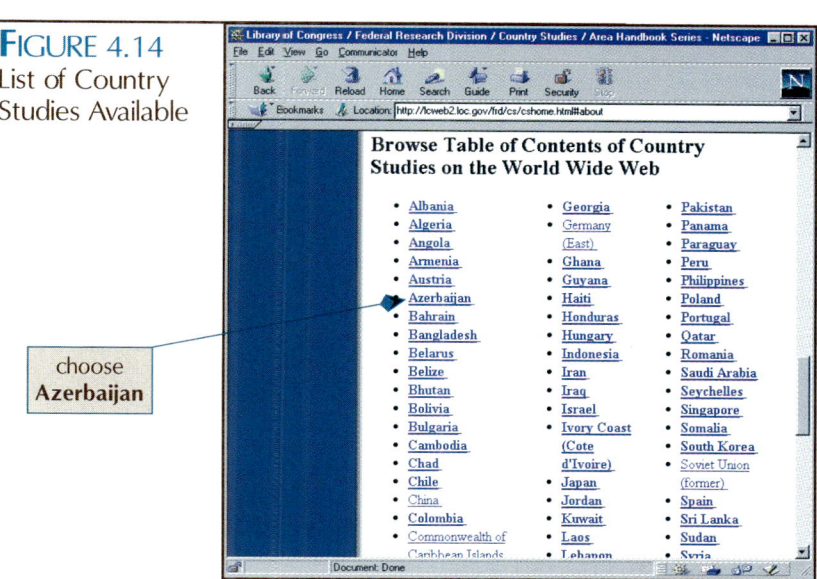

choose
Azerbaijan

5 Explore the country study for Azerbaijan by searching it by keyword.

If you want to search for a specific topic within the country study, you can search by keyword. In keeping with our topic in the last example, let's see if there is any information on refugees in the country study.

✈ In the search form, type in **refugees** and click on **SEARCH**, as shown in Figure 4.15.

FIGURE 4.15
Search Form with **refugees** Typed In

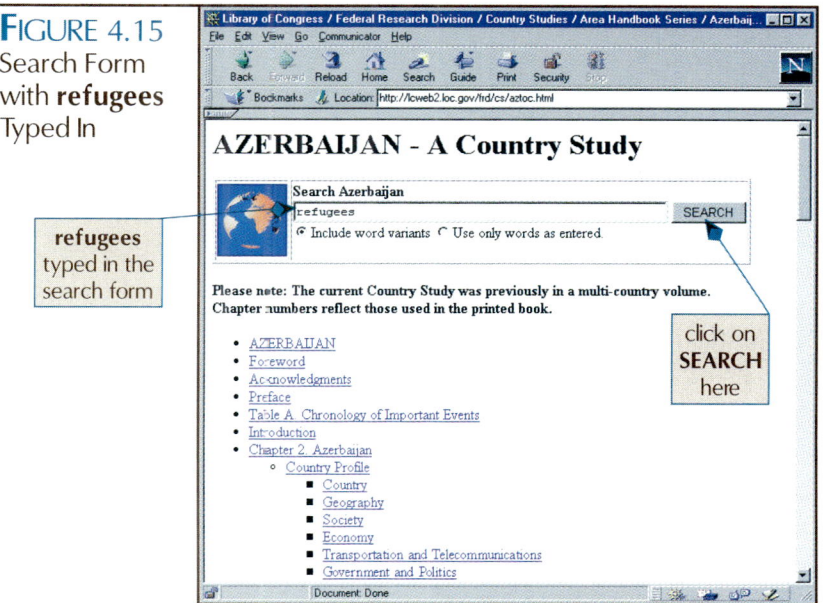

refugees
typed in the search form

click on
SEARCH
here

Figure 4.16 shows the results of the search. You can click on any of the 13 resulting hyperlinks to view the parts of the country study that contain the word **refugees** in the text.

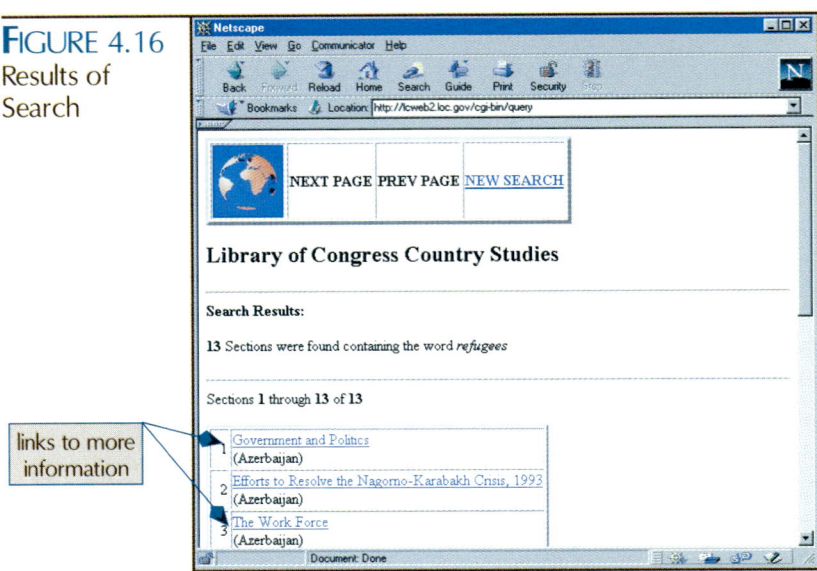

FIGURE 4.16
Results of Search

NEXT PAGE PREV PAGE NEW SEARCH

Library of Congress Country Studies

Search Results:

13 Sections were found containing the word *refugees*

Sections 1 through 13 of 13

links to more information

1 Government and Politics
(Azerbaijan)
2 Efforts to Resolve the Nagorno-Karabakh Crisis, 1993
(Azerbaijan)
3 The Work Force
(Azerbaijan)

End of Example 4.2

Directories and virtual libraries can be useful if you have a broad subject and aren't sure how to narrow it down. They are also helpful if you want to get a general idea about what resources are available and can help you focus your topic that way. Virtual libraries are especially useful as a starting point for research on a particular topic or a place to find subject guides, reference works, and specialized databases. But if you want to zero in quickly on Web pages that are specifically related to your topic, or if your topic is multifaceted or extremely detailed and you know which keywords you want to use, a search engine is what you need. In the following sections, we'll discuss search engines and give a brief overview of the most common keyword search features.

Search Engines and Meta-Search Tools

Search engines are tools that use computer programs called *spiders* or *robots* to automatically gather information on the Internet to create the search engine databases. Spiders go out on the Internet and locate hyperlinks that are available to the public. These hyperlinks are retrieved and put into a database that you can search by using a search engine. Robot programs were created because the number of Internet documents has increased so rapidly that people can't keep up with indexing them manually. Each of the major search engines handles a huge amount of data because they all attempt to do the same thing: index as much of the Web as possible.

There are advantages to computer-generated databases. They are frequently updated, give access to very large collections, and are the most useful tool for providing comprehensive search results. If you are looking for a specific concept or phrase, or if your topic is multifaceted, a search engine is the best place to start. You would be smart to look in more than one, because each engine gives different results.

The major search engines are:

TABLE 4.4

The Major Search Engines

Search Engine	URL
AltaVista	http://www.altavista.com
Excite	http://www.excite.com
HotBot	http://www.hotbot.com
Infoseek	http://infoseek.go.com
Lycos	http://www.lycos.com
Northern Light	http://www.northernlight.com
WebCrawler	http://www.webcrawler.com

Search Engine Similarities

All of the major search engines are similar in that each one has a *search form* where you enter keywords, phrases, or proper names. After clicking on **search**, **submit**, **seek**, or some other command button, the database returns a collection of hyperlinks to your screen, which are usually listed according to their *relevance* to the keyword(s) you typed in, from the most relevant link to the least relevant. Search engines determine relevancy in different ways. Generally, it's determined by how many times the search terms appear in the document. All search engines have online help to get you acquainted with their search features. Two commonly supported search features are *Boolean searching* and *phrase searching*. Other search features available in many search engines include field searching, truncation searching, and proximity searching.

BOOLEAN OPERATORS. In some search engines, if nothing is typed between two words, the search engine assumes that an OR is between them. This is what we'd refer to as a *default setting*. In order to override this feature, you'd either have to type **AND** between the words or put a + before both words, depending on the search features supported by the search engine.

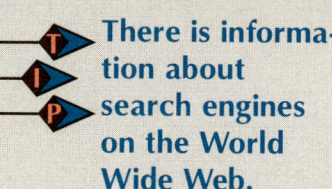

There is information about search engines on the World Wide Web.

+ "Search Engine Watch" http:// searchenginewatch .com/

+ "Comparing Search Engines" http://www .hamline.edu/ library/bush/ handouts/com- parisons .html

+ "Lost in Cyberspace" http://www. newscientist.com/ keysites/ networld/ lost.html

TABLE 4.5

Boolean Operators

Boolean Operator	Functions
AND	Placing **AND** between keywords in your search expression will narrow the search results. For example, **canoes AND kayaks** would narrow your search so that you would retrieve only those sites that have both words—*canoes* and *kayaks*—in them.

127

Instead of building their own databases, meta-search tools use the databases of the major search engines and directories that already exist on the Internet and provide the user with search forms or interfaces for submitting queries to these search tools.

OR	Placing **OR** between keywords broadens your search results. For example, **canoes OR kayaks** would retrieve those sites that have either word—*canoes* or *kayaks*—in them.
NOT	Placing **NOT** in a search expression will also narrow a search. For example, **canoes NOT kayaks** would retrieve those pages that have the word *canoes*, but not the word *kayaks*, in them.

PHRASE SEARCHING. Let's say you are searching for information on chaos theory. If you type in the words **chaos theory** separated by a space, some search engines may assume that you are in effect saying **chaos AND theory**, while other search engines may assume that you mean **chaos OR theory**. Your search results would not be very precise because the words *chaos* and *theory* could appear separately, not as a phrase, throughout the document.

- Most search engines support phrase searching and require double quotation marks around the words in the phrase. In our example, we would type **"chaos theory"**.

- Searching by phrase guarantees that the words you type in will appear adjacent to each other, in the order in which you type them.

Search Engine Differences

The major search engines differ in several ways:

- index size

- search features (many search engines support the same features but require you to use different *syntax* in order to initiate them)

- frequency of updates to the database

- relevancy algorithms

- overall ease of use

It is important to know these differences because in order to do an exhaustive search of the World Wide Web, you must be familiar with a few different search tools. No single search engine can be relied upon to satisfy every type of query.

META-SEARCH TOOLS. It can be confusing and time-consuming to do your search in several databases, especially if you have to keep track of all of their differences. To solve these problems, database providers have come up with meta-search tools. *Meta-search tools* allow you to search several

search engines simultaneously; they are often called *parallel-search tools* or *unified search interfaces*. After you simply submit your query, the parallel-search tool collects the most relevant sites from each database and sends them to your screen. Instead of building their own databases, meta-search tools use the databases of the major search engines and directories that already exist on the Internet and provide the user with search forms or interfaces for submitting queries to these search tools. Table 4.6 shows the most popular parallel-search tools and their URLs.

Some sites list World Wide Web search tools and their search forms separately, so you can search them one at a time. These sites are called *all-in-one search tools*. These resources can be helpful for keeping up-to-date with new databases on the Web. The most popular all-in-one search tools are shown in Table 4.7.

The Internet Sleuth is listed as a parallel-search tool and an all-in-one search tool because it offers hundreds of general and

128

TABLE 4.6

Parallel-Search Tools and Their URLs

Parallel-Search Tool	URL
Dogpile	http://www.dogpile.com
Internet Sleuth	http://www.isleuth.com
MetaCrawler	http://www.go2net.com/search.html
ProFusion	http://profusion.ittc.ukans.edu
SavvySearch	http://www.cs.colostate.edu/~dreiling/smartform.html

TABLE 4.7

All-in-One Search Tools and Their URLs

All-in-One Search Tool	URL
All-in-One Search Page	http://albany.net/allinone
Internet Sleuth	http://www.isleuth.com/
Search.Com	http://www.search.com/

specialized databases all in one place. You can either search them individually or choose several to search at one time. Figure 4.17 shows how the Internet Sleuth is organized and some of the search options available.

At this point, it would be helpful to give you an example of how search features work. This example will focus on how to create a *search expression* using the features discussed above: phrase searching and Boolean searching.

FIGURE 4.17
The Internet Sleuth: A Meta-Search Tool

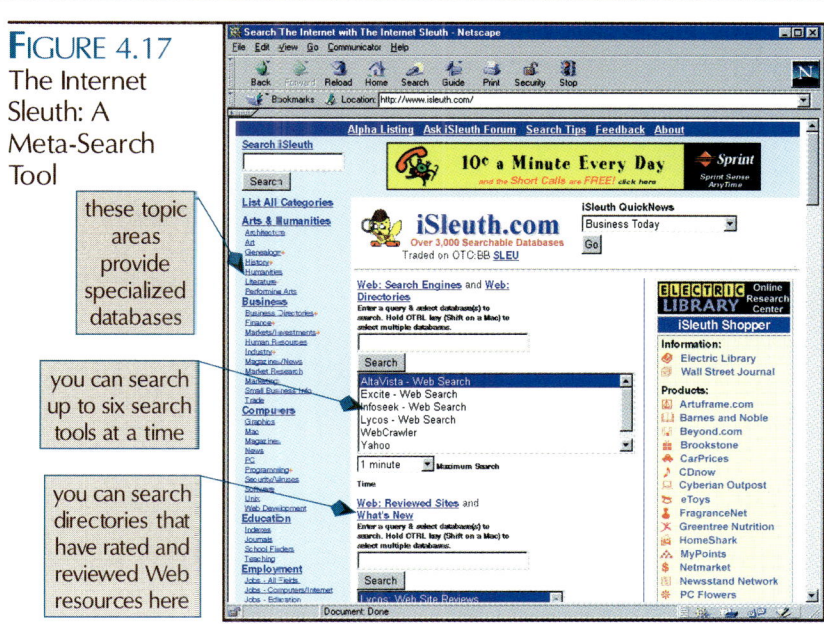

these topic areas provide specialized databases

you can search up to six search tools at a time

you can search directories that have rated and reviewed Web resources here

EXAMPLE 4.3

Using a Search Engine to Find Information

In this example, we're going to continue searching for information about refugees and human rights in Azerbaijan. For a multifaceted search like this, a search engine is the best tool to use. We'll use the search engine database called HotBot. HotBot indexes every word in the Web pages that are included in its database. In order to retrieve the most relevant results, we'll use Boolean operators and phrase searching, two of the most useful search features.

We'll follow these steps:

1. Go to the home page for HotBot.

2. Read the help section to determine which search features are supported.

3. Type a search expression in the form provided.

4. Examine the results and click on the one that appears to be most relevant.

◆❶ Go to the home page for HotBot.

The home page for HotBot should look similar to the one pictured in Figure 4.18.

➕ Click on the location field. The URL of the current Web page will be highlighted. Now you can type in the URL for HotBot.

➕ Type **http://www .hotbot.com** in the location field and press **Enter**.

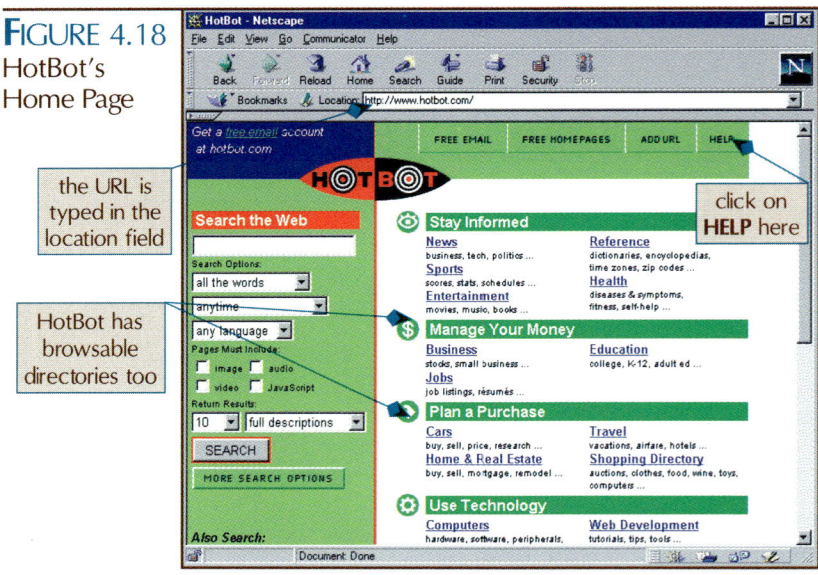

FIGURE 4.18 HotBot's Home Page

◆❷ Read the help section to determine which search features are supported.

Before we type in a search expression in the search form, we need to think a bit about how we're going to construct the search request. First of all, we want to search for *human rights* as a phrase. We also need to find the words *refugees* and *Azerbaijan* in the Web pages. Therefore, we need to find out if HotBot supports Boolean searching and phrase searching. The best place to look is the help section.

✈ Click on **HELP** as shown in Figure 4.18.

Your screen will display several hyperlinks that provide different types of information about HotBot. The most useful hyperlink for search help is the Search Tips link.

✈ Click on the hyperlink titled **Search Tips**.

Figure 4.19 shows the search tip categories.

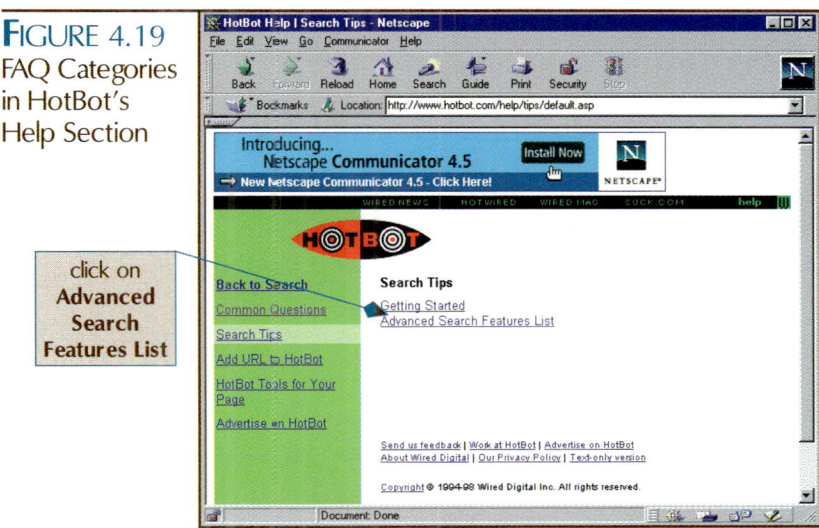

FIGURE 4.19
FAQ Categories in HotBot's Help Section

The most useful category for our needs is the link titled **Advanced Search Features List**.

✈ Click on **Advanced Search Features List**, as shown in Figure 4.19.

After reading about which search features HotBot supports, we can conclude that

✦ HotBot requires quotation marks around words that must appear next to each other, in the order specified. This means that you would place quotes around a phrase.

✦ HotBot also supports Boolean searching, which allows you to search using AND, OR, and NOT. In order to perform a Boolean search, you need to select **Boolean phrase** from the pull-down menu on the home page that is located below the search form.

✦ HotBot is mostly case insensitive. This means that you don't need to capitalize proper nouns.

As you become more adept at searching and more familiar with the particular search tool you're using, it may not be mandatory for you to check the help section.

After you're finished looking at the help screens, scroll up to the top of the screen.

- To return to HotBot's home page, click on **Back to Search.**

5 Type a search expression in the form provided.

- Type the following search expression in the search form provided on HotBot's home page: **"human rights" and azerbaijan and refugees**

- Click on the arrow below the search form. Choose **Boolean phrase** from the list of choices, as shown in Figure 4.20.

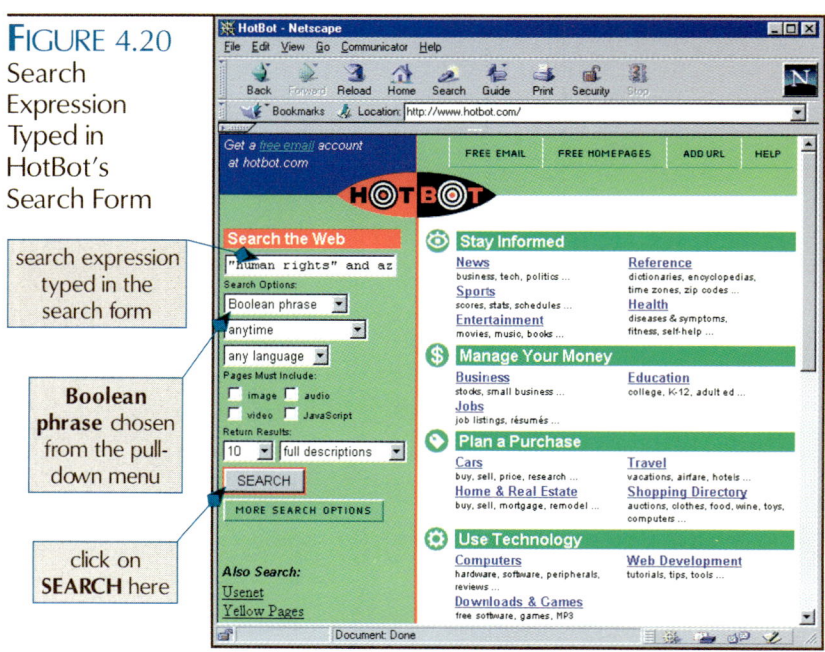

FIGURE 4.20 Search Expression Typed in HotBot's Search Form

search expression typed in the search form

Boolean phrase chosen from the pull-down menu

click on **SEARCH** here

- Click on **SEARCH** and wait for HotBot to deliver links to Web pages that match your search query.

This search will result in links to Web pages that have the phrase *human rights* and the words *Azerbaijan* and *refugees* in them. You can see the search keywords typed in the search form in Figure 4.20.

132

4 Examine the results and click on the one that appears to be most relevant.

Figure 4.21 shows the first few results. Search engines list results according to relevancy. Note that the first on the list is 99 percent relevant to the search expression.

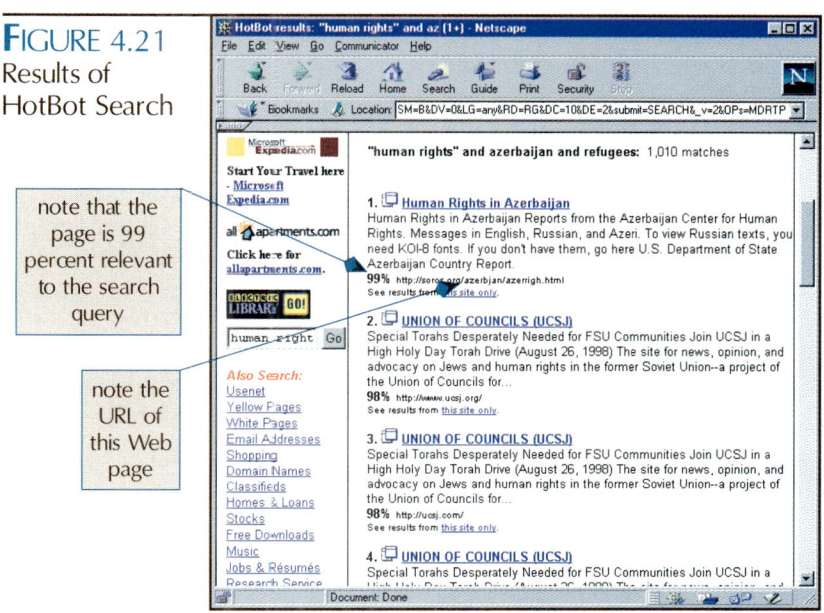

FIGURE 4.21
Results of HotBot Search

Note the first hyperlink that appears on the list of results in Figure 4.20. Your results may be different. This Web page, according to HotBot, is the most relevant. "Human Rights in Azerbaijan" consists of hyperlinks that focus on Azerbaijani refugees and human rights issues. By looking at the first part of the URL, **http://www.soros.org**, you can determine that an organization has published this information. Before you bookmark the site and use it to further your research, you might want to look up **www.soros.org** and find out what this organization does and why it is interested in Azerbaijan's human rights problems. By doing this, you will get an idea of any possible bias the information may contain.

End of Example 4.3

In Example 4.3 we searched HotBot for relevant Web pages focusing on the human rights situation for Azerbaijani refugees. Since we wanted to search for the two words *human rights* as a phrase, we needed to use a search engine that supported phrase searching. We found out by looking in HotBot's help section that it does support phrase searching as long as the phrase is enclosed in quotation marks. HotBot also supports Boolean searching, which we needed in our search

FIGURE 4.22
newsBOT

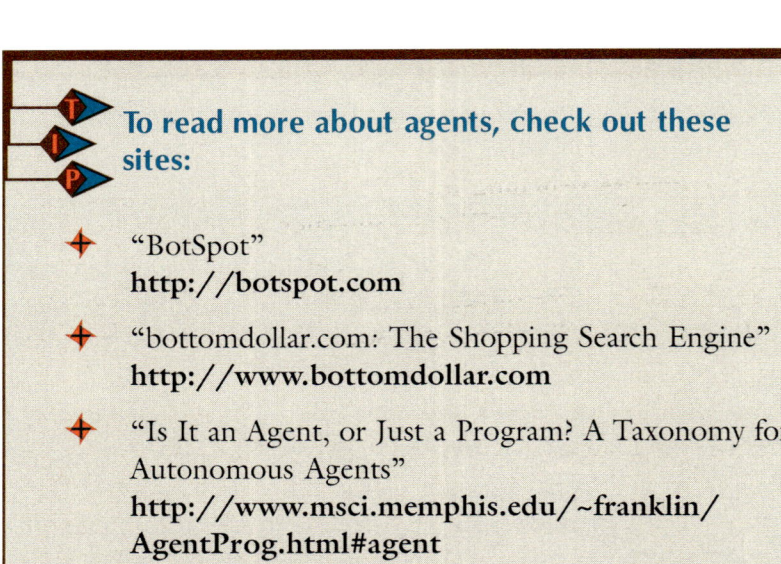

the news sources are searched every 15 minutes

click here to access the entire list of stories by site

expression as well. The Boolean operator used in this search expression was the operator AND. AND narrows results, while OR expands them.

Intelligent Agents

Searching the Web can be a time-consuming and overwhelming task. If you find yourself performing repetitive searches, you may want to use agents to help you. *Agents* are software entities that gather information or accomplish tasks without your intervention. You tell an agent what actions you want performed and the agent then executes them on your behalf. Agents can perform the repetitive tasks of searching databases, retrieving and filtering information, and delivering it back to you. For example, an agent might compare airfare prices for a particular destination that you request and send the lowest fare to your desktop. These agents are sometimes referred to as *intelligent agents*, *personal agents*, or *bots* (short for *robots*). An example of an agent is NewsHub, with the URL **http://www .newshub.com**, shown in Figure 4.22. The NewsHub agent automatically searches for news stories from several of the world's best news sources every 15 minutes. It sorts the stories into categories such as health, science, financial, technical, and so forth. NewsHub also provides customizable versions to corporations for distributing information to their employees and others.

NewsHub searches several sites simultaneously, just as meta-search engines do. You can read the articles according to

Several types of search tools are available on the World Wide Web. These tools—directories and virtual libraries, search engines and meta-search tools, agents, and specialized databases,—are all **useful ways to find information.**

news source if you click **by site**, as shown in Figure 4.22

Summary

This chapter introduced several types of search tools available on the World Wide Web. These tools—directories and virtual libraries, search engines and meta-search tools, specialized databases, and agents—are all useful ways to find information. Directories, sometimes referred to as subject catalogs, are topical lists of selected Web resources organized in a hierarchical way. Directories differ from search engines in one major way: people, not computer programs, collect and maintain the information included in directories. Directories cover small portions of the Web. In fact, directories are small collections of resources compared to the huge databases that search engines access and search. Browsing directories can be a very effective way to find the resources you need, especially if you're sure where the information you're searching for will appear on the World Wide Web.

Virtual libraries are directories that contain collections of resources that librarians or information specialists have carefully chosen and organized in a logical way. Virtual libraries typically provide an organizational hierarchy with subject categories to facilitate browsing. The main difference between virtual libraries and directories is that virtual libraries are much smaller, since the resources included are very carefully selected. The people who organize virtual libraries are usually on the lookout for three major types of information: subject guides, reference works, and specialized databases.

Search engines are tools that use computer programs called spiders or robots to automatically gather information on the Internet and create full-text databases from that information. Spiders go out on the Internet and locate hyperlinks that are available to the public. Spiders then load these resources into a database, which is searchable by using a search engine. Each of the major search engines handles a large amount of data because they all attempt to do the same thing: index as much of the World Wide Web as possible. With meta-search tools, the user can search several search engines simultaneously or access a list of separate search forms for each search engine that allows the user to search one database at a time.

Intelligent agents are useful for performing repetitive tasks witout user intervention, such as searching databases, retrieving and filtering information, and other operations on the user's behalf. ✦

Selected Terms in This Chapter

agent
all-in-one
    search tool
Boolean searching
default setting
directory
hierarchy
intelligent agent
meta-search tool

parallel-search tool
personal agent
phrase searching
reference work
relevance
robot (bot)
search engine
search expression
search form

specialized database
spider
subject category
subject guide
syntax
top-level category
unified search
    interface
virtual library

1. Use the Librarians' Index to the Internet, **http://sunsite .berkeley.edu/internetindex**, to look for the blue book for automobiles. Try to find it by typing in keywords and by browsing the subject categories. What categories did you go through to find it? Explain why either browsing or searching was easier.

2. Browse Yahoo!, **http://www.yahoo.com**, for a list of home-brewer organizations. Write down the top-level category and all the subcategories that you clicked on to reach the list.

3. Use WebCrawler, **http://www.webcrawler.com**, to look for the home page of Mary Washington College. First, search for it by typing in **Mary Washington College**. Note how many results were returned. Then try the search again with quotation marks around the phrase. How were the results affected? Why?

4. Use the Argus Clearinghouse, **http://www.clearinghouse .net**, to find a subject guide on Celtic music. What is the URL of the subject guide? When was it updated?

5. Go to AltaVista, **http://www.altavista.com**, and search for Web pages on the presence of the Coca-Cola Company in foreign countries. Read the help section in AltaVista. Do you need to use Boolean operators? Phrase searching? Write the search expression that you used.

6. Use Northern Light, **http://www.northernlight.com**, to find information on the reasons why the Australian mala, a small wallaby, is an endangered species. Write down the search expression you used and how many results were obtained. Click on one of the folders that appear on the left side of the screen along with the results. Which folder did you click on? Were the contents of the folder more or less relevant to your search request?

7. Browse Excite's directory, **http://www.excite.com**, to find a list of AIDS/HIV resources. Find the three most relevant sites and make a note of their URLs.

8. Use HotBot, **http://www.hotbot.com**, to search for information on Nelson Mandela. Use the pull-down menu to help you search for a person's name. Write down the URLs for the three most relevant Web pages you found.

9. Use the meta-search tool Internet Sleuth, **http://www.isleuth.com**, to find the U.S. Government Manual. Access it and search for information on the Central Intelligence Agency. Make sure you read the search tips. How did you type in the search request? There are two choices for viewing the text. You may select **TXT** or **PDF**. The PDF (portable document format) option is available only if you have Adobe Acrobat installed on your computer.

10. Use PubMed, **http://www.ncbi.nlm.nih.gov/PubMed/**, to search for journal articles on the subject of labyrinthitis. Limit your search to articles published within the past 12 months. How many articles resulted from this search? Go back to PubMed's home page and choose **Advanced Search**. Use this mode to search for articles on the subject of blepharitis. How many results did you obtain? Now limit the results of this search to articles written in English. How many results do you have now?

chapter 5

S E A R C H
STRATEGIES
FOR SEARCH
ENGINES

Chapter 4 gave you an overview of the different types of search tools on the World Wide Web. This chapter will focus on one of the most popular types of tools: search engines. Search engines employ computer programs called spiders or robots to build their databases. Search engines are the most used databases on the Web because they give access to the largest collections and provide the most comprehensive results. This chapter will include the following sections:

- **Search Engine Databases**

- **Search Features Common to Most Search Engines**

- **Output Features Common to Most Search Engines**

- **A Basic Search Strategy: The 10 Steps**

In this chapter, we'll cover search engine databases in detail. Why is it so important to learn how to search these databases? Search engines are the most powerful search tools on the World Wide Web, with the most popular being those that access the largest databases. Many also index Usenet newsgroups, FTP, and Gopher sites. None of the search engines are exactly alike. Some are better for certain kinds of information than others. Maybe you've tried a few search engines and have found that some engines retrieve too many documents that aren't pertinent. Perhaps at other times they don't retrieve enough information. This chapter should clear up some ambiguities you may have about why some searches work well and others don't.

The Major Search Engine Databases on the World Wide Web

- AltaVista
  http://www.altavista.com

- Excite
  http://www.excite.com

- HotBot
  http://www.hotbot.com

- Infoseek
  http://infoseek.go.com

- Lycos
  http://www.lycos.com

- Northern Light
  http://www.northernlight.com

- WebCrawler
  http://www.webcrawler.com

Search Engine Databases

Knowing how search engine databases are indexed can help you select the most appropriate tool for your research needs, retrieve the most relevant information, and understand why results vary from one database to another.

Indexing

In directories, site managers and *cybrarians* assign keywords to Web pages. They describe a Web page with a few words. This *keyword indexing* enables you to find that page if any of the words you type in match the words used to describe the page.

In search engines, a computer program, called a spider or robot, gathers new documents from the Web. The program retrieves hyperlinks that are attached to these documents, loads them into a database, and indexes them using a formula that differs

How a Spider Works —Searching the Internet for New Documents

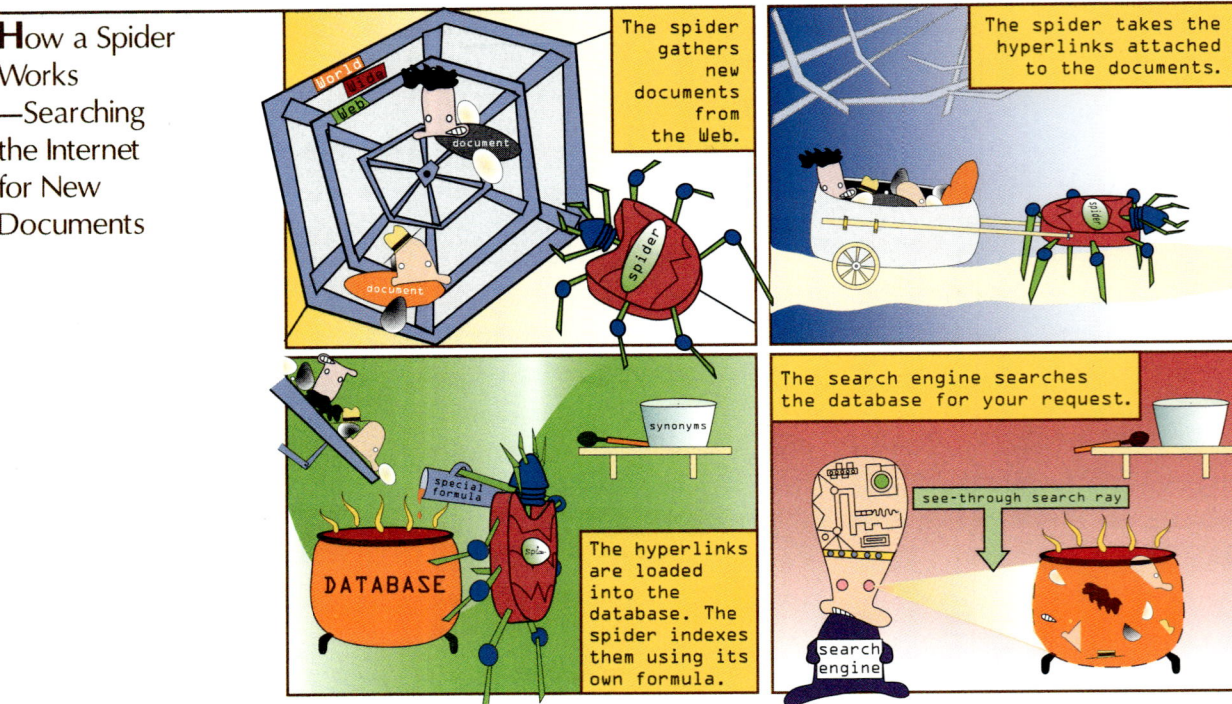

The spider gathers new documents from the Web.

The spider takes the hyperlinks attached to the documents.

The hyperlinks are loaded into the database. The spider indexes them using its own formula.

The search engine searches the database for your request.

from database to database. The search engine then searches the database according to the request you enter. Although robots have many different ways of collecting information from Web pages, the major search engines all claim to index the entire text of each Web document in their databases. This is called *full-text indexing*. All of the major search engines are full-text databases.

Some robot programs are intuitive; they know which words are important to the meaning of the entire Web page, and some of them can find synonyms to the words and add them to the index. Some full-text databases, such as Excite, use a robot that enables them to search on con-

cepts, as well as on the search query words. In some search engines, the robot skips over words that appear often, such as prepositions and articles. These common words are called *stop words*.

Some search engines allow Web page submitters to attach meta-tags to their pages. *Meta-tags* are keywords that describe the page but may not appear on the page. They appear only in the HTML source document. Meta-tags allow Web pages that don't have a lot of text in them to come up in a keyword search.

When to Use Search Engine Databases

Search engines are the best tools to use when you are looking for

very specific information or when your research topic has many facets. Directories are helpful when you are looking for general and single-faceted topics. Usually when you need information on a very detailed or multifaceted subject, however, a search engine will give you not only more information, but also the most precise and up-to-date information possible. Even though most of the major search engine databases attempt to index as much of the Web as possible, each one has a different way of determining which pages are most relevant to your search request. In one database, a relevant document may be fiftieth on the list; in another database, the document may be first. In order to retrieve the most relevant documents, you should become familiar with many search engines and their features.

Search Features Common to Most Search Engines

It's important to understand the different search features before you begin using a search engine for research. The reason for this is that each search engine has its own way of interpreting and manipulating search expressions. In addition, many search engines have default settings that you may need to override if you want to obtain the most precise results. Because a search can bring up so many words, it is very easy to have a lot of hits with few that are relevant to your query. This is called *low precision/high recall*. You may be satisfied with having very precise search results with a small set returned. This is defined as *high precision/low recall*. Ideally, using the search expression you enter, the search engine would retrieve all of the relevant documents you need. This would be described as *high precision/high recall*.

Search engines support many search features, though not all engines support each

hiking AND camping

hiking OR camping

one. If they do support certain features, they may use different syntax in expressing the feature. Before you use any of these search features, you need to check the search engines' help pages to see how the feature is expressed, if it is supported at all. We will now list the most common search features and explain how each feature is used.

Boolean Operators

We have already used Boolean operators in some of our searches. Knowing how to apply Boolean operators in search ex-

pressions is extremely important. The diagrams show the different operators and how they are used.

Use an AND between search terms when you need to narrow your search. The AND indicates that only those Web pages having both words in them will be retrieved. Some search engines automatically assume an AND relationship between two words if you don't type AND between them. This would be a *default setting* of the search engine.

An OR between search terms will make your resulting set larger. When you use OR, Web pages that have either term will be retrieved. Many search

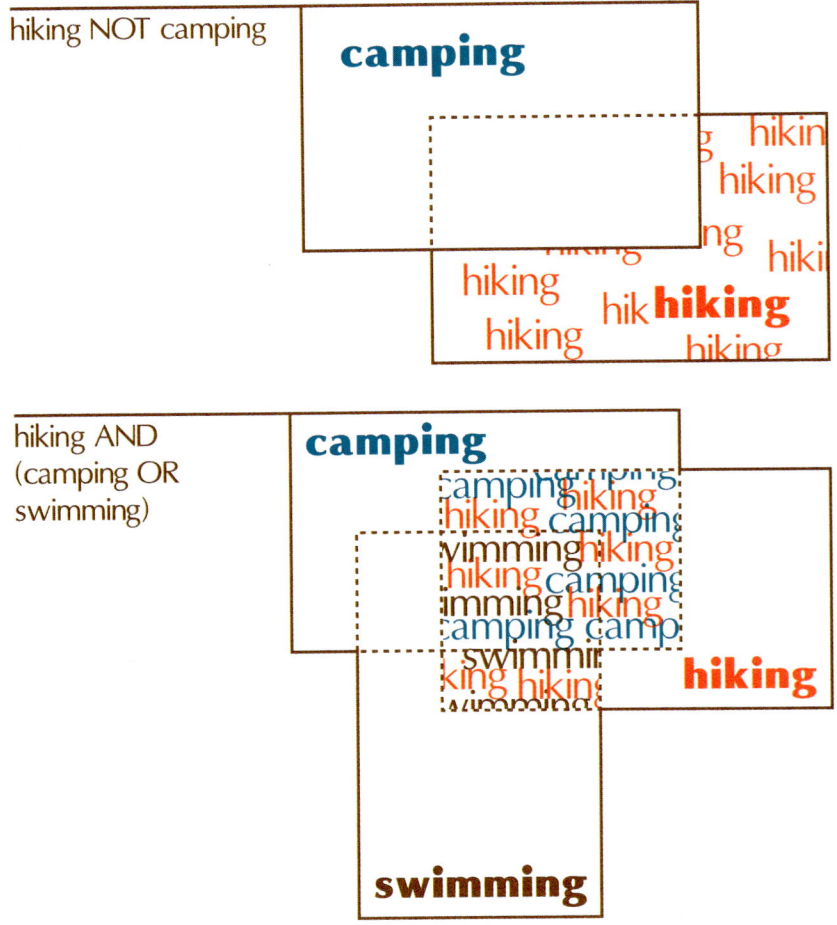

hiking NOT camping

camping

hiking AND
(camping OR
swimming)

camping

hiking

swimming

parentheses indicate that *camping* or *swimming* will be processed first, and that this result will be combined with *hiking*. If the parentheses were not there, the search engine would perform the search from left to right. All pages with both the words *hiking* and *camping* would be found first, and then all pages with the word *swimming* would be included. This would give you an unacceptable result, so you must be careful when using nested Boolean logic.

Implied Boolean Operators

Implied Boolean operators, or pseudo-Boolean operators, are shortcuts to typing AND and NOT. In most search engines that support this feature, you would type + before a word or phrase that must appear in a document and - before a word or phrase that must not appear in a document.

Phrase Searching

A *phrase* is a string of words that must appear next to each other. *Global warming* is a phrase, as is *chronic fatigue syndrome*. Use phrase-searching capability when the words you are searching for must appear next to each other and must appear in the order in which you

engines automatically place an OR between two words if there is nothing typed between them. This would be a default setting of the search engine.

The NOT operator is used when a term needs to be excluded. In the example at the top, Web pages with both *hiking* and *camping* in them would not be retrieved. Some search engines require an AND in front of the NOT. In this case, the expression would be written like this: **hiking AND NOT camping**.

This example shows *nested Boolean logic*. Use this logic when you need to include ANDs and ORs in one search statement. For example, say that there is a term that must appear in your results. You may want to search for this term along with a concept that you can describe with synonyms. To do this, you would need to tell the search engine to find records with two or more synonyms and then to combine this result with the first term. Here, the typed them. Most search engines require double quotation marks to differentiate a phrase from words searched for by themselves. The two phrases mentioned above would be expressed as: **"global warming"** and **"chronic fatigue syndrome"**. Phrase searching is one of the most helpful search features, as it increases the chance that your search will have relevant results.

Proximity Searching

Proximity operators are words such as NEAR and WITHIN. For example, you are trying to find information on the effects of chlorofluorocarbons on global warming. You might want to retrieve results that have the word *chlorofluorocarbons* very close to the phrase *global warming*. By placing the word NEAR between the two segments of the search expression, you would achieve more relevant results than if the words appeared in the same document but were perhaps pages apart. This is called *proximity searching*.

Truncation

Truncation is the process of looking for multiple forms of a word. Some search engines refer to truncation as *stemming*. For example, if you were re-

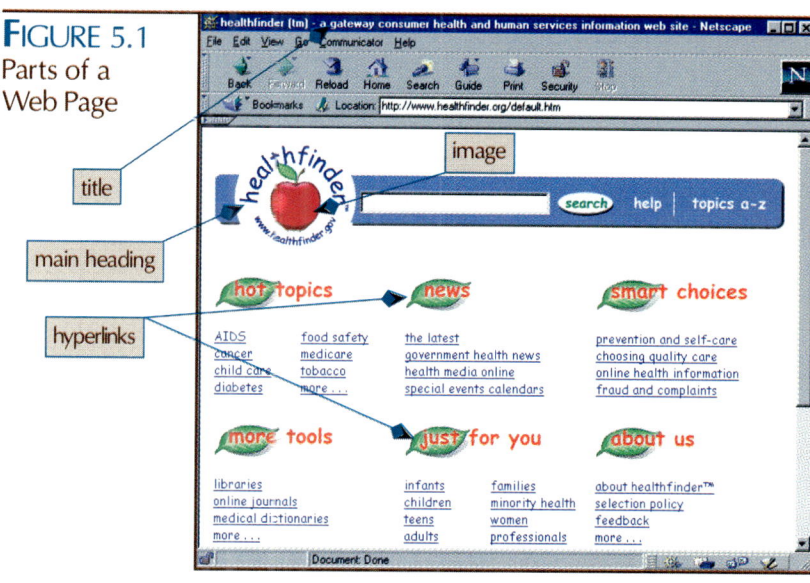

FIGURE 5.1
Parts of a Web Page

searching postmodern art, you might want to retrieve all records that have the root word *postmodern*, as well as *post-modernist* and *postmodernism*. Most search engines support truncation by allowing you to place an asterisk (*) at the end of the root word. You would need to see the help screen in the search engine you are using to find out which symbol is used. In our example, we would type **postmodern***. Some search engines automatically truncate words. In those databases, you would type **postmodern** and be assured that all the endings would also be retrieved. In these cases, truncation would be a default setting of the search engines. If you didn't want your search expression to be truncated, you would need to override the default fea-

ture. You would find out how to do this by reading the search engine's help screens.

Wildcards

Using *wildcards* allows you to search for words that have most of the word in common, except for maybe a letter or two. For example, we might want to search for both *woman* and *women*. Instead of typing **woman OR women**, we could place a wildcard character (most often an asterisk) to replace the fourth letter. It would look like this: **wom*n**.

Field Searching

Web pages can be broken down into many parts. These parts, or *fields*, include titles, URLs, text, summaries or annotations (if present), text, and so forth. (See Figure 5.1.) **Field searching** is the ability to limit your search to certain fields. This ability to search by field can increase the relevance of the retrieved records. For example, let's say you wanted to search the Web for an image of a comet. You could, in the search engines that support this feature, limit your search results to Web pages that contain images that have the word *comet* in their file names.

Case Sensitivity

Case sensitivity is an important feature that can lead to a much more precise search, especially if you are looking for proper names such as Sting, the Who, or Brad Pitt. Some search engines recognize capitalization, and some do not. If the search engine you are using doesn't recognize capitals, just think of the results you'd get by entering **sting** in the search query box.

Concept Searching

Concept searching occurs when a search engine automatically searches for Web pages that have terms similar to the ones you entered in the search query box. Excite supports this feature.

Limiting by Date

Some search engines allow you to search the Web for pages that were added to the database between certain dates. In **limiting by date**, you can find only the pages that were entered in the past month, in the past year, or in a particular year.

Output Features Common to Most Search Engines

The way a search engine displays results can help you decide which search engine to use. The following features are common to many engines, but as we saw earlier with the search features, the engines all have different ways of determining and showing these features.

Relevancy Ranking

Most search engines measure each Web page's relevance to your search query and arrange the search results from the most to the least relevant. This is called **relevancy ranking**. Each search engine has its own algorithm for determining relevance, but it usually involves counting how many times the words in your query appear in the Web pages. In some search engines, a document is considered more

relevant if the words appear in certain fields, for example, the title or summary field. In other search engines, relevance is determined by the number of times the keyword appears in a Web page divided by the total number of words in the page. This gives a relevancy percentage, and the page with the largest percentage appears first on the list of results.

Annotations or Summaries

Some search engines include short descriptive paragraphs of each Web page they return. These annotations, or summaries, can help you decide whether or not to open a Web page, especially if there is no title for the Web page or if the title doesn't describe the page in detail.

Results Per Page

In some search engines, the **results per page** option allows you to choose how many results you want listed per page. This can be a time saver, because it sometimes takes a while to go from page to page as you look through results.

Sorting Results

Some services allow you to choose how you want your results sorted—by relevance, URL, location, organization, folders, and so forth. This feature is known as *sorting*.

Duplicate Detection

It is not unusual to retrieve several instances of the same Web page in your results. Some search engines detect these duplicates and remove them. In meta-search engines or unified search interfaces, *duplicate detection* is a common feature.

Modification of Search Results

Some search engines will insert a copy of your search request on the first page of your results to make it easier for you to modify the query if you so desire. With others, you may be required to return to the original search form before making this *modification of search results*. Some search engines allow you to search only the results of an earlier search, which can be extremely helpful.

Meta-tag Support

Some search engines acknowledge keywords that a Web page author has placed in the meta-tag field in the HTML source document. This means that a document may be retrieved by a keyword search, but that the search expression may not appear in the document.

A Basic Search Strategy: The 10 Steps

The following list provides a guideline for you to follow in formulating search requests, viewing search results, and modifying search requests. These procedures can be followed for virtually any search request, from the simplest to the most complicated. Some search requests may not require you to go through a formal search strategy. If you want to save time in the long run, however, it's a good idea to follow a strategy, especially when you're new to a particular search engine. A basic search strategy can help you get used to each search engine's features and how they are expressed in the search query. Following the 10 steps will also ensure good results if your search is multifaceted and you want to get the most relevant results. The strategy may help you to avoid sifting through the same information more than once.

The 10 steps of the basic search strategy are as follows:

1. Identify the important concepts of your search.

2. Choose keywords that describe these concepts.

Search tips:

If you feel that your search has yielded too few Web pages (low recall), there are several things to consider:

- Perhaps the search expression was too specific; go back and remove some terms that are connected by ANDs.

- There may be more terms to use. Think of more synonyms to OR together. Truncate additional words if possible.

- Check spelling and syntax (a missing quotation mark or parenthesis).

- Reread the help pages.

If your search returns many results that are unrelated to your topic (high recall/low precision), consider the following:

- Narrow your search to specific fields, if possible.

- Use more specific terms; for example, instead of *cancer*, use the specific ◆

145

Evaluate sources before deciding to use them.

Step 8 of the search strategy focuses on evaluating the results of your search. While each Web page should be carefully evaluated before you use the information, there are a couple ways to quickly evaluate your results to see if you are on the right track:

+ Open the first few Web pages and execute the Find command (click on **Edit**, then **Find**) in each to see how your search terms are used.

+ Note the domain names of the first few URLs. Are they primarily ◆▶

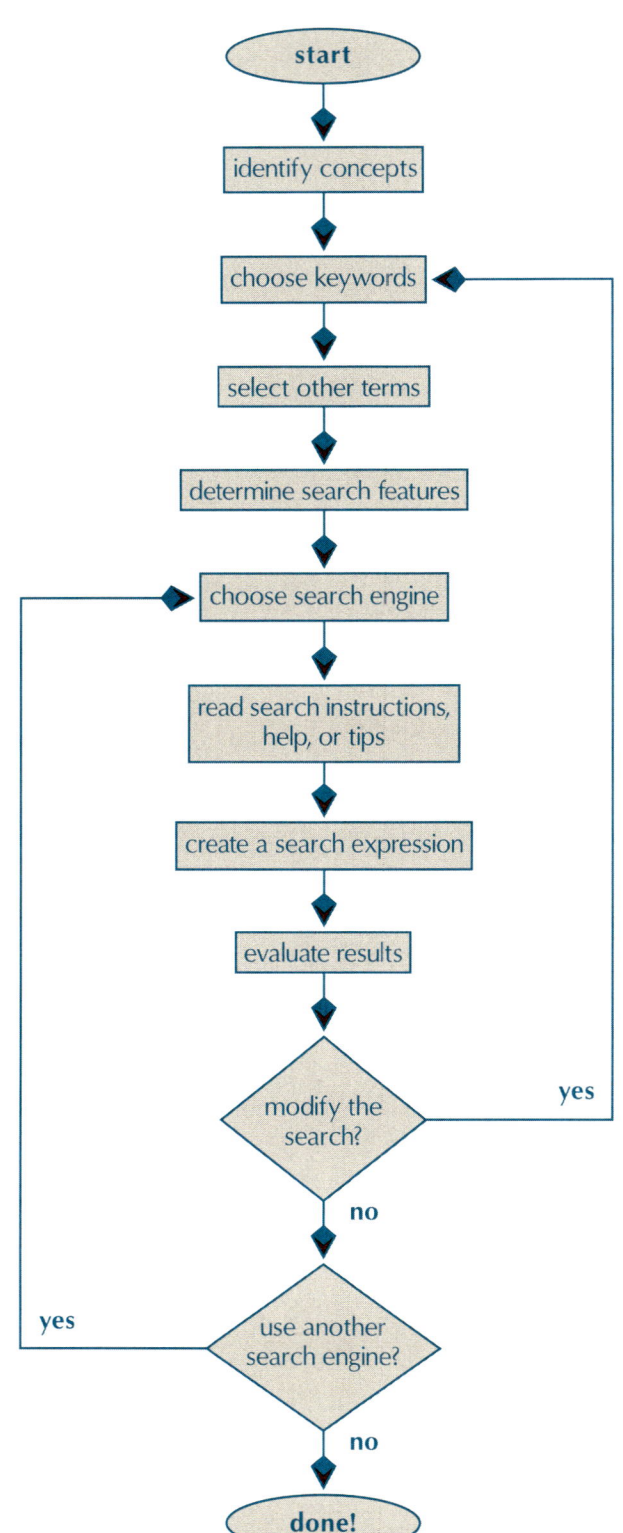

3. Determine whether there are synonyms, related terms, or other variations of the keywords that should be included.

4. Determine which search features may apply, including truncation, proximity operators, Boolean operators, and so forth.

5. Choose a search engine.

6. Read the search instructions on the search engine's home page. Look for sections such as "Help," "Advanced Search," "Frequently Asked Questions," and so forth.

7. Create a search expression using syntax that is appropriate for the search engine.

8. Evaluate the results. How many hits were returned? Are the results relevant to your query?

9. Modify your search if needed. Go back to Steps 2 through 4 and revise your query accordingly.

10. Try the same search in a different search engine, following Steps 5 through 9 above.

In order to explain these concepts in the most practical way, we'll do an example of the same search in two full-text databases.

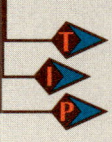

commercial (**.com**), educational (**.edu**), or organizational (**.org**) sites?

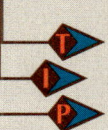

Be flexible.

Remember that the Web is always changing and that your results may differ from those shown here. Don't let this confuse you. The examples demonstrate fundamental skills that don't change, even though the number of results obtained or the actual screens may look different. ◆

EXAMPLE 5.1

Search Strategies in AltaVista and Northern Light

In this example, we are going to search for resources on a multifaceted topic. We want to find Web pages that focus on how self-esteem relates to young girls' likelihood of developing eating disorders. There has been a lot of research in the past 10 years about how changes in modern life affected hurt teenage girls' development, and we'd like to see if any of this research has been published on the Web.

Following the basic search strategy, we need to examine the facts of our search, choosing the appropriate keywords and determining which search features apply. Then we'll go to the search engine and read the search instructions. We'll explore AltaVista first, then we'll perform the same search (using the appropriate syntax) in Northern Light. Let's see how these two search engines handle this multifaceted topic. In the first part of the example we'll follow these steps, which correspond to all 10 steps of the basic search strategy:

❶ Identify the important concepts of your search.

The most important concepts of this search are the development of eating disorders in adolescent girls and the way this is related to their lack of self-esteem.

❷ Choose the keywords that describe these concepts.

The main terms or keywords include the following: teenage girls, self-esteem, and eating disorders.

❸ Determine whether there are synonyms, related terms, or other variations of the keywords that should be included.

For teenage: adolescent, adolescence.
For eating disorders: anorexia nervosa, bulimia.
For self-esteem: self-respect.

TABLE 5.1

Formulation of the Search Strategy

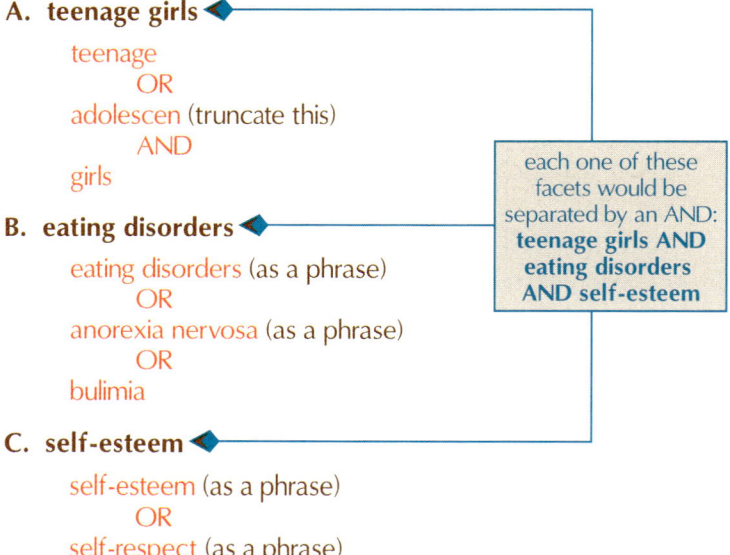

A. **teenage girls**
  teenage
        OR
  adolescen (truncate this)
        AND
  girls

B. **eating disorders**
  eating disorders (as a phrase)
        OR
  anorexia nervosa (as a phrase)
        OR
  bulimia

C. **self-esteem**
  self-esteem (as a phrase)
        OR
  self-respect (as a phrase)

each one of these facets would be separated by an AND: **teenage girls AND eating disorders AND self-esteem**

❹ Determine which search features may apply, including truncation, proximity operators, Boolean operators, and so forth.

When developing a search expression, keep in mind that you place **OR** between synonyms and **AND** between the different concepts, or facets, of the search topic. If you write down all the synonyms you can think of, it may help with the construction of the final search phraseology. Table 5.1 shows the three major concepts, or facets, of the search topic with their synonyms, connected with the appropriate Boolean operators. Keep in mind there can be different ways to express the same idea. For example, for the facet teenage girls, you could say **"teenage girls" OR "adolescen* girls"** instead of **(teenage OR adolescen*) AND girls**. Note that by using the truncated word **adolescen**, we would retrieve

148

the words *adoiescent* and *adolescence*. Before you get online, take a few minutes to determine whether you have used all the search features that you possibly can. It can save you a lot of time in the long run.

5 ▶ Choose a search engine.

✚ Click on the location field, key in **http:// www.altavista.com**, and press **Enter**.

In this example, we are going to search AltaVista first. This search engine supports full Boolean searching, which is a search feature we need for this topic. AltaVista's advanced search mode has a large search form, which makes it easier to type in a lengthy search expression.

6 ▶ Read the search instructions on the search engine's home page. Look for sections such as "Help," "Advanced Search," "Frequently Asked Questions," and so forth.

AltaVista has two search modes: simple and advanced. The simple search mode only supports implied, or pseudo-Boolean, searching. This means that you could perform an AND and NOT search by typing **+** before the word if it has to appear in each of the results, and **-** before words that you don't want in the results. Since our topic involves many ORs, we will need to do an advanced search.

When you open AltaVista, you will see the simple search form. You'll access the help section from this screen. Then you'll want to look at the search instructions for its advanced search capabilities.

✚ Click on the **Help** hyperlink.

Scroll down the page until you see the Advanced Search example, as shown in Figure 5.2.

✚ Click on the hyperlink **Advanced Help**.

FIGURE 5.2
Help for Advanced Searches in AltaVista

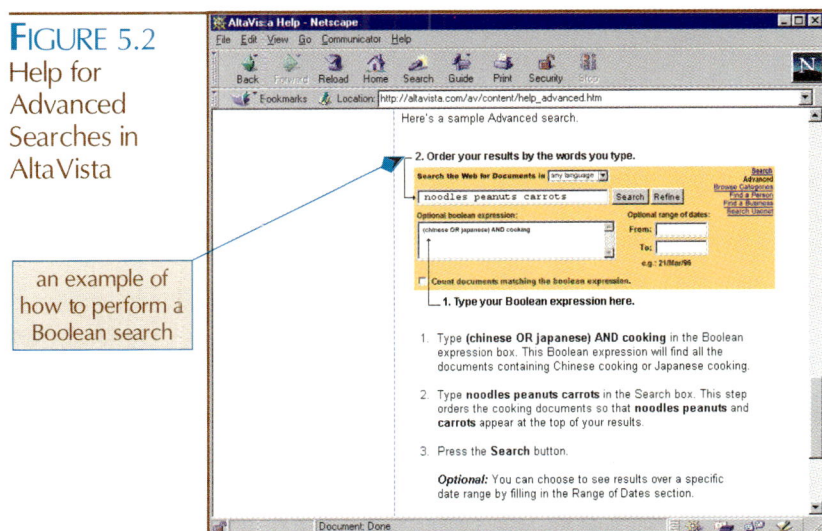

149

After reading the extensive help screens in AltaVista, you can start determining how to construct your search expression. In addition to reviewing how to combine Boolean operators with phrases and parentheses, you'll need to find out how AltaVista truncates words. You'll also need to read the section on ranking, or ordering your results. This is a crucial part of AltaVista's advanced search mode. You must type words in the Search box that you want to have in the first documents returned to you. If you don't, the results will be listed in any order, and the first documents may not be as relevant as the last documents returned.

7 Create a search expression using syntax that is appropriate for the search engine.

Now that you've read the search help, it's time to formulate the search expression. It will help to write it out before you type it in the search form. Here is a possible way to express this search:

> **(teenage or adolescen*) and girls and ("eating disorders" or "anorexia nervosa" or bulimia) and ("self-esteem" or "self-respect")**

Keep in mind that you can always modify your search later. Let's try entering it in AltaVista's advanced search form.

✦ Click on the **Back** icon twice to return to AltaVista's home page.

Make sure all of the quotation marks are present and that you've closed all of the parentheses properly. Check your spelling and determine whether you have ANDs and ORs in the proper places.

✦ Enter the search expression in the form, as shown in Figure 5.3.

FIGURE 5.3 Advanced Search in AltaVista with Search Expression Entered

✦ In the form under **Enter Ranking Keywords in**, type in the phrase **"eating disorders"** as shown in Figure 5.3.

✦ Click on **Search**.

8 Evaluate the results. How many hits were returned? Are the results relevant to your query?

Note the number of hits this search has returned to your screen. Look at a few of the titles. Do they appear to be relevant? Figure 5.4 shows the first few. Because the Web is always changing, the results shown may not be the same ones that you retrieve.

Click on the title of the first result on the list.

FIGURE 5.4
Results of
AltaVista
Search

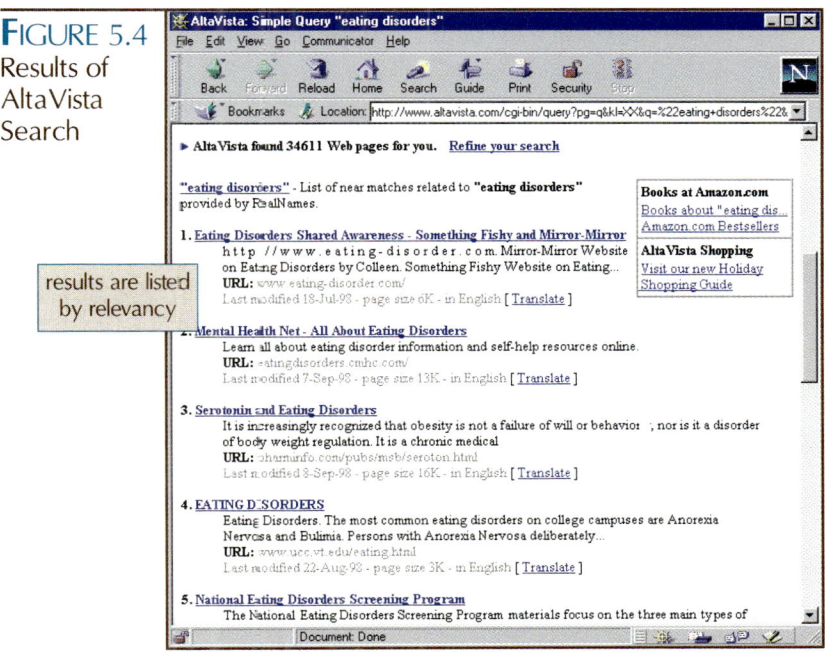

Examine the first page that appears on your screen. Is the information relevant to the search query? Scroll down to the bottom of the page and click on the arrows to see the next page of results, as shown in Figure 5.5. Look through the results on this page to determine whether they seem relevant.

FIGURE 5.5
Navigating
Search Results
in AltaVista

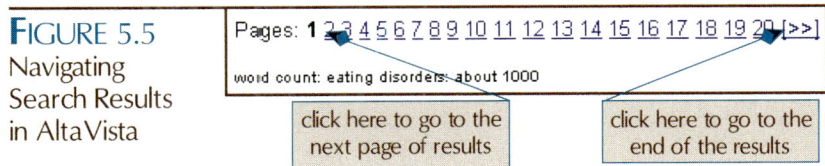

9 Modify your search if needed. Go back to Steps 2 through 4 and revise your query accordingly.

The results seem relevant, and the number of hits is an adequate set with which to work. You may, however, want to limit the results by date. You could do this by going back to the search query screen and typing a date in the space provided.

10 Try the same search in a different search engine, following Steps 5 through 9 above.

Since our topic is multifaceted and requires a powerful search engine, we'll do the same search in Northern Light.

End of first part of Example 5.1

Northern Light, **http://www.northernlight.com**, is a full-text database that not only indexes World Wide Web documents, but also includes a fee-based database containing about a million articles from about 2,000 sources. These sources include journals, newspapers, books, and other types of publications. If you want to view a document from this special collection, you will be charged a fee. The cost per article ranges from $1 to $4. You can subscribe to the service for a small fee per month that covers the cost of obtaining up to 50 documents. Northern Light has another unique feature—the way results are organized. In addition to listing the results of your search by relevancy, Northern Light organizes the results for you in subject folders. These folders provide a way for you to screen or filter your results, and can help with information overload. These folders are created anew with each search you perform, so the headings vary depending on the subject matter. There are four major kinds of folders: type, subject, source, and language. A type folder might be "press releases" or "job advertisements." A subject folder may be "global warming" or "epidemics." Source folders would resemble something "www.globalchange.org" or "commercial sites." A language folder will group non-English language sites together, which is another helpful feature. We'll follow these steps, which correspond to Steps 6 through 9 of the basic search strategy:

1. Read the search instructions on the search engine's home page. Look for sections entitled "Help," "Advanced Search," "Frequently Asked Questions," and so forth.

2. Create a search expression using syntax that is appropriate for the search engine.

3. Evaluate the results. How many hits were returned? Are the results relevant to your query?

4. Modify your search if needed. Revise your query accordingly.

5. End the session.

Read the search instructions on the search engine's home page. Look for sections such as "Help," "Advanced Search," "Frequently Asked Questions," and so forth.

First we need to open Northern Light.

➕ Click on the location field, type **http://www.northernlight.com**, and press ⏎**Enter**.

➕ On the home page for Northern Light, click on **HELP/HINTS**.

scroll down until you see **Boolean Search Help**

Your screen should look like the one in Figure 5.6.

FIGURE 5.6
Northern Light Help

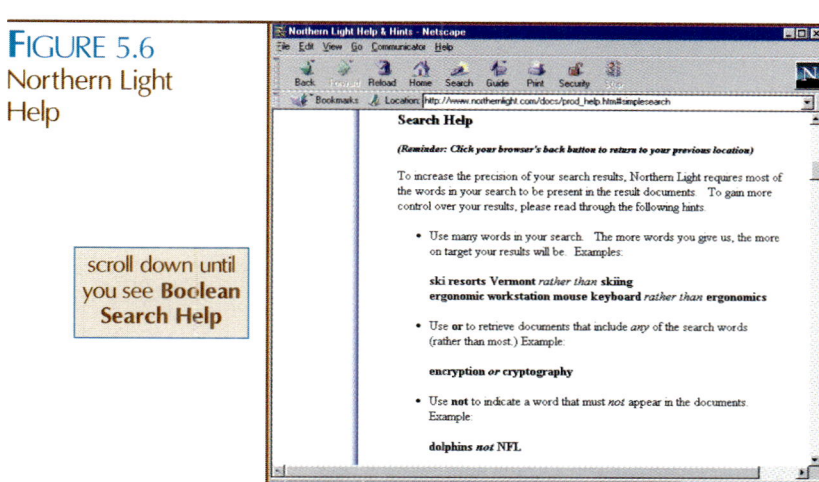

➕ Scroll down the page until you see the hyperlink **Boolean Search Help**, and click on it.

Your screen should look like the one pictured in Figure 5.7.

FIGURE 5.7
Boolean Search Help in Northern Light

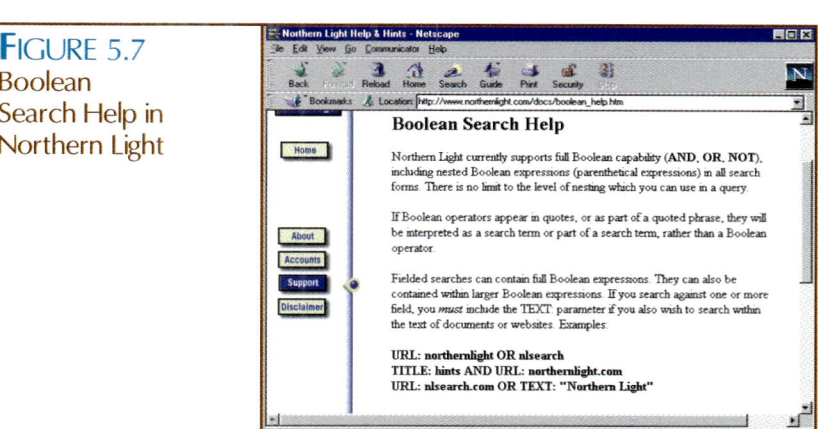

◆ Create a search expression using syntax that is appropriate for the search engine.

➕ After checking out the help pages, return to Northern Light's home page by clicking on **Home**, located on the left side of the screen.

Now you are ready to start searching for your topic in Northern Light. We know that Northern Light supports phrase searching and Boolean searching, so we won't need to change our concepts. In fact, we can type in the exact search expression that was used in the AltaVista search. The only thing that is different is Northern Light's search form is much smaller than AltaVista's.

✚ Type the following search expression in the search form provided: **(teenage or adolescen*) and girls and ("eating disorders" or "anorexia nervosa" or bulimia) and ("self-esteem" or "self-respect")**

✚ Click on **SEARCH**.

Look at the results of the search query, as shown in Figure 5.8. Your results may be different.

FIGURE 5.8
Northern Light Search Results

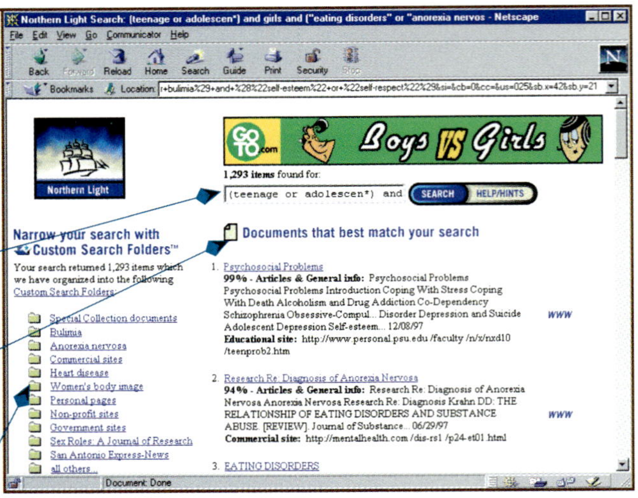

search expression typed in here

results listed by relevancy in all categories

click on the **Women's body image** folder

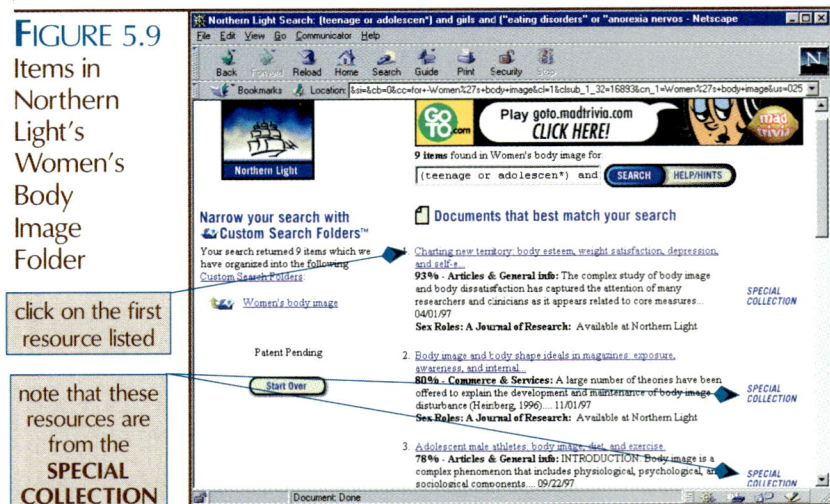

◆ Evaluate the results. How many hits were returned? Are the results relevant to your query?

✚ Click on the **Women's body image** folder, as shown in Figure 5.8.

The results on the right side of the screen are listed by relevancy. Along the left side of the screen are the custom search folders. One of the folders looks particularly promising: **Women's body image**. Let's see what's inside this folder.

FIGURE 5.9
Items in Northern Light's Women's Body Image Folder

click on the first resource listed

note that these resources are from the **SPECIAL COLLECTION**

Figure 5.9 shows a partial list of the resources in this folder. Note that the first three resources are from the **SPECIAL COL-LECTION**. This means that you will have to set up an account with Northern Light in order to read the full articles.

Let's access the first resource listed.

＋ Click on the first resource listed, **Charting new territory: body esteem weight satisfaction, depression, and self-e…**.

Figure 5.10 shows a summary of this article, which is from the journal *Sex Roles: A Journal of Research*. There is a summary, or abstract, of the article. If you want to purchase this article, you'll need to click on the hyperlink **Purchase Document**.

FIGURE 5.10
Document Summary of an Article in Northern Light's Special Collection

click here to purchase the article

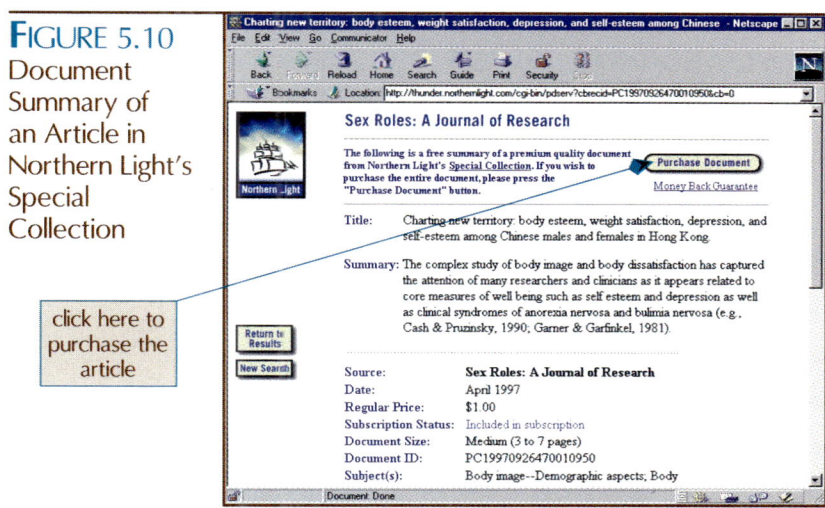

◆4 Modify your search if needed. Go back to the search form and revise your query accordingly.

◆5 End the session.

You can end the session now or continue to the next example.

＋ To end the session now, click on **File** on the menu bar, and select **Exit** from the menu.

End of Example 5.1

As we saw in this example, AltaVista and Northern Light handle multifaceted search queries in similar ways. In some ways, the AltaVista search form makes it easier to perform a search. The large form allows you to type in a long search expression with ease (if you have read the search help carefully). Northern Light supports most of the same search features that AltaVista does. The two major differences are that Northern Light's results are organized into folders and its collection includes selective resources that you can pay for.

There are pros and cons to using any of the search engines. Sometimes it comes down to which service you are more comfortable using. In the following two examples, we'll be searching for the same topic in two very different databases: Infoseek and MetaCrawler. Infoseek is a full-text search engine database, whereas MetaCrawler is a meta-search tool, which allows you to search several search engines simultaneously. In performing searches in each of these indexes, we will follow the steps laid out in the basic search strategy.

EXAMPLE 5.2

Search Strategies in Infoseek

We'll be searching for the same information that we did in Example 5.1—how self-esteem relates to teenage girls' likelihood of developing eating disorders. In Example 5.1, we already did Steps 1 through 4 of the basic search strategy, so we'll now do the following steps, which correspond to Steps 5 through 10 of the strategy:

1. Choose a search engine.

2. Read the search instructions on the search engine's home page. Look for sections such as "Help," "Advanced Search," "Frequently Asked Questions," and so forth.

3. Create a search expression using syntax that is appropriate for the search engine.

4. Evaluate the results. How many hits were returned? Are the results relevant to your query?

5. Modify your search if needed. Revise the query accordingly.

6. Try the same search in a different search engine.

7. End the session.

▶ Choose a search engine.

We'll be searching Infoseek, another popular search engine. Infoseek doesn't support Boolean searching as AltaVista and Northern Light do, but it does allow for the use of implied Boolean operators—the + and the −. These operators represent the Boolean AND and NOT, but there is no OR capability in Infoseek. This makes it difficult to search for synonyms. Infoseek does allow you to search the results of a previous search, which is one way around this limitation. Let's go to Infoseek and see how it handles our topic.

✦ Click on the location field, type **http://infoseek.go.com**, and press **Enter**.

View the Infoseek home page, as shown in Figure 5.11.

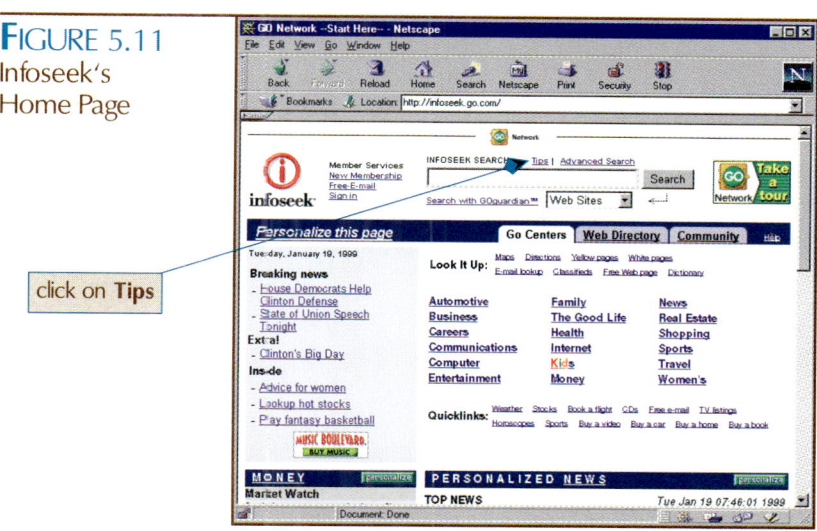

FIGURE 5.11
Infoseek's
Home Page

click on **Tips**

2 Read the search instructions on the search engine's home page. Look for sections such as "Help," "Advanced Search," "Frequently Asked Questions," and so forth.

Click on **Tips**, as shown in Figure 5.11.

Now scroll to the bottom of the page and click on **Quick Reference to Syntax**.

You can read through the tips if you like.

The "Quick Reference to Syntax" page appears in Figure 5.12. From reading the search tips, we determine the following:

- Infoseek supports phrase searching by requiring that quotes be placed around words that must be together or hyphens between adjacent words.

- A + should be placed in front of a word or phrase that must be present in the Web pages found.

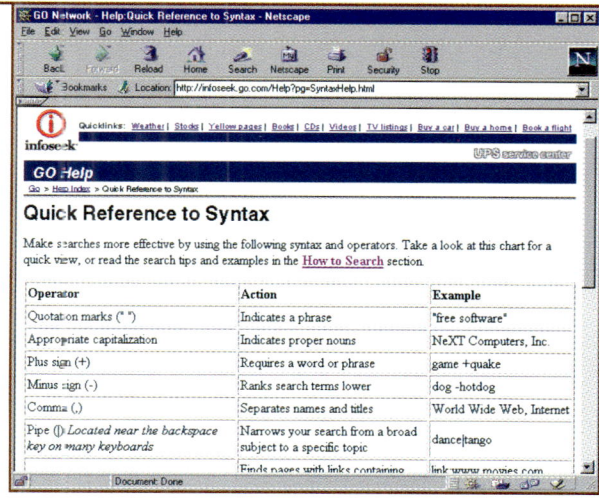

FIGURE 5.12
Search Help
in Infoseek

3 Create a search expression using syntax that is appropriate for the search engine.

Since full Boolean searching isn't supported, it's better to not type in too many words or phrases at this point. If we typed in **+"anorexia nervosa" +bulimia +"self-esteem"** in addition to the two

➕ Click on the **Infoseek** icon at the top of the page.

➕ Type **+"teenage girls" +"eating disorders"** and click on **Search** as shown in Figure 5.13.

phrases below, we would be requiring that *all* of the phrases and words appear in the Web pages, which might give us too few results. It's best to start out with fewer terms at first and to see what results we obtain. We can always modify our results later.

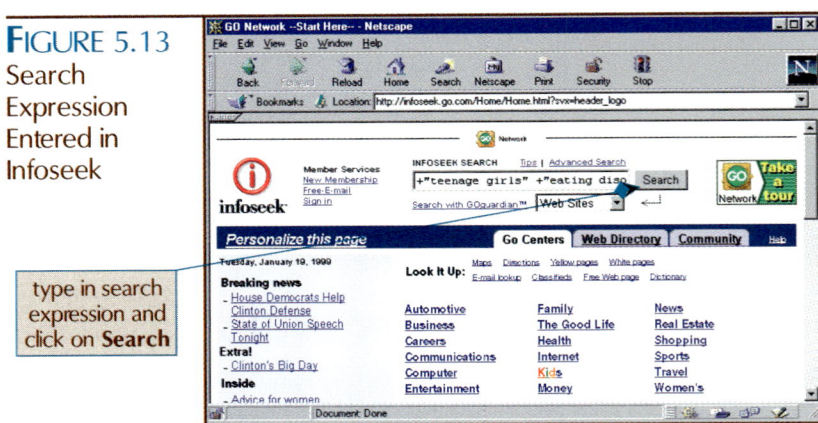

FIGURE 5.13 Search Expression Entered in Infoseek

type in search expression and click on **Search**

④ Evaluate the results. How many hits were returned? Are the results relevant to your query?

This search retrieved some relevant hits. A few of the results appear in Figure 5.14. Don't be surprised if you obtain different results.

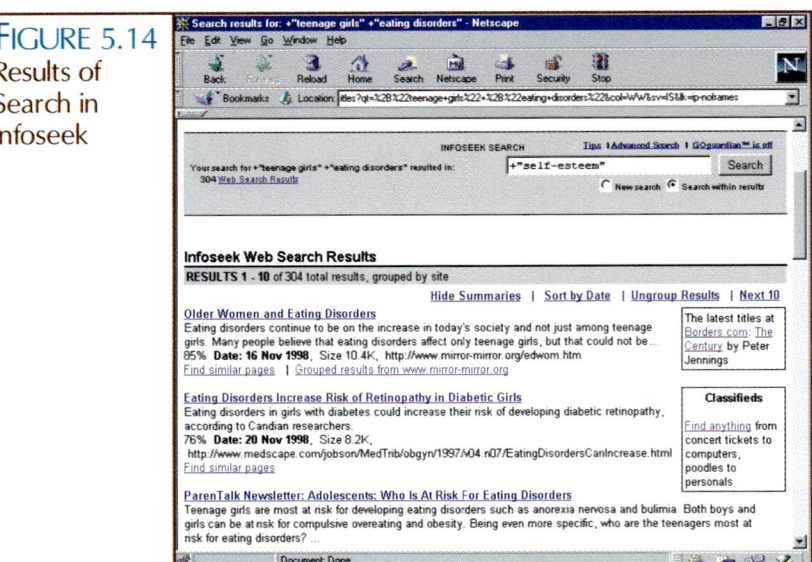

FIGURE 5.14 Results of Search in Infoseek

⑤ Modify your search if needed. Revise the query accordingly.

Infoseek allows you to search only the results of a search. Let's say that of the documents that the search retrieved, you want to know which ones contain the phrase *self-esteem*. All that is required is to type **+"self-esteem"** in the search form provided and to indicate that only these results should be searched. Let's do that now.

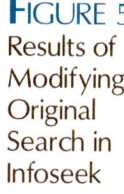 In the search form provided, type **+"self-esteem"**, as shown in Figure 5.14.

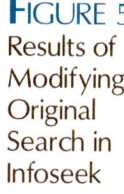 Click on the button next to **Search within results**.

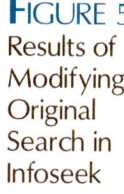 Click on **Search**.

Figure 5.15 shows the results of this modification. Remember that you may have different results, because the Web is always changing.

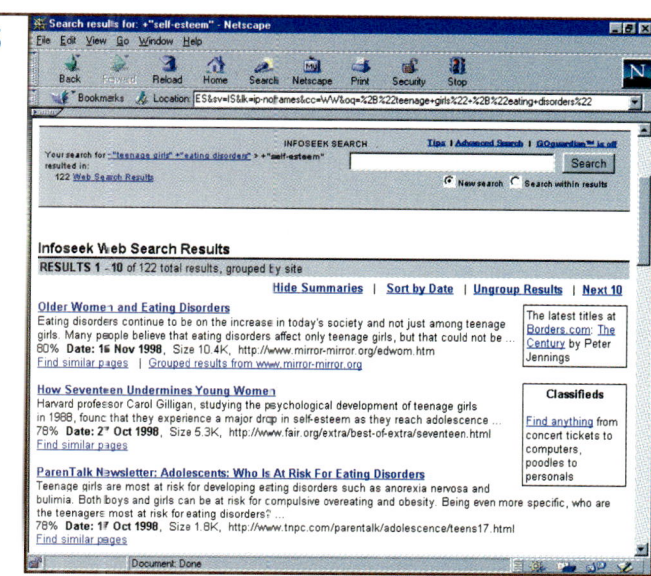

FIGURE 5.15
Results of Modifying Original Search in Infoseek

6 Try the same search in a different search engine.

Next we're going to try the same search in MetaCrawler in Example 5.3.

7 End the session.

You can exit the Internet now or go on to the next example.

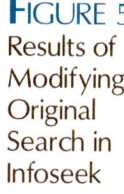 To exit now, click on **File** on the menu bar, and select **Exit** from the menu.

End of Example 5.2

Infoseek proved to be an effective search engine. We obtained fewer results than in AltaVista or Northern Light, because there is no OR capability in Infoseek. The use of the Boolean OR expands results, whereas the use of AND or + narrows results.

EXAMPLE 5.3

Search Strategies in MetaCrawler

In this example, we'll look for information on the same topic in MetaCrawler. As stated before, MetaCrawler is a meta-search tool. Also known as parallel-search tools or unified search interfaces, meta-search tools don't create their own indexes. They merely provide a search interface so that you can use several search engines and directories at the same time with one search expression. Currently, MetaCrawler searches five different databases: AltaVista, Excite, Lycos, WebCrawler, and Yahoo!. Meta-search tools can be very useful for single-word subjects but unreliable for multiterm, multifaceted searches, such as the one we have been using in this chapter. Let's see how MetaCrawler handles our topic. We'll be following Steps 5 through 10 of the basic search strategy, as we did in Example 5.2.

1. Choose a search engine.

2. Read the search instructions on the search engine's home page. Look for sections or hyperlinks such as "Help," "Advanced Search," "Frequently Asked Questions," and so forth.

3. Create a search expression using syntax that is appropriate for the search engine.

4. Evaluate the results. How many hits were returned? Are the results relevant to your query?

5. Modify your search if needed. Revise the query accordingly.

6. Try the same search in a different search engine.

7. End the session.

◀▶ Choose a search engine.

✚ Click on the location field and type in the URL for MetaCrawler's home page, **http://www.go2net.com/search.html**, and press **Enter**.

Let's go to MetaCrawler.

Your screen should look like the picture in Figure 5.16.

FIGURE 5.16
MetaCrawler's
Home Page

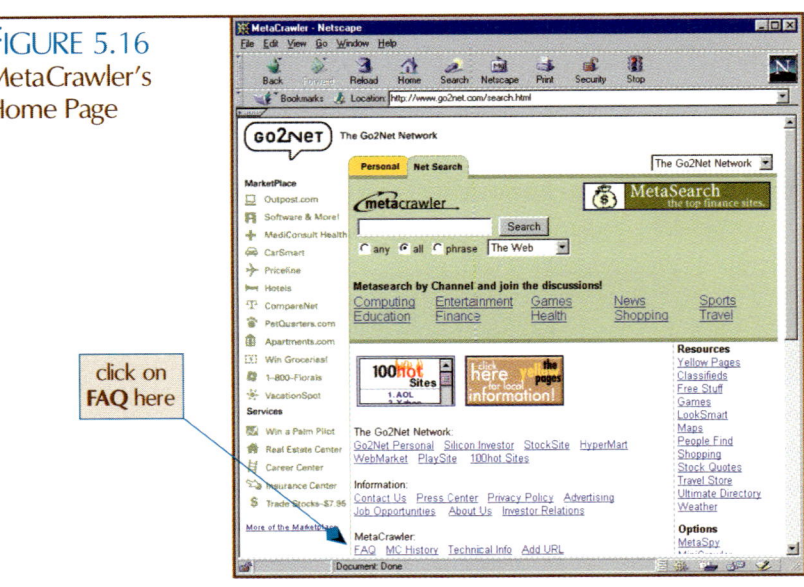

2 Read the search instructions on the search engine's home page. Look for sections or hyperlinks such as "Help," "Advanced Search," "Frequently Asked Questions," and so forth.

In order to find out how to use MetaCrawler, read its documentation.

✛ Click on **FAQ** on the left side of the screen, as shown in Figure 5.16 (scroll down the page if necessary).

Here you will notice that MetaCrawler uses implied Boolean operators (+ and –) and that phrase searching, using double quotation marks, is a supported feature. See Figure 5.17.

✛ Scroll down and click on the hyperlink **How can I refine MetaCrawler searches?**

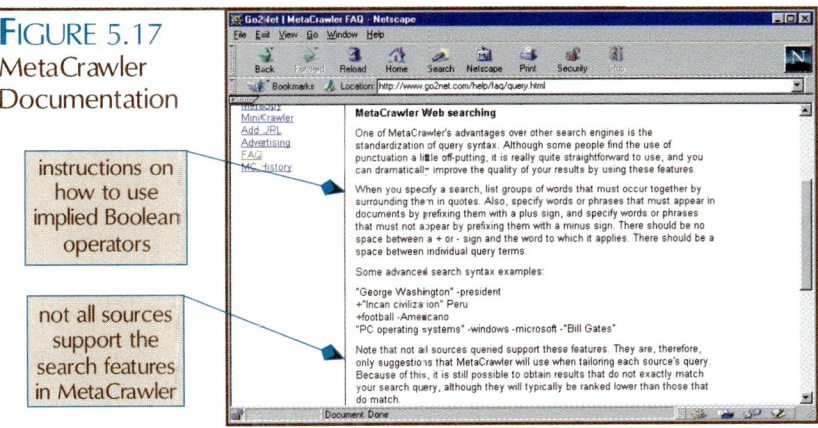

FIGURE 5.17
MetaCrawler Documentation

instructions on how to use implied Boolean operators

not all sources support the search features in MetaCrawler

3 Create a search expression using syntax that is appropriate for the search engine.

First, we need to find MetaCrawler's search form.

✛ Scroll to the bottom of the "FAQ" page.

By using this search expression and choosing **all**, you are telling MetaCrawler to find all the Web pages in which each of these three phrases occurs. The **+** in front of each phrase indicates that the phrase *must* appear somewhere in the Web pages.

✛ Type the following search expression in the search form:
+"teenage girls"
+"eating disorders"
+"self-esteem"

✛ Click on **all**.

✛ Click on **Search**.

This will initiate your search request. See Figure 5.18.

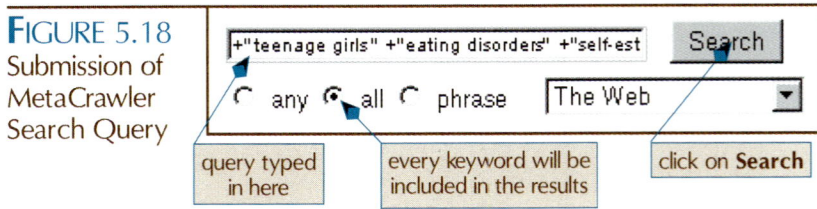

FIGURE 5.18
Submission of
MetaCrawler
Search Query

query typed in here

every keyword will be included in the results

click on **Search**

As MetaCrawler conducts the search, it will list on the screen the different search tools it has searched so far along with the number of the results found in each one. You can't always rely on these results, however. If MetaCrawler says there are zero results in a certain database, this isn't necessarily true. Sometimes the search query in MetaCrawler doesn't coincide with the search features supported in the individual databases. When the results appear, they are listed by relevance and not by the search engine or directory in which they were found. MetaCrawler should detect and weed out duplicates. Figure 5.19 depicts how the results will be listed. Remember that your results may differ from those shown here.

4 Evaluate the results. How many hits were returned? Are the results relevant to your query?

After looking through the results, we decide to modify our search to see if we can get more hits.

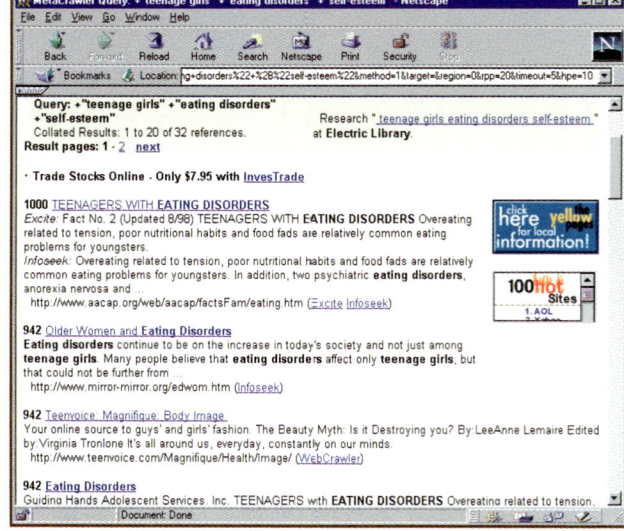

FIGURE 5.19
MetaCrawler
Results

5 Modify your search if needed. Revise the query accordingly.

Since MetaCrawler does not support nested Boolean searching, it may be unwise to add too many synonyms for the words we've already entered. We could add one more term, **bulimia** for example, and then change the search option to **any** instead of **all**. The danger would be that some of the results may not be as relevant as we would like. In effect, this would be the same as placing an OR between each word instead of an AND.

Let's modify our search by adding the extra keyword and changing the search options.

— Scroll to the bottom of the page.

The revised search query screen should look like Figure 5.20.

— Place the cursor at the very beginning of the search query box and type **+bulimia**. Make sure there is a space between **+bulimia** and **+"teenage girls"**.

FIGURE 5.20
Modification of MetaCrawler Search

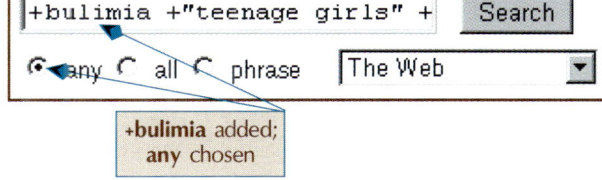

+bulimia added; any chosen

— Click next to **any**.

Figure 5.21 shows the first few results. Note that, at the time of this search, changing the search options returned fewer results.

— Click on **Search**.

FIGURE 5.21
Results of Modifying Search in MetaCrawler

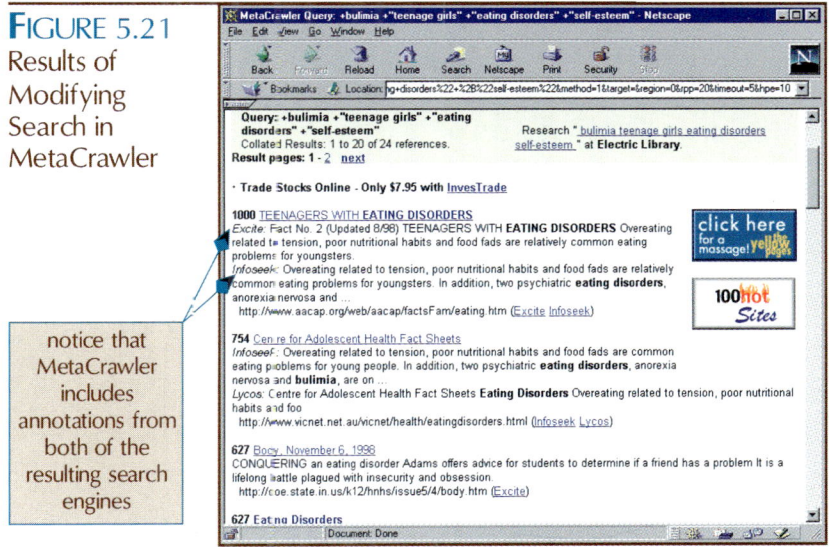

notice that MetaCrawler includes annotations from both of the resulting search engines

⟩ **6** Try the same search in a different search engine.

If you like, you can try the same search in a different search engine on your own.

⟩ **7** End the session.

— Click on the **File** menu and select **Exit**.

End of Example 5.3

It is important to understand the major search features, such as Boolean logic, phrase searching, truncation, and others. Read each search engine's documentation before you enter the search request in the query box.

In Examples 5.1, 5.2, and 5.3, we searched for information on the same topic in four different search engines. Each one had its own particular syntax and individual search and output features. We saw the importance of reading each search engine's documentation before beginning the search. All of the search engines gave relevant results, but none of them gave the same results.

Summary

Search engines are tools that search databases. These search engines have been created by computer programs, commonly referred to as spiders or robots. These spiders go out onto the World Wide Web and put every single word of every Web page they find into a database. With the help of our search request, the search engine then searches this full-text database for us. Some databases are not full-text, but instead consist of selected words from Web documents.

In either case, each search engine accesses its database differently. Even though many search engine databases claim to cover as much of the Web as possible, the same search performed in more than one database never returns the same exact results. If you want to do a thorough search, you should become familiar with a few of the different search engines. Toward this end, it is important to understand the major search features, such as Boolean logic, phrase searching, truncation, and others, and which features are available in the various search engines before you start your search. It is also necessary to read each search engine's documentation before you enter a search request in the query box. You may want to check the documentation often, since search engines are constantly changing their search and output features.

It can help to try your search in a meta-search tool if you're not overly concerned about obtaining precise and comprehensive results. By using meta-search tools, you can gather hits from several databases at once.

In this chapter, we introduced the basic 10-step search strategy that can help you formulate search requests, submit them to search engines, and modify the results retrieved. We have focused on the major search engines on the World Wide Web, but there are several hundred other search engines on the Web that search smaller databases. In addition, there are other search engines that are not free to the public; they require passwords or subscription costs. Our intent in this chapter was to give you a foundation in searching any database, no matter whether it is large or small, fee-based or not. All of the steps in the basic search strategy apply to any database. ◆

Selected Terms in This Chapter

case sensitivity
concept searching
default setting
duplicate detection
field
field searching
full-text indexing
high precision/high recall

high precision/low recall
implied Boolean operator
keyword indexing
limiting by date
low precision/high recall
meta-tag
modification of search
   results

nested Boolean logic
proximity searching
relevancy ranking
results per page
sorting
stop word
truncation
wildcard

1. Using the advanced search mode in AltaVista, **http://www.altavista.com**, and Infoseek, **http://infoseek.go.com**, look for relevant resources on the following:
   a. the writings of Jack London
   b. the ebola virus
   c. chronic fatigue syndrome
   d. symptoms of decompression sickness

   Write down the first three Web pages retrieved by both search engines. Were any the same? Write down the search expression you used for each topic in the two databases. For each topic, list any problems you had and how many times you modified the search request in each search engine.

2. Do a simple search in AltaVista, **http://www.altavista.com**, for resources on asteroids. How many Web pages were returned by your search? Narrow the results by clicking on **Refine your search**. Select two or three words that you wish to require in the results and redo the search. What happened to the number of search results returned to your screen?

3. Find documents that deal with the economic benefits of historic preservation. Perform the search in Northern Light, **http://www.northernlight.com**, and MetaCrawler, **http://www.go2net.com/search.html**. Write down the search expressions you used in each database.

4. Using AltaVista, **http://www.altavista.com**, find the periodic table of elements. How many hyperlinks did you find? Compare two of the periodic tables you found. Which one was easier to use? Why?

5. In Northern Light, **http://www.northernlight.com**, use all of steps in the basic search strategy to perform a search on the following topic: "The problems encountered in deep sea diving." Give special consideration to finding possible synonyms and using truncation. Write down the steps you took.

165

What problems, if any, did you encounter? Did you need to modify your search strategy? If so, how did you do this?

6. Using the advanced search mode in AltaVista, **http://www.altavista.com**, search for information about Newt Gingrich. Find Web pages in which his name appears near the word *ethics*. Then limit your search to those Web pages that were entered into the database since October 1, 1996. How many search results did you obtain? Look at the first couple of pages. Do they appear to be relevant? Go into at least two Web pages and use Find in Page to do a search inside the Web page, looking for the words *Newt Gingrich*. Did the words appear in the documents? *Hint:* **Find in Page** is found under **Edit** in the menu bar.

7. Use MetaCrawler, **http://www.go2net.com/search.html**, to find information on baby boomers and social security. How many results did you obtain? Write down the first three Web page titles in the results list and their URLs. Write down the search expression you used.

8. Using the advanced search mode in AltaVista, **http://www.altavista.com**, look for information on how mad cow disease causes Creutzfeldt-Jakob disease in humans. Keeping in mind that mad cow disease is also known as bovine spongiform encephalopathy, incorporate this into your search in the correct way. Write down the search expression that you used and the total number of hits retrieved. Did the results appear to be relevant to your search request? Write down three of the most relevant titles with their URLs.

9. Open Lycos, **http://www.lycos.com**, and find information on whether there is an increasing number of youth gangs in cities in the United States. Try to determine whether there has been an increase in juvenile crime and violence in America, and if so, what the reasons are. Write out the search strategy, and explain how you entered the

information in Lycos. Did you need to modify your search to obtain the most relevant results? If so, how did you modify it?

10. Using the advanced search mode in AltaVista, **http:// www.altavista.com**, find information on a new drug that has been developed by Glaxo-Wellcome (a pharmaceutical company) for AIDS and HIV. The drug is commonly referred to as 1592, or 1592U89. Write out the search expression you used. Open a Web page or two and find 1592 or 1592U89 somewhere in the document using the Find in Page function in Netscape. Now try to find similar information using Infoseek, **http://infoseek.go.com**. Write out the search expression you used and the number of results received.

WRITING YOUR OWN WEB PAGES

In this chapter we'll talk about the basics of creating Web pages. You've seen lots of different Web pages as you've been browsing and searching the World Wide Web, and you may have been curious about how they're made. You'll see that it's a straightforward process to design and put together a basic Web page. A Web page is fundamentally an ordinary text or ASCII file, so special tools or programs aren't absolutely necessary. We'll go over the material you need to get started and also discuss proper style, how to get your pages on the Web, how to publicize your pages, and resources that can help you do more.

What turns an ordinary text file into a Web page? Two things: a Web browser and instructions or tags written in HTML (hypertext markup language). To better understand this, let's review the way your browser works with Web pages. The Web browser is a client program that sends requests to a server program. Whether you click on a hyperlink or type in a URL (open a location), your browser, the client, sends a request to a computer that's running the server program. The request is in a form taken from a URL. The server sends back a file to your computer, which passes it on to the browser. That file contains text, links to images, and hyperlinks. The format of the text on the page, the images you see on a page, and the hyperlinks are specified using HTML. The browser interprets the HTML and displays the page. If the HTML says to display a word or phrase in the file in bold font, for example, the browser does it. If the HTML tags say to display an image (and the image can be anywhere on the Web), the browser takes care of that as well. If the tag says that what follows is a hyperlink to some other page, the browser displays the text as a hyperlink and associates it with the specified URL. Hyperlinks on a page can be to other pages or other types of files, such as sound or video files, images, and even some interactive programs. Even if the Web page is a local file, a file on your computer, it has the same format and the browser interprets it in the same way as a Web page anywhere on the Internet.

To summarize: Web pages are text or ASCII files in which HTML (hypertext markup language) is used to specify the format of the Web page, images to be displayed, hyperlinks, and possibly other elements. A Web browser interprets the HTML in the file and then displays the Web page.

A Web page is a text file that contains HTML codes or tags. The HTML tags give the browser **instructions about how to display or represent information** in the file. The text file is also called the source for the Web page.

Since Web pages are text files we don't necessarily need any special tools or editors to create them. You'll find it's easier to create more complicated Web pages using editors designed for that purpose, but you can get along with any word processor or editor that can create text files. (If you're using Microsoft Windows, then Notepad, available through **Applications**, is sufficient.) You'll also find that you can see the way HTML is used to put together any Web page by first selecting **View** from the menu bar and then choosing **Page Source**.

Now let's go on to the details. We'll include figures and examples, and create some Web pages as we go along. The Web pages will be saved in local files and viewed with the Web browser.

Description of a Web Page

A *Web page* is a text file that contains HTML codes or tags. A *text file* is a file that contains plain printable characters. The *HTML tags* give a browser instructions about how to display or represent information in the text file. The text file is also called the *source* for the Web page.

The name of the source file has to end with the extension **.htm** or **.html**. Some examples are **resources.htm**, **mvtool12 .htm**, **index.html**, and **weather .html**. If the name doesn't have that form, HTML tags may be ignored. It is possible for a Web page to contain no HTML tags; in that case, the text is displayed in plain form and there's no title on the Web page.

Figures 6.1 and 6.2 show the source for a Web page and the Web page as it's displayed by the browser. Several items have been labeled so you can see the relationship between the HTML tags and what's displayed by the browser. You can learn a few things about using HTML from looking at the source (Figure 6.1) and how it's displayed by the browser (Figure 6.2). Here are a few things to notice:

◆ The HTML tags are contained in angle brackets (< >); for example, **<TITLE>** and **<IMG SRC="intcover.gif">**.

◆ Many HTML tags come in pairs. One tag in the pair uses a slash (/), such as **<I>** and **</I>** or **<H1>** and **</H1>**. The first tag tells the browser to start (**<I>**) and the second to stop (**</I>**) displaying the text between them in italic font.

◆ To write comments or notes in a document that you don't want to show up in the window, surround the comments with **<!--** and **-->**.

◆ Looking at the page displayed by the browser, you can see that carriage returns and spaces are generally ignored by the browser. You can use the HTML tag **<P>** to indicate the start of a new paragraph.

◆ **<A HREF="URL">** ... text ... **</A>** is an HTML tag for a hyperlink. Any URL may be used between the quotation marks.

◆ **<IMG SRC="file name">** is an HTML tag for an image. Put the name of the file or a hyperlink to a file containing the image between the quotation marks.

The page was written using the accessory Notepad, although any editor that would create and save a text file could have been used. In this case the file's name is **try1.htm** and it's in the directory **inetbk** on Drive **C:**. The Web page was displayed by selecting **Open Page...** from the pull-down

FIGURE 6.1
Source for
Web Page

```
<HTML>
<HEAD>
<TITLE> Web page title</TITLE>
</HEAD>
<BODY>
<H1> This is a Level-1 heading.</H1>
<H6> This is a Level-6 heading. </H6>
<!-- HTML has 6 levels of headings, H1 is the largest and H6 is the
smallest -->
<!-- By the way, tags that start like this one are for the author's
comments -->
<!-- They don't show up in the Web page -->
Hello!
<P>
My name is Ernest Ackermann.
My first book with Franklin, Beedle & Associates was published
April, 1995. The title is
<I> Learning to Use the Internet</I>,
there is a

<A HREF="http://www.mwc.edu/ernie/lrn-net.html">
home page for the book </A>
, and
here is a picture of the cover!
<IMG SRC="intcover.gif">

<P>
Just for fun, here's a hyperlink to the
<A HREF="http://www.comcentral.com">home page for the Comedy Channel </A>.
<P>
This is the last line that will show up through the Web browser.
</BODY>
</HTML>
```

start a Web page
with the tag <HTML>

title for the Web page—text surrounded
by <TITLE> and </TITLE>; every page
should have a title

use <I> and </I> to
display text in italic

HTML tag for a hyperlink; note that it starts with
<A HREF="URL"> and ends with </A>—the
text in between is displayed as a hyperlink

HTML tag to
display an image

end a Web page with
the tag </HTML>

menu you see after clicking on **File** in the menu bar.

The hyperlinks reference other Web pages on the World Wide Web. The URL used for the image **intcover.gif** means that the image is stored in a file with that name in the directory **inetbk** on Drive **C:**. The URL format for a file uses the vertical bar | after C, **C¦**, to represent **C:**.

The URL in the **<IMG SRC="URL">** tag could have linked to any image on the Internet. That same image could have been displayed using the tag **<IMG SRC="http://www.mwc.edu/ernie/InternetToday/intcover.gif">**, since the file is accessible through the Web server at

FIGURE 6.2

Web Page, Source Shown in Figure 6.1, as Displayed by Web Browser

title for the Web page; every page should have a title

image displayed here

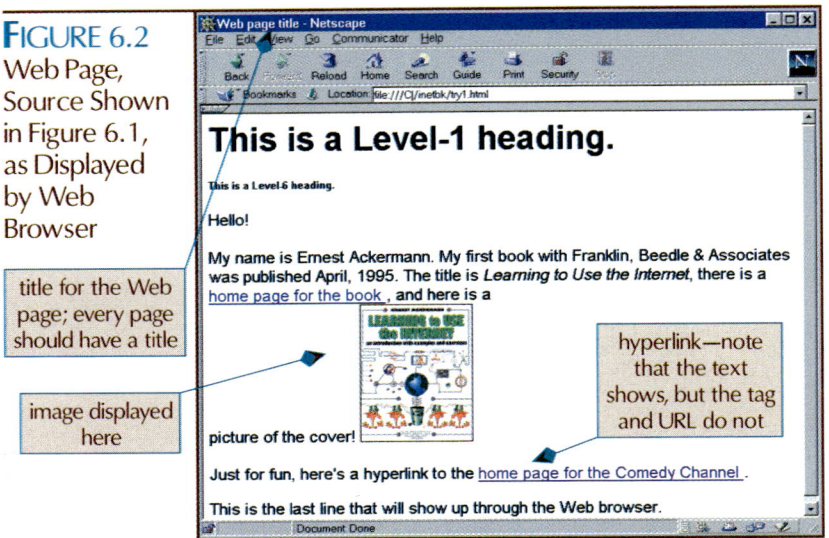

This is a Level-1 heading.

This is a Level-6 heading.

Hello!

My name is Ernest Ackermann. My first book with Franklin, Beedle & Associates was published April, 1995. The title is *Learning to Use the Internet*, there is a home page for the book , and here is a

picture of the cover!

hyperlink—note that the text shows, but the tag and URL do not

Just for fun, here's a hyperlink to the home page for the Comedy Channel .

This is the last line that will show up through the Web browser.

FIGURE 6.3

View Document Source Window for Web Page in Figure 6.2

```
<HTML>
<HEAD>
<TITLE> Web page title</TITLE>
</HEAD>
<BODY>
<H1> This is a Level-1 heading.</H1>
<H6> This is a Level-6 heading. </H6>
<!-- HTML has 6 levels of headings, H1 is the largest and H6 is
the smallest -->
<!-- By the way, tags that start like this one are for the
author's comments -->
<!-- They don't show up in the Web page -->
Hello!
<P>
My name is Ernest Ackermann.
My first book with Franklin, Beedle & Associates was published
April, 1995. The title is
<I> Learning to Use the Internet</I>,
there is a
<A HREF="http://www.mwc.edu/ernie/lrn-net.html">
home page for the book </A>
, and
here is a picture of the cover!
<IMG SRC="intcover.gif">

<P>
Just for fun, here's a hyperlink to the
<A HREF="http://www.comcentral.com">home page for the Comedy
Channel </A>.
<P>
This is the last line that will show up through the Web browser.
</BODY>
</HTML>
```

www.mwc.edu. The browser retrieves the file from the server through the Internet using the URL **http://www.mwc.edu/ ernie/InternetToday/intcover .gif** and then displays it. The person viewing the page won't necessarily know where the file holding the image is located. That information can be found by looking at the source for the Web page or by reading the information that's displayed when **Page Info** is selected from the **View** pull-down menu in the menu bar.

Figures 6.1 and 6.2 give you a basic idea of what a Web page contains, what HTML tags look like, and how HTML tags can be used. Regardless of how advanced or complex a Web page can be, remember that it contains the text you see on a page, HTML tags, and other items called *elements*. The elements can be images, hyperlinks to audio files, hyperlinks to files on your computer, hyperlinks to other parts of the document, hyperlinks to other portions of the Web, or interactive programs, scripts, and files that use inline plug-ins.

Viewing the Source Version of a Web Page

You can view the source version of any Web page. This lets you see the HTML used to create the page. It is a straightforward process. Click on **View** from the menu bar and then choose **Page Source**. Figure 6.3 shows what you'd see if you chose to view the source of the Web page shown in Figure 6.2.

Figure 6.3 shows the same text as Figure 6.1, but in a different format. Viewing the document source with Netscape shows the HTML tags and URLs in a different font and color, making them easy to pick out.

Viewing the source is a good way to see how a Web page is constructed and to learn from the work of others. It's not intended to be used for copying someone else's work. A Web page belongs to the author just like anything else, such as a book or tape that someone has created and developed. If you see something you like, view the source, study how it was done, and then adapt the techniques you see to your own work.

Introduction to HTML

Web pages are written using **HTML (*hypertext markup language*)**. HTML consists of a collection of instructions, called *tags*, that the Web browser interprets to display a Web page.

The commands or instructions are written in HTML, but the effects of the tags aren't seen until a Web browser or some program interprets the HTML. For example, the tags **<B>** and **</B>** placed around text indicate that the enclosed text is to be displayed in bold format. So if

`Be sure to follow the <B>Yellow Brick Road</B> to get to Oz.`

were part of a Web page, it would be displayed as

Be sure to follow the **Yellow Brick Road** to get to Oz.

Other examples of HTML are shown in the previous two sections of this chapter.

The commands and the way browsers interpret HTML have more to do with the organization of a document rather than with its format. A number of commands can control the way text is displayed but HTML emphasizes the hypermedia aspects of the World Wide Web—extra spaces, tabs, and line length, for example, are generally ignored by HTML; the text is made to fit within the browser's window.

HTML does contain the commands or tags to create hyperlinks from one part of a Web page to another part of the same page and to create hyperlinks to other Web pages or resources on the Internet. In other words, these hyperlinks are embedded into or become part of the Web page. ***Uniform Re-***

source Locators (***URLs***) are used to create the ***hyperlinks***. The same process of embedding hyperlinks in a document is used to embed images. The text, images, and hyperlinks are called *elements* of a Web page.

Web pages are stored in plain text files; they contain ordinary printable characters. A number of tools and Web page editors to help create and write Web pages are listed in the Yahoo! directory section "Computers and Internet:Software:Internet:World Wide Web:HTML Editors," **http://www.yahoo.com/ Computers_and_Internet/ Software/Internet/World _ W i d e _ W e b / H T M L _Editors/**. These can be useful, but they're not necessary. The pages can be written using any word processor or editor that can save information as a text file. When the file is saved its file

extension should be **.htm** or **.html**.

We'll write the HTML and Web page using a simple ***text editor***, save the file as a text file, and then view it with the Web browser. This way we'll be able to concentrate on the basics. You'll find HTML is not difficult. Organizing a body of material and developing an effective design are the harder tasks. We'll give some pointers about style and list some resources for style guides on the Web later.

In this section we'll concentrate on the HTML tags that do basic formatting, create lists, include hyperlinks to other Web pages and resources, and include images in Web pages. After you understand the basics and have some confidence, you'll be ready to go forward on your own.

Some aspects of HTML not covered here include Web page

173

FIGURE 6.4
Outline of Head and Body Sections of a Web Page

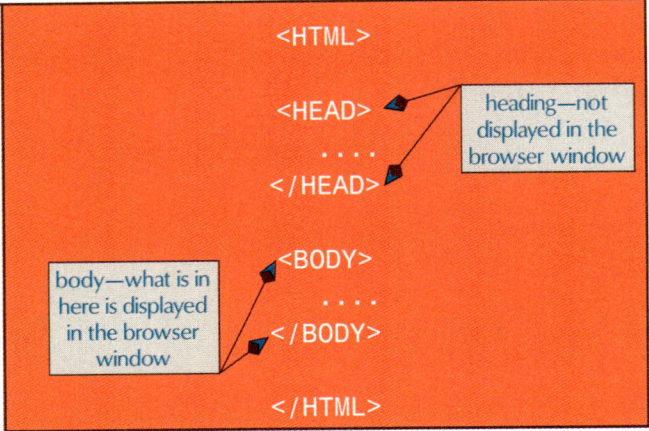

elements such as tables, image maps, forms, JavaScripts, Java applets, and inline plug-ins. They're best covered in a book that focuses on HTML. When you're ready to use them, consult some of the Web guides to HTML listed on page 207.

General Form of HTML Tags

Almost all HTML tags begin with the character < (right angle bracket) and end with the character > (left angle bracket). The exceptions are the tags that represent special individual characters, such as the right or left angle bracket. Some of the tags come in pairs; they surround or enclose text. The second tag is like the first except that there's a slash (/) after <. The text in between is treated some special way. For example, the text in between the tags **<I>** and **</I>** is displayed in italic font. You can see this in Figures 6.1 and 6.2. Some tags may occur singly and cause

an action. In Figures 6.1 and 6.2 we see that **<P>**, which causes a new paragraph to start, acts that way. We've written the tags in uppercase, but HTML ignores the case of the letters in a tag. Remember, though, that in a URL, it's very important to use the proper case for names of files.

To summarize: Most HTML tags are enclosed between < and >. Some tags occur in pairs. The second is like the first except a slash is used after < to indicate it's the matching tag; for example, **<I>** and **</I>**. Other tags may occur as single entities, such as **<P>**. Tags can be written using upper- or lowercase letters; HTML ignores the case of letters in a tag. In URLs you have to pay strict attention to the case of the letters.

Structure of a Web Page—Head and Body

Each Web page ought to start with the tag **<HTML>** and end

with **</HTML>**. Between those tags, a Web page has two distinct parts: the head or heading, which gives some information about the Web page, and the body, which contains the elements or content of the Web page. The title of the Web page, for example, goes in the heading section. The other information that may be put in the heading concerns issues that are more advanced than those we're dealing with here. Use the tags **<HEAD>** and **</HEAD>** to denote the heading of the Web page, and use **<BODY>** and **</BODY>** to mark off the body of the page. The items in the heading section aren't displayed as part of the Web page. Figures 6.1 and 6.3 show the proper use of the tags to declare the document as being written in HTML and to denote the heading and body sections. Figure 6.4 gives a brief outline.

Title

Every Web page needs a title. The title doesn't appear as part of the Web page, but it is visible at the very top of the browser window, as shown in Figure 6.2. It's important to give a page an appropriate title, because the title is the name that appears in a bookmark list, the title is the name that appears when someone uses a search engine to find the page, and the title is significant when a searching program looks for pages that are relevant to a search word or phrase. The title is put between the tags **<TITLE>** and **</TITLE>** in the heading section of a Web page, as shown in Figure 6.1.

Author's Comments

The author of a Web page can include comments that are part of the source for the page but aren't displayed when the browser is displaying the page. Comments are useful as notes about how the page was constructed or what might need to be changed in the future. Comments serve as reminders not only to the person writing the page but also to anyone who might have to modify the page. Professional computer programmers learn early in their training that they need to include comments as part of a computer program so the next person who has to perform some maintenance on it can understand the purpose and methods of the program. The same holds true for Web pages. Comments need to be surrounded by **<!--** and **-->**, as shown in Figures 6.1 and 6.3.

Headings

Web pages can be given a rigid structure. You can start with a top-level heading and then have several levels of subheadings. One rule used for constructing a Web page is restate the title at the top of the body section as a Level-1 heading using the tags **<H1>** and **</H1>**, then give a Level-2 heading using **<H2>** and **</H2>**, then a third-level heading, and so on. There are six levels of headings using the tags **<H1>**, **<H2>**, **<H3>**, and on through **<H6>**. The different levels of headings control the size of the characters displayed. In Figure 6.1 we used **<H1>** and **<H6>**, and you can see the difference in Figure 6.2. Figure 6.5 shows a portion of the source for the Web page shown in Figure 6.6. Here the title was restated as a Level-3 heading, **<H4>** was used for the subheadings, and **<H6>** was for the small lettering of the illustrator's name.

FIGURE 6.5
Source for Web Page in Figure 6.6

<H3> used for top-level heading

<H4> used for subheadings

<H6> used for illustrator's name in small print

FIGURE 6.6
Web Page with Source in Figure 6.5

Level-3 heading displays slightly larger than Level-4

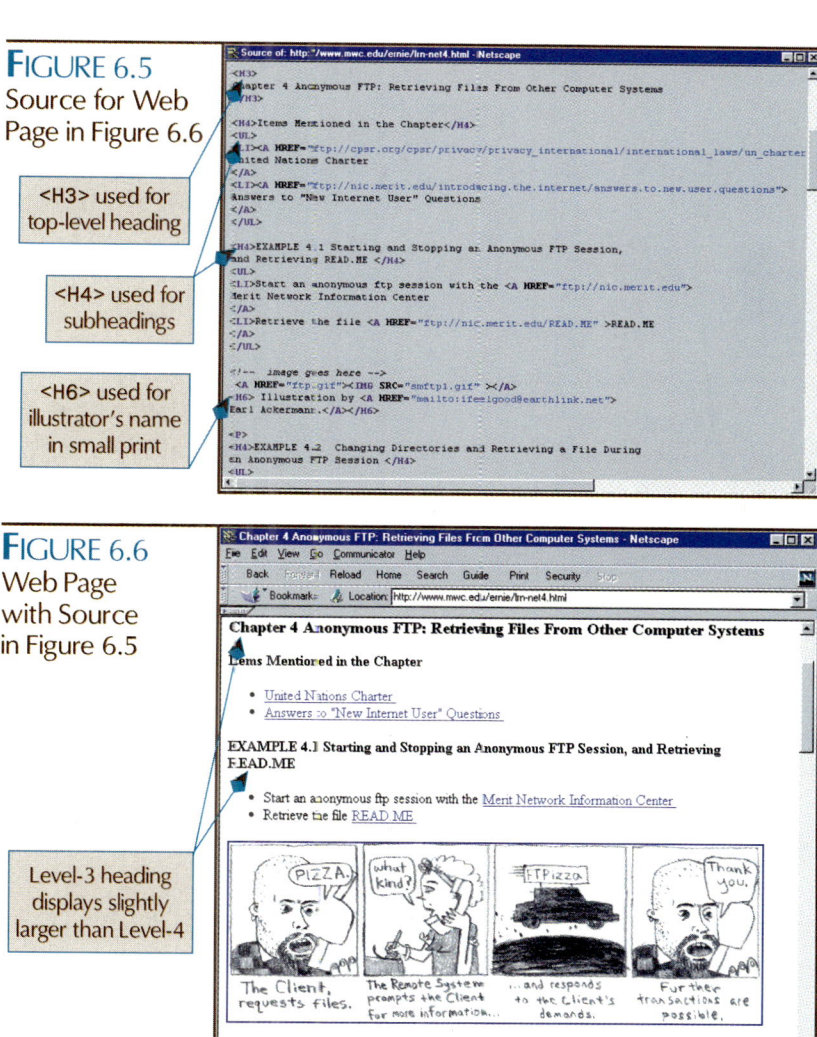

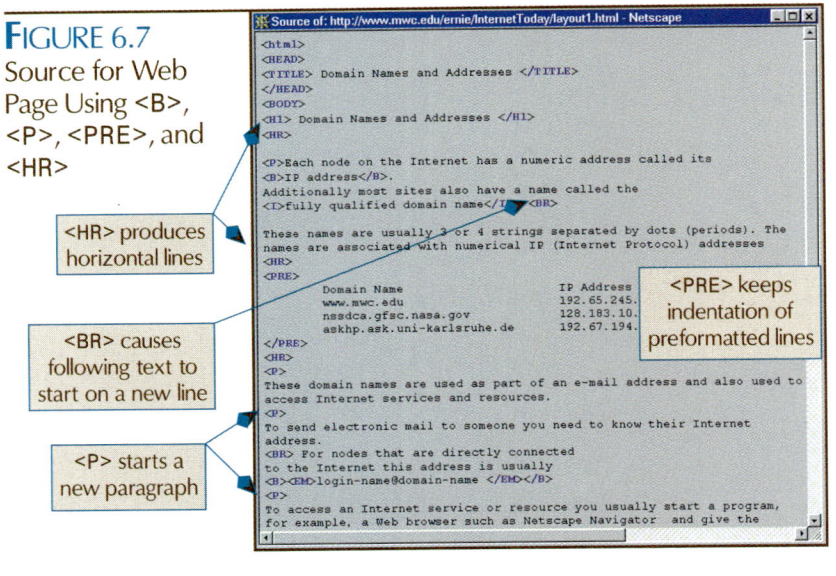

<HR> produces
horizontal lines

 causes
following text to
start on a new line

<P> starts a
new paragraph

<PRE> keeps
indentation of
preformatted lines

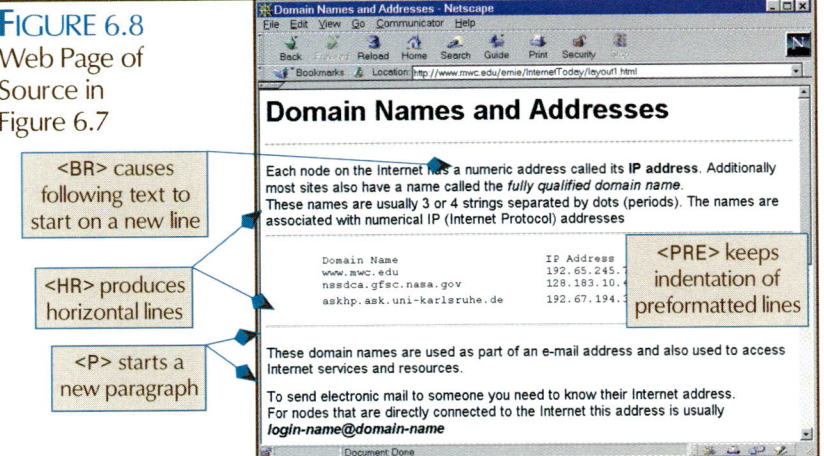

 causes
following text to
start on a new line

<HR> produces
horizontal lines

<P> starts a
new paragraph

<PRE> keeps
indentation of
preformatted lines

Paragraphs, Line Breaks, and Horizontal Lines

Blank spaces on a line and blank lines in a source document don't show up when an HTML document is displayed by a Web browser; they're ignored. The source documents in Figures 6.1 and 6.5 contain blank spaces and lines that don't appear in the Web pages as shown in Figures 6.2 and 6.6. The advantage to this is that lines are adjusted or formatted by the browser so they fit nicely within the window. There's also a disadvantage: You need to use an HTML tag to specifically mark the beginning of a paragraph or the end of a line.

Use <P> to mark the beginning of a paragraph. When the browser interprets this tag, a blank line is displayed, and the text following <P> starts on a new line. <P> has been used in all the examples shown above. Another way to think about this is that <P> is used to separate paragraphs.

Use <BR> to separate lines. The text following the tag <BR> is placed at the beginning of the next line in the browser's window.

The tag <HR> puts a horizontal line on the Web page. Like <BR>, it can be used to separate lines. Often it's used to separate sections of a Web page. The length of the horizontal line is automatically adjusted so it's always the width of the window.

Figures 6.7 and 6.8 show the document source and the browser view of a page that uses <BR>, <P>, and <HR>. These tags can be placed anywhere on a line or between lines. None of the tags has a matching tag.

Character Formatting—Italic, Bold, and Emphasized

HTML tags can be used to display parts of the text in bold or italic font. To display text in bold font surround it with the tags <B> and </B>. To display text in italic font use the tags <I> and </I>. Both of these are used in the source document shown in Figure 6.7. The tags <EM> and </EM> are also used to display text in italic font. The portion of the source in Figure 6.7 that reads **<B><EM>login-name @domain-name </EM></B>** displays the enclosed text in bold and italic font.

Why use **<EM>** and not **<I>** for italic font? Some browsers don't display text in italic font, and some people think it's better to use the tag **<EM>** to let the browser determine how the text will be displayed. **<EM>** means *emphasize* to a browser and many browsers will display the text in italic. If a browser can't display text in italic font, it will use some other font to emphasize the text. There are other tags that behave this way; **<STRONG>** and **<B>** can usually be used in place of each other.

Preformatted Text

Blank spaces on a line (except for the one necessary for proper punctuation) and blank lines are ignored when an HTML source document is displayed as a Web page. That way the text can be automatically adjusted by the browser so it looks good in different sizes of windows. Sometimes, though, you want to have certain spacing or indenting. Use the HTML tag **<PRE>** to tell the browser not to automatically rearrange or format the text. Putting **<PRE>** and **</PRE>** around text indicates that it's preformatted, and the browser shouldn't change the

way it's to be displayed. Text within the tags is displayed in a fixed-width font, usually Courier, and looks different from other text displayed by the browser. Figure 6.7 shows the use of the tags **<PRE>** and **</PRE>**, and Figure 6.8 shows how Netscape displays the text.

Quoted Text

To display quoted text in the Web browser, use the HTML tags **<BLOCKQUOTE>** and **</BLOCKQUOTE>**. As an example, Figure 6.9 shows a portion of the source document for the Web page displayed in Figure 6.10.

FIGURE 6.9
Source Code Showing Use of
<BLOCKQUOTE>
and
</BLOCKQUOTE>

```
Civil disobedience is certainly not a new notion, and there's a long
tradition of times when history has shown it to be necessary and reason-
able. The authors of the <I>Declaration of Independence</I> stated
conditions under which they felt civil disobedience is justified.
<BLOCKQUOTE>

"Prudence, indeed, will dictate that Governments long established should
not be changed for light and transient causes; and accordingly all expe-
rience hath shown that mankind are more disposed to suffer, while evils
are sufferable than to right themselves by abolishing the forms to which
they are accustomed. But when a long train of abuses and usurpations,
pursuing invariably the same object, evinces a design to reduce them
under absolute Despotism, it is their right, it is their duty, to throw
off such Government, and to provide new Guards for their future security."
 - Declaration of Independence
</BLOCKQUOTE>

References to other sources justifying civil disobedience are given at
the end of this chapter.
```

FIGURE 6.10
Web Page Showing Effect of `<BLOCKQUOTE>` and `</BLOCKQUOTE>`

notice the effect of using `<BLOCKQUOTE>` and `</BLOCKQUOTE>`

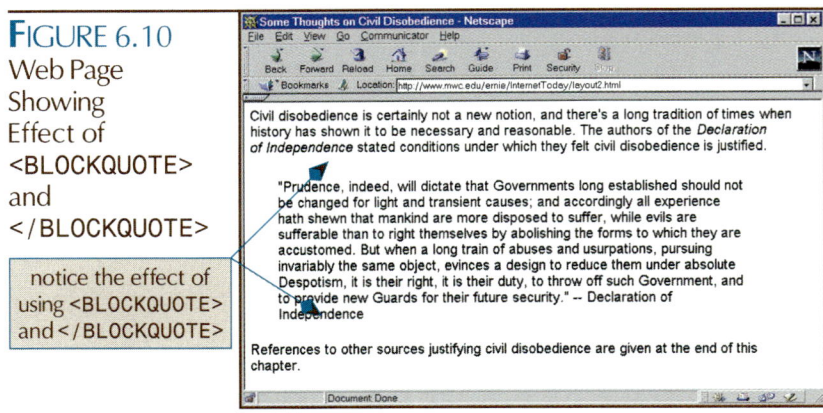

FIGURE 6.11
Example of Using HTML to Produce Ordered List

```
What is the Internet?
We'll look at it from these points of view.
<OL>
<LI> From a social point of view.
<LI> From a practical point of view empha-
sizing resources.
<LI> From a technical point of view.
</OL>
```

FIGURE 6.12
Ordered List on Web Page

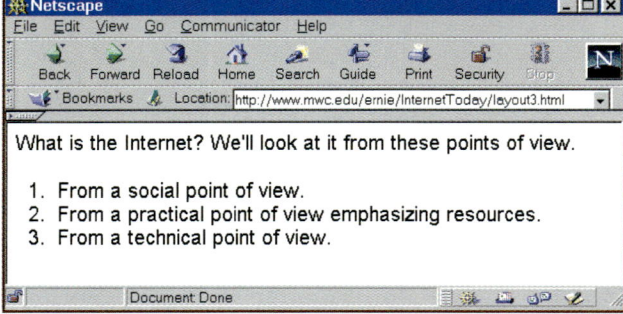

Special Characters

Here's a question for you. If a Web browser interprets the character < as the beginning of an HTML tag, then how can we display < on a Web page? HTML has ways of representing that and other special characters. Use

<   to represent   <
>   to represent   >
&   to represent   &
" to represent   "

There are many other special characters that can be represented with HTML. These are part of standards for sets of codes that are set by the ISO (International Organization for Standardization). Two sources for a complete list of ways to represent special characters in HTML are "Martin Ramsch - iso8859-1 table," **http://www.uni-passau.de/~ramsch/iso8859-1.html**, and "ISO8859-1/HTML Stuff," **http://ppewww.ph.gla.ac.uk/~flavell/iso8859**.

Lists

HTML has tags for several different types of lists—sequences of items, with each item on its own line. Additionally, the lists can be nested so one type of list is inside another. The types of lists supported by HTML are as follows:

- Ordered (numbered) lists
- Unordered lists
- Descriptive lists

Hey! We just used an unordered list to show the types of lists you can represent with HTML.

ORDERED OR NUMBERED LISTS. Ordered lists are lists in which each item is numbered. You don't need to do the numbering; the Web browser does this automatically. The first item on the list is numbered 1.

If you change the list and add items, the browser takes care of renumbering them correctly. It's no surprise that ordered lists are also referred to as numbered lists.

The rules for using HTML to construct ordered lists are as follows:

1. An ordered list starts with the tag **<OL>** and ends with the tag **</OL>**.

2. Each item in the list starts with **<LI>**.

Figure 6.11 shows a simple example of using these rules, and Figure 6.12 shows how it would be displayed.

UNORDERED LISTS (BULLETED LISTS). Each item in an unordered list is marked with a dot called a *bullet*. The term *unordered* means the items aren't numbered, but they do appear in the order given in the source document. These lists also go by the names *unnumbered lists* or *bulleted lists*.

The rules for using HTML to construct unordered lists are as follows:

1. An unordered list starts with the tag **<UL>** and ends with the tag **</UL>**.

2. Each item in the list starts with **<LI>**.

FIGURE 6.13
Example of Using HTML to Produce Unordered List

```
This is an example of an <B>unordered
list</B>.
<P>
What is the Internet?
We'll look at it from these points of
view.
<UL>
<LI> From a social point of view.
<LI> From a practical point of view empha-
sizing resources.
<LI>From a technical point of view.
</UL>
```

FIGURE 6.14
Unordered List on Web Page

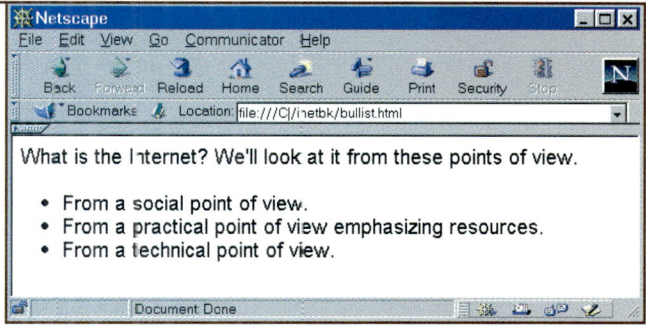

Figure 6.13 shows a simple example of using these rules, and Figure 6.14 shows how it would be displayed.

DESCRIPTIVE LISTS (INDENTING). Each item in a descriptive list has a title and then an indented description of the title. The items aren't marked with numbers or dots (bullets) as are ordered and unordered lists.

The rules for using HTML to construct descriptive lists are:

1. A descriptive list starts and ends with the tags **<DL>** and **</DL>**, respectively.

2. The descriptive title for each item starts with the tag **<DT>**.

3. The indented description for a title is marked with **<DD>**.

Figures 6.15 and 6.16 are examples of descriptive lists.

You can also use descriptive lists to write bibliographies in HTML. Figure 6.17 shows the source code for the bibliography shown in Figure 6.18.

FIGURE 6.15
Example of
Using HTML
to Produce
Descriptive
List

```
This is an example of a <B>descriptive
list</B>.
<P>
What is the Internet?
We'll look at it from these points of view.
<DL>
<DT> From a social point of view.
<DD> Consider the Internet in terms of individuals and groups
of users. We'll focus on using the Internet for communica-
tion and the virtual communities that have arisen in recent
times.
<DT> From a practical point of view emphasizing resources.
<DD> Consider the Internet as a vast storehouse of information.
We'll also stress the fact that the information isn't only
"on the shelf", but that there are lots of people to answer
questions and give support.
<DT> From a technical point of view.
<DD> Here's where we give an introduction to some of the tech-
nical details and issues. We'll look at the Internet as a
network of networks, explain how the networks can communicate,
and cover some details about connecting to the Internet.
</DL>
```

FIGURE 6.16
Web Page Using
Descriptive List

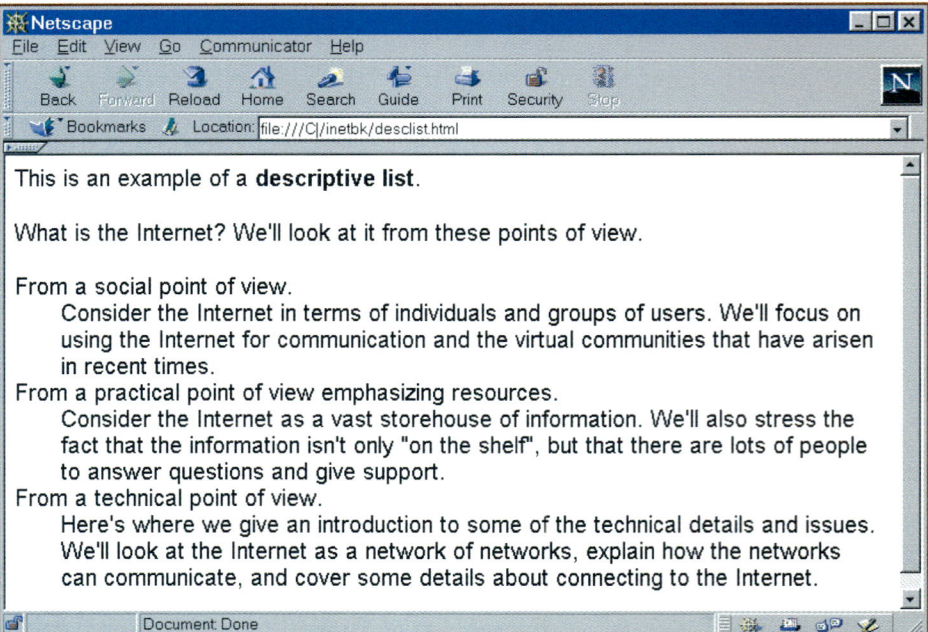

180

```
<H3>Bibliography</H3>


<DL>
<DT>Ackermann, Ernest C. (1995).
<DD><I>Learning to Use the Internet</I>,
Wilsonville, OR: Franklin, Beedle &amp; Associates.

<DT> Comer,Douglas
<DD><I>The Internet Book: Everything You Need to Know about
Computer Networking and How the Internet Works</I>,
Englewood Cliffs NJ: Prentice-Hall

<DT>Groves, Dawn(1995).
<DD><I>The Web Page Workbook</I>,
Wilsonville, OR: Franklin, Beedle &amp; Associates.

<DT>Liu, C., Peek, J., Jones, R., Buus, B, and Nye, A. (1994)
<DD><I> Managing Internet Information Services: World Wide
Web, Gopher, FTP, and More</I>,
Sebastopol, CA: O'Reilly &amp; Associates
```

FIGURE 6.18
Web Page
Bibliography

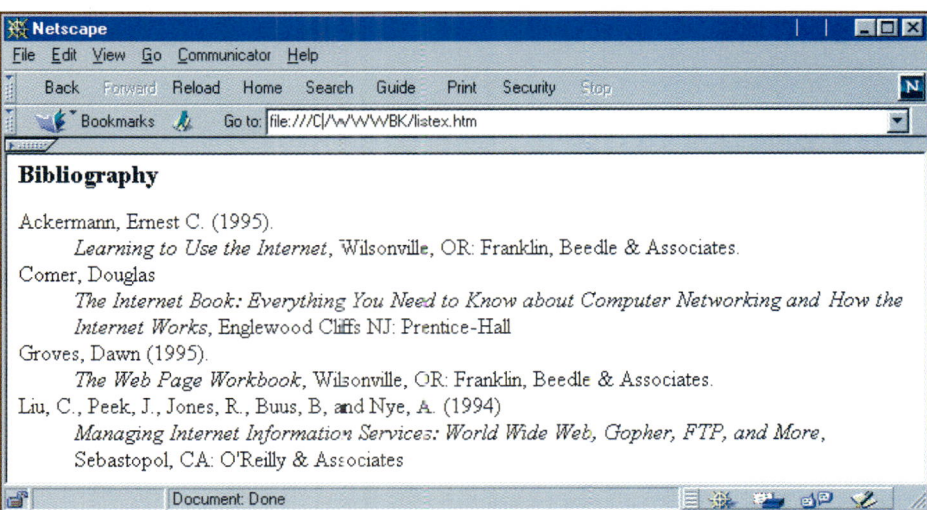

NESTED LISTS. Any of the types of lists mentioned can be nested; that is, one put inside another. You'll notice that the symbol used to mark items in un- ordered lists changes shape when these lists are nested. Here's an example showing nested lists. Figure 6.19 shows the source and Figure 6.20 the portion of the Web page shown in the source. Here we have one ordered (num- bered) list with several unordered lists nested inside. We've marked the first nested list in Figure 6.19.

HTML was designed to allow for the **construction of hypertext, hypermedia documents, or Web pages**. One of its strong points is that with it we can create hyperlinks from one part of a Web page to another Web page, a resource on the World Wide Web, or another part of the same page.

FIGURE 6.19
Source for
Web Page
in Figure 6.20

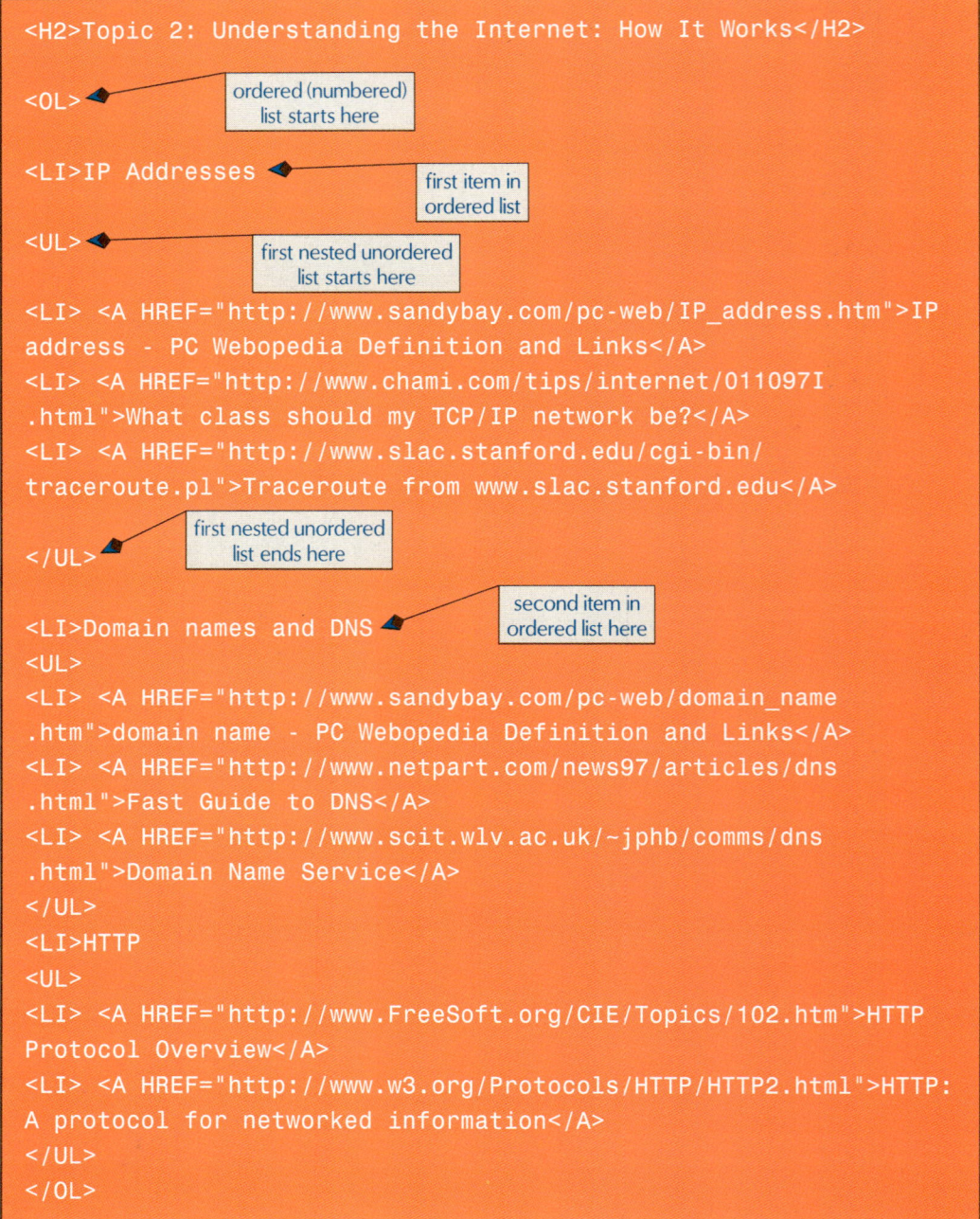

```
<H2>Topic 2: Understanding the Internet: How It Works</H2>

<OL>

<LI>IP Addresses

<UL>

<LI> <A HREF="http://www.sandybay.com/pc-web/IP_address.htm">IP
address - PC Webopedia Definition and Links</A>
<LI> <A HREF="http://www.chami.com/tips/internet/011097I
.html">What class should my TCP/IP network be?</A>
<LI> <A HREF="http://www.slac.stanford.edu/cgi-bin/
traceroute.pl">Traceroute from www.slac.stanford.edu</A>

</UL>

<LI>Domain names and DNS
<UL>
<LI> <A HREF="http://www.sandybay.com/pc-web/domain_name
.htm">domain name - PC Webopedia Definition and Links</A>
<LI> <A HREF="http://www.netpart.com/news97/articles/dns
.html">Fast Guide to DNS</A>
<LI> <A HREF="http://www.scit.wlv.ac.uk/~jphb/comms/dns
.html">Domain Name Service</A>
</UL>
<LI>HTTP
<UL>
<LI> <A HREF="http://www.FreeSoft.org/CIE/Topics/102.htm">HTTP
Protocol Overview</A>
<LI> <A HREF="http://www.w3.org/Protocols/HTTP/HTTP2.html">HTTP:
A protocol for networked information</A>
</UL>
</OL>
```

Labels in figure: ordered (numbered) list starts here; first item in ordered list; first nested unordered list starts here; first nested unordered list ends here; second item in ordered list here

Hyperlinks

HTML was designed to allow for the construction of hypertext, hypermedia documents, or Web pages. One of the advantages of HTML is that with it we can create hyperlinks from a resource on the World Wide Web to another Web page or from one part of a Web page to another part of the same Web page. We'll cover both of these types of hyperlinks in this section.

FIGURE 6.20
Web Page Using
Nested Lists

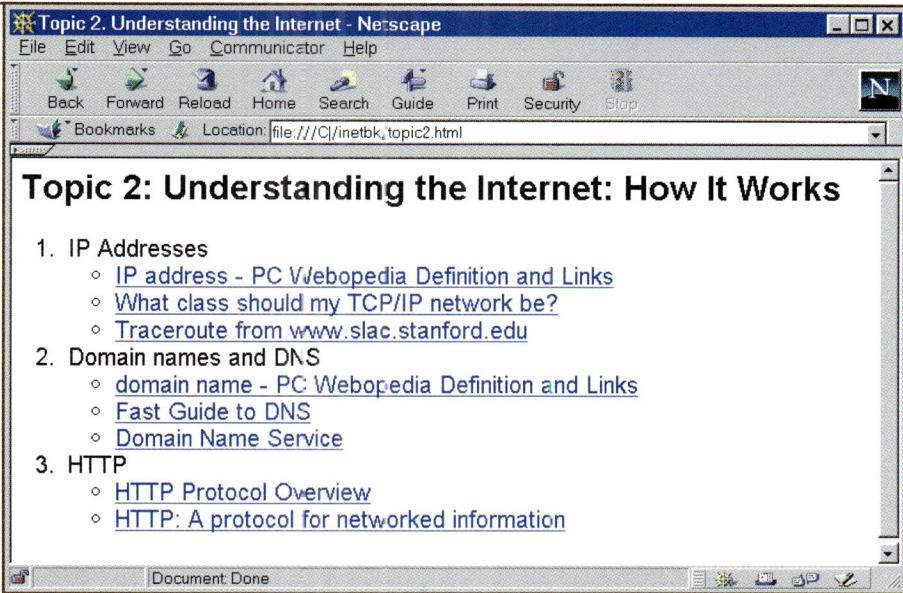

A Web browser would display that HTML as:

The home page for Ernest Ackermann has a link to materials for workshops and tutorials.

HYPERLINKS TO OTHER RE-SOURCES ON THE WEB. To use HTML to represent a hyperlink to a resource on the Web, you use two tags, with text or an image between them.

The first tag starts with **<A HREF="** and includes the URL or link for the resource. The matching tag is **</A>**. As you've already seen, many HTML tags appear in pairs.

We'll look at an example before giving the rules for these types of tags.

Here's an example of the HTML tags used for creating a hyperlink:

```
The home page for <A HREF="http://www.mwc.edu/ernie/index.html">
Ernest Ackermann</A> has a link to materials for workshops and tutorials.
```

A Web browser would display that HTML as:

The home page for Ernest Ackermann has a link to materials for workshops and tutorials.

If someone clicked on **Ernest Ackermann** in the browser's window, the browser would open the location and go to the resource given by the URL.

The HTML rules for creating hyperlinks are generalizations of the example above.

+ The first tag has the form **<A HREF="URL">**. A URL for an actual Web page is substituted

for **URL** between the pair of quotation marks (**"**).

+ The closing tag is **</A>**.

+ The tags aren't visible on the Web page.

+ The text between the two tags appears on the Web page as underlined or highlighted text.

+ If there's an image between the two tags, its border is highlighted.

+ Clicking on the text or image opens the location or takes the user to the Web resources given by the URL.

Figures 6.21 and 6.22 show the use of HTML tags for hyperlinks from a Web page to other resources on the Web. Figure 6.21 shows the HTML source, and Figure 6.22 shows the Web page. There are hyperlinks to sites at more than one location—a Web page can contain hyperlinks to many different locations and resources. Near the bottom of the page an image is used within the tags for a hyperlink, otherwise the hyperlinks all appear as text. We'll discuss displaying images in the next section. You'll notice that this uses some HTML tags we've discussed before. Try to predict what the page will look like before looking at Figure 6.22.

FIGURE 6.21
Source for
Hyperlinks
Example

```
<b>Got a question? Want to make a comment? </b>
<UL>
 <LI><a href="http://www.digicool.com/arttalk/main">
   Please use the Guest Book</a>
</UL>
<HR>
<A HREF="http://www.mwc.edu/ernie/sg/sgswebacc.html">
 Statistics </A>
about visitors from the WWW.
<HR>
Steve Griffin Retrospective <BR>
September 29 - November 5  <BR>
duPont Gallery, duPont Hall <BR>
<A HREF="http://www.mwc.edu/index.html">
 Mary Washington College </A>
Galleries <BR>
Fredericksburg, VA 22401
<P>
Opening Reception (in real space) <BR>
Thursday, September 28 <BR>
5:00 - 7:00 PM
<HR>
<A HREF="http://www.mwc.edu/ernie/sg/credits.html">
 Credit Where Credit's Due</A>
<HR>
<P><EM>Steve Griffin Retrospective Home Page <BR>
Mary Washington College Galleries <BR>
Fredericksburg, VA 22401 <BR>
URL:http://www.mwc.edu/sgexhibit.html</EM>
<P>
For more information, email Ernie Ackermann at
<A HREF="mailto:ernie@mwc.edu"> ernie@mwc.edu</A>
```

some of the hyperlinks are represented here as text

```
<P>
<A HREF="http://www.mwc.edu/ernie/sg/virtual.html">
<IMG ALIGN=LEFT SRC="http://www.mwc.edu/ernie/sg/return.gif">
</A>
Go to Home Page for Steve Griffin Retrospective Virtual Exhibit URL:
<A HREF="http://www.mwc.edu/ernie/sg/virtual.html">
http://www.mwc.edu/ernie/sg/virtual.html</A>
```

this hyperlink takes the user to the same Web page as the one that uses the image, except the hyperlink here is represented as text

HYPERLINKS TO OTHER PARTS OF THE WEB PAGE.

HTML can also be used to create hyperlinks between several parts of the same document. This is useful when dealing with a long document. Hyperlinks for a table of contents or list of sections can take the reader to specific parts of the document. Hyperlinks within a document are also appropriate when constructing a glossary—a list of terms and definitions—to allow the reader to consider some items in context.

Making a link from one part of the document to another section involves link tags and an anchor tag. The anchor marks a spot within the document, and the link tags are ties to that specific anchor. Figure 6.23 shows an example of the source for these types of hyperlinks, and Figure 6.24 shows how they would be displayed by a Web browser.

Clicking on a hyperlink in Figure 6.24 takes the user to a portion of the document marked by anchor tags. Looking

FIGURE 6.22
Web Page Produced by Source in Figure 6.21

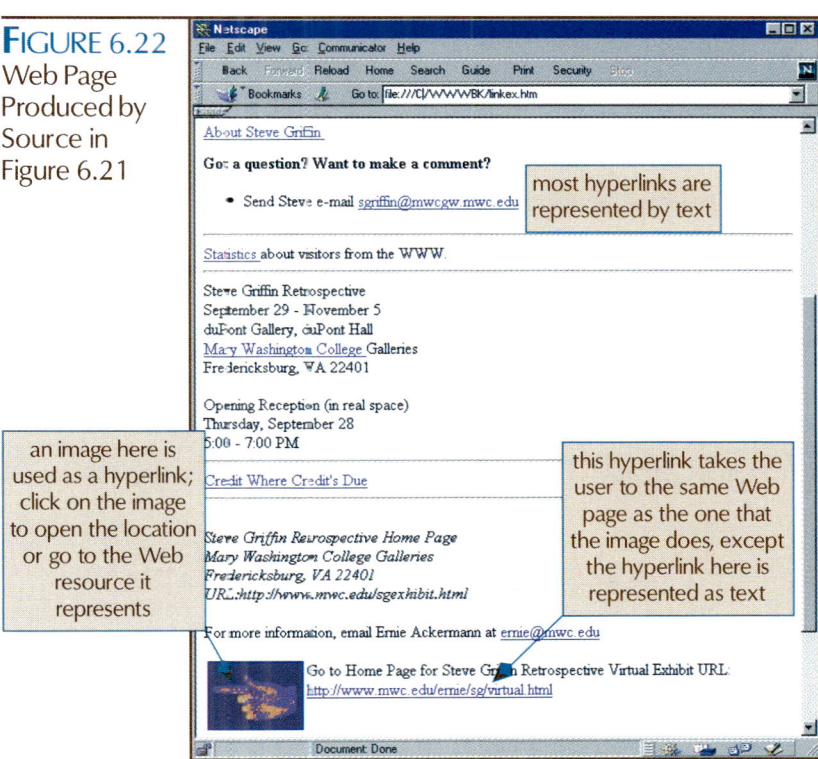

most hyperlinks are represented by text

an image here is used as a hyperlink; click on the image to open the location or go to the Web resource it represents

this hyperlink takes the user to the same Web page as the one that the image does, except the hyperlink here is represented as text

T I P The name of the file tells the browser the type of resource.

In the preceding figures you've seen hyperlinks to several resources. If the name of the file holding the resource ends with **.html** or **.htm**, the browser displays it as a Web page. If the name ends with **.gif**, it's displayed as an image. In order to have the ◆

browser display or play (if the resource is an audio or video file) correctly, the file needs to be named properly. The proper name depends on the file extension, the characters after the dot (.) near the end of its name. Here's a list of file types with the proper extensions. You or your audience will need the proper helper files to deal with the resources. You may need additional helper programs or plug-ins to work with the file types follwed by an asterisk (*).

Extension	Type of Resource
.au	AU audio file
.aiff	AIFF audio file
.wav	WAV audio file *
.ra, .ram	Real Audio audio file *
.gif	GIF image file
.jpg	JPEG image file
.tif	TIFF image file *
.xbm	XBM bitmap image
.txt, .text	Plain text
.htm, .html	HTML document, Web page
.pdf	Adobe Acrobat format *
.ps	PostScript *
.mpg, .mpeg	MPEG movie *
.mov	QuickTime movie *

at the example in Figure 6.23 you see:

- Anchor tags have the form **<A NAME= "word">** portion-of-document **</A>** where *word* is some term that's used in the link tags. When the link is selected the page is displayed starting here.

- Hyperlinks to portions of a document have the form **<A HREF= "#word">** text or image **</A>**. Clicking on the hyperlink takes the user to the portion of the document where the anchor word's definition appears.

The # character identifies the link as going to a portion of a document. The hyperlinks we've shown here are within one document or Web page. You can use the same idea to set up hyperlinks to portions of

FIGURE 6.23
Source for Hyperlinks Within Document

```
<B><A NAME="anonymousftp">Anonymous FTP</A>:</B> A means of using
<A HREF="#ftp" >FTP</A> (file transfer protocol) in which a user
starts an FTP session with a remote host, gives the login or user name
&quot;anonymous&quot;, and the <A HREF="#email">email</A> address as a
password.

<P>

<B>Archie:</B> An information service which helps to locate a
file which can then be retrieved by <A HREF="#anonymousftp">anonymous FTP
</A>.
```

defines the anchor named **anonymousftp** to be tied to the text **Anonymous FTP**

link to the anchor **email** defined elsewhere

link to the anchor **anonymousftp** defined above

FIGURE 6.24
Web Browser Display of Source in Figure 6.23

```
Anonymous FTP: A means of using FTP (file transfer protocol) in which a
user starts an FTP session with a remote host, gives the login or user
name "anonymous", and the email address as a password.


Archie: An information service which helps to locate a file which can
then be retrieved by anonymous FTP.
```

other documents, provided the document has anchors defined in it. The material in Figure 6.23 was taken from the Web page whose URL is **http://www .mwc.edu/ernie/glossary .html**. If we wanted to make a hyperlink from another Web page to the portion of the glossary that gives the definition of anonymous FTP we'd use the URL **http://www.mwc. edu/ernie/glossary.html #anonymousftp** in a link, as shown below.

```
Before 1990, you needed to learn how to use
<A HREF="http://www.mwc.edu/ernie/glossary.html#anonymousftp">
anonymous ftp </A>to access most of the material on the Internet.
```

Images

A Web browser is capable of displaying images as part of a Web page. The basic HTML tag to use for an image has the form **<IMG SRC="URL">** or **<IMG SRC="file-name">** where *URL* is the URL of a file or *file-name* is the name of a file on your computer that contains the image. Browsers can display images that are in GIF or JPEG format. The browser determines the format only by the name of the file. If the image is in GIF, store it in a file whose name ends with **.gif**. For an image in JPEG format, store it in a file whose name ends with **.jpg**.

We've used HTML tags for images that appear in Web pages for some of the previous figures:

- Figure 6.5
  <A HREF="ftp.gif"> <IMG SRC="smftp1 .gif"></A>

- Figure 6.21
  <IMG ALIGN=LEFT SRC="http://www .mwc.edu/ernie/sg/ return.gif">

The second URL uses a fully qualified domain name. The first uses a relative name, the name of a file, for the URL. An advantage to using a relative URL is that it's easier to type in. A disadvantage is that the image has to be in the same directory as the Web page. That restricts the location of pages and images. If you're working with a small number of images and Web pages, this isn't too

 **Make sure others can find your images and hyperlinks.**

Try to avoid using a URL or file name that references a local file in terms of its location on your computer without giving the Internet address of the computer. An example of this would be the HTML tag **<IMG SRC="file:///C:mypics/ greatpic.gif">**.

That tag instructs the browser to display a file on the computer that's being used to run the Web browser. That means if readers aren't using the computer that holds the file, they won't be ◆▶

187

able to see it! If you want the image or the hyperlink to be accessible from other computers on the Internet you need to use a URL that includes the domain name of the system that's running the Web server.

If the image were to be displayed as part of a Web page with the URL of **http://www.circlea .com/nicestuf/coolpage .html**, for example, put the image in the same directory or folder as the Web page and make its tag **<IMG SRC="greatpic .gif">**.

hard to deal with, but it can get difficult to manage with complex designs. To read more about using relative names versus fully qualified names, look at the section of the Web page "Composing Good HTML," **http://www.cs.cmu.edu/ ~tilt/cgh**, by Eric Tilton that deals with this subject.

You can also give directions to the browser as to where the accompanying text will be displayed in relation to the image. Text can be displayed aligned at the top, middle, or bottom of an image. It's usually displayed to the left of the image. Use **ALIGN=BOTTOM**, **ALIGN =MIDDLE**, or **ALIGN=TOP** within the tag **<IMG SRC ="..">**; for example, **<IMG ALIGN=TOP SRC="http:// www.mwc.edu/ernie/ InternetToday/intcover .gif">**. With these types of alignments only one line is displayed in the specified position and the remaining text (if there is any) is displayed beginning under the image. It's also pos-

sible to align text with the entire image, starting at the top, using **ALIGN=LEFT** or **ALIGN =RIGHT**. This puts the image to the left or to the right of the text.

The method of alignment is easier to think about when you see some examples, and we'll look at a Web page that contains some images that are aligned differently. The page we'll look at is accessible through the URL **http:// www.mwc.edu/ernie/ InternetToday/demoalign .html**. (Remember how to go to a page if you know the full URL? Click on the location field to highlight the URL of the current Web page, type the URL in the dialog box, and then press Enter.)

Figure 6.25 shows the effect of using these three tags along with some accompanying text:

```
<IMG ALIGN=TOP SRC="http://www.mwc.edu/ernie/sg/fleethum.gif">
<IMG ALIGN=MIDDLE SRC="http://www.mwc.edu/ernie/sg/fleethum.gif">
<IMG ALIGN=BOTTOM SRC="http://www.mwc.edu/ernie/sg/fleethum.gif">
```

Note that if the size of the font or window were changed, the results would be different.

What we see here depends on those items as well as the screen resolution (number of pixels).

Figure 6.26 demonstrates the use of left and right alignment using the following tags:

```
<IMG ALIGN=LEFT SRC="http://www.mwc.edu/ernie/sg/fleethum.gif">
<IMG ALIGN=RIGHT SRC="http://www.mwc.edu/ernie/sg/fleethum.gif">
```

Background Colors and Images

Using HTML, you can set the background for a Web page so that it is a solid color or an image. You do this by setting an attribute in the **<BODY>** HTML tag. For example, to have a white background on a Web page use the tag **<BODY BGCOLOR="WHITE">**. To set the background of a Web page to an image, say one that's in the file **mwc.gif**, use <**BODY BACKGROUND="mwc.gif"**>. Only one of these, **BGCOLOR** or **BACKGROUND**, may be set in the <**BODY**> tag since the background will be either a color or an image, but not both. Setting a color or an image as the background on the Web page displays all the other text or images on top of the background.

The rules for the file name that's used with **BACK-GROUND** are the same as for any image used in HTML. The file name can be a fully qualified URL with domain name and path or it can be relative to the location of the file that holds the source for the Web page. Take a look at the Web page with URL **http://www.mwc .edu/ernie/InternetToday/ background.html** to see an example.

Colors may be designated by name—such as white, blue, or palegoldenrod—or they can be designated by a six-digit hexadecimal (base 16) numeral. Most folks are more comfortable with the names for colors. Netscape has a guide that lists the names of 256 colors in the Web page "Color Values," **http:// developer.netscape.com/docs/ manuals/communicator/ jsguide4/colors.htm**. (That's how we know the names

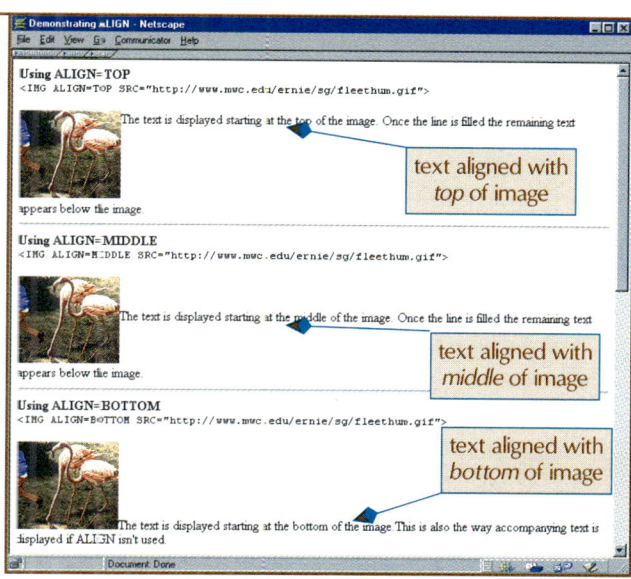

FIGURE 6.25 Alignment at Top, Middle, and Bottom of Image

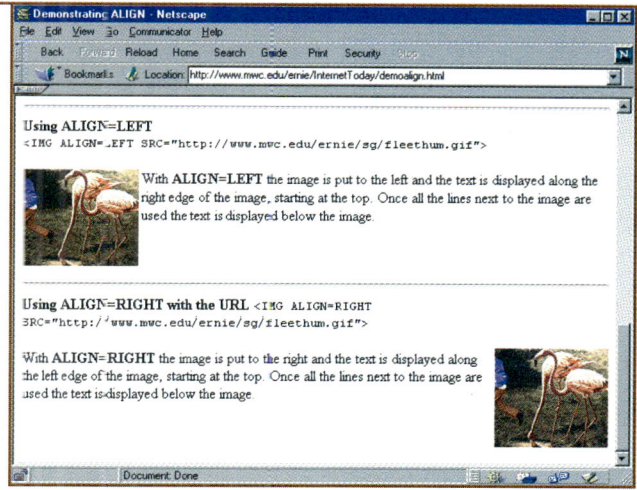

FIGURE 6.26 Demonstrating `ALIGN=LEFT` and `ALIGN=RIGHT`

palegoldenrod and papayawhip can be used for colors!) The six-digit numeral indicates the amount of red, green, and blue in the color. The colors are formed in a similar way to how light is mixed. By that we mean that giving the highest value to all three colors (designated by #FFFFFF) results in white, and giving the least value to each

(designated by #000000) results in black. The first two characters after the # represent the amount of red, the next two the amount of green, and the last two the amount of blue. Using hexadecimal digits allows for 16 * 16 possibilities for each of the three colors and thus 16^6 (over 16 million) possible colors. Before you get too carried away with the many color possibilities remember that many people view Web pages on a monitor that may display only 256 colors. Two places to refer to for advice and more information about using color in Web pages are:

♦ "AnnaBella's HTML Help - Colors" by A. Ramsden
http://www.geocities.com/Heartland/Plains/6446/color.html

♦ "The Browser Safe Color Palette" by Lynda Weinman
http://www.lynda.com/hex.html

Table 6.1 lists the tags we've mentioned above.

TABLE 6.1

HTML Tags

Tag	Purpose
<BODY>, </BODY>	Marks the body of the document; what is displayed in the browser window.
<HEAD>, </HEAD>	Marks the heading section; contains a description of the document.
<HTML>, </HTML>	Marks the HTML portion; first and last tags in the file.
<TITLE>, </TITLE>	The document title is put between these tags.
<! -- .. -->	Contains comments about the document; nothing is displayed.
<H1>, </H1>	Level-1 headings in the body section; largest font for heading. There are six levels of headings: **<H1>** ... **<H6>**, each one displayed smaller than the previous one with H6 being the smallest.
<P>	Starts a new paragraph.
** **	Starts a new line.
<HR>	A horizontal line; looks like a divider between sections or items on the page.
<I>, </I>	Italic text.
<EM>, </EM>	Emphasized text, often displayed as italic.
<B>, </B>	Bold text.
<BLOCKQUOTE>, </BLOCKQUOTE>	Extended quotation.
<PRE>, </PRE>	Preformatted text.
<, >, &	Represent the special characters <, >, and &.
<OL>, </OL>	Ordered or numbered list.
<UL>, </UL>	Unordered or bulleted list.
<LI>	Marks a list element in an ordered or unordered list.
<DL>, </DL>	Descriptive or indented list.
<DT>	Marks an item in a descriptive list.

<DD>	Describes an element in a descriptive list.
<A HREF="URL">, </A>	Used to create a hyperlink. The text or image between the tags is represented as the hyperlink on the Web page. When it's selected the actual URL given in place of *URL* is used to access a resource on the Web.
<IMG SRC="URL">	Used to display an image as part of a Web page. The actual URL given in place of *URL* represents an image file.

URL Formats

When you're writing Web pages you'll probably want to include hyperlinks to other resources on the World Wide Web. You saw in the section above on hyperlinks that you do that by using a tag in the form of **<A HREF ="URL">** where a specific URL is substituted for *URL*. We'll give the formats for URLs for different services or protocols on the Web later in this section.

Before going into the different formats for URLs, here's a quick review of the concept and general format of a URL. The purpose of a URL is to give the location and the means to get to a resource on the Internet. The Web browser uses it to access items, and it's becoming common to see it used as a way to let people know about a resource, source of information, or advertisement. You'll find it helpful to think of a URL as having the form

```
how-to-get-there://where-to-go/what-to-get
```

Its general form is

```
service://domain-name-of-site-supplying-service/full-path-name-of-item
```

Essentially this is like a sign pointing to something on the Internet. Starting at the far left, the portion of the URL up to the colon (:) tells what type of Internet service to use. The Internet domain name or address of the site supplying the information comes just after the characters **://**. After the first single slash, you have the full path name of the item. One of the key items of a URL is the type of service or protocol it represents.

Here's a list of different URL types. You may not have come across some of these services or resource types before; each is covered more in depth elsewhere in the text. Look for more information in the appropriate chapter.

Resources for finding personal Web pages.

There are several Web-based collections of personal Web pages. Most of these services allow you to list or register your personal Web page as well as search for other's Web pages. Some of the collections are

✦ "One Nation WorldWide"
http://www .onww.com/

Resource or Service	URL Begins With	Example
Web pages	http://	http://nmaa-ryder .si.edu/artdir/ treasures.html Selections from the

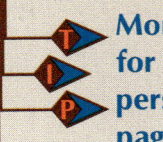

More resources for finding personal Web pages.

- "Personal pages WorldWide" http://www .utexas.edu/ world/ personal/ index.html
- "Who Where? Personal Home Pages Directory" http:// homepages .whowhere .com/

A directory of places to find personal Web pages is:

- "Yahoo—Society and Culture : People : Personal Home Pages" http:// dir.yahoo .com/Society _and_Culture/ People/Personal _Home_Pages/ Web_Directories

Two interesting articles about why people create personal Web pages:

- "The World Wide Web as Social Hypertext" by Tom Erickson

		permanent collection of the National Museum of American Art.
FTP (Chapter 7)	ftp://	ftp://ftp.jpl.nasa.gov/ pub/images/browse/ A directory of images from NASA Jet Propulsion Laboratory's public information FTP archive.
Gopher (Chapter 7)	gopher://	gopher://gopher .loc.gov The Library of Congress' Gopher Server.
Telnet (Chapter 7)	telnet://	telnet://locis.loc.gov Search holdings of Library of Congress. telnet://world @psupen.psu.edu Pen pages. Use the login name *world* once you're connected. telnet://culine .colorado.edu:860 Schedule for the National Hockey League. 860 is a port number.

Two other services—email and Usenet news—have URLs, but their URLs are in a slightly different format. They do not include the **://**.

Resource or Service	URL Begins With	Example
Email (Chapter 3)	mailto:	mailto:ernie@mwc .edu Send an email message to the address ernie@mwc.edu.

Usenet news	news:	news:rec.food.cooking URL to access the articles in the newsgroup **rec.food.cooking.**

EXAMPLE 6.1

Writing a Web Page

Now that we know something about HTML, HTML tags, and URLs, we'll put together a Web page. This Web page could be called a *personal home page* because it gives information about an individual. Lots of folks—probably thousands—have personal home pages. It's a way of letting others on the Internet know about you. An example of an excellent personal home page is "Jan's Home Page," **http://www.tile.net/jan**, created by Jan Hanford.

In this example we'll create a Web page that gives some personal and work-related information. We'll break up the information into three sections:

A. Name, email address, work address and phone number, and description of the type of work one does.

B. List of personal interests with hyperlinks to some appropriate Web sites.

C. List of some interesting or favorite Web sites.

We'll include an image file (a photo). At the end of the page we'll include the name and email address of the person who created the page, an email address for readers to use if they have any questions about the Web page, and the date the Web page was last modified or changed.

You create the Web page by typing the HTML tags and text into a file on your computer using an editor or word processor. No matter what software

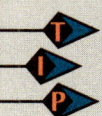

More resources for finding personal Web pages.

http://www.pliant.org/personal/Tom_Erickson/SocialHypertext.html

✦ "Personal Home Pages and the Construction of Identities on the Web" by Daniel Chandler **http://www.aber.ac.uk/~dgc/webident.html**

you use to create the page, your work is saved in a text or *ASCII* (*American Standard Code for Information Interchange*) file. The name of the file ends with the extension **.htm**. The image used here was created by starting with a photograph and putting it into a scanner, which created an image file. It's a picture of one of the authors. He's not that good looking, but if you want a copy of it to use for practice go to his home page, **http://www.mwc.edu/ernie**, put the mouse pointer on his picture and [Shift]+click (press [Shift] and click with the left button on the mouse), and you'll be able to save it in a file on your computer.

We're going to write the page in stages: first we'll write the HTML statements, then we'll save them to a file, and finally we'll use the Web browser to view what we've done so far. We'll use the text editor Notepad, which is part of the basic accessories for a Microsoft Windows system. Use whatever editor or word processor you'd like.

The steps we'll follow for this example are:

1. Start the editor.

2. Type the HTML for the heading section and the HTML and text for the items in Section A.

3. Create a **WebPages** directory.

4. Save the work into a file named **webpage1.htm**.

5. Use the Web browser to view the page.

6. Add the necessary HTML tags to create hyperlinks.

7. Repeat the previous three steps for Sections B and C.

8. Add the image near the top of the page and other information at the end of the page.

Now carry through with the steps.

 Start the editor.

Click the **Start** button, highlight **Programs**, highlight **Accessories**, and click on **Notepad**.

If you're using Microsoft Windows 95 or 98, click on the **Start** button, move the pointer to **Programs**, then move the pointer to **Accessories** and click on **Notepad**. If you're using a previous version of Windows, double-click on the icon **Accessories** and then double-click on the icon for **Notepad**.

Once Notepad starts you'll see a window similar to the one shown in Figure 6.27, except there won't be any text in the window.

❷ Type the HTML for the heading section and the HTML and text for the items in Section A.

✈ Just start typing the HTML and tags necessary for the items in Section A as shown in Figure 6.27.

Figure 6.27 shows the HTML tags and text necessary to have the items we mentioned in Section A displayed by a viewer.

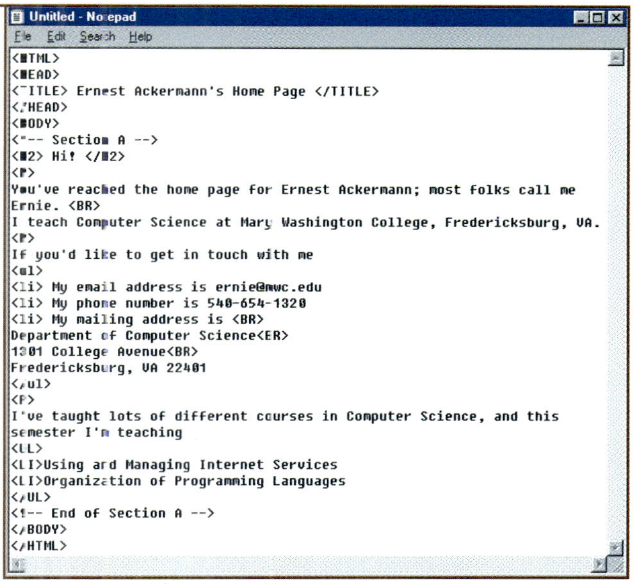

FIGURE 6.27
Initial Text and HTML Tags for Web Page

```
<HTML>
<HEAD>
<TITLE> Ernest Ackermann's Home Page </TITLE>
</HEAD>
<BODY>
<!-- Section A -->
<H2> Hi! </H2>
<P>
You've reached the home page for Ernest Ackermann; most folks call me
Ernie. <BR>
I teach Computer Science at Mary Washington College, Fredericksburg, VA.
<P>
If you'd like to get in touch with me
<ul>
<li> My email address is ernie@mwc.edu
<li> My phone number is 540-654-1320
<li> My mailing address is <BR>
Department of Computer Science<ER>
1301 College Avenue<BR>
Fredericksburg, VA 22401
</ul>
<P>
I've taught lots of different courses in Computer Science, and this
semester I'm teaching
<LL>
<LI>Using ard Managing Internet Services
<LI>Organization of Programming Languages
</UL>
<!-- End of Section A -->
</BODY>
</HTML>
```

To look at what's been done so far with a Web browser, you need to save the work to a file. To save a file while using Notepad, click on **File** in the menu bar, choose **Save As**, and then give a file name. You'll want to be sure of two things:

1. The name of the file ends with **.htm** or **.html**, such as **webpage1.htm**.

2. You know the name of the directory or folder that holds the file so you can find it later.

❸ Create a **WebPages** directory.

✈ Open Windows Explorer. Click the drive in which you wish to create the directory. From the menu bar, click on **File**, highlight **New**, and click on **Folder**. Key in **WebPages** and then press **Enter**.

If you have the opportunity, be sure to select an appropriate folder to hold the file. You might want to create a folder named **WebPages** to hold your work. Just to be specific for this example, the work will be saved in a file named **webpage1.htm** in a folder (directory) named **WebPages**.

195

4 Save the work into a file named **webpage1.htm**.

After you select **Save As** a dialog box will appear on the screen. Type **C:\WebPages\webpage1.htm** in the portion of the dialog box labeled **File name**. A dialog box is shown in Figure 6.28.

✛ Select **File**, then **Save As**. In the **File name** box, key in **C:\WebPages \webpage1.htm**.

5 Use the Web browser to view the page.

Be sure the Web browser is started. You don't have to connect to the Internet to view the file holding the Web page since it's a local file.

✛ Click on **File** in the menu bar and then select **Open Page**.

A dialog box will appear on the screen. It may not be set to the folder (directory) **WebPages**, which holds the file we want to view. If that's the case, type **C:\WebPages** in the open spot labeled **File name** and press **Enter**. After that you'll see a dialog box similar to the one in Figure 6.28.

✛ Click on **Choose File**.

FIGURE 6.28
Dialog Box

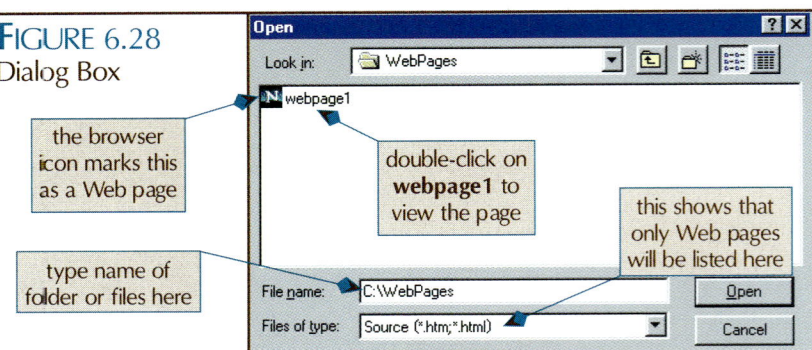

the browser icon marks this as a Web page

double-click on **webpage1** to view the page

this shows that only Web pages will be listed here

type name of folder or files here

✛ Double-click on the file name **webpage1**.

Double-clicking on the file name **webpage1** brings the Web page you've written to the Web browser. It's shown in Figure 6.29.

FIGURE 6.29
Web Browser View of **webpage1.htm**

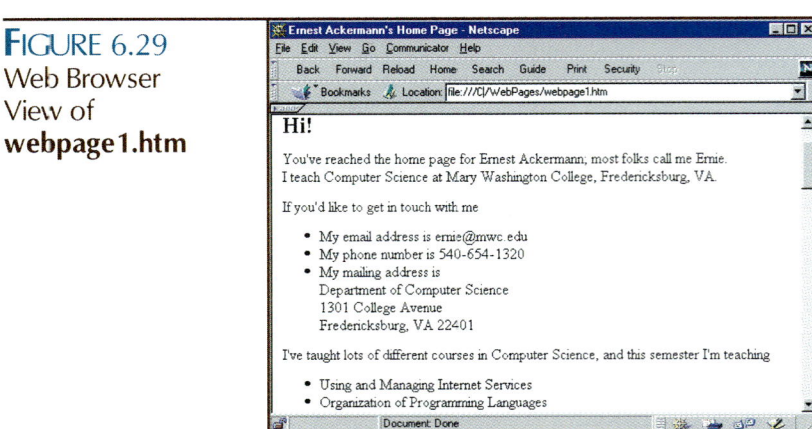

How do you like it? It's not bad, but we're going to change it just a little by adding some hyperlinks. Since the college has a home page, we'll add a hyperlink to that through the college's name and we'll also add a hyperlink so folks can send email by clicking on the email address on the screen. To do that we have to:

1. Use a word processor to edit the file holding the Web page.

2. Save the changes.

3. View the Web page with the browser again.

If both the editor and the browser are still on the screen, you have to click on the appropriate windows to use them. Otherwise, you need to start them.

⑥ Add the necessary HTML tags to create hyperlinks.

✚ To add hyperlinks to the page, return to Notepad and key in the HTML as shown to the right. Select **File** from the menu bar, click **Save**, then return to Netscape and click on **Reload** to view your changes.

To add the hyperlinks, we'll edit the source so that it now reads

```
I teach Computer Science at
<A HREF="http://www.mwc.edu">
Mary Washington College</A>,
Fredericksburg, VA.
…
<li> My email address is
<A HREF="mailto:ernie@mwc.edu">ernie@mwc.edu</A>
```

As you make changes to **webpage1.htm**, it's a good idea to keep viewing it. When you're trying new things, it's useful to be able to make changes and see what they look like almost immediately.

Figure 6.30 shows the portion of **webpage1.htm** with the hyperlinks added. We've pointed out the tags to add. Figure 6.31 shows the Web page as displayed by the browser.

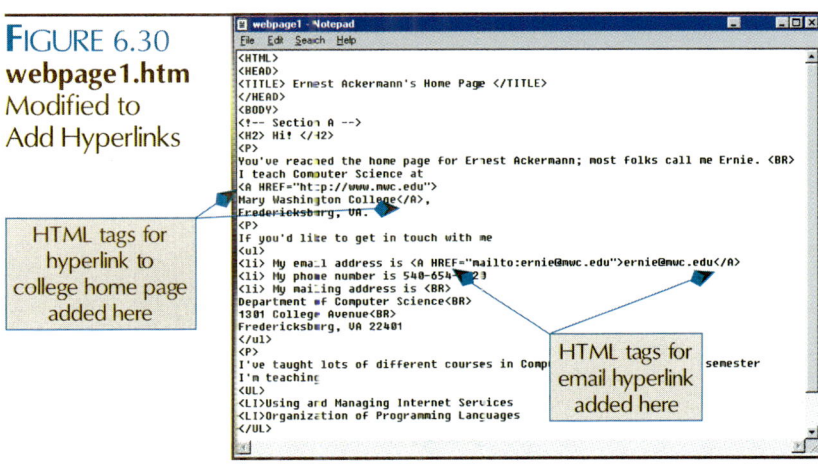

FIGURE 6.30
webpage1.htm
Modified to
Add Hyperlinks

HTML tags for hyperlink to college home page added here

HTML tags for email hyperlink added here

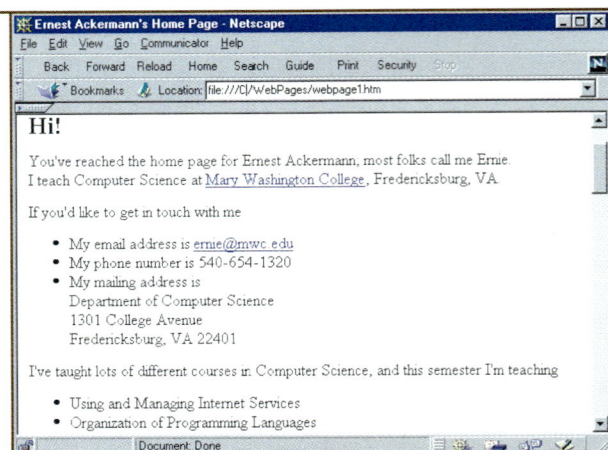

FIGURE 6.31
Viewing
webpage1.htm
After Saving
Changes and
Reloading

Repeat the previous three steps for Sections B and C.

Return to Notepad and key in the HTML and tags necessary for Sections B and C, as shown in Figure 6.32. Be sure to save your changes. In the browser window, click on the **Reload** button to view the additions to the Web page.

Now we need to add Sections B and C. In each case, you've got to add the text and HTML tags to the file **webpage1.htm** by using the editor or word processor to type in the changes. Be sure you save the changes. After each change you may want to view your work as we did above by clicking on the icon labeled **Reload** in the Netscape toolbar. Copies of recently viewed Web pages are kept in an area on the disk called the cache (there's likely to be a directory by that name in the folder that holds the browser program). When you ask to view a Web page, the browser checks to see if it's in the cache and uses that copy instead of going out on the Internet to get a new copy. This makes for faster display of some pages, but doesn't always give you the most recent version of a page. Clicking on **Reload** goes to the source for the page and brings in a new copy.

Figure 6.32 shows the HTML tags and text we've added for Sections B and C. Figure 6.33 shows the view through the browser.

FIGURE 6.32
Sections B
and C

```
webpage1 - Notepad
File  Edit  Search  Help
<HR>
<!-- Section B -->
<H3>Hobbies & Interests </H3>
In addition to teaching and working at the College I also like to spend time enjoying my
hobbies <B>gardening</B> and <B>photography</B>.<BR>
Here are a few gardening links I find useful.
<UL>
<LI> <A HREF="http://hammock.ifas.ufl.edu/txt/fairs/vh/17547.html">
Organic Vegetable Gardening</A>
<LI> <A HREF="http://www.av.qnet.com/~supak/org.htm">
Organic Gardening</A>
<LI> <A HREF="http://www.gardenweb.com/spdrsweb/">
The Garden Spider's Web</A>
<LI> Usenet newsgroup <A HREF="news:rec.gardens"> rec.gardens</A>
</UL>
I also enjoy photography -- got my first darkroom kit when I was 14. Here are a few
photography exhibits on the Web.
<UL>
<LI> <A HREF="http://www.nypl.org/research/chss/spe/art/photo/abbottex/abbot.html">
Berenice Abbott</A>
<LI> <A HREF="http://www.book.uci.edu/AdamsHome.html">
Ansel Adams: Fiat Lux</A>
<LI> <A HREF="http://interact.uoregon.edu/MediaLit/FA/MLVisul">Photographic Media</A>
<LI> <A HREF="http://www.cmp.ucr.edu/netscape.html">
UC/Riverside Museum of Photography</A>
</UL>
<!-- End of Section B -->
<HR>
<!-- Section C -->
<H3>Links to Other Places on the Web</H3>
These are a few places on the Web that I go to for information.
<UL>
<LI> <A HREF="http://www.webactive.com/webactive/home.html">
Web Active: What's New in Activism Online</A>
<LI> <A HREF="http://www.newslink.org/spot.html">
NewsLink, lists of Web sites for newspapers, magazines, broadcasters</A>
<LI> <A HREF="guide.infoseek.com"> InfoSeek Guide - Searching</A>
<LI> <A HREF="http://senplib.ucsd.edu/aboutnet/aboutnet.html"> UCSD Science and Engineering
Library - About the Net</A>
</UL>
```

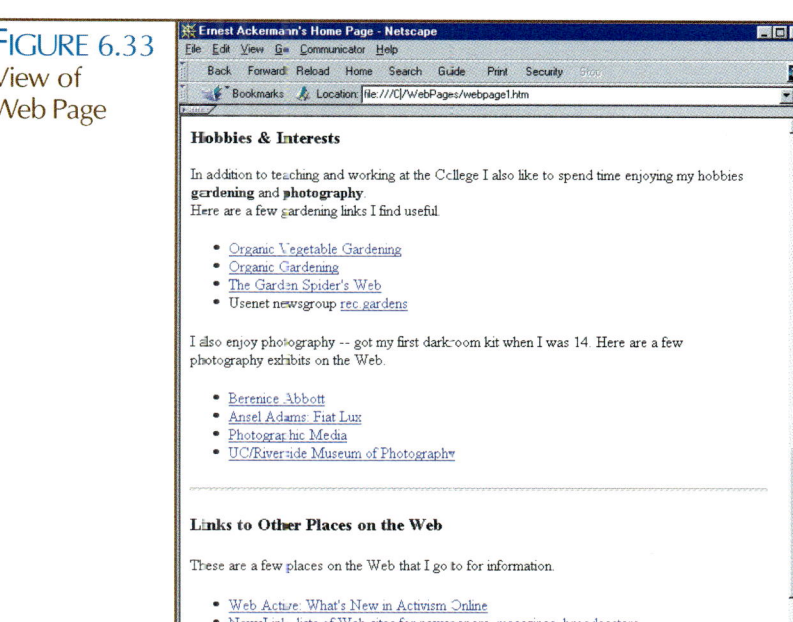

FIGURE 6.33
View of
Web Page

Add the image near the top of the page and other information at the end of the page.

To add the additional information to the page, return to Notepad and key in the HTML as shown to the right. Once again, save your changes before returning to Netscape and clicking on **Reload**.

We're going to add a picture at the top of the page and some information at the end. The picture is in a file in GIF (graphic interchange format) and we'll use an **IMG SRC** tag to display it. The information at the end includes an email address to use if readers have questions about the Web page, the name and email address of the person who created the page (it's always a good idea to sign your work), and the date the Web page was last modified or changed.

To add the image, we'll include the HTML tag for the image between the lines

```
<P>
You've reached the home page for Ernest Ackermann; most
folks call me Ernie. <BR>
```

in the source. With this addition the source now contains

```
<P>
<IMG ALIGN=RIGHT SRC="picture.gif">
You've reached the home page for Ernest Ackermann; most
folks call me Ernie. <BR>
```

Using **SRC="picture.gif"** implies the image is in the same directory as the Web page. We've made sure that's the case, so the Web page now looks like the one shown in Figure 6.34.

199

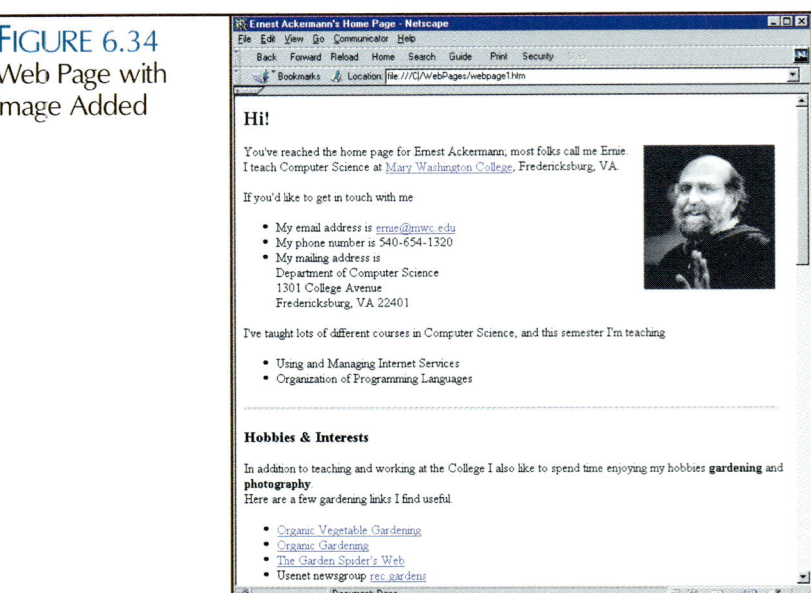

FIGURE 6.34
Web Page with
Image Added

To add the other information, we'll go to the line before

```
</HTML>
```

and add

```
<HR>
Please send any questions or comments about this page to
<A HREF="mailto:ernie@mwc.edu">ernie@mwc.edu </A> <BR>
Web page written and developed by Ernest Ackermann.<BR>
Last time anything was changed here: Saturday, March 28,
1998.<BR>
Thanks for visiting!
```

Figure 6.35 shows the end of the Web page after that material has been added to **webpage1.htm**.

FIGURE 6.35
New View of
Web Page

new material
displayed here

We've significantly changed the look of our Web page by adding hyperlinks, different types of lists, and an image. Let's call it done.

End of Example 6.1

Example 6.1 showed one possibility for a Web page design. A page to represent a business or organization needs to concentrate more on presenting an image of the organization, the services offered, and a means to get the reader involved in requesting information, services, or products. A page that focuses on a theme (such as guitars) or an event (such as an art exhibit) needs to present information, provide a means for folks to participate, and include hyperlinks to related resources or Web pages. Some pages are pure whimsy, entertainment, or playfulness. No matter what type of Web page you're constructing, think carefully about its purpose and design and search for Web pages with a similar topic or purpose before writing. We can learn a lot from looking at each other's work.

Tools to Help Create Web Pages

You saw in the previous section that to create Web pages you need an editor or word-processing program that lets you save your work in text or ASCII format. In fact, that's all you need to create relatively simple pages. When you have to create lots of pages or pages with lots of HTML, you'll want to use something that makes the task easier.

There are several programs that can help you create Web pages. Working with them is like working with a word processor. They have a menu bar and toolbar that let you create the page as you'd see it through a Web browser. The tags are often inserted automatically. For example, to create a hyperlink, you highlight text, click on the icon to create a link, and type the URL for the link in a dialog box. Several of the programs are shareware or make evaluation copies available on the World Wide Web. The current version of Netscape Communicator includes Composer, an easy to use, *visual Web page editor*. Several popular word-processing and spreadsheet programs include tools to save documents in HTML format. These are useful for situations in which a number of documents have to be converted or when documents have to be produced in two formats—for the printed page and for the Web.

To see lists of sites that provide tools for creating Web documents take a look at:

- "Resources for Creating Web Sites" **http://home .netscape.com/ browsers/createsites/ index.html**

- The Web Developer's Virtual Library, "VL-WWW: HTML_Editors" **http:// wdvl.internet.com/ Vlib/Authoring/ HTML_Editors.html**

- "Yahoo!—Computers and Internet : Software : Internet : World Wide Web : HTML Editors" **http:// dir.yahoo.com/ Computers_and _Internet/Software/ Internet/World _Wide_Web/ HTML_Editors/**

Style Guides—How to Do It Right, How to Do It for Impact, and How to Make It Portable

Now that you've learned the basics of creating a Web page, you ought to consider issues of style. That means thinking about how to create a Web page that is enjoyable to look at, easy to read, and effective. Creating an effective Web page deals with issues of content, HTML, and design, because the page has text, hyperlinks, and images. The two primary components are effective language and two dimensional design or layout skills. You'll also need an understanding of the technical issues involved in creating and viewing Web pages—a good understanding of HTML and the characteristics and limitations of Web browsers.

One difficulty with designing a Web page is that a number of technical conditions that affect the way a page looks can't be controlled—size and type of font set by the user, number of colors displayed on a monitor, and screen resolution of a monitor. Options can be set on a Web browser controlling the type and size of font used to display text, so text that looks "just right" in terms of size and placement may appear differently to different users.

There's no control over the type of monitor or display used to view a Web page. Some monitors will be set to display 16 colors, some 256 colors, and some millions of colors. An image that looks great on a display capable of displaying lots of colors may not look very good when fewer colors are available. The screen resolution or number of pixels in the viewing window affects the way the Web page appears. Images and text have their dimensions ultimately specified in terms of pixels regardless of what's being used to view them. The greater the number of pixels, the finer the resolution. An image on a screen with a resolution of 1,024 by 768 pixels will generally look better and be sharper than an image on a screen with a resolution of 800 by 600 pixels or 640 by 480 pixels. So an image that's 300 by 400 pixels, say, will appear much smaller on a screen whose resolution is 1,024 by 768 pixels than it will appear on a screen with a resolution of 640 by 480 pixels. Furthermore, the size of the browser window can be changed by the user. So as you design a page you need to think about what it will look like on different types of monitors and with different user configurations.

A middle-of-the-road approach would be to design a Web page so it looks good on a monitor that displays 256 colors and has a resolution of 800 by 600 pixels. Compromises have to be made, because it's impossible to predict the type of monitor used and the way the Web browser options are set.

There are also a number of style elements that you can control to create appealing and effective Web pages.

✦ **Use HTML that most browsers can deal with.**

The HTML presented in this chapter can be interpreted by most browsers, but other HTML tags aren't always interpreted in the same way by all Web browsers. So the HTML you use in a Web page ought to be chosen to give the page the format you'd like and be viewable in that format by most Web browsers; not everyone will be using Netscape Navigator. Try viewing a Web page with different browsers to learn what works best.

There is no agreement on all aspects of HTML among the different Web browsers. What works in one browser may not work in another. You've probably seen comments on some pages that say the page is "optimized for Netscape" or "works best with Netscape." That's because some tags are used that the Netscape browser understands, while other browsers don't. Likewise there are HTML tags that some browsers interpret while the Netscape browser doesn't. (That's one of the reasons we're concentrating on basic HTML, tags that most browsers recognize, in this chapter.) Why do we have these differences? The features that one browser can support and others cannot are what distinguish one browser from another. At the present time there are several companies that want to establish themselves as the leader in the field of providing Web browsers. Netscape has held that position. Its move to give its browser the capabilities to interpret interactive elements and elements with animation, such as JavaScript, Java applets, and inline plug-ins, was meant to allow it to keep that position. Microsoft with its browser, Internet Explorer, soon followed Netscape's lead. Most browsers support the tags in HTML version 3.0, and there is an international effort to get HTML 4.0 adopted by the primary Web browsers. To read more about current trends and

developments regarding HTML look at the Web page "Hyper-Text Markup Language Home Page," **http://www.w3.org/**.

✦ **Use relatively small images and limit the number of images in a Web page.**

It can take many bytes to represent an image, which means it may take a long time for someone to view a Web page with many images or a large image. We'll calculate how long it would take to display an image whose size is 54K (kilobytes) being received on a computer that's using a 28.8 Kbps (kilobits per second) modem. The modem can receive information at a rate of about 28,800 bits per second. Since each byte consists of 8 bits, the modem can receive information at $28,800/8 = 3,600$ bytes per second. Since the size of the file holding the image is approximately 54,000 bytes, it takes $54,000/3,600 = 15$ seconds to deliver the image to the browser. Notice we're ignoring any delay due to Internet traffic. Some, but not all, folks might be willing to wait that long for the image. If several images that size are on the page, the wait becomes unreasonable. One thing to do is to represent the image on the page by a

small version called a thumbnail. Another possibility is to reduce the number of colors in the image (this is also called reducing the color depth) so the image can be represented with fewer bytes. Either can be made into a hyperlink to the full image. This gives access to the image in all its glory, but doesn't necessarily delay viewing the entire Web page.

✦ **Use proper grammar and spelling.**

You want your page to be effective and well received. Grammatical or spelling errors don't give a good impression of you and can turn off a reader pretty quickly.

✦ **Use proper spacing and emphasis.**

Let the spacing reflect the organization of the text and content of the Web page. If the page has several distinct sections, separate them with a horizontal rule (**<HR>**) or blank spaces. Use bold or italic font appropriately. Section headings ought to be emphasized as well as important subsections or words. On the other hand, you need not overdo the use of spacing, horizontal rules or shadow lines, and emphasized text. Because something can be done, doesn't mean it has to be done.

- **Include an email address for comments, the name of the author/designer/producer, the URL for the page, and the date the Web page was last modified.**

These items are usually placed at the end of the Web page. The email address is there in case someone reading the page has a question or suggestions about the Web page or its content. You can use the mailto URL to give the email address a hyperlink; clicking on it will bring up a window to create an email message. Web pages ought to contain the name(s) of the person(s) responsible for developing the Web page. It gives credit and responsibility where they are due. The URL for the page is included so that someone reading it will know how to reach it on the Web in case the page is printed or reproduced in some other manner. Knowing when something was changed last is helpful for readers to keep track of the most recent version of a document, and it also gives an indication of how timely the content of the Web page is.

- **Rather than create long documents,** create a collection of shorter ones with a table of contents.

The difficulty with long documents is that they may take a long time to transfer before they can be viewed, and it's more time consuming to scroll or page through to find appropriate information. It's generally better to divide a long Web page into several smaller ones, and provide a contents page, making the items in the table of contents hyperlinks to the appropriate sections.

- **Think about what you're going to write, and think about the layout before writing the HTML.**

There's no substitute for planning and good design. Take the time to think about what you want to do and how you can do it.

Here's a list of selected HTML style guides available on the World Wide Web:

- "About the Artist," **http://www .ankiewicz.com/ artist/WebRant .html,** by K. Ankiewicz. Information and opinions about using images.

- "Composing Good HTML," **http://www.cs .cmu.edu/~tilt/cgh,** by E. Tilton. The author says this doesn't "purport" to be a style guide, but it contains lots of excellent information on topics such as "Common Errors" and "Things to Avoid."

- "Elements of HTML Style," **http://www.book .uci.edu/Staff/ StyleGuide.html,** by J. K. Cohen. Gives the basic rules for HTML style. Also contains hyperlinks to other style documents.

- "Guide to Style," **http://www.sun .com/styleguide,** by R. Levine. A helpful guide from some of the staff at Sun Microsystems.

- "Sucky to Savvy," **http://jeffglover .com/ss.html,** by J. Glover. An item-by-item guide to style elements in Web pages with recommendations for their use.

- "Why the Web Sucks II,"

http:// www.spies.com/ ~ceej/Words/ rant.web.html, by C. J. Silverio. Silverio doesn't mince words, and her opinions are sound. Includes hyperlinks to examples of good and bad Web pages.

✦ "Yale C/AIM Web Style Guide," **http://info.med .yale.edu/caim/ manual/index.html**, by P. J. Lynch and S. Horton. The most complete and authoritative style manual available on the Web. A must to read and put into your bookmark list for future reference.

Putting Your Information on the WWW

To make your Web pages available to everyone else on the Internet, the Web page and all supporting files have to be placed on the computer that's acting as the Web server. That computer is running the software and has the Internet connections so that information on it can be retrieved by using a URL that starts with **http://**. Most Internet service providers provide this service to their customers, either for an extra fee or for free. If you're at an educational institution or commercial organization, there are likely to be specific procedures and policies you have to follow to make your Web page available to the rest of the WWW. You'll have to check the policies and procedures for your situation.

Once you put your page(s) on a Web server, you're a (Web) published author! One of the great things about the Internet is that it's almost as easy to be an information provider as it is to be an information consumer. There are a number of ways to publicize your Web page. If your Web page is a personal page, you can list it at any site mentioned in the tip on pages 191–93.

If the Web page is the home page for a business, organization, event, or anything else then it's not appropriate to use those services. There are lots of other services to use and other ways to publicize a Web page.

You can announce your page by submitting it to several special locations on the World Wide Web: What's New Web pages, Web directories, and search engines. These services give you forms to fill out telling the URL for your page, your name and email address, and some descriptive information about the Web page. Depending on the workload, it may take a service several days or even weeks to list your Web page. There's generally no charge to have a Web page listed by these services. Some services are selective about what's listed and may not list the page. "Netscape What's New," **http:// home.netscape.com/ netcenter/new.html**, lists only selected sites, ones which they consider are advancing the technology of the Web. This contrasts with "What's New Too!" **http://nu2.com**, which lists any announcement that's sent. Most of the directories we've mentioned in Chapter 4 accept submissions of URLs, and Yahoo! makes a daily list available of recently added Web pages, **http://www.yahoo .com/new**. When you submit a request to be listed in a directory you'll also have to pick the category that has the page listing. To choose the appropriate category, find pages on the same or similar topic within the directory and use the same category. You can also submit an announcement of your page to a mailing list and to Usenet newsgroups.

In addition to the individual services and sites, there are Web pages that can be used to submit a URL to several at once. Three of these are:

- ✦ "Information City Promote Your Site" **http://www .FreeReports.net/ submit.html**

- ✦ "SiteOwner.Com" **http://siteowner .linkexchange.com**

- ✦ "Submit It!" **http://www. submit-it.com**

Some directories have designated sections you can use to announce or publicize a Web page. Two of these are:

- ✦ The section "Internet > Web publishing > Site promotion" in the Infoseek directory **http:// infoseek.go.com/ internet/ web_publishing/ web_site_promotion**

- ✦ The section "Computers and Internet: Internet:World Wide Web:Announcement Services" in the Yahoo! directory **http://www. yahoo.com/ computers_and _internet/internet/ world_wide_web/ announcement _services**

Three documents that give a comprehensive list of services and sites to use for announcing a Web page are:

- ✦ "FAQ: How to Announce Your New Web Site" **http://ep.com/ faq/webannounce .html**

- ✦ "How To Publicize Your Web Site Over The Internet" **http://www .samizdat.com/ public.html**

- ✦ "Internet Infoscavenger's Search Engine Pointers" **http://www .infoscavenger.com/ engine.htm**

Getting your Web page announced properly can take some work, but people are going to have to know about it in order to find it among the millions of pages on the World Wide Web.

Resources for More Information on Creating Web Pages

There's lots of help on the World Wide Web for creating Web pages and using HTML. Most of the major directories

(such as Yahoo! or Excite) have sections on the topic, several discussion groups and newsgroups deal with HTML and authoring at basic and advanced levels, and there are several tutorials you can use with a Web browser to help you learn. We'll give some more details about each of those areas below. In addition to what follows, you'll want to check your favorite library or bookstore—either in person or via the Internet—for books that deal with designing and constructing Web pages and Web sites.

LISTINGS IN DIRECTORIES. Look at these sections of directories for information about HTML:

- ✦ "Excite Computers and Internet / Web Page Design" **http://www. excite.com/ computers_and _internet/internet/ web_page_design**

- ✦ "The Virtual Library of WWW Development" **http://wdvl.internet .com/Vlib**

DISCUSSION GROUPS. Discussion groups are a way to share information and get questions answered. All the communication is carried on through email. For more information about using a discussion group see the Web page **dgroups.html** on the disk included with this book. Refer to these discussion groups for information about HTML:

- ❖ "HTML-L, HTML Assistance Mailing List"
  To subscribe, send email to
  listserv@vm3090 .ege.edu.tr
  with the body of the message being
  SUBSCRIBE HTML-L your-full-name.

- ❖ "ADV-HTML, Advanced HTML Discussion List"
  To subscribe, send email to
  listserv@ua1vm .ua.edu
  with the body of the message being
  SUBSCRIBE ADV-HTML your-full-name.

A list of other discussions groups is kept in the document "World Wide Web Mailing Lists," **http://www.w3.org/ Mail/Lists.html**.

NEWSGROUPS. Usenet newsgroups are another way to share information and get questions answered through group discussion. The disk included with this book contains general information about Usenet newsgroups and instructions for getting your browser set for Usenet newsgroups. To read it use your browser to open the Web page **Usenet.htm** on the disk. There are several newsgroups that deal with the issues of authoring Web pages:

- ❖ **comp.infosystems. www.authoring .html**
  Discussion of issues related to HTML in terms of usage, standards, etc.

- ❖ **comp.infosystems. www.authoring.images**
  Discussion of issues related to the use of images within Web pages.

- ❖ **comp.infosystems .www.authoring .misc**
  Discussion on any topics related to writing Web pages.

TUTORIALS AND GUIDES. There are several very good guides and tutorials for creating Web pages:

- ❖ "A Guide to URLs"
  http://www .netspace.org/ users/dwb/url-guide.html
  A useful guide to the different URL formats.

- ❖ "GDLabs Design-O Rama"
  http://www .glassdog.com/ design-o-rama/
  An interesting and lively set of lessons and commentary about Web site design and construction.

- ❖ "Know the Code: HTML for Beginners"
  http://www.cnet .com/Content/ Builder/Authoring/ Basics/
  A straightforward introduction from CNET's builder.com.

- ❖ "NCSA—A Beginner's Guide to HTML"
  http://www.ncsa .uiuc.edu/General/ Internet/WWW/ HTMLPrimer.html
  An excellent tutorial to take you through the basics of using HTML.

Summary

Web pages are text or ASCII files in which HTML, hypertext markup language, is used to specify the format of the Web page, images to be displayed, hyperlinks, and possibly other elements. A Web browser interprets the HTML in the file, called the source file, and then displays the Web page. So one part of the task of writing Web pages is learning how to use HTML to design and implement appropriate and effective pages.

The source file for a Web page consists of text, URLs, and other elements along with tags or directives written according to the rules of HTML. Most HTML tags are enclosed between < and >. Some tags occur in pairs with the second being like the first, except a slash is used after < to indicate it's the matching tag; for example, <I> and </I>. Other tags occur as single entities, such as <P>. Tags can be written using upper- or lowercase letters; HTML ignores the case of letters in a tag. In URLs you have to pay strict attention to the case of the letters. An HTML document ought to have two parts, a heading and a body. The heading contains the title for the Web page, and the body holds the content—what will be displayed on the Web page. HTML tags can be used for some control over vertical spacing, such as ending lines and starting paragraphs, but otherwise most horizontal and vertical spacing within a source file is ignored. The browser takes care of fitting the page within its window. HTML tags are also used to specify up to six levels of headings in a document and control whether text is displayed in bold, italic, or plain font. Lists—numbered, with bullets, or descriptive—can be specified with HTML tags. HTML is also used to create and specify hyperlinks and place images within a Web page. The hyperlinks start with a tag of the form **<A HREF ="URL">** (where you substitute an actual URL for *URL*), followed by text or a tag for an image, and then terminated with **</A>**. The following:

```
It appears that <A HREF="http://www.mwc.edu/ernie/index.html">
Ernest Ackermann</A> is the culprit!
```

would appear on a Web page as

It appears that <u>Ernest Ackermann</u> is the culprit!

Clicking, in the Web page, on **Ernest Ackermann** would cause the browser to open the location associated with **http://www .mwc.edu/ernie/index.html**. Images are put into Web pages by using a tag in the form of **<IMG SRC="URL">** where the URL of an image is substituted for *URL*. The image needs to be either in GIF or JPEG format to be displayed by the Web browser. Text can be aligned with an image, either at the top, middle, or bottom. Images can be placed to the left or right of text. HTML does have lots of other tags; we've covered the most basic ones in this chapter.

Since a source file is in text format, it can be created with any editor or word processor that allows you to save a file in text or ASCII form. No special program to create a Web page is necessary, but when there's lots to do or you have to convert from another format to a Web document, it's useful to have a program designed to create Web pages. Some are available as shareware, some free, and some must be purchased before using them. Several directory lists of these programs are given.

Learning HTML is one part of being able to create interesting and effective Web pages. You also need to be concerned with the content and the layout of the content. Two dimensional design skills are as important as technical skills.

How a Browser Interprets HTML

The source with text, hyperlinks, and html tags for images	Your browser takes in all the elements from the source	Your browser proudly displays the Web page to you

There are a number of technical items over which the Web page designer or author has no control such as the resolution and number of colors available on the monitor used to view the Web page. A number of tips for good style are listed along with a list of style guides available on the Web.

Putting a page on the World Wide Web means that the file(s) that contain the text, images, and other elements on the page have to be placed on a computer that's acting as a Web server. You need to check with your organization, school, business, or Internet service provider to find out the policies and appropriate procedures for your situation. Once the page is accessible through the World Wide Web or Internet and its URL has been assigned, you can start announcing or publicizing it. A list of several different ways to announce a Web page have been given previously in this chapter.

Designing, creating, or writing a Web page is generally very satisfying. You create something and then let millions of folks around the world see it. Before making the page available to the world, you can develop it on your computer and view it with your Web browser. When you need help or want to pursue the topic further there are a number of resources, guides, newsgroups, and mailing lists on the Web to give help in creating or authoring Web pages. What fun! ✦

Selected Terms in This Chapter

American Standard Code for Information Interchange (ASCII)
element
HTML tag
hyperlink

hypertext markup language (HTML)
personal home page
source
text editor

text file
Uniform Resource Locator (URL)
visual Web page editor
Web page

1. a. Does your organization, school, company, or Internet service provider have a home page? What's the URL?
   b. Take a look at the source view for the Web page in question a. What's in the heading section?
   c. To whom do you send email for suggestions or comments?
   d. When was the page last modified?

2. Suppose you've created a personal home page.
   a. Find out the steps necessary to get the page on the World Wide Web.
   b. What are the rules for the page's content? Can you put anything at all on the page?

3. Make some modifications to the Web page in Example 6.1.
   a. Replace the items in Section A so it describes what you do professionally or the classes you're taking.
   b. Replace the items in Sections B and C to reflect your interests.
   c. If you've got a picture or image in digital form, replace the image that was used in the text.

4. Suppose the file named **bobo.gif** holds an image in GIF, and it's in the folder or directory named **c:\exercise**. To answer the following questions, supply the HTML tags to accomplish the task described.
   a. Write the HTML necessary and sufficient to display the image as part of a Web page.
   b. Write the HTML necessary and sufficient so the image appears on the page as a hyperlink without any attached text. When someone clicks on it, the current Web page is replaced by a page consisting only of the image.
   c. Write the HTML necessary and sufficient so the image appears as part of a Web page. Next to the image are the words "enter at your own risk." The words

function as a hyperlink to **http://www.mwc.edu/~ernie/funhouse.html**, but clicking on the picture does nothing.

5. Write the HTML necessary to display the list
   Dave
   Marsha
   John
   Rita
   Ernie

   a. as
      1. Dave
      2. Marsha
      3. John
      4. Rita
      5. Ernie

   b. as
      • Dave
      • Marsha
      • John
      • Rita
      • Ernie

   c. as
      1. Dave
      2. Marsha
         • John
         • Rita
      3. Ernie

6. Create a Web page that's
   a. a personal Web page for your instructor, spouse, or boss.
   b. a Web page for a small business.
   c. a Web page for a major entertainment or sports figure.
   d. a Web page for a candidate for political office.

7. The Argus Clearinghouse, **http://www.clearinghouse.net**, is a Web site and virtual library—it collects, reviews, and rates sources. The rating system it uses is described on the Web page "Ratings System," **http://www.clearinghouse.net/ratings.html**.

a. Use the Clearinghouse's rating system to evaluate each of the following Web sites:

- ✚ BUBL Link 610 Medical sciences, medicine
  http://link.bubl.ac.uk/medicine/
- ✚ On Health
  **http://www.onhealth.com/ch1/
  0,1091,,00.htm**
- ✚ Martindale's Health Science Guide
  **http://www-sci.lib.uci.edu/~martindale/
  MedicalResources.html**
- ✚ Medical Matrix
  http://www.medmatrix.org/index.asp

b. Is the Clearinghouse's rating system useful in helping decide which of the Web sites would be more suitable for you? Why or why not?

8. The HTML tag **<BODY BACKGROUND="URL">**, where *URL* is the URL of an image file, makes that file the background for the Web page. That's the way some folks put a colorful background on their Web pages. Take a look at the source for the Web page at **http://www.mwc.edu/ernie/InternetToday/background.html** for an example of the use of a background color.

a. Using a Web page you've written change the tag **<BODY>** to **<BODY BACKGROUND="http://www.mwc.edu/ernie/purp.gif">** and view the resulting Web page.

b. You may want to use other backgrounds. A collection of backgrounds is available at Texture Land, **http://www.meat.com/textures/**. Go to that site, retrieve a texture, and use it in one of your Web pages.

9. A World Wide Web service named CRAYON (**http://crayon.net**), which stands for CReAte Your Own Newspaper, lets you create a newspaper by automatically constructing a Web page based on your choices of news sources.

a. Using CRAYON, create a Web newspaper for your-self. Print a copy of the source document.

b. Without using CRAYON, create a Web newspaper for yourself.

c. Create a newsletter that carries information about a specific topic. For example, you might want to create one about health, bicycling, a specific sport, a specific type of music, or stock market prices.

10. Create a Web page that tells the reader about an interest or a hobby of yours. Make it interesting and informative. Include hyperlinks to some of the most important Web pages and WWW resources related to the subject or hobby.

11. Suppose you're in the business of creating Web pages for others. Design and build a Web page that describes your services and shows your work.

TELNET, FTP, AND GOPHER

As we've seen, there are lots of resources and information on the World Wide Web. But remember that the popularity of the World Wide Web is a fairly recent development. Mosaic, the first graphical Web browser made available to the public, was released in November 1993, and people were using the Internet for 20 years before that. Information was and is still shared on the Internet through the services or protocols Telnet, FTP, and Gopher. *Telnet* allows login access to another computer on the Internet. It's used to execute programs (like database searches) on remote computers. *FTP, file transfer protocol*, is the basic means of copying a file from one computer system to another. *Gopher*, made available in 1991, became an extremely popular service because it gave access to information and services on the Internet through a relatively easy-to-use menu system. These days most resources are available through a Web-browser interface and there are few active Gopher sites.

Protocols are the rules by which clients and servers on the Internet exchange information. Each service has different protocols. You can tell the protocol being used by looking at the URL for a resource. You would use the URL **http://lcweb .loc.gov**, for example, to go to the home page for the Library of Congress. The protocol here, **http**, brings a Web page, with images and formatted text, to your browser. The Library of Congress also provides access to its resources through:

Telnet: The URL **telnet:// locis.loc.gov** connects you to a remote computer so you can search the library's holdings.

FTP: Use the URL **ftp:// lcweb.loc.gov** to copy files without viewing them first.

Gopher: The URL **gopher:// lcweb.loc.gov** takes you to a menu-oriented (little text and no images) interface to basically the same information available on a Web page.

Telnet

When you are working on a computer connected to the Internet, you are part of a system of networks composed of over 40 million computers. Networks are often designed to allow users on one computer in the network to access information or run programs on another computer on the network. The Internet allows for that possibility through the service named Telnet. The service was created so that an Internet user at one site (the local site) could access facilities, software, or data at another site (the remote site). When you use Telnet on your computer to contact another computer system on the Internet, it's as if you are directly connected to the remote system. Naturally, you have to have permission to use the remote system. Some sites require a login name and a password, whereas others don't.

Telnet gives access to several bulletin boards and community network systems, online databases, and some library catalogs. When you use Telnet you're going to log in to another computer system, and you will have to use the commands for that system. Sometimes that takes you into unfamiliar territory. You'll also find that the response from the remote system may not seem smooth or may be slow. Some of that has to do with the fact that you're communicating with the remote system over the Internet.

What you type and the response from the remote system is transmitted as a collection of packets that have to be sent, received, and assembled. Because of these limitations, you may want to use Telnet only when the resource you need isn't available any other way. Many of the services that used to be available only through Telnet are now available as Web pages and are generally easier to use that way.

Here are some examples of resources available through Telnet:

Library of Congress	**telnet://locis.loc.gov**	**Search for materials available through the Library of Congress. No login name or password is required.**
PENpages	**telnet://penpages.psu.edu**	**Search for and retrieve information from agricultural, health, teaching, and other databases. This service is provided by the College of Agriculture of the Pennsylvania State University and the Pennsylvania Department of Education. You type the word world when you see the prompt Username:.**
Weather underground	**telnet://cirrus.sprl.umich.edu:3000**	**Retrieve weather reports.**

The Form of a URL for Telnet

You can see from these examples that the URL for a Telnet resource starts with the word **telnet**, a colon (**:**), and two slashes (**//**), as in **telnet://**.

That's followed by the domain name or IP address of the computer system that provides the service available through Telnet. In some cases the domain name is followed by a colon (:) and a number, as in **telnet://cirrus** **.sprl.umich.edu:3000**, the URL for the Weather underground at the University of Michigan. That number at the end is called a *port number*. This form is used at some remote sites so an Internet user doesn't have to give a login name. The remote site automatically starts a program or service when your Telnet client makes the connection. You need to know this form if you're going to open the location and type in the URL yourself. In many cases, however, you'll probably use Telnet by clicking on a hyperlink in a Web document.

Configuring Your Browser for Telnet

In order to use Telnet with your Web browser, you need a Telnet program on your computer with the proper option so the browser knows the name of the file to use for Telnet applications. To see if your browser is set for Telnet use, start the browser, click on the location field, and type in one of the URLs listed above. If you get connected, then all is well. If you get the message "Unable to find application," then Telnet isn't available. Once you have a Telnet client on your computer you can set Netscape to work with it by clicking on **Edit** in the menu bar, selecting **Preferences**, clicking on **Navigator**, and then clicking on **Applications**. Then click on **New Type** and fill in **URL:Telnet Protocol** for **Description of type**, put only a space in the fields **File extension** and **MIME Type**, and put the path to the Telnet application files in

the field **Application to use**, as shown in Figure 7.1.

There may be a copy of Telnet on your computer. First, ask whether Telnet is on your computer or if it came with the software you received from your Internet provider. The standard installation of Windows 95 puts a Telnet program in the directory or folder **Windows**. If that doesn't help, see if you can find a Telnet program already on the computer. Use the tools for searching directories and folders for a program or application whose name starts with **Telnet**. If you're using Windows 95, select **Windows Explorer** from the Start menu, click on **Tools** from the menu bar, then select **Find** and then **Files or Folders**. Type **telnet*** for the name of the file to find. This may tell you if a copy of a Telnet client is on your computer. (A Telnet program could be on the computer under a different name.) If you find a copy, note its location so you'll be all set when we get to the section describing how to configure Netscape Navigator to use Telnet.

If there is no copy of Telnet on your computer, you might want to retrieve one from the Internet. There are several available; some are shareware and some are freeware. If the program is shareware, you're encouraged to copy it to your

computer, try it for a while, and then send the author a fee for a full-fledged version of the program. If the program is freeware, you can copy it to your computer and use it without any cost.

These steps tell you how to get a copy of Telnet from the Internet, install it, and set the proper Netscape Navigator preference so you can use it. If you already have a copy of Telnet on your computer go to Step 4.

1. Find a location on the Internet that has Telnet programs to fit into your environment.

If you're working in a Windows environment, you can find a collection of programs that work well at the "Terminals and Telnet" section of WinFiles.com, a large collection of shareware for Windows 95/98 computer systems. Use the URL **http://www.winfiles.com/apps/98/terminals.html** for information about several Telnet programs. (WinFiles.com is a popular shareware site, and it's worth a visit to the home page, **http://www.winfiles.com**.)

For other sources, take a look at the Web site "Nerd's Heaven," **http://boole.stanford.edu/nerdsheaven.html**. It lists several resources for shareware and freeware.

2. Retrieve a Telnet program.

There are likely to be several Telnet programs listed at one site. How to decide which to choose? Be sure you pick a program that will work in your environment—for example, don't select a program designed for a Macintosh computer to use with Windows 95. You'll also want to be sure to select one that emulates or mimics a **vt100** terminal. A number of resources available through Telnet require vt100 emulation. Other things that might affect your choice are the program's features and its cost. We'll work here with the shareware program NetTerm. It works well and is inexpensive. It's available at several places on the Internet. One spot is the NetTerm Web page "Downloads," **http:// starbase.neosoft.com/ ~zkrr01/html/downloads .html**.

After you retrieve shareware you can take your time evaluating the program. If you decide to use it regularly, register the program and send payment to the author.

Regardless of which Telnet package you choose, retrieve the program. After clicking on a hyperlink for the program, you might get the message "No Viewer Configured for File Type:

application/x-zip-compressed" from Netscape Navigator. That's because the file holding the program is stored in compressed format using a program named PKZIP or WinZip, and your Web browser doesn't have those programs installed as helper programs to automatically uncompress the file after it's been transmitted. That's just fine; select the option that lets you **Save File...** A **Save As..** dialog box pops up for you to specify the folder to use to store the file. Create a new folder to hold the file and save it there. Working with compressed files is discussed in the section in this chapter on FTP. If PKZIP or WinZip isn't on your computer or network, you'll have to retrieve one of them from the Internet as well. A URL for a version of PKZIP is **http://www.pkware.com/ download.html**, and a URL for a version of WinZip is **http:// www.winzip.com/ddchome .htm**. Use the URL **http:// www.pkware.com** to read more about PKZIP, and use the URL **http://www.winzip.com/ winzip** to go to the WinZip home page.

3. Uncompress and install the Telnet program.

After retrieving the program you'll have to uncompress it and then install the software. Let's say

you've retrieved the file **nt32427i.exe** from **http:// starbase.neosoft.com/ ~zkrr01/html/downloads .html**. It's in *zipped* format—you need to *unzip* it—but it's stored as a self-extracting zip file. With a compression program on your computer all you have to do is click on the name of the file and follow the instructions to install the file. The setup program takes care of everything and should install the program NetTerm. You can now safely delete the folder you created to hold the file you downloaded from **starbase .neosoft.com**.

4. Set the preferences for Netscape Navigator.

Click on **Edit** in the menu bar, select **Preferences**, click on **Navigator**, and then click on **Applications**. That brings up the applications panel. Then click on the button labeled **New Type** and fill in **URL:Telnet Protocol** for **Description of type**, put only a space in the fields **File extension** and **MIME Type**, and put the path to the Telnet application files in the field **Application to use**. We show the entries filled in the "New Type" form in Figure 7.1. There we typed **c:\Netterm\netterm .exe %1** since that's where we put the NetTerm program. If you're going to use the Telnet that's included with Windows 95, you'd type **c:\windows\ telnet.exe %1** instead.

After it's typed in click on the button labeled **OK**. That makes Netscape aware of the program you'll be using for Telnet.

If you find these steps too difficult, ask for some help from a friend or local expert.

After you've set up Telnet it's ready to be used when necessary. Suppose you were perusing the Library of Congress' Web site and came upon the Web page "The Library of Congress Catalogs," **http://lcweb .loc.gov/catalog**. That page describes different ways to search the Library of Congress catalogs. One way to search is by giving commands to search and browse the catalogs. This is done through LOCIS, (the Library of Congress Information System). We point out two hyperlinks in Figure 7.2. One is a hyperlink that starts a Telnet session to LOCIS and the other describes LOCIS. The Library of Congress has a Web page that gives some pointers. Suppose you want to search for books by a particular author or search on a specific subject. If you click on the hyperlink shown in Figure 7.2, you'll go to a Web page that has a hyperlink to LOCIS as well as some tips about using LOCIS and using Telnet from a Web browser. From there you'll

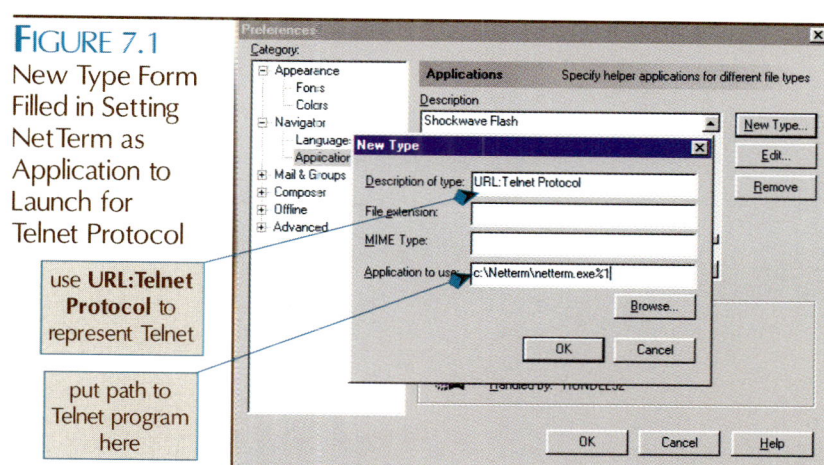

FIGURE 7.1
New Type Form Filled in Setting NetTerm as Application to Launch for Telnet Protocol

use **URL:Telnet Protocol** to represent Telnet

put path to Telnet program here

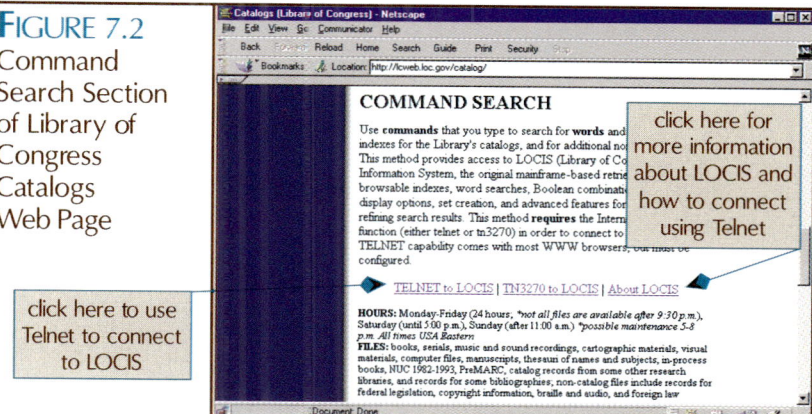

FIGURE 7.2
Command Search Section of Library of Congress Catalogs Web Page

click here to use Telnet to connect to LOCIS

be able to search information held by the Library of Congress by using Telnet.

Here's another possible scenario. A friend tells you how you can look up weather reports for the U.S. by using Telnet to connect to **cirrus.sprl.umich .edu** at port **3000**. You click on the location field, type in **telnet://cirrus.sprl.umich .edu:3000**, press , and away you go. Figure 7.3 shows the location field filled in with the URL for accessing weather reports.

Be flexible.

Remember that the Web is always changing and that your results may differ from those shown in the examples. Don't let this confuse you. The examples demonstrate fundamental skills that don't change, even though the results obtained or the actual screens may vary. ◆

FIGURE 7.3
Location Field
Filled in with
URL for NHL
Schedules

Bookmarks   Go to: telnet://cirrus.sprl.umich.edu:3000

EXAMPLE 7.1

Using a Telnet Client

In this example we're going to use a Telnet client program—one that's on your computer—to access a site on the Internet. Specifically, we'll contact LOCIS at the Library of Congress. We won't give the details of using LOCIS because that's not really pertinent to using the Telnet client. We'll leave that to you to explore on your own.

We're going to be using the Telnet client that comes with Windows. We're assuming that the browser is started and set to access the Windows Telnet client when it comes across a Telnet URL. That's the way Netscape is usually set up on a computer.

We're going to connect to the Library of Congress Information System, LOCIS. You can browse or search some of the library catalogs available through the Web site for the Library of Congress.

Assuming that Netscape Navigator is already started, here are the steps to follow:

1. Go to the Library of Congress' Web page, "The Library of Congress Catalogs."

2. Select the hyperlink **Command Search**.

3. Start a Telnet session by clicking on the hyperlink **Telnet to LOCIS**.

4. Select an item from the menu.

5. End the Telnet session.

◆ Go to the Library of Congress' Web page, "The Library of Congress Catalogs."

✚ Click on the location field; it will change color.

Figure 7.4 shows a portion of the Web page. We'll click on the hyperlink **Command Search** to get to the portion of the page that has a hyperlink to LOCIS. Before doing that you may want to take a look at some of the other sections of this Web page. For example, the hyperlink **Other Research Tools** takes you to a list of other tools you may want to use in a research project.

✦ Type in **http://lcweb .loc.gov/catalog** and press Enter.

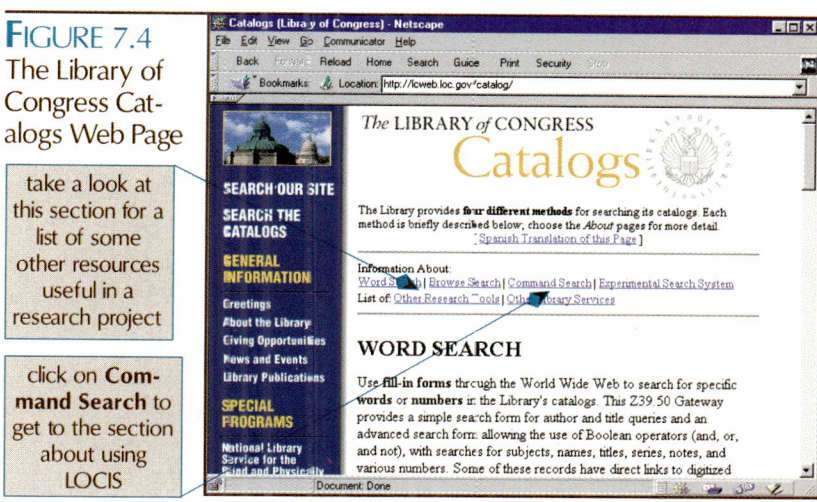

FIGURE 7.4
The Library of Congress Catalogs Web Page

take a look at this section for a list of some other resources useful in a research project

click on **Command Search** to get to the section about using LOCIS

② Select the hyperlink **Command Search**.

Selecting **Command Search** takes you to the portion of the Web page with easy access to LOCIS. We show that in Figure 7.2.

✦ Click on the hyperlink **Command Search**.

③ Start a Telnet session by clicking on the hyperlink **Telnet to LOCIS**.

The pointer turns to a hand. The URL for that hyperlink shows in the status bar. The URL is **telnet://locis.loc.gov**. Clicking on the hyperlink starts a Telnet session using the Internet domain name or address **locis.loc.gov**. If at another time when you were not using a Web browser you wanted to get to the Library of Congress Information System by using a Telnet client program you would use the address **locis.loc.gov**. Now use the browser to make the connection.

✦ Move the mouse pointer to the hyperlink **Telnet to LOCIS**.

✦ Click on **Telnet to LOCIS**.

That starts your browser's Telnet program. The Telnet program will attempt to contact the site **locis.loc.gov**, and in a short period of time you ought to see a window with contents similar to Figure 7.5.

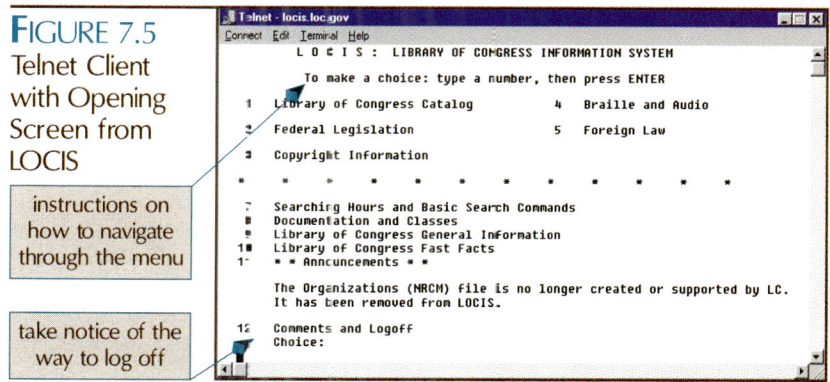

FIGURE 7.5
Telnet Client with Opening Screen from LOCIS

instructions on how to navigate through the menu

take notice of the way to log off

4 ▶ Select an item from the menu.

At this point you've established a Telnet session with the computer system whose Internet domain address is **locis.loc.gov**. You are logged in to that computer system just as if you were using a terminal that was directly connected to the computer. You are, of course, connected through the Internet. If you remember, in Chapter 1 we noted that the Internet is a packet-switched network. All Telnet activity between your computer and the remote computer is transmitted through packets, and those packets may take different paths through the Internet. The Telnet protocol and transmission control protocol (TCP) create the illusion of a direct connection.

Enough of that for now. It's time to explore LOCIS. But before we do, take some time to read what's on the opening screen and pay special attention to instructions on how to log out or quit the Telnet session. In this case we see that by typing **12** we can log off. Why don't you select an item from the menu to browse a section of LOCIS?

5 ▶ End the Telnet session.

We know from what we've read earlier and what's on most of the LOCIS screens that typing **12** will take us to the main menu. Suppose we're at the main menu.

✦ Type **12**; press Enter.

That brings up a screen to tell us how we can send in comments about LOCIS. We also see that there's one more step to end the session. It's the same as the previous step.

✦ Type **12**; press Enter.

This enables us to log off of the LOCIS system, and a pop-up box appears in the Telnet window as shown in Figure 7.6. The box tells us the connection to LOCIS was lost or terminated. To end the session and get back to the Web browser we need to close the pop-up box and the Telnet window.

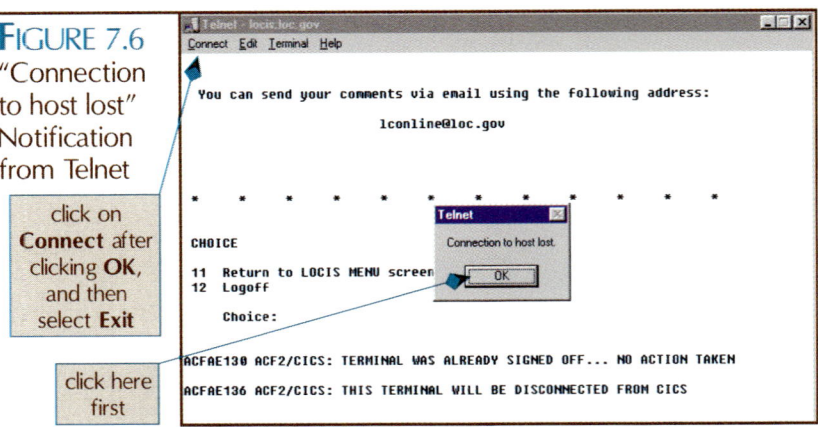

FIGURE 7.6 "Connection to host lost" Notification from Telnet

click on **Connect** after clicking **OK**, and then select **Exit**

click here first

Telnet - locis.loc.gov
Connect Edit Terminal Help

You can send your comments via email using the following address:

lconline@loc.gov

*   *   *   *   *   *   *   *   *   *   *   *

CHOICE

Telnet
Connection to host lost.
OK

11   Return to LOCIS MENU screen
12   Logoff

Choice:

ACFAE130 ACF2/CICS: TERMINAL WAS ALREADY SIGNED OFF... NO ACTION TAKEN

ACFAE136 ACF2/CICS: THIS TERMINAL WILL BE DISCONNECTED FROM CICS

✦ Click on **OK** in the pop-up box.

This should close the Telnet window.

✦ Click on **Connect** in the menu bar of the Telnet window and select **Exit**.

End of Example 7.1

FTP

FTP, which stands for file transfer protocol, is one of the basic Internet services. It's designed to copy files from one computer system to another. A primary reason for creating the Internet was to allow researchers to exchange ideas and results of their work. FTP allows that sharing of information, data, or any sort of file.

In this section we'll look at using *anonymous FTP* to retrieve copies of files from another site on the Internet. The term *anonymous* means anyone on the Internet can copy files from a computer system without being a registered user of that system. In that way it's just like displaying or saving a Web page from some other site on the World Wide Web. A big difference between HTTP, the protocol used on the World Wide Web, and FTP is that FTP was created at a time when most Internet users had a fair amount of experience using computers, so it doesn't provide very much in the way of

a user-friendly interface. But it's an efficient way to copy files. Anonymous FTP allows you to retrieve files that are publicly available from another computer system on the Internet. Systems that allow anonymous FTP sessions are called *anonymous FTP sites*, and the collections of files they make available are called **FTP archives**.

Before HTTP and Gopher, FTP was about the only way to copy files on the Internet. You could send a file as part of an email message, but that's not really the same thing. If I want to retrieve a file at your site and it's coming to me by email, I have to send email to your site to request the file and the file has to be packaged up as part of a message and then sent to me. With anonymous FTP, a group of files is made available to the general public. Anyone can contact the computer system, request a file, and have it sent to them. The length of time it takes to transfer depends on the size of the file and the speed of the Internet connection or modem at the

sender's and receiver's sites, but it is as fast as retrieving a comparably sized Web page.

Do we still need to use FTP? Yes. FTP can be used to transfer any type of file. It's commonly used nowadays to distribute software throughout the Internet. Most of these software programs are available as *shareware*, which means that you retrieve (download) the program from an archive, use it, and purchase it if you find the program useful. FTP is an efficient way to transfer files when you know the exact name and location of the file—and that's all included in its URL. Using FTP, you can also transfer a file from your computer to another. This is called *uploading* a file. When you upload, you usually have to give a login name and password to the other computer system; it's not the same as anonymous FTP. This turns out to be a good way to work on one computer and transfer your work to another. Some people use this technique to update or create Web pages. They do their work on one computer and then transfer the files to a computer that acts as a Web server.

In this section we'll look at:

- Understanding the URL Format for FTP

- Downloading a File by Anonymous FTP

- Locating FTP Archives and Other Sites for Finding Software

- Downloading and Working with Files from Software Archives

- Using an FTP Client

Understanding the URL Format for FTP

These days, much of the access to files by FTP is through a Web browser. As you know, that means you need to be familiar with the URL format for FTP. Here is the general form of a URL for anonymous FTP:

ftp://name-of-ftp-site/ directory-name/file-name

Note the following features:

- The URL for anonymous FTP starts with **ftp://**.

- The name of the FTP site follows **//**.

- The directory name starts with the first single **/** and ends at, but does not include, the last **/**.

- The name of the file follows the last **/**.

- All the slashes (/) go in the same direction and slant to the right.

Suppose a friend tells you, "I found this picture of Mars with great detail and colors. You can get it by anonymous FTP at the FTP site for the Jet Propulsion Laboratory, **ftp.jpl.nasa.gov**. You'll want to get the file **marglobe.gif**. It's in the directory **pub/images/browse**. There are also some animations at the same site in **pub/images/anim**." You'd like to view the image, and she's told you everything you need to retrieve it. The URL for that file is **ftp://ftp.jpl.nasa.gov/pub/images/browse/marglobe.gif**.

Matching this to the general URL form for FTP, we have

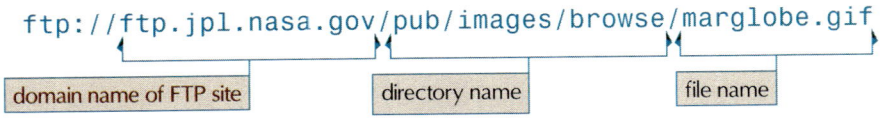

ftp://ftp.jpl.nasa.gov/pub/images/browse/marglobe.gif

domain name of FTP site   directory name   file name

FIGURE 7.7
FTP Archive Displaying Directory Files

click here to go to the higher level directory **/pub/images**

click on any of these to view the file

the file **marglobe.gif** is further down the list; use the scroll bar to get to it

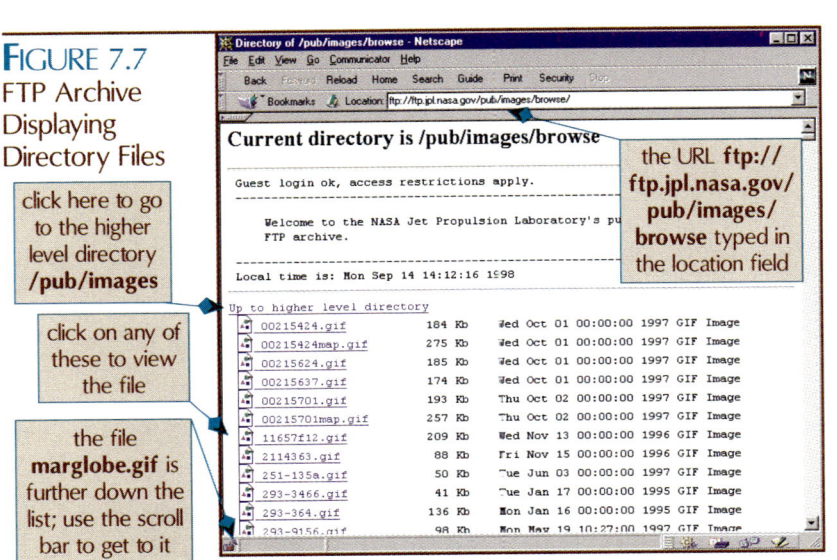

You can also use a URL to refer to a directory. For example, if you use the URL **ftp://ftp.jpl.nasa.gov/pub/images/browse**, the Web browser displays a list of all the files and subdirectories in the directory **/pub/images/browse**. The contents of this directory appear in Figure 7.7. Each file or subdirectory is represented as a hyperlink, and you can view it or listen to it by clicking on its name, provided your system has the appropriate software and hardware.

Downloading a File by Anonymous FTP

There are two ways to retrieve a file (that is, copy it from a remote site to the computer you're using).

Method 1: View the File First, and Then Save It Using the File Menu

If you type a file's URL or click on a hyperlink, the file will be transferred to the Web browser. This is useful if you want to view the file before you save it, but the file will be transferred to your computer first. If the browser is configured to display or play a file of that type, you'll see (and hear, if possible) the file's contents in the Web browser window. Some examples of files of this type are text files, Web pages that are text files with HTML commands, or GIF or JPEG image files.

The file may also be displayed in a window that belongs to another program called a *helper application*. If there is no helper application installed to display the file, a message box pops up saying "No Viewer

Configured for File Type." If the file is displayed in the browser window, select **Save As** from the **File** pull-down menu in the menu bar. This opens a **Save As** dialog box on the screen. Select the name of the directory or folder in which you want to save the file, and then click on the button labeled **Save**. If the file comes up in the window for another application, such as Microsoft Word, save it through the commands for that application. See the tip to the right on how to handle a file type that doesn't match any type that your browser can work with.

Method 2: Save the Hyperlink in a File Without Viewing It by Using the Right Mouse Button or Shift and Click

If there is a hyperlink to the file in the Web browser's window, you can save the hyperlink. To retrieve the file without viewing it, put the mouse pointer on the hyperlink and press the right mouse button. When a menu pops up, choose **Save Link As**. This opens a **Save As** dialog box on the screen Set the directory or folder name, and then click on the **Save** button.

Another way to do this is to place the pointer on a hyperlink. Then hold down the Shift key, click on the hyperlink, and release

What to do when "No Viewer Configured for File Type" pops up.

The message "No Viewer Configured for File Type" means you have a file type that your browser doesn't know how to handle. Select the option that lets you save to disk. A **Save As** dialog box opens, asking you to specify the folder in which you want to store the file. If you want to open the file, be sure you have the necessary hardware and software to uncompress and display or play the file after it has been sent. There are lots of variations for the necessary equipment and programs, so we can't cover all of them here. If you have everything you need, you configure the browser so that it knows what to do with that file type in the future. Netscape's online help has instructions for configuring specific helper applications. In Netscape 4, click on the **Edit** menu, click on **Preferences**, select the **Applications** panel, and click on the **Help** button. For Netscape 3, click on the **Options** menu, select **General Preferences**, choose **Helpers**, and click on the **Help** button. ◆

the **Shift** key. This immediately opens a **Save As** dialog box. You can save it to the file you've specified on your computer.

The following activity goes through the steps involved in downloading a file by anonymous FTP when using a Web browser.

EXAMPLE 7.2

Retrieving a File by Anonymous FTP

In this activity, we'll retrieve the file that we mentioned previously, the one containing an image of Mars. We will retrieve the file using the two methods mentioned above to demonstrate how each is done.

Suppose the browser is already started and ready for use. Using the first method, we'll retrieve the file by typing the URL **ftp:// ftp.jpl.nasa.gov/pub/images/browse/marglobe.gif**. Web browsers can display files of this type. The file will be displayed, but it won't be saved into a file that we can use again until we select **Save As** from the **File** pull-down menu in the menu bar and set the folder and file name for it. In this case, we will view the file's contents before saving it.

Then we'll use the second method to save the same file. We'll enter the URL for the directory that contains the file, **ftp:// ftp.jpl.nasa.gov/pub/images/browse/**, find the file's hyperlink, and use the right mouse button to retrieve it. Retrieving a file this way is quicker, because the browser doesn't have to display it first.

Here are the steps we'll follow using the first method:

1. To view the file, type its URL in the location bar.

2. Save the image in a file on your computer.

3. Once you have chosen an appropriate folder, you need to save the file.

The steps we'll follow using the second method are:

1. Go to the Web page with the hyperlink we want.

2. Find the entry for **marglobe.gif**.

3. Save the file **marglobe.gif**.

Method 1: View the File First

▶ To view the file, type its URL in the location bar.

If the URL is correct and the image is still available, the browser will display the image of Mars.

✛ Click on the location field, type **ftp://ftp.jpl.nasa .gov/pub/images/ browse/marglobe.gif**, and press **Enter**.

❷ Save the image in a file on your computer.

You can now save this image in a file on your computer.

✛ In the menu bar, click **File**.

The File menu opens.

✛ Select **Save As** from the menu.

A **Save As** dialog box appears, as shown in Figure 7.8.

The next step is to store the file in an appropriate folder or directory. You can save the file in the current folder. Alternately, you could select or create another folder to hold the image. Figure 7.8 shows the file being stored in a folder named **images**. Store the file wherever you like. It is a good idea to have one folder for all items of a similar type or a collection of files related to a project. That way it's easier for you to find the file the next time you want it.

❸ Once you have chosen an appropriate folder, you need to save the file.

FIGURE 7.8
Save As Dialog Box for Saving **marglobe.gif**

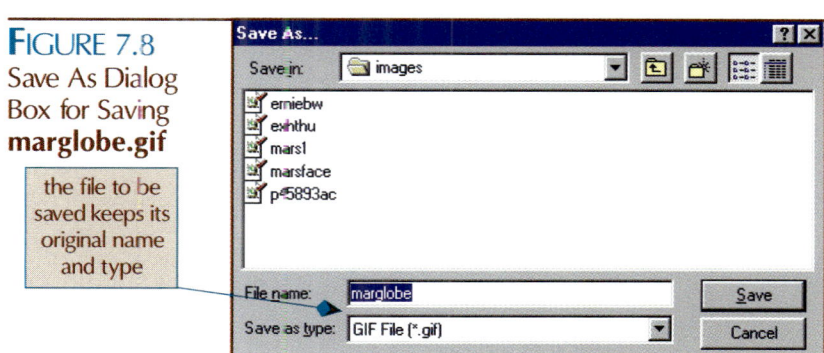

the file to be saved keeps its original name and type

✛ Click on the button labeled **Save**.

Method 2: Save the Hyperlink in a File Without Viewing It

❶ Go to the Web page with the hyperlink we want.

This connects you by anonymous FTP to the archive server at **ftp.jpl.nasa.gov** and displays the listings of the directory **/pub/ images/browse**, as shown in Figure 7.7.

✛ Click on the location field, type **ftp://ftp.jpl.nasa .gov/pub/images/ browse/**, and then press **Enter**.

❷ **Find the entry for marglobe.gif.**

There are several ways to locate a specific string of text. You could browse the listings by pressing the down arrow key ⬇ or the **PgDn** key or by using the vertical scroll bar. A more direct way is to use **Find** to let the browser locate it.

✛ Press **Ctrl**+**F**, or click on the **Edit** menu and select **Find in Page**. Type the name of the file to retrieve, and then click on the **Find Next** button.

The browser will take you to the first occurrence of whatever you entered, if that string is in the text portion of the Web page.

✛ If there is more than one match, press **Ctrl**+**G** to go to the next match until you find the hyperlink. Click on **Cancel** to close the **Find** dialog box.

You'll eventually reach the portion of the listing that resembles what is shown in Figure 7.9.

FIGURE 7.9
Directory Listing Showing Hyperlinks

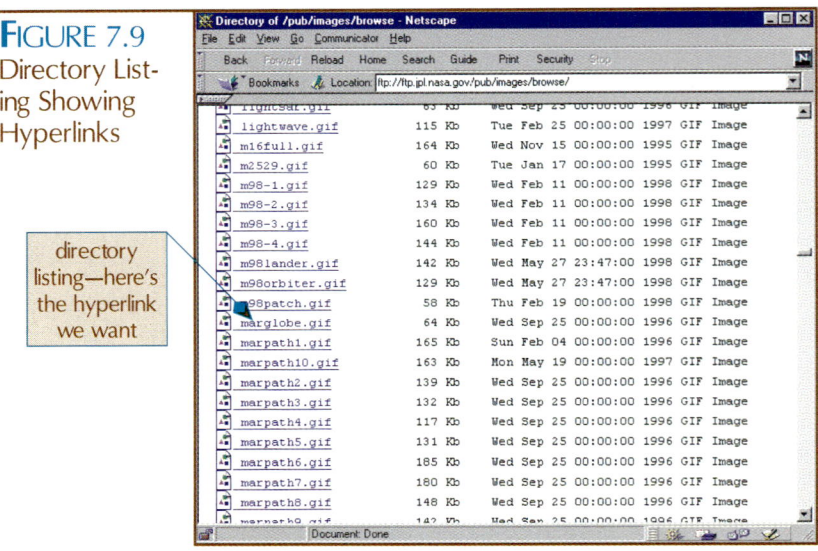

The listing in Figure 7.9 contains an icon for each file. The icons here indicate that the files are images. This listing also contains the size of each file, the date it was last modified, and an annotation describing the file type.

You can now retrieve the file.

❸ Save the file **marglobe.gif**.

✛ Position the cursor or mouse pointer over the name **marglobe.gif**.

The cursor turns into a hand when it's sitting on a hyperlink.

+ Press the right mouse button and select **Save Link As** from the pop-up menu.

+ A **Save As** dialog box appears, as shown in Figure 7.8. Select the proper folder or directory for the file and click on the button labeled **Save**.

A box labeled **Saving Location** appears on the screen. That box keeps you updated about the progress of the transfer from the remote site to your computer.

Congratulations! You've successfully retrieved a file by anonymous FTP.

End of Example 7.2

In Example 7.2, we used a Web browser to retrieve a file by anonymous FTP. You follow the same steps to retrieve any type of file. In this case, because the image comes from NASA, it is available for your personal use. Before using it for any commercial purposes, be sure to obtain permission. You can retrieve files by anonymous FTP at no cost, but having retrieved a file doesn't give you the right to use it any way you'd like. The information in these files needs to be treated in the same way as information that's part of a book, newspaper, audio recording, or video recording.

Locating FTP Archives and Other Sites for Finding Software

In the previous activity, we used an FTP archive to retrieve a file.

An archive is a collection of directories arranged according to some scheme. A common arrangement is for the top level to be sorted by the type of computer system (such as Mac, PC, and Unix) and for the levels below that to be ordered according to the type of software (such as games, utilities, and Internet). You start at the home or root directory and, by clicking on hyperlinks that represent folders or directories, you move to or browse through the archive. Once you've located the file you want, you can download it using one of the methods described in Example 7.2.

There are several well-established and reliable FTP archives in the world. The following list is representative of the general purpose archives. The first has a search form available so you can find files in the archive. The second has a Web page interface

that you use to go through the archives. The last is a more traditional type of listing; the items are well organized, but you have to find your own way.

+ "UIArchive," University of Illinois at Urbana-Champaign **http://uiarchive.cso.uiuc.edu**

+ "Wuarchive," Washington University in St. Louis **http://ftp.wustl.edu**

+ "Garbo archives," University of Vaasa, Finland **ftp://garbo.uwasa.fi**

Because millions of files are available through FTP, you can appreciate how difficult it is to find the name of a file and its archive without some automated search tool. In 1990, Peter Deutsch, Alan Emtage, and Bill Heelan at McGill University created a service named Archie and released it for public use. Archie is available with an interface specially designed for use with a Web browser. You enter the name or a portion of the name of the file you're looking for. Archie returns a collection of hyperlinks to files or directories that match the name used in the search box. For more information on using Archie, look at the Web page for Archie's home, "Bunyip Information Systems," **http://www.bunyip .com/products/archie**. Here's a list of a few Archie servers. Try one!

- "Archie Search at Bunyip"
  http://archie.bunyip .com/archie.html

- "ArchiePlex Form at FUNet"
  http://www.funet .fi/funet/archie/ archieplexform.html

- "FTP Search v4.0"
  http://ftpsearch .lycos.com

Using Archie is all well and good, provided you know the name or a portion of the name of the file you're seeking. Sometimes you need to guess what the name might be. But it can still be difficult. A better approach is to arrange files in categories according to their function—such

as sound files, desktop utilities, games, HTML editors, and so forth—and a description of each. If there is a way to search the collection by file names and descriptions, then we have a more useful service.

Several of these are available on the Web. We'll look at some in the next examples and in the exercises. Many of the files accessible through these sites are software, programs, or collections of programs and other files, which are distributed as shareware. The files are in either executable form (their names end with **.exe**) or compressed form (their names end with **.zip** or **.gz**). We'll show you how to work with them in the next section. Here are a few sources on the Web that list FTP and software or shareware archives:

- "Librarians' Index to the Internet"
  http://sunsite .berkeley.edu/ internetindex, then select **Computers**, **Software**

- "nerd's HEAVEN: The Software Directory"
  http://boole .stanford.edu/ nerdsheaven.html

- "Yahoo! Top: Computers and Internet: Software: Shareware"

http://www.yahoo .com/computers_and _internet/software/ shareware

Downloading and Working with Files from Software Archives

Several services on the Web act as archives and distributors of software in the form of shareware or *freeware* (software that may be used and distributed at no cost). Each service supplies links to the programs; when you click on the link, the software is transferred to your computer, essentially by FTP. In other words, you select the software you'd like, and you then use a Web browser to download it to your computer.

Shareware Often Comes in Packages

Most of the files in the archives are *packages*, or collections of related files. They are in packages because to install, run, and use a single program usually requires several files, such as program libraries, instructions for installing and registering the program, and online help files. When you retrieve a program, you get all the files you need combined in one package.

The files or packages are processed by a *compression* program, which reduces the total number of bytes necessary to represent the information in the package. Reducing the size of a file makes it take less time to download the file. Because of this compression, you must do two things to the package after you receive it: uncompress it and extract the individual files from the package.

Compressed files or packages have names that usually end in **.zip**. Two popular compression programs are PKZIP and WinZip (which are both shareware). You will definitely want a copy of either of those utilities. As you might guess, they are both available in compressed format, as packages.

How can we extract the files necessary for those compression programs or similar packages? These and many other packages are in what are called *self-extracting archives*. The package's file name ends in **.exe**. When you click on the name, it starts extracting its own components. For example, the software for the Netscape and Microsoft browsers are in that format.

This compressed format isn't used only with programs. Any single file or collection of files can be compressed and transmitted in that compressed format. In the course of writing this book, we used this technology. Because each chapter has so many images,

the files were quite large. We put each chapter and the images into a single package and then compressed it using either PKZIP or WinZip. We used FTP to send the compressed packages to the publisher.

Downloading and Installing Software

Here are the steps involved in downloading and installing shareware or freeware programs and associated files:

- Find the program you want to retrieve in a software archive.

- Create a folder or directory to hold the program from the archive on your computer.

- In the software archive, click on the hyperlink to the program. As soon as you indicate where it should go using a **Save As** dialog box, it will be transferred to your computer.

- If the file name ends in **.exe**, then it's likely a self-extracting archive. Locate it using Windows Explorer and double-click on it. It will either install itself—follow the instructions—or it will extract its parts into the current directory.

- If the file name ends in **.zip**, then you have to use a program such as PKZIP or WinZip to extract the components. You usually select the folder or directory in which they will go.

- In either case, look for a file with a name similar to **Readme** or **Instructions** to see what steps you need to take to install the program or to work with the files in the package. In many cases, the extracted files need to go through some other processing by a program named **Setup** before they are ready to use.

- Be sure to check the program and associated files for computer viruses. Many of the archives check files for viruses before making them available to the public, but you ought to check them yourself.

Obtaining a Copy of PKZIP or WinZip

You can see from the above steps that you'll need a copy of PKZIP or WinZip, but you don't need both.

To get a copy of PKZIP, go to the home page for PKWARE,

You will want a program that **checks files for computer viruses**. Several are available, and you can get shareware versions to evaluate and decide which you like best.

http://www.pkware.com. Spend a little time reading about PKZIP, the way it works, and file compression in general. Click on the hyperlink that takes you through the steps of downloading the software. Store it in a new folder only for PKZIP. Once it has finished downloading, there will be a new application (program) in the folder. Click on it and follow the instructions. It will install itself in a directory or folder. Once it's installed, go to that directory using Windows Explorer, and read the file named **Readme**, which contains information about the files you've installed. The program's name is PKZIP; click on it when you need to use it.

To get a copy of WinZip, go to the home page for Win-Zip with the URL **http://www.winzip.com**. Spend a little time reading about WinZip, how it works, and the topic of file compression. Click on the hyperlink that takes you through the steps of downloading the software. Store it in a new folder only for WinZip. Once it's finished downloading there will be a new application (program) in the folder. Click on it and it will lead you through the steps of installing the program in a folder on your computer. The name of the program is WinZip; click on it

when you need to uncompress a file.

Acquiring Antivirus Software

You will want a program that checks files for computer viruses. Several are available, and you can get shareware versions to evaluate and decide which you like best. One, F-PROT, makes its software free to individuals; commercial customers or organizations must pay for using it. Three sites that offer shareware versions of their antivirus and virus protection software are:

- ◆ "F-PROT, Data Fellows" **http://www.datafellows.com**

- ◆ "Norton AntiVirus, Symantec" **http://www.symantec.com/nav/index_downloads.html**

- ◆ "VirusScan for Windows 95, McAfee" **http://download.mcafee.com/**

If you don't have an antivirus program on your computer, visit one of the sites, download the most recent version, and install it. All of the antivirus programs from the sites listed above come as com-

pressed packages. After you download one of these, you'll need to use the software to uncompress and extract the files into a folder. Once you have done that, look for a file with a name such as **Readme** to get instructions on how to install the software. In many cases, you can install the programs on your system by clicking on an application or program in the folder named **Setup**. You follow the same steps for installing these programs as for almost any other software that you download.

Using Software Archives and FTP Search Services

In an earlier section of this chapter, we listed the URLs of some lists of software archives or sites in which you find software to download through FTP.

WHAT YOU'LL FIND IN THE ARCHIVES. Software archives maintain their own collections of files, and FTP archives have hyperlinks to the files, which are usually stored at the Web site for the person or organization that markets the software. Both types include a search form so you can search the collection for files, and several also have reviews, descriptions, and links to the software arranged into categories so you can browse the items accessible through the archive.

The files are usually arranged in categories according to the type of software, such as games, Internet, utilities, and personal use. Sometimes they are also arranged according to the type of operating system they're designed for, such as MS-DOS, Windows 3.x, Windows 95/98/NT, or Macintosh.

Some archives are dedicated to programs for a particular operating system, and some only to Internet software. Two examples are WinFiles.com, which specializes in software for Windows 95/98/NT systems, and TUCOWS, which has software to be used for working with the Internet. ZDNet Software Library is a good example of a full-featured software archive with extensive reviews of many of the items it lists.

Here's a list of a few archives:

General:

✦ "DOWNLOAD.COM"
http://www
.download.com

✦ "FILE MINE"
http://www.
filemine.com

✦ "FilePile"
http://www
.filepile.com

✦ "SHAREWARE.COM"
http://www
.shareware.com

✦ "ZDNet Software
Library"
http://www
.zdnet.com/swlib

Specialized:

✦ "Stroud's Consummate
Winsock Applications"
http://cws.internet
.com

✦ "TUCOWS"
http://www
.tucows.com

✦ "WinFiles.com"
http://www
.winfiles.com

BEFORE YOU DOWNLOAD. We're going to demonstrate downloading and installing some software in Example 7.3. Before you download software, you need to answer a few questions for yourself.

✦ **Is the program appropriate for my computer system?**

Most of the software archives include a description of the system requirements for the software you'll download. Check that you have enough memory (RAM) to run the program (some require 16 megabytes to run properly) and that you have the correct operating system. Software that's developed for a Windows 95/98/NT system won't work properly if it's installed on a system running Windows 3.1 or on a Macintosh system.

✦ **Do I have enough storage space on my disk to hold the software?**

Again, look at the system requirements to see that you have enough disk space to hold the new program along with your other software.

✦ **Do I meet the software licensing requirements?**

Most software is available as shareware to anyone, but some software is available only to educational or nonprofit institutions. The software will likely come with a licensing agreement; you'll need to read this and decide whether to consent to it.

✦ **Do I have permission to install the software?**

If you're working on your home computer, then there's probably no problem. However, if you're working on a computer that's owned by your school or company—which is probably shared with others—check local policies to see whether you may install new software on the computer.

Check to see if you have the proper software, such as **PKZIP or WinZip**, to extract the parts of the package. Oftentimes, this will be stated in the description of the software.

✦ **Do I have the software I need to install the software?**

Check to see if you have the proper software, such as PKZIP or WinZip, to extract the parts of the package. Oftentimes, this will be stated in the description of the software. Also look at the name of the package. If its file extension is **.zip**, then you'll need a program such as the ones we've mentioned to install it.

✦ **Will the software have a detrimental effect on other software on my computer?**

This isn't always easy to answer until the software is installed, in which case it may be too late. Read as much as you can about the software before installing it to see if it will have a detrimental impact on existing programs or system configuration. Be sure you can check it for viruses before installing it.

✦ **Will I be able to uninstall the program if things don't go well?**

These days, most software comes with a program that makes it easy to remove the primary program and all associated files if and when you need to do this.

Now we'll go through the steps involved in downloading and installing software from an archive.

EXAMPLE 7.3

Downloading and Installing Software from a Software Archive

We've been searching for and finding information on the World Wide Web throughout this book. In many instances, we've added some resources to our bookmark list. The list has grown and needs some organization and management. We know we can do this through our browser, but we're interested in seeing if there is some software that has better tools for organizing and managing our bookmark collection. In this activity, we'll go to one of the software archives, find something we'd like to try, check to see that it's appropriate to download and install, and then go through the steps necessary to install it. Here are the steps we'll follow in this example:

1. Go to the home page for the ZDNet Software Library.

2. Search the library for software dealing with bookmarks.

3. Select software to download and check the system requirements.

4. Download the software.

5. Install the software.

Of course, we'll want to try the program at some point, but we won't show that here.

We'll assume that the Web browser is started and displayed on the screen.

◆ Go to the home page for the ZDNet Software Library.

✚ Click on the location field, type **http://www .zdnet.com/swlib**, and press **Enter**.

The ZDNet Library is a large, well-organized, and well-maintained software archive. We use the URL for its home page, **http:// www.zdnet.com/swlib**, to access the software library or archive. The home page appears in Figure 7.10. We're going to search for software dealing with bookmarks in the next step. The term **bookmarks** is entered in the search form in Figure 7.10.

FIGURE 7.10
Home Page for ZDNet Software Library

click here for help with downloading and using the archive

you can browse the archive by topic

type the search term here and press **Enter**

featured archives can be found here

We see from the home page that we can search or browse the archive either by type of software or by type of computer system. Several types of software and individual programs are listed. We also see there's a **Help** hyperlink and a hyperlink called the **Easy Download Guide**. We know from using other search services that it's a good idea to click on **Help** (or any type of search guide available on the service's home page) and do some reading before we continue.

✚ Click on the hyperlink **Easy Download Guide**.

We'll follow the steps listed there after we select the software to download. In the next step, we'll start searching for software that deals with bookmarks, but it's worth spending a little time to browse some of the categories.

➋ Search the library for software dealing with bookmarks.

➕ Go back to the home page for ZDNet Library.

➕ Type **bookmarks** in the search box, and click on **SEARCH**.

You can search for software by typing a keyword or phrase in the search box and clicking on the button labeled **SEARCH**.

➌ Select software to download and check the system requirements.

A portion of the Web page listing the search results appears in Figure 7.11. It's worth taking some time clicking on the hyperlinks for some of the packages to read the ZDNet Library review. In addition to a link to the review, we see the date the software was added to the archive, its rating, and the number of downloads (other folks retrieving the software) listed. To be specific we'll click on the hyperlink for **WebTabs v1.0f**.

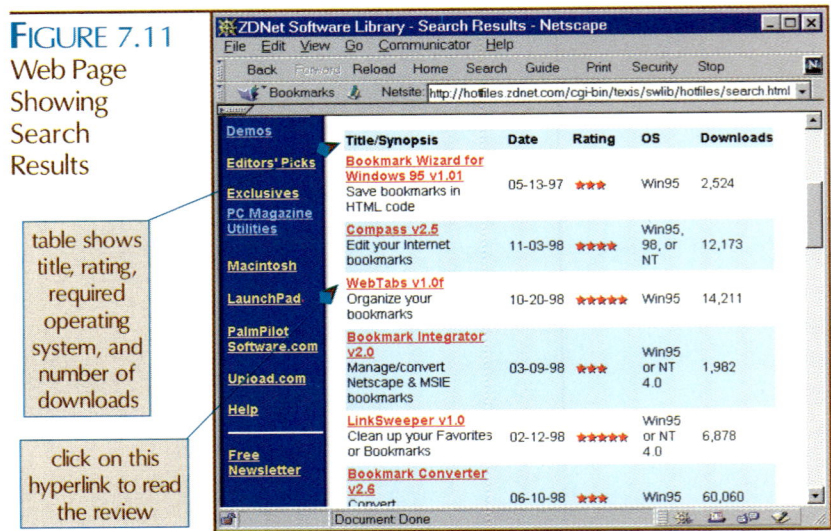

FIGURE 7.11 Web Page Showing Search Results

table shows title, rating, required operating system, and number of downloads

click on this hyperlink to read the review

➕ Click on the hyperlink **WebTabs v1.0f**. You may need to scroll to the bottom of the first page of results and click on the button **Hits 26–50** to find the WebTabs link.

The Web page for WebTabs is shown in Figure 7.12. The entire Web page isn't shown there, but after reading all of it, we see that it is designed to run on a computer that uses a Windows 95 operating system and that in compressed form it takes up 2,394,171 bytes— roughly 2 megabytes. Once it's expanded, we can expect it to take up about twice as much space, and we need to decide if we have enough disk space to install it. If after reading the review we feel the software will be useful to us, it is appropriate for our computer, and we have enough space for it, then we can start downloading it.

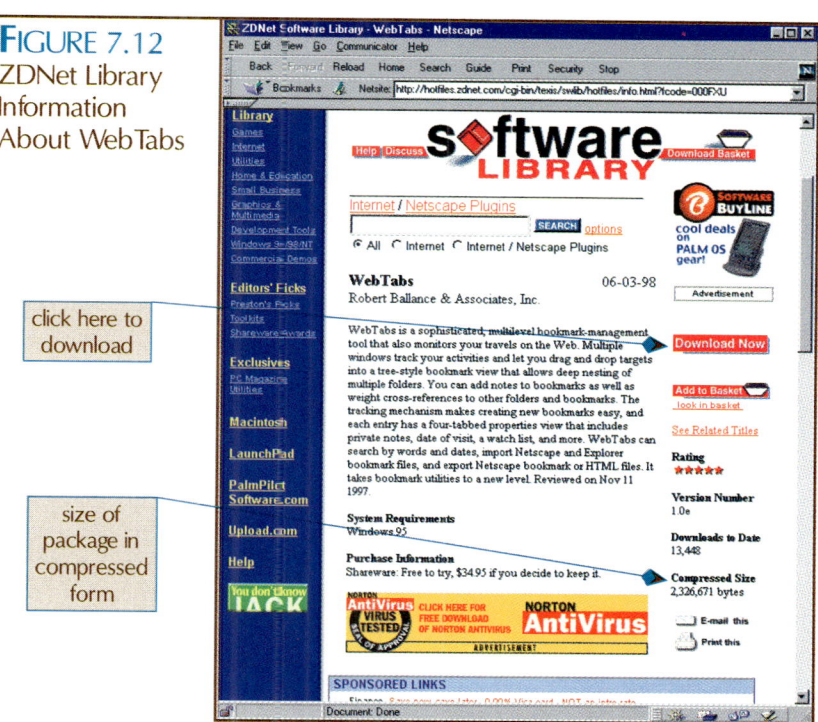

FIGURE 7.12
ZDNet Library Information About WebTabs

click here to download

size of package in compressed form

◆ **Download the software.** We're going to follow the steps in the ZDNet download guide.

✦ First we'll create a folder to hold the software package. We're using Windows 95 so first we open Windows Explorer by clicking on the **Start** button, selecting **Programs**, and then choosing **Windows Explorer**.

✦ We'll use Windows Explorer to display the contents of Drive C:. Click on **File** in the menu bar, select **New**, and then click on **New Folder**.

The window you'll see appears in Figure 7.13. If you're using other software to manage your files, read the instructions in the download guide.

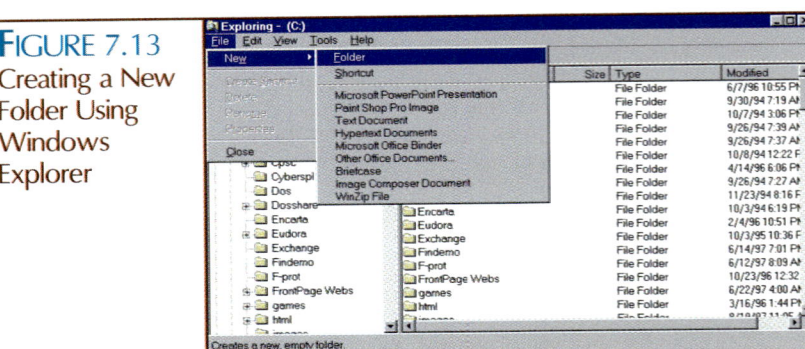

FIGURE 7.13
Creating a New Folder Using Windows Explorer

A new folder is created. We'll name it **WebTabs**.

✚ Type **WebTabs** for the folder's name and press ⟨Enter⟩.

Now we're ready for the second step in the download process. We can use the browser to transfer the file from ZDNet Library to our system. Be sure the Web page shown in Figure 7.12 is displayed on your computer.

✚ Return to the browser window and click on the hyperlink **Download Now**.

The browser will attempt to transfer the file to your computer using FTP. You'll likely get a dialog box message such as "Unknown file type" or some other warning. In any case we will click on a button that lets us save the file to disk. If you were using a browser other than Netscape, you might get a different message. You want to save the file to your disk. Click on a button that lets you do this. A **Save As** dialog box will appear.

✚ Use the controls in the **Save As** dialog box to select the **WebTabs** folder, as has been done in Figure 7.14. Then click on **Save**.

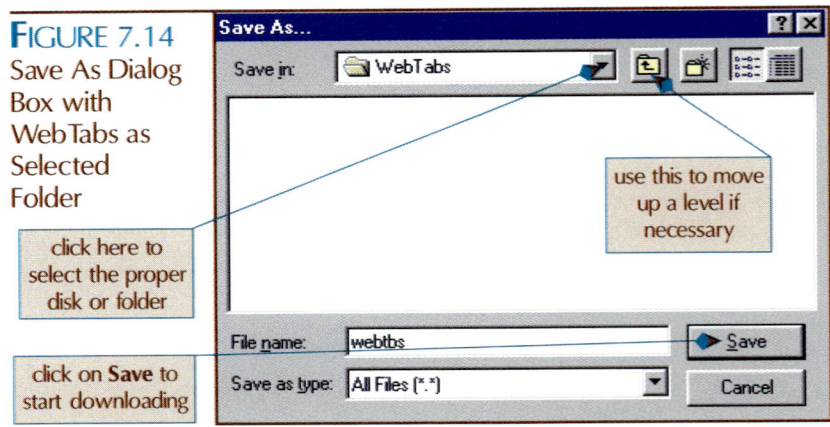

FIGURE 7.14
Save As Dialog Box with WebTabs as Selected Folder

click here to select the proper disk or folder

use this to move up a level if necessary

click on **Save** to start downloading

A window titled "Saving Location" pops up on the screen to show the estimated time it will take to download the file and the progress of the download. Depending on the speed of your modem, how busy the server is at ZDNet, and current Internet traffic, it could take a few minutes or longer (up to an hour in extreme cases) to download the file. Figure 7.15 shows the **Saving Location** box. It shows that the download is about 25 percent finished. We can estimate that it will take about 15 to 20 minutes for the download.

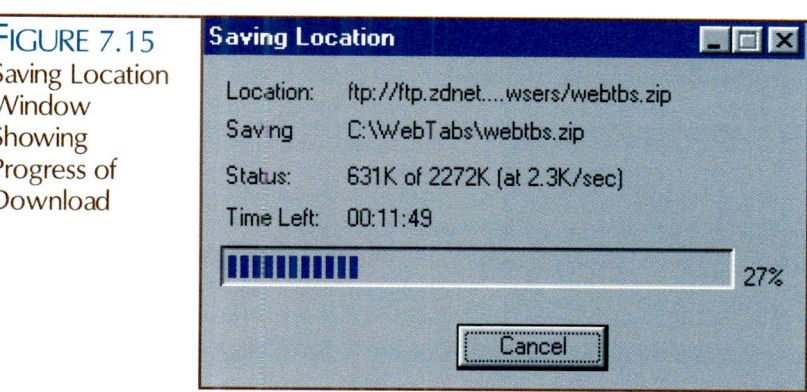

FIGURE 7.15
Saving Location
Window
Showing
Progress of
Download

When that box closes, we're ready to install the software.

❺ ▶ Install the software.

The downloaded file will be in the **WebTabs** folder we created on Drive C:. To view the file, use Windows Explorer to open **WebTabs**.

✚ Use Windows Explorer to open the folder **WebTabs**.

The listing indicates that the file is a compressed, or zip, file, as shown in Figure 7.16. It will appear this way if we've installed WinZip on our computer. If we had installed PKZIP instead, it would still be listed as a compressed file.

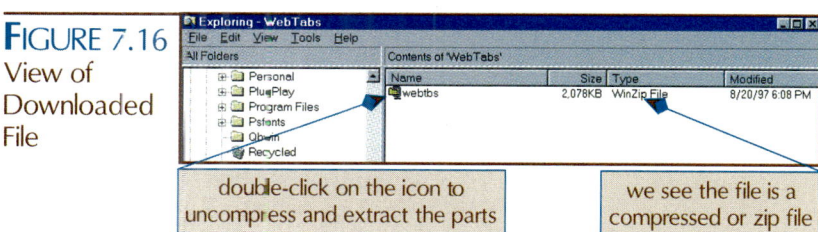

FIGURE 7.16
View of
Downloaded
File

✚ Double-click on the **webtbs** icon.

Double-clicking on the icon starts WinZip. If WinZip was installed with the Wizard option, then the software will take us step-by-step through extracting the parts of the package and installing the software. If not, click on **Extract** to extract and uncompress the files. In either case, extract all the files to this directory. Figure 7.17 shows the contents of the folder **WebTabs** after the files have been extracted (and we've pressed the key **F5** to refresh the folder display).

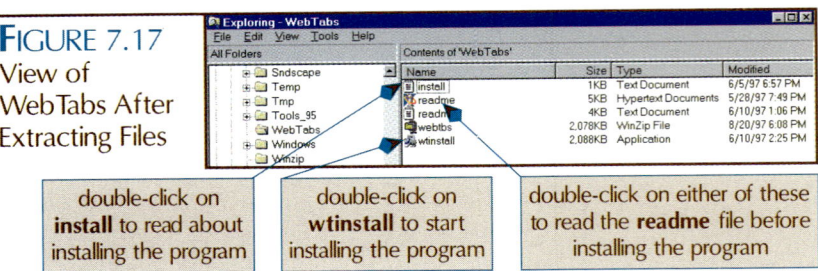

FIGURE 7.17
View of
WebTabs After
Extracting Files

Before going any further, we'll read some of the documentation that comes with the software.

Double-click on the icon for readme.

Double-clicking on either icon labeled **readme** allows us to read the contents of that file. It describes some of the program's features and requirements.

Double-click on the icon for install.

Double-clicking on the **install** icon opens a brief document that tells us about the installation file, **wtinstall**. The document also says that an uninstall program will be available so that we can remove the program and all its parts when we want to do this. We might, for example, decide that we don't want to purchase the program after the shareware trial period ends—after 30 days, in this case.

Now we're ready to install the program so that we can use it. When we double-click on the **wtinstall** icon, a program will start to lead us through the installation process. We will take all the usual options as the installation or setup program proceeds.

Double-click on the icon for wtinstall.

A setup program starts. When it finishes, the WebTabs program will be installed in the folder **C:\Program Files\WebTabs**, and **WebTabs** will be added to our **Start** menu. It's instructive to use Windows Explorer to see what's in the folder **C:\Program Files\WebTabs**. You'll see the program, and you'll need to click on its icon to start it. You will also see a program or application named **Unwise**; double-click on its icon to remove WebTabs from the system.

One more thing: Now that we've installed WebTabs, we don't need the files in the folder **C:\WebTabs** anymore. It's safe to delete that folder at this point.

End of Example 7.3

In Example 7.3, we downloaded and installed a program from a software archive. The steps we followed were fairly typical, although the details can change, depending on the program downloaded and the software archive used. We installed the program by clicking on an icon labeled **wtinstall**. In most other cases, we'll click on an icon labeled either **Setup** or **Install**.

Using an FTP Client Program

In the examples and activities discussed so far in this chapter, we have used FTP through the Web browser. That may be all you need to search for and retrieve information from the Web or Internet using FTP. Sometimes, though, you may want to use an FTP program that's separate from the browser. To use an FTP program this way, you'll still need an Internet connection from your computer. The program you run will download files from a server or upload files from your computer to a server. This is the sort of client/server interaction we discussed in Chapter 1. The FTP program you use acts as a client.

When you work with an FTP client to contact another computer (called the *server* or *host*), you'll need to have certain pieces of information. The following list explains what you must know.

✦ **You'll need the Internet domain name or address of the server, or host.**

The client uses the *domain name* to contact the server. Earlier in the chapter, in the section "Understanding the URL Format for FTP," we pointed out the domain name portion of a URL that implies the use of FTP.

✦ **If you're going to be downloading software, you'll need a user name and a password on the host.**

If you're using anonymous FTP, the user name is "anonymous" and the password is your email address. If you're going to download some files from your user account on the server system, you'll use your assigned user name and password.

✦ **If you're going to be uploading files to another computer, you'll need a user name and password on the host.**

The user name and password enable you to upload files to a directory or folder that isn't necessarily available to the public.

Of course, you'll also need an *FTP client* for your computer. Several are available as shareware, but one in particular is highly recommended. It's WS_FTP, and it's free for personal use. To get a copy appropriate for your system, go to the Junod Software home page, **http://www.gabn.net/junodj**. John A. Junod has written and continues to maintain WS_FTP. Several very good guides to using WS_FTP are available on the Web. Here's a short list:

✦ "Installing and Configuring WS_FTP" **http://usats.com/learn/ftp.shtml**

✦ "Using WS_FTP For Windows" **http://www.imaginarylandscape.com/helpweb/ftp/wsftp.html**

✦ "WS FTP v4.5" **http://riceinfo.rice.edu/Computer/Facilities/Colleges/PC/WSFTP/WSFTP.html**

We'll briefly go over how to use WS_FTP, but look at some of these guides for more help when you're ready.

First download and install the appropriate version of the software from Junod Software. Use the techniques discussed in Example 7.3.

Once the program is installed, you start it by selecting it from the **Start** menu, clicking on an icon on your desktop, or clicking on an icon in a folder. Which one of these you choose depends on how it was installed. When it starts, a session profile pops onto the screen.

Figure 7.18 shows a session profile for connecting to a system with the host name (same as the domain name) **www .mwc.edu**. The user id or login name for this user is **ernie**. A password isn't typed in here; it will be typed in when the host system is contacted. If a password were saved with this profile, then anyone using the computer could access the files belonging to user **ernie** on **www.mwc.edu**. If this were to be an anonymous FTP session, then the box labeled **Anonymous** would be checked. You can select other servers with different profiles by clicking on the button to the right of the profile name.

To contact the host, click on the button labeled **OK**. Acting as a client, WS_FTP attempts to contact the host system. Another window pops up that

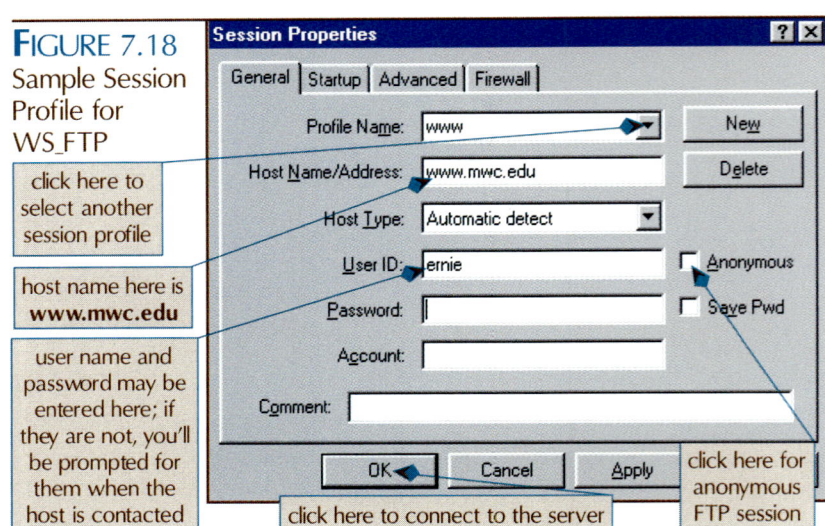

FIGURE 7.18 Sample Session Profile for WS_FTP

click here to select another session profile

host name here is **www.mwc.edu**

user name and password may be entered here; if they are not, you'll be prompted for them when the host is contacted

click here to connect to the server

click here for anonymous FTP session

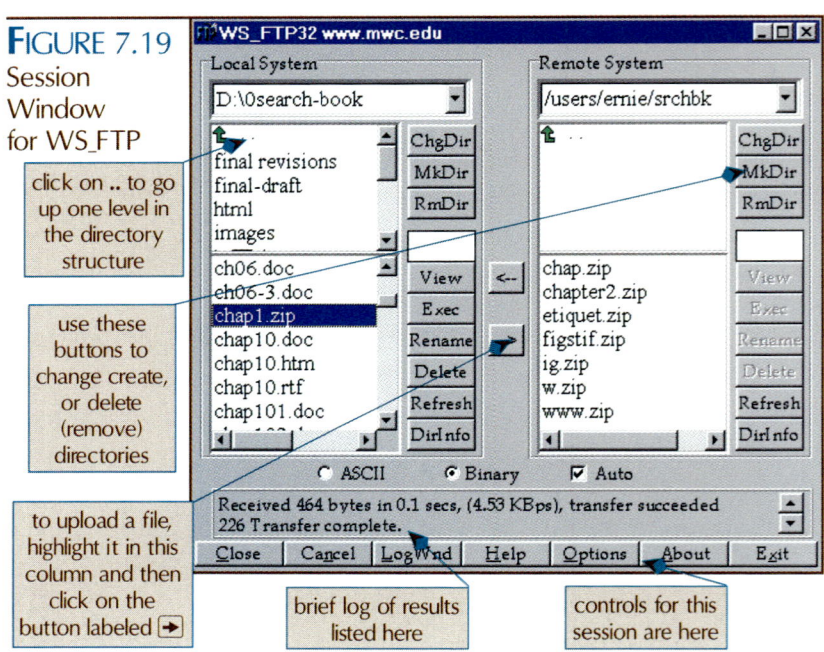

FIGURE 7.19 Session Window for WS_FTP

click on .. to go up one level in the directory structure

use these buttons to change create, or delete (remove) directories

to upload a file, highlight it in this column and then click on the button labeled ➡

brief log of results listed here

controls for this session are here

shows whether the host has been contacted. The user then has control over the transfer of files.

Figure 7.19 shows the window that appears when WS_FTP starts an FTP session with **www.mwc.edu**. The left col-

umn lists the files in the current folder of your computer, the client. The right column lists the files in the directory with which you've connected on the host computer.

You can choose a file to transfer by selecting it from the

FIGURE 7.20
Transfer Status
Window

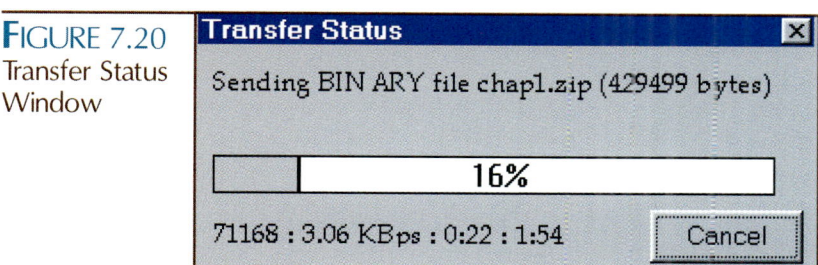

appropriate column. You'll see that there are scroll bars to let you scroll through the list of files and directories on both the client and host computers. In each column, the subdirectories of the current directory are listed in the upper panel and the files are listed in the lower panel.

Suppose we want to upload the file named **chap1.zip** from the client computer—that's the computer you're using—to the host computer. As shown in Figure 7.19, we highlight **chap1.zip** and click on the button labeled ➡. In doing so, we move the file from the client (listed on the left) to the host (listed on the right).

After we click on ➡, a **Transfer Status** dialog box pops up showing information about the transfer of the file from one computer to another via the Internet. Figure 7.20 shows the window for the upload we've been discussing. The items shown include the total number of bytes to transfer, the number transferred so far, the rate of transfer, how much time has elapsed so far, and the esti-

mated remaining time. That window remains on the screen until the transfer is complete. To stop the transfer, click on the **Cancel** button.

To download a file, select the directory on the local system that will hold the file, highlight the name of the file in the list on the right, and click on ⬅.

WS_FTP is an example of an FTP client. It presents a graphical user interface for transferring files between a client and server. Other client programs have a strictly text-based interface. With those, you use the command *get*, as in **get etiquet.zip**, to download a file. You use the command *put*, as in **put chap1.zip**, to upload a file.

Gopher

Like the WWW, Gopher puts the focus on the information, not on learning a number of different techniques. A Gopher server provides a menu to represent the information and resources it has available. You work with one or more menus, choosing items

that are documents (files), directories, links to other Internet sites, tools to help you find information, or other Internet services. You don't have to know many techniques to use Gopher; most of the time you only need to be able to choose items from a menu. Eventually, you come to a menu item representing a text document, image, or other type of file.

Some sources for more information about Gopher are

✦ "Gopher FAQ"
   **http://
   gopher.mtholyoke.
   edu:70/1m/about/
   moregopher/gfaq**

✦ "gopher—PC Webopaedia Definition and Links"
   **http://www
   .pcwebopedia.com/
   gopher.htm**

✦ "Guide to Network Resource Tools: Exploring tools—Gopher"
   **http://www.
   terena.nl/libr
   /gnrt/explore/
   gopher.html**

ABOUT GOPHER. Gopher software was created and developed at the University of Minnesota to allow users to browse and retrieve documents in a campus environment. The gopher is the mascot of the University of Minnesota; that may be connected to how the software got its name. You can also think of the software working, tunneling, or burrowing its way through the Internet, in the same way a gopher tunnels through the earth.

USING GOPHER. When you're using a Web browser to access a Gopher site, the items on the menu are hyperlinks. The items are represented by text with icons indicating the type of Internet service or resource available by following the link. When you come to a link that represents a file (rather than another menu), you can view it, save it to a file, or print it by the same methods as for any other file accessible with your Web browser. Figure 7.21 shows a Gopher menu in the browser window.

The WWW has become more popular than Gopher, and the information on the WWW is presented in a more effective manner. Gopher sites can only display text menus. When you use the WWW, you work in a hypertext or hypermedia environment. Sometimes the items you select are part of other sentences or paragraphs. These links to other Internet resources are presented in context, rather than as a list or menu. Gopher also hides many of the details of mak-

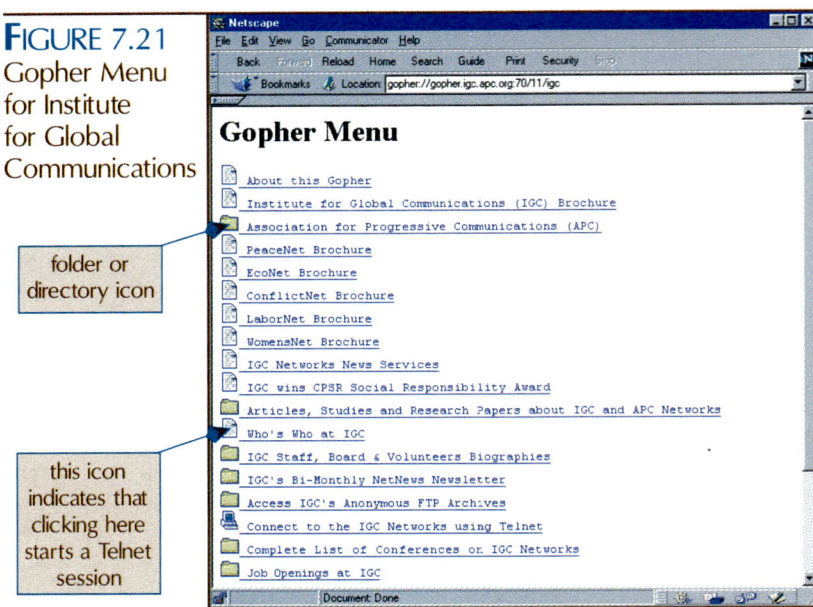

FIGURE 7.21
Gopher Menu for Institute for Global Communications

folder or directory icon

this icon indicates that clicking here starts a Telnet session

ing connections to different Internet sites and using Internet services. However, when you're using Gopher you're always dealing with menus, so you have to work according to the ways the menus are defined. The entries on menus can't be very long, which means they may not be descriptive; you sometimes end up choosing a menu item that doesn't represent the type of information you wanted. Some sites are discontinuing their Gopher servers to concentrate on providing information as Web pages.

URL Format for Gopher

A URL for a Gopher site begins with **gopher://** followed by the Internet domain name of the site. For example, **gopher://gopher**

.loc.gov/ is the URL for the Gopher server at the Library of Congress. The URL in the form **gopher://internet-site-name/** takes you to the home Gopher menu for a site if there is one.

Locating Resources Available Through Gopher

An extensive list of sites accessible through Gopher is the Web page "Gopher Jewels," **http://galaxy.einet.net/GJ**. Some of those sites are still active, but many have moved their information to a Web server. Since most of the information available through Gopher is also accessible on the World Wide Web, you can use the search engines listed in Chapter 4 to find resources available through Gopher.

Several excellent collections of information available through Gopher have been developed. These collections are often called *subject trees*; they're like the World Wide Web directories discussed in Chapter 4. A list of several subject trees is maintained at Tradewave Galaxy whose URL is **http://galaxy.einet.net/GJ/subject-trees.html**.

Summary

This chapter discussed three established protocols used to share information on the Internet—Telnet, FTP, and Gopher. These protocols were used before the WWW was developed, and they're still used in situations where they are most effective or appropriate. They can be used by selecting hyperlinks in the Web browser window or typing a URL to start them.

Telnet was created so that a person at one computer on the Internet could log into and use the programs and services of another computer on the Internet. There are several applications where this is useful, such as searching databases or library catalogs. The Telnet connection between two computer systems is a virtual connection; packets representing the portions of a session are passed between the

two systems. This sometimes makes the session slow or seem choppy. It's best to use Telnet when that's the only way to access a resource; many Telnet services are being converted over to be accessible as Web pages.

A URL for a resource accessible through Telnet has the form **telnet://internet-site-name**:

> *Example:*
> **telnet://locis.loc.gov**

or the form **telnet://internet-site-name:port-number**:

> *Example:*
> **telnet//cirrus.sprl.umich.edu:3000**

Some Telnet sites require you to supply a login name and perhaps a password; others use a port number. You can start a Telnet session by typing the URL or clicking on a hyperlink, but Telnet doesn't run inside a Web browser window, and it isn't always included with Netscape Navigator. You may have to retrieve a shareware or freeware version of Telnet and then configure Netscape Navigator.

FTP stands for file transfer protocol. Along with Telnet and email, it is one of the three basic services on the Internet. It's used to share files or copy files from one site on the Internet to another. It's most effective when the name of the remote site, the directory, and the file are known;

FTP isn't designed for browsing. Anonymous FTP is the term used when a file can be copied from one computer to another without giving a login name or a password. Collections of files available by anonymous FTP are called anonymous FTP archives.

To retrieve a file by anonymous FTP, use a URL in the form **ftp://name-of-ftp-site/directory-name/file-name**, for example, **ftp://ftp.jpl.nasa.gov/pub/images/browse/marglobe.gif**. To look through a directory use a URL in the form **ftp://name-of-ftp-site/directory-name/**, for example, **ftp://ftp.jpl.nasa.gov/pub/images/**. When you use FTP with a Web browser and you give the URL for a file, the browser attempts to display the file and then you can save it to your computer. Files available by anonymous FTP are classified as being text (ASCII) files or binary files. Text files contain only printable, readable characters, like the ones on this page. Binary files contain information that's meant to be processed by a computer (such as programs, compressed files, archives, or collections of files) or files that can be viewed or heard (such as images, video, or audio).

Literally trillions of bytes of information, programs, and resources are available through anonymous FTP. Archie, one of the first Internet search programs, is a tool specifically designed for searching anonymous FTP archives. When you supply a keyword, the names of the files, directories, and sites in the database are searched. Several other search services and software libraries search a database that holds descriptions and reviews of software available through anonymous FTP. Some of the software archives also have entries arranged by the type of program (for example, antivirus programs) or by the operating system (for example, Windows 95 or Macintosh).

Transferring a file from a remote computer to the computer you're using is called downloading a file. That's what you do when you retrieve a program from an FTP archive. Many of the programs depend on a number of auxiliary files to be run and used effectively, such as online help. These files are put together into a package, and the contents are compressed to allow for easier and faster storage and transfer.

After you retrieve one of these packages of software, you need to process it to extract the components. If the package name ends with **.exe**, then it's a self-extracting archive. Click on the name of the package, and it will unpack itself. If the name ends with **.zip**, you'll need to use a program such as PKZIP or WinZip.

Once the files are extracted, you will run a program (application) to install the program. To be safe, you'll also want to scan the software for computer viruses before you install it. Look for a file with a name such as **Readme**, and read it before you install the program. It may help you decide whether the program is appropriate for you and your computer system. Finally, look for a program—often named **Setup** or **Install**—that you'll run to install the program.

The Gopher system was designed to deliver documents in an academic environment. It was developed at the University of Minnesota and is available on a wide variety of computer systems. You work with a menu system to retrieve information. The menus are available through the Web browser once you fol-low a hyperlink to a Gopher server or give the URL for a Gopher server on the Internet. The items on the menu are hyperlinks, and thus can be of a variety of types—file, directory, BinHexed Macintosh file, DOS binary archive, uuencoded file, Telnet session, image file, Web page, or index-search server. Gopher was developed before the WWW. It allows access to a variety of services and resources on the Internet in much the same way as Web browsers do, except that with Gopher you're always dealing with a menu. With a Web browser you deal with hypertext and hypermedia, so presenting, delivering, and discovering information are more effective on the WWW than they could be in "gopher-space" (the collection of material available through Gopher menus).

The basic form of a URL for Gopher is **gopher://gopher-server-name**; as an example, **gopher://gopher.tc.umn.edu**. Since you trace through menus to get to items, the URLs for some items available through Gopher can be complex. ◆

Selected Terms in This Chapter

anonymous FTP	file transfer protocol (FTP)	Gopher
compression	freeware	shareware
domain name	FTP archive	Telnet
	FTP client	upload

Telnet

1. Find the subway route you need to follow to get from a given location to another in Paris. Do the same thing for a subway route in Boston. Impossible? Not if you use Telnet to contact the Subway Navigator. To do that, use **telnet://metro.ratp.fr:10000**. Once you're connected, choose either French or English as the language used for the menus.
   a. Choose France/Paris as the city and find the subway route from Notre-Dame de Lorette to Champs Elysees. Which lines (trains) should you take? Which stops will you pass through? Where do you change trains? How long will it take?
   b. Now answer the same questions for the route from the airport to the Fenway area in USA/Boston.

2. The previous exercise had you look up subway routes using Telnet. Did you notice that service is also available as a Web page? Use the URL for the "Subway Navigator" (**http://metro.ratp.fr:10001**) and look up the same routes as in Exercise 1. Describe the benefits of using the Web interface rather than the Telnet interface.

3. You can use Telnet to get weather reports for cities in the U.S. and weather information about cities in other countries. Use the URL **telnet://cirrus.sprl.umich.edu:3000** to start a Telnet session with the Weather underground at the University of Michigan. When you first contact the site, pressing **Enter** displays a full menu of options and keying in a three-letter city code displays the forecast for that city.
   a. The code for Dodge City, Kansas, is DDC. What's the forecast for Dodge City?
   b. What's the forecast for Orlando, Florida?
   c. What information does the Weather underground offer about cities in Central and South America?

(handwritten margin note: Organization or Comm.)

4. Free-Nets are community-based organizations that provide free or low-cost access to the Internet. Look at the ones listed on the Web page "List of Community Networks," **http://ofcn.org/networks/By_State.txt.html**. Find one located in or near where you live. Use Telnet to connect to that Free-Net. Describe the services and resources available.

Using Telnet to Search Libraries and Databases

5. You've got to do some research on Beethoven's works. Your challenge is to come up with a list of five or more references—author, title, and call number—that deal with Beethoven's chamber music. Probably any book about Beethoven will contain the topic, but the references you find ought to be specific to chamber music. Luckily, the Beethoven Bibliography Database is accessible by Telnet. Here's how to reach it. First use Telnet to go to **sjsulib1 .sjsu.edu**. Use **lib** if you're prompted for a login name; select **O** on the main menu, and then select **Beethoven Bibliography Database**. You'll want to do a search by subject, a search by keyword, or perhaps a search by genre.

6. The National Institutes of Health Library in Bethesda, Maryland, makes its catalog available through Telnet; use **telnet://nih-library.nih.gov**. No password is required to log in. Once you're connected, select **NIH Library Catalog** and you'll see a menu such as:

> **A > AUTHOR**
> **T > TITLE**
> **S > SUBJECT**
> **C > CALL #**
> **W > WORDS in the title**
> **V > VIEW your circulation record**
> **I > Library INFORMATION**
> **D > DISCONNECT**

a. Search the catalog for books or journals whose author has the same last name as yours. If nothing meets that criterion, search for items by an author whose name is close to yours. The catalog system will let you know what is close. Write down the title, author, and call number of three items.

b. Suppose you need to do some research on the topic of AIDS. Do a subject search and report the title, author, and call number of five items.

c. Do a word search on the topic of AIDS and report back the title, author, and call number of five items different from the ones you reported in part b.

FTP

7. Use your Web browser to retrieve the document whose URL is **ftp://cpsr.org/cpsr/privacy/privacy_international/ international_laws/un_charter.txt**.

   a. What is it about?
   b. What is the domain name of the site being contacted?
   c. What protocol is used to transfer the file? Explain.
   d. Find the same document at a Web site that uses a different protocol for transferring the file to your browser.

8. Homophones are words that sound the same but that are spelled differently. For example, *here* and *hear* are homophones. Can you think of a hundred more? A list of homophones is available by anonymous FTP at **ftp://crl .nmsu.edu/CLR/lexica/homophones/homophones .txt**.

   a. Retrieve the list and browse through it. List a few homophones.
   b. What is the domain name here?
   c. Use the URL **ftp://crl.nmsu.edu/CLR** to find out the name and purpose of this anonymous FTP archive.

d. Can you find another list of homophones on the Web? Give the URL.

9. Retrieve a copy of "Anonymous FTP Frequently Asked Questions (FAQ) List," **ftp://rtfm.mit.edu/pub/usenet-by-group/news.answers/ftp-list/faq**.

   a. The FAQ contains an answer to this question: "What types of FTP information are available?" Write a summary of the answer.

   b. Give a brief synopsis of the copyright notice you see when you connect by anonymous FTP to the directory **/pub/usenet-by-group** at **rtfm.mit.edu**.

10. Internet standards documents are often stated in documents called Request for Comments (RFC).

    a. Retrieve the file **1855.txt** from **ftp.isi.edu** in the directory **/in-notes**. Start with the URL **ftp://ftp.isi.edu** and work from there.

    b. What does that document have to say about FTP? (*Hint:* Look in Section 4.1 of the RFC.)

11. Health care for pets too!

    a. Write down the steps necessary to retrieve the file named **health-care.Z** from the directory **/usenet/news.answers/dogs-faq** at **ftp.uu.net**.

    b. Retrieve the file. It is compressed. If you have a program that can uncompress it, use that now. You can get a version of it in uncompressed form from either **rtfm.mit.edu** under the directory **/pub/usenet-by-group/news.answers/dogs-faq**, or from **ftp.univ-lyon1.fr** in the directory **/pub/faq/by-name/dogs-faq**.

    c. There is a similar file about health care for cats. Can you find it?

12. Retrieve a copy of the file with the URL **ftp://nic.merit.edu/introducing.the.internet/answers.to.new.user**

.**questions**. Using that file, write a one- or two-sentence answer to each of the following questions.

a. What is the difference between the *Internet* and an *internet?*

b. What is an advantage of the domain name system (DNS)?

c. What is Archie?

d. How is Archie different from FTP?

e. What is Gopher?

13. Using any two of the Archie servers mentioned in the text, use the string **Africa** to request an Archie search with an exact match.

a. Which server gave the most results?

b. Which server gave the results that would be most useful to you?

14. Using the images available through URL **ftp://ftp.jpl .nasa.gov/pub/images/browse**, collect the URLs for images of all the planets in the solar system. Put them in one bookmark folder.

15. Do you know about Neko? Go to the software archive "FilePile," **http://filepile.com/nc/start**. Search for a program that lets you experience Neko. What is Neko? What are the system requirements for using the program? Download and install it. Be sure to select your operating system as part of the search form on FilePile's home page.

16. Do you need an alarm while you're using your computer?

a. Go to the software archive "ZDNet Library," **http:// www.zdnet.com/swlib**, and search for programs that act as alarm clocks. Choose one program to download, and explain why you made that choice. Download and install the program. Did it work as you anticipated it would? If you're not happy with it, remove it from your computer system.

b. Go to the software archive FILE MINE, **http://www.filemine.com**, and search for an alarm clock program. Choose one program to download, and explain why you made that choice. Download and install the program. Did it work as you anticipated it would? If you're not happy with it, remove it from your computer system.

c. Write a few sentences comparing the features of the two archives. Which do you prefer? Why?

Gopher

17. Select one of the Gopher subject trees listed at URL **http://galaxy.einet.net/GJ/subject-trees.html**, as mentioned in the text. By saving hyperlinks in the bookmark list and/or creating a Web page, put together your own subject tree. The tree doesn't have to be elaborate or too complex. Pick five areas or subjects that interest you and collect at least three hyperlinks in each area.

18. Use the URL **gopher://gopher.well.sf.ca.us** to connect to the WELLgopher.

a. Follow the link **About this gopherspace** to find out about WELLgopher. One of the items describes WELLgopher as an experiment. What type of experiment? What is the editorial policy and when was it written?

b. Go back to the main menu. Go to the menu entitled **Communications and Media**. Describe what you find there.

c. Visit a few of the other menus. Now what can you say about the experiment attempted by WELLgopher? Have they accomplished their goals? Explain your answer.

chapter 8

SOCIAL ISSUES, LEGAL ISSUES, AND SECURITY

The Internet and the World Wide Web encompass many cultures and points of view. Given the rapid growth in the number of online users, it's only to be expected that rules, regulations, and laws will be established to govern the use of the Internet and World Wide Web. In this chapter, we'll cover these topics:

+ **Privacy and Civil Liberties**

+ **Intellectual Property and Copyright**

+ **Internet Security**

It's easy to get excited about using the Internet and the Web. They're vivacious, interesting, and important places to work, learn, do business, and just have fun. The World Wide Web always seems to have something new. You find not only new resources, but also better services and programs, making the WWW and the Internet easier to use and more powerful. There's also a great deal of diversity; different cultures, nations, and outlooks are represented on the Internet. All these things make for an exciting environment, but as the Internet and the World Wide Web become more popular and the number of users increases, it's reasonable to expect rules, regulations, and laws governing their use. You also have to consider the effect the Internet has on our lives, our communities, and society as its use becomes more widespread. In this chapter we'll discuss a few of these issues associated with using the Internet and the World Wide Web.

The explosive growth of the World Wide Web and the inclusion of commercial networks and services into the Internet have been accompanied by an astounding increase in the population of Internet users. Many of the new users feel that networks and computers, like a public utility, should be available anywhere, reliable, and easy to use. As the Internet becomes available to a much wider portion of the population, older modes of behavior on the Internet have changed. Commercial activity and advertising are firmly established as common Internet activity. Businesses are determining effective and secure ways of engaging in commerce on the Internet. As the use of the Internet becomes more widespread in the areas of education, research, business, and recreation, issues of security, reliability, ownership, and liability become more important. Many local laws and international agreements are directly applicable to Internet activities. On the other hand, this is a rather new medium using technology that came into existence after many applicable laws were written. New laws and agreements recognizing these changes and differences are being established.

The Internet and the World Wide Web have grown rapidly from a research project into something that involves millions of people worldwide. Much of the Internet's usefulness comes from the fact that users and service providers depend on each other and need to support each other. Hopefully, that sort of sharing and respect will continue. Your behavior, your expectations of others, and your activities will make the difference.

Privacy and civil liberties are often defined in terms of their expression or environment. Laws in the United States dealing with privacy and expression in printed form **need to be modified** to take into account new media and new means of transmitting information.

Privacy and Civil Liberties

What's reasonable to expect in terms of *privacy* and civil liberties as they relate to use of the Internet? Your initial response might be that you expect the same protection of your privacy and the same *civil liberties*—such as freedom of expression, safeguards against the arbitrary exercise of authority, and protection from abusive or offensive actions—on the Internet as you have in your other dealings in society. Codes of behavior or rules of etiquette have developed on the Internet over the years.

In some cases laws have been adopted to provide the same level of protection of privacy and guarantees of civil liberties for working with electronic media as with any other media. An important point is that privacy and civil liberties are often defined in terms of their expression or environment. The laws in the United States dealing with privacy and expression in printed form (on paper) need to be changed to suit electronic communications. Laws need to be modified to take into account new media and new means of transmitting information. Furthermore, the people who develop, act on, and enforce laws need to be informed of the impact of technological changes.

We'll cover a few of the important issues related to privacy and civil liberties—email privacy, unwarranted search and seizure, and offensive messages and libel.

Email Privacy

When you send a message by email, the message is broken into packets and the packets are sent out over the Internet. The number of packets depends on the size of the message. Each message has the Internet address of the sender (your address) and the address of the recipient. Packets from a single message may take different routes to the destination, or may take different routes at different times. This works well for the Internet and for you. Since packets are generally sent through the best path, depending on the traffic load on the Internet, the path doesn't depend on certain systems being in operation, and all you have to give is the address of the destination.

The packets making up an email message may pass through several different systems before reaching their destination. This means there may be some places between you and the destination where the packets could be intercepted and examined. Since all the systems have to be able to look at the address of the destination, each system could be able to examine the contents of the message. If you're using a computer system shared by others or if the system at the destination is shared by others, there is usually someone (a system administrator) capable of examining all the messages. So, in the absence of codes of ethics or without the protection of law, email could be very public. Needless to say, you shouldn't be reading someone else's email. Most system administrators adopt a code of ethics under which they will not examine email unless they feel it's necessary for support of the systems they administer. The truth of the matter is they are generally too busy to bother reading other people's mail.

ELECTRONIC COMMUNICATIONS PRIVACY ACT. One example of a law to ensure the privacy of email is the *Electronic Communications Privacy Act* (*ECPA*) passed in 1986 by Congress. It prohibits anyone from intentionally intercepting, using, and/or disclosing email messages without the sender's permission. The ECPA was passed to protect individuals from having their private messages accessed by government officers or others without legal permission. That bill extended the protections that existed for voice communications to non-voice communications conveyed

How Public Key Encryption Works

You write a message.

You encrypt the message. Anyone with access to the public key can do this.

The message is put in an unreadable form.

You send the message.

the Internet

Only someone with the private key can decode the message.

through wires or over the airwaves. You can, of course, give your permission for someone to access your email. However, law enforcement officials or others cannot access your email in stored form (on a disk or tape) without a warrant, and electronic transmission of your email can't be intercepted or "tapped" without a court order. The ECPA does allow a system administrator to access users' email on a computer system if it's necessary for the operation or security of the system. The ECPA then gives the system administrator the responsibility to allow no access to email passing within or through a system without a court order

or warrant. She can and indeed should refuse any requests to examine email unless the proper legal steps are followed.

ENCRYPTION. When you send a message by email it's often transmitted in the same form you typed it. Even though it's unethical and illegal for someone else to read it, the message is in a form that's easy to read. This is similar to sending a message written on a postcard through the postal service. One way to avoid this is to use encryption to put a message into an unreadable form. The characters in the message can be changed by substitution or scrambling, usually based on

some secret code. The message can't be read unless the code and method of encryption are known. The code is called a key. Many messages are encoded by a method called public key encryption. If you encrypt a message and send it on to someone, that person has to know the key to decode your message. If the key is also sent by email, it might be easy to intercept the key and decode the encrypted message.

With public key encryption there are two keys, one public and the other private. The public key needs to be known. To send a message to a friend, you use her or his public key to encrypt the message. Your friend then uses her or his private key to decode the message after receiving it. Suppose you want to send an encrypted message to your friend Milo. He tells you his public key; in fact, there's no harm if he tells everybody. You write the message and then encrypt it using Milo's public key. He receives the message and then uses his private key to decode it. It doesn't matter who sent the message to Milo as long as it was encrypted with his public key. Also, even if the message were intercepted, it couldn't be read without Milo's private key. It's up to him to keep that secret. Likewise, if he wanted to respond, he would use your public key to encrypt the message. You would use your private key to decode it.

You can obtain a version of public key encryption software called PGP, for Pretty Good Privacy. It's freely available to individuals and may be purchased for commercial use. There are some licensing restrictions on the use of the commercial versions in the United States and Canada. Furthermore, United States State Department regulations prohibit the export of some versions of this program to other countries. In fact, current restrictions in the United States prohibit the export of most encryption methods, while other countries allow the export of encryption methods

and algorithms. Some people feel strongly that these policies should be changed for the sake of sharing information and allowing common encryption of sensitive and business messages, but others don't agree.

To read more about PGP, take a look at these:

- ✦ "PGP and what it does" by David Rosoff **http://www.arc .unm.edu/~drosoff/ pgp/pgp.html**

- ✦ "Protect your Privacy with PGP" by Victoria Hall Smith **http://www .cnet.com/Content/ Features/Howto/ Privacy**

- ✦ "Where To Get The Pretty Good Privacy Program (PGP) FAQ" **http://www .cryptography.org/ getpgp.htm**

One issue that needs to be resolved is whether it should be possible for law enforcement or other government officials to decode encrypted messages. Some argue that because of the need to detect criminal action or in the interests of national security, the means to decode any messages should be available to the appropriate authorities. Others argue that individuals have the right to privacy in their com-

munications. In the United States, the issue has been decided in favor of government access in the case of digital telephone communications. The issue hasn't been settled yet for email or other forms of electronic communications.

Here's a list of some extensive resources for information about electronic privacy:

- ✦ "6.805/STS085: Readings on Encryption and National Security" **http://www-swiss .ai.mit.edu/6095/ readings-crypto.html**

- ✦ "6.805/STS085: Readings on Privacy Implications of Computer Networks" **http://www-swiss .ai.mit.edu/6095/ readings-privacy.html**

- ✦ "EPIC Online Guide to Privacy Resources" **http://www.epic .org/privacy/privacy _resources_faq.html**

- ✦ "The Privacy Pages" **http://www.2020tech .com/maildrop/ privacy.html**

Privacy on the Web

It's easy to get the impression that you're browsing the Web and using Internet services in an anonymous manner. But that's not the case. Every time you visit a Web site, some information about your computer system is transmitted to the server. When you fill out a form the information you provide is passed to a server. Some Web sites track the activities of users through the use of *cookies*, information that's passed between a computer that's using a Web browser and a Web server. You also need to be aware of the risks involved with giving out personal information through email, chat groups, and forms. Since it may be difficult to know with whom a person is communicating, you need to be especially careful about disclosing personal information. Children especially need to know about and be informed of the risks and dangers involved with using the Internet.

WHAT HAPPENS WHEN YOU GO TO A WEB SITE—WHAT THE SERVER KNOWS. When you go to a Web site, either by clicking on a hyperlink or by typing in a URL in the location field, your browser (the client program) sends a request to a Web server. This request includes the IP address of your computer system, the URL of the file or Web page you've requested, and the time the request was made. If you click on a hyperlink from a Web page, the URL of the Web page is also passed to the server. All of this information is kept in log files on the server. It's possible to have the log files analyzed and track all access to a Web server.

THE TRAIL LEFT ON YOUR COMPUTER. We've seen that each server keeps log files to identify requests for Web pages. So in that sense you leave a trail of your activities on each of the Web servers that you contact. There's also a trail of your activities kept on the computer you use to access the Web. Recently accessed Web pages and a list of the URLs accessed are kept in the *cache*—a folder or directory that contains recently viewed Web pages, images, and other resources, and the *history list*. If you're using a computer to access the Web in a public place, such as a lab or library, then it's possible for someone to check on your activities.

✦ **Cache.**

Most Web browsers keep copies of recently accessed Web pages, images, and other files in a folder or directory called the cache. When you return to a Web page you've visited recently, the browser first checks to see if it's available in the cache and retrieves it from your computer rather than retrieving it from a remote site. It's much faster to retrieve a Web page from the cache rather than from a remote site. This is convenient, but it also leaves a record of your activities. It is possible to clear the cache whenever you'd like using the Preferences panel. To do that bring up the Preferences panel by clicking on **Edit** in the menu bar and selecting **Preferences**. Next bring up the Cache panel by clicking on **Advanced** and then clicking on **Cache**; and finally clear the disk cache by clicking on **Clear Disk Cache**.

✦ **History list.**

The Web browser keeps a record of the path you've taken to get to the current location. To see the path and select a site from it, click on **Go** in the menu bar. The browser also keeps a list of all the Web pages visited recently in the history list. To bring up the history list, press Ctrl+H from the keyboard or click on **Communicator** from the menu bar and select **History** from that menu. This list is kept around for a time period specified in days. The number of days an item may be kept on the list is set in the Preferences panel category titled Navigator. To get to the spot where you can set it, click on **Edit** in the menu bar, select **Preferences**, and then click on **Navigator**. You can also clear the history list from this panel by clicking on **Clear History**.

COOKIES. A cookie is information that's passed between a Web server and a Web browser program. Netscape developed the term and the method for working with cookies. The collection of cookies on your computer is (usually) kept in a file named **cookies.txt**. A Web server requests and/or writes a cookie to your computer only if you access a Web page that contains the commands to do that. You have the option to not accept any cookies, to accept cookies that only get returned to the server that put a cookie on your computer, or to be warned before accepting a cookie. To do that click on **Edit** in the menu bar, select **Preferences**, and then click on **Advanced**.

Cookies are sometimes viewed as an invasion of privacy, but they are useful to you in some cases. Suppose you want to visit a site frequently that requires you to give a password or a site that you can customize to match your preferences. Hypertext transfer protocol (HTTP) is used when you visit a Web site. When a Web page is requested, a virtual connection is made between the client and the server so the server can deliver the Web page. Once the page has been transmitted, the connection is terminated. If you visit a site again—in a few days or a few seconds—the server, through

HTTP, has no information about the previous visit (except for the log file's record of the URL for the page). Cookies can be used to keep track of your password or the preferences you've set for every visit to that site. That way you don't have to enter the same information each time you visit.

✦ To get more information about cookies take a look at the Webopedia entry on cookies at **http://www.webopedia.com/cookie.htm**.

Unwarranted Search and Seizure

Suppose a person is suspected of having illegal items on a computer system, such as pirated software, credit card numbers, telephone access codes, stolen documents, or proprietary information, and law enforcement officials obtain a court order or warrant to search or confiscate the materials. What are reasonable actions?

✦ Is it reasonable to confiscate all the disks connected to or networked to the suspect's computer system?

✦ Is it reasonable to confiscate all the suspect's computer equipment including the main computer, printers, modems, and telephones?

✦ If the items are removed from the premises for searching, how much time should pass before they are returned?

✦ If the suspect's system is part of a bulletin board or email system with messages for other, presumably innocent persons, should those messages be delivered to the innocent parties?

The answers to these and some related questions depend on the laws governing permissible searches and seizures. The actions taken in cases such as these also depend on how well the technology is understood by the courts and law enforcement officials. For example, the Fourth Amendment to the United States Constitution guards against unreasonable searches and seizures of property. In 1990, all the computer equipment and files of one company, Steve Jackson Games, were confiscated and searched by the United States Secret Service. The warrant application released later showed that the company was not suspected of any crime. However, the law enforcement officials, in their fervor to deal with "computer crime," appeared to disregard accepted civil liberties. Some of this was undoubtedly because they were unfamiliar with the technology at that time. A printer or modem, for example, can't store anything once the power is turned off, so there is no need to confiscate those items if one is searching for what might be illegal information. These actions and the related court cases point out the need to keep the officers of the legal system informed and educated regarding the uses and capabilities of technology.

The Electronic Frontier Foundation (EFF) was formed in 1990 to, among other things, bring issues dealing with civil liberties related to computing and telecommunications technology to the attention of the public at large, legislators, and court and law enforcement officials. It is a nonprofit public interest organization. Use the URL **http://www.eff.org** to access the home page of the EFF and **http://www.eff.org/pub/** to view their library of publications and other materials available on the Internet. They have also provided legal services and opinions in cases similar to the one described above.

Offensive Material and Libel

OFFENSIVE AND ABUSIVE EMAIL. Virtually all codes of etiquette, ethics, and policies for acceptable use of networked computer facilities include state-ments that prohibit sending offensive or abusive messages by email. This is, naturally, similar to the codes of behavior and laws we adhere to in other, everyday communications. One difference between dealing with this sort of behavior on the Internet versus other vehicles of communication, such as the telephone or postal service, is that no one is in charge of the Internet—it is a cooperative organization. If you have a problem with someone at your site, talk with your supervisor, their supervisor, your system administrator, or your Internet service provider about it. If the problem comes from another site, send email to the address **postmaster@the.other.site**, and talk with the system administrator at your site or your supervisor about it. (You substitute the Internet domain name of the site in question for *the.other.site.*) Individuals have been arrested and prosecuted for making threatening remarks by email. Civil suits and charges have been filed against individuals in cases of harassment, abuse, and stalking.

SEXUALLY EXPLICIT MATERIAL AND PORNOGRAPHY.

Some material available on the Internet may be classified as sexually explicit or pornographic. It's not surprising since there's a large number of people using the World Wide Web and the Inter-net with varying preferences, interests, and cultural perspectives. Also, as with other media, there is a market for it. In the past most of this material was available through Usenet newsgroups whose names clearly identified the content, for example, **alt.binaries.nude.celebrities**.

With the increase in popularity of the WWW, many commercial Web sites that traffic in explicit videos, phone sex, and items with sexually explicit themes have been set up. In fact these so-called "XXX-rated" sites were among the first to be successful commercial ventures on the Web. Most of these sites have a home page warning that the related pages contain material some might find offensive or inappropriate. The home page often contains a form where the user states that she/he is at least 18 or 21 years of age. The commercial sites charge a fee for access. The fee is generally charged to a credit card or some other electronic account. It's not difficult to find this material on the Internet, but in almost every case it has to be sought out; people using the Internet aren't coerced or tricked into viewing it.

The focus of the debate about this so-called "cyberporn" has been whether it's appropriate for the material to be readily available to children and whether it's appropriate to pass laws that

While filters may be helpful, keep in mind that some sites may be screened that might have useful material. The American Library Association has stated that if the library were to use filters, they would be restricting access to information.

restrict the content of the Internet. There are a number of programs that can be installed on a computer to restrict the material that can be accessed on the World Wide Web. The programs work with lists of Web pages and ways of describing the content of Web pages to filter material.

Two sources of information about these programs and related topics are:

+ "Filtering Facts"
  http://www .filteringfacts.org

+ "PEDINFO Parental Control of Internet Access"
  http://www.uab.edu/ pedinfo/Control.html

While filters may be helpful, keep in mind that some sites may be screened that might have useful material. For example, Web pages that address gay teenagers, safe sex information, drug legalization, and controversial issues may not appear in the results list because certain words have been filtered out and therefore made inaccessible. Also, certain medical topics like breast cancer may be avoided because the words that describe these medical conditions and body parts may be on the filter list. It is for this reason that the American Library Association has stated in "Access to Electronic Information, Services and Networks: An Interpretation

of the Library Bill of Rights," **http://www.ala.org/alaorg/ oif/oif_q&a.html**, that if a library were to use filters, it would be restricting access to information. The ALA feels that it's the library's role to provide access to information and let users choose what they want to read, hear, or see. Opponents of this view say that libraries don't generally collect pornography in book or magazine form, so why should libraries allow this material to be accessed on the Internet?

The culture of the Internet has fostered personal rights and liberties, so some argue its content should not be restricted or censored. There are laws banning or restricting pornography; some countries have more stringent laws than others, and some laws restrict the distribution of the material. Private networks such as AOL and Prodigy sometimes enact their own rules regarding content. One online service filtered out messages containing the word "breast," but rescinded that action due to complaints from users who found information and discussions relating to breast cancer very valuable.

It seems that the current debate regarding pornography and civil liberties on the Internet will be continued for some time. The President of the United States signed legislation that had been approved by Congress, the Com-

munications Decency Act of 1996, that made it illegal to transmit certain materials on the Internet. The term used in the legislation is "indecent" material. This legislation presents some problems—monitoring the Internet would greatly increase the expense and complexity of maintaining current networks; the term "indecent" is open to many interpretations. On June 27, 1997, in Reno vs. American Civil Liberties Union, the U.S. Supreme Court ruled that this act abridged the freedom of speech that is protected by the First Amendment. The court stated, "The interest in encouraging freedom of expression in a democratic society outweighs any theoretical but unproven benefit of censorship." You can read this opinion at **http://www.ciec .org/SC_appeal/opinion .shtml**. This opinion held that the Internet should not be viewed as a broadcast medium like television or radio, but a medium in which individuals are guaranteed free speech. Here are a few sites for more information about these topics:

+ "Cyberporn Debate"
  http://www2000 .ogsm.vanderbilt.edu/ cyberporn.debate.cgi

+ "Internet Censorship"
  http://epic.org/free _speech/censorship

- "Technology and Freedom"
  http://www.freedomforum.org/technology/welcome.asp

INAPPROPRIATE BUSINESS PRACTICES.

There was a time before the late 1980s when commercial traffic was not allowed on the Internet. Now the use of the Internet for commercial activities is commonplace. It's not unusual for Web pages to carry advertisements. Usenet and email discussion groups developed on the Internet in the late 1970s and early 1980s in an atmosphere free from marketing and advertising. Some (relatively few) Usenet newsgroups and discussion groups tolerate commercial announcements. Most of these groups are adamantly opposed to any selling or advertising, and unsolicited marketing is met with strong resistance. This resistance has included attempts to have the advertiser dropped by their ISP and flooding the advertiser's mailbox with email messages.

Advertising and commerce is allowed on the Internet, but most users prefer that it be done in clearly identified newsgroups, discussion groups, or Web pages.

An inappropriate commercial posting to a newsgroup or an unsolicited commercial email is called *spam*. The term is also used to mean a message sent to many unrelated newsgroups, discussion groups, or individual email addresses. Because email can be composed and is sent by a computer, it's relatively easy to send several thousand messages in less than an hour. Naturally, it's annoying to get this "junk" email or posting to groups. It's also costly to the person receiving the spam, and, unfairly, not very costly to the person sending the email. The receiver bears the cost in several ways:

- Time spent sifting through email or postings that are junk.

- Time spent retrieving email messages or newsgroup postings from a server (this is particularly a problem for people who pay for Internet service according to how long they maintain an Internet connection).

- Time spent waiting to connect to sites and retrieve Web pages because traffic is slowed on the Internet due to the spam being sent.

- Possibly higher charges from an ISP since an ISP has to store the mail or group postings until they are read.

Spam is more than an annoyance; it slows other traffic on the Internet and imposes a cost on the receiver (dealing with the unsolicited commercial email or newsgroup postings) at little cost to the sender. Some estimates put the cost of spam at over thirty million dollars per year.

Some legislation dealing with spam is pending in the U.S. Congress. Identifying spammers and notifying their Internet service providers is sometimes helpful in dealing with the problem. Several major ISPs have instituted policies that attempt to prohibit spam from their servers (but still it's the ISP's customers that have to eventually pay the bill for that). In 1997 one ISP, EarthLink, successfully mounted a legal challenge against Cyber Promotions, Inc., in order to stop the company from sending unsolicited email to its customers or using the ISP's networks for distributing unsolicited email. In 1998 Cyber Promotions was ordered to pay EarthLink two million dollars.

The Coalition Against Unsolicited Commercial Email (CAUCE) is an all-volunteer organization that supports legislative and technical solutions to eliminating spam. Visit their Web site "Join the Fight Against Spam," **http://www.cauce.org**, for more information. The Web site "Get that spammer,"

http://kryten.eng.monash.edu.au/gspam.html, by Julian Byrne contains lots of information about ways to track down and stop spammers.

LIBEL. Some libel suits have been filed based on postings to Usenet or some other network. One person or company feels that another has slandered them or falsely attempted to damage their reputation. Once again, you would expect the same laws or rules for libel in the society at large to be applied to network communications. That's generally the case, but an interesting issue comes up, centering around whether the company or organization that maintains a computer telecommunication system is responsible for libelous or even illegal messages posted there. In the United States the courts have generally drawn an analogy between these systems and a bookstore. The owner of a bookstore is not responsible for the contents of all the books in the store, and likewise, the management of a commercial networked system on the Internet has not been held responsible for all messages on its system. On the other hand, some commercial network systems claim to screen all messages before they're posted. In that case they may be held accountable for libelous messages. Also, consider that

telephone companies aren't held responsible for the speech on their equipment since they fall into the category of a "common carrier." However, television and radio stations are responsible for the content of their broadcasts.

Intellectual Property and Copyright

You know there is a wealth of files, documents, images, and other types of items available on the Internet. They can be viewed, copied, printed, downloaded, saved in a file, or passed on to others. Just because we can copy or duplicate information we find on the Internet, is it legal or ethical to do so? Many, if not most, of these items don't exist in a physical form, so perhaps the issues about ownership that depend on something having a physical form don't make sense. But ownership of these items, whether they have a physical form, does make sense in terms of intellectual property. There are a number of laws and agreements throughout the world to protect intellectual property rights.

Only the owners of information can grant the right to copy or duplicate materials. This is called the copyright. Many documents on the Internet contain a statement asserting the document is copyrighted and give

permission for distributing the document in an electronic form, provided it isn't sold or made part of some commercial venture. The copyright laws of the United States, the Universal Copyright Convention, or the Berne Union generally protect items that don't contain such statements. Most copyright conventions or statutes include a provision so individuals may copy of portions of a document for short-term use. If information is obtainable on the Internet and there is no charge to access the information, it often can be shared in an electronic form. That certainly doesn't mean you can copy images or documents and make them available on the Internet, or make copies and share them in a printed form with others. Quite naturally, many people who create or provide material available on the Internet expect to get credit and be paid for their work.

One issue that may need to be resolved is the physical nature of information on the Internet. In most cases, it exists on one disk and is viewed in an electronic form. It has no tangible, physical form when it's transmitted. Copyright law in the U.S. specifies that copyright protection begins once the work is in "fixed form," so the original portion of these works is protected by copyright. The notion of fixed form is much easier to determine with more traditional works that exist in a physical form, such as books, poems, stories, sound recordings, or motion pictures. Naturally, it seems reasonable to say a work is in fixed form when stored on a disk, but can we say the same about material being transmitted through several networks? If the work only existed on a disk, if that was the only way to obtain the work, then it's clear when the work is being copied and who may be copying the disk. On the other hand, if the information can be accessed through the Internet, one may not know if it is being copied and stored. Current laws and conventions were written for works that exist in some definite physical form, and the nature of that form may make it difficult or time consuming to make unauthorized copies. But information transmitted on the Internet or other networks is very easy to copy. When you copy something in digital form, you make an exact duplicate. Each copy is as good as the original. The ease with which works can be copied and distributed may require a law different from current copyright statutes.

Not all cultures have the same attitudes about ownership of information. Some cultures have a long tradition of sharing information and works created by individuals. Other groups feel all information should be free, and so they think it's appropriate to make works available only if there is no charge for the use of the works. The worldwide nature of the Internet and other networks requires addressing these cultural differences. When the United States deals with some countries, it may withhold a certain level of trading status if they don't abide by international copyright conventions.

These resources give more information about copyright and intellectual property rights:

- ✦ "Copyright Basics" **http://lcweb.loc .gov/copyright/ circs/circ1.html**

- ✦ "INFORMATION POLICY: Copyright and Intellectual Property" **http://ifla.inist.fr/ II/cpyright.htm**

Internet Security

When you use a computer system connected to the Internet, you're able to reach a rich variety of sites and information. By the same token, any system connected to the Internet can be reached in some manner by any of the other computer systems connected to the Internet. Partaking of the material on the Internet also means that you have to be concerned about the security of your computer system and other systems. The reason for concern about your system is obvious—you don't want unauthorized persons accessing your information or information belonging to others who share your system. You want to protect your system from malicious or unintentional actions that could destroy stored information or halt your system. You don't want others masquerading as you. You need to be concerned about the other systems' security so you can have some faith in the information you retrieve from those systems and so you can conduct business transactions. A lack of security results in damage, theft, and, what may be worse in some cases, loss of confidence or trust.

Maintaining security becomes more important as we use the Internet for commercial transactions or transmitting sensitive data. Internet services (as well as other software) aren't always completely tested for security flaws and sometimes security problems will be discovered. While it's exciting to be at the cutting edge, there's some virtue in not adopting the latest service or the latest version of software until it has been around for a while. This gives the Internet community a chance to discover problems. There are several organizations that are dedicated to finding, publicizing, and dealing with security problems. Two in the United States are

- ✦ "CERT (Computer Emergency Response Team)" **http://www.cert.org** Part of the Software Engineering Institute and operated by Carnegie Mellon University for the Department of Defense.

- ✦ "CIAC (Computer Incident Advisory Capability)" **http://www.ciac.org** Maintained by the U.S. Department of Energy.

For a list of similar organizations throughout the world take a look at "FIRST Team Contact Information," **http://www .first.org/team-info**.

In the section "Privacy and Civil Liberties" we mentioned some of the security or privacy problems associated with email. Since information is passed from system to system on the Internet, not always by the same path or through designated secure systems, it can be monitored. Furthermore, you can't always be sure that the address on email hasn't been forged. It appears that an important way to keep transactions secure is to use encryption techniques. These are similar to the ones discussed in that same section on privacy and civil liberties.

If you access the Internet by logging into a computer system, your primary defense against intrusion is your password. You need to choose a password that will be difficult to guess. This means choosing a password that's at least six characters long. You'll also want to use a password that contains upper- and lowercase letters and some nonalphabetic characters. Additionally, the password shouldn't represent a word, and it shouldn't be something that's easy to identify with you such as a phone number, room number, date of birth, or license number. Some bad choices are **Skippy**, **3451234a**, or **gloria4me**. Better choices might be **All452on**, **jmr!pmQ7**, or **sHo$7otg**. Naturally, you have to choose something you'll remember. Never write down your password; doing that makes it easy to find.

Persons who try to gain unauthorized access to a system are called *crackers*. A cracker will, by some means, get a copy of the password file for a system containing the names of all the users along with their passwords. (In some cases the permissions on a password file are set so anyone can read it. This is necessary for certain programs to run. Fortunately, the passwords are encrypted.) Once a cracker gets a copy of a password file, she will run a program that attempts to guess the encrypted passwords. If a password is an encrypted version of a word, a word in reverse order, or a word with one numeral or punctuation mark, it is not too difficult for the program to decipher it. If a cracker has one password on a system, she or he can gain access to that login name and possibly access other portions of the system from there. So, in addition to creating a good password, you need to change it regularly.

Since connecting a network to the Internet allows access to that network, system administrators and other persons concerned with network security are very concerned about making that connection. One device or part of a network that can help enhance security is called a *firewall*. A firewall can be a separate computer, a router, or some other network device that allows certain packets into a network. (Remember that all information is passed throughout the Internet as packets.) By using a firewall and configuring it correctly, only certain types of Internet services can be allowed through to the network. Organizations with firewalls often place their WWW, FTP, and other servers on one part of their network and put a firewall system between those servers and the rest of the network. The firewall restricts access to the protected internal network by letting through only packets associated with certain protocols. Email can still be delivered and sometimes Telnet to the internal network is allowed. If you are on the protected portion of the network, behind the firewall, then you can access Internet and WWW sites on the Internet, but they may not be able to gain direct access to you. Firewalls also perform logging and auditing functions so that if security is breached, the source of the problem may be determined.

To find out more about firewalls, read "Internet Firewalls Frequently Asked Questions," **http://www.v-one.com/documents/fw-faq.htm**.

You don't need to be paranoid about security, but you do need to be aware of anything that seems suspicious. Report any suspicious activity or changes to your directory or files to your system administrator. The system administrator can often take actions to track down a possible break in security. Be suspicious if you're asked for your password at unusual times. You should be asked for it only when you log in. Never give your password to anyone. If a program changes its behavior in terms of requiring more information from you than it did before, it could be that an unauthorized user replaced the original program with another. This is called a *Trojan horse*, because of the similarity of the program to the horse in the classic Greek tale. What appears to be benign can hide some malicious actions or threats.

One type of program that causes problems for Internet users is called a *virus*. A virus doesn't necessarily copy your data or attempt to use your system. However, it can make it difficult or impossible to use your system. A virus is a piece of code or instructions that attaches itself to existing programs. Just like a biological virus, a computer virus can't run or exist on its own, but must be part of an executing program. When these programs are run, the added instructions are also executed. Sometimes the virus does nothing more than announce its presence; in other cases the virus erases files from your disk. A virus moves from system to system by being part of an executable program. Be careful where you get programs. You can obtain a program that scans your system for viruses and also checks programs you load onto your system for known viruses. Use these virus-scanning programs to check new programs you load on your system. Also be sure to have a backup copy of your files so they can be restored if they're inadvertently or maliciously erased.

Getting documents and images from other sites on the Internet won't bring a virus to your system. It comes only from running programs on your system. Viruses can exist in executable programs and also have been found in word-processing documents that contain portions of code that are executed, called macros. For more information on viruses, check the hyperlinks at "Anti-Virus Web Sites," **http://www.virusbtn.com/AVLinks/sites.html**, maintained by *Virus Bulletin*, an international bulletin dealing with prevention, identification, and removal of computer viruses.

Internet security is very important to many users, as well it should be. We need to make sure that messages are private and that monetary transactions and data sources are secure. Laws and acceptable codes of conduct enforce some of these concerns.

A good document about security and privacy is "Identity, Privacy, and Anonymity on the Internet" by L. Detweiler. It's available in three parts at the URL **http://www.uni-giessen.de/faq/archiv/net-privacy.part1-3/msg00000.html**.

Giving Out Information About Yourself and Your Family

There are a number of situations in which you may be asked or

Any information you put into a form will be passed to a Web server and find its way into a database. Disclosing your street or email address to a business sometimes results in your receiving junk mail. You can't be sure **how the information will be used** or marketed unless the organization gathering the data makes explicit guarantees.

tempted to give out personal information. These can range from being asked to fill out a form to download some software or sign up for a service on the Web to being asked for your address or phone number through email or a chat group. Any information you put into a form will be passed to a Web server and find its way into a database. Disclosing your street address to a business sometimes results in your receiving junk mail, and disclosing your email address may result in your getting unsolicited junk email, or *spam* as it's called. You can't be sure how the information will be used or marketed unless the organization gathering the data makes some explicit guarantees. We hear about and come across situations of fraudulent practices and schemes that swindle money from unsuspecting individuals in our daily lives, and we're just as likely to come across those types of situations when were using the Internet. It's relatively easy to create an Internet or Web presence that makes an individual, a company, or an organization appear to be legitimate and trustworthy. Because of this we need to be all the more skeptical and cautious when conducting personal or commercial dealings on the Internet.

More dangerous situations can arise when we develop a relationship with someone through email or a chat group. These can arise because when we're communicating with someone on the Internet most of the communication is through text. We don't get to hear the person's voice or see them. We may see a picture, they may tell us about them, but we may never know with whom we are communicating. For example, I may be involved in a long series of email messages or have several conversations in a chat room with a person who claims to be my age and gender. The person may even send me a photograph. It could be that the person is totally misrepresenting their true self. So we need to be very careful about giving out any personal information, and we certainly wouldn't make arrangements to meet the person without having the meeting take place in a public location and without taking other precautions.

Children particularly need to discuss these issues with their parents, and they need to understand clearly stated rules about not giving out any personal information or telling someone where they go to school or play. The Web page "Staying Street Smart on the Web," **http://www.yahooligans.com/docs/safety**, is a good place to find information about Internet safety issues for children and parents.

Common sense tells us not to give out personal information, home phone numbers, or home addresses to people we don't know. We're likely not to do that in our daily lives when we don't know the person who is asking for the information, and it's just as important to apply the same rules when we're using the Internet or the World Wide Web. The Internet and the Web give us lots of opportunities for learning, recreation, and communication. We don't need to be rude or unfriendly, but we do need to be careful, safe, and secure.

Summary

The Internet has had a tradition of sharing. This includes sharing data, sharing services, exchanging email, having free and generally open discussions, and bringing together ideas and opinions from a diverse population. The rules for behavior, policies for acceptable use, and laws pertaining to activities on the Internet have developed over time. In some cases policies and laws have been adopted from other media, and in other cases the unique qualities of the Internet and electronic communications have been taken into account in establishing laws and policies.

During the transmission of information on the Internet, the information or communication is divided into packets of bytes (characters) that are sent from one system to another. The packets may pass through several different systems, may take different routes to arrive at a destination, and transmissions from one site to another may take different routes at different times. This opens the possibility for intercepting and examining email or other transmissions. Be careful about what you say in email, and think about using encryption techniques so that only the recipient can read the email. Laws such as the Electronic Communications Privacy Act (ECPA) have been adopted in some countries to ensure the privacy of electronic communications. The ECPA makes it illegal to intercept or read other people's email and requires that government officials obtain a warrant or court order before searching, seizing, or intercepting electronic communications. Laws regulating slander, libel, threats, and harassment deal with electronic communications as well.

The Internet has grown very rapidly, with a sharp increase in the number of users and a change in the makeup of that population. It continues to become more inclusive, representing users from different countries, cultures, and work groups. This causes some strains between some groups of users and others whose actions seem contrary to past acceptable modes of behavior. For example, in the past the Internet was almost free of commercial transactions, and now commercial uses are condoned and encouraged.

In most cases, the information available on the Internet is the intellectual property of someone or some organization and is protected by copyright laws. Check to see if there are any copyright notices on information. Some of it can be shared in an electronic form, provided the author is given credit and it's not modified. Problems arise because it's so easy to make copies of information available in electronic form. There are very few, if any, ways to know whether a copy has been made. This issue needs to be resolved. Some suggest using methods of encryption to protect against unauthorized copying or dissemination.

Internet security is an important issue for a variety of reasons, including an individual's desire for privacy, the increased use of the Internet for commercial transactions, and the need to maintain the integrity of data. If you access the Internet by logging into a computer system, you need to take care to choose a password that will be difficult to guess. Furthermore, you should notice and report any unusual circumstances or modifications.

The Internet is an important place to learn, work, and enjoy yourself. Some of its strengths have come from the diversity in the user population because there is no central control and because there is two-way access. If you can receive information, you can produce information! The Internet has been relatively free of regulation, but it has codes of ethics and acceptable use policies to make it a reasonable and safe place for a variety of activities. As the Internet grows and changes, it needs to maintain its sources of strength and vitality. Whether it will maintain its character will depend on the concerns and actions of its users. ✦

Selected Terms in this Chapter

cache
civil liberties
cookie
cracker

Electronic Communications
  Privacy Act (ECPA)
firewall
history list

privacy
spam
Trojan horse
virus

These exercises are all small projects. They're meant to give you some focus in thinking about the issues raised in this chapter and to involve you in accessing some Internet sites and resources appropriate to the topics in this chapter.

Acceptable Use Policies

1. a. Does your organization have a statement of policies or procedures for acceptable use of the Internet?

   b. If your answer to part a was yes, get a copy of that policy and read it. Which of the policies would you recommend be changed? Explain your answer.

   c. If your organization doesn't have a policy, then list three or more items you think ought to be in such a policy.

2. Several sites on the Internet have copies of acceptable use policies. You can browse through a list for schools (K–12) by using the URL **gopher://riceinfo.rice.edu:1170/11/More/Acceptable**. Retrieve or browse two of those policies.

   a. How do these policies compare with each other?

   b. What changes would you recommend making to either of the policy statements?

3. Retrieve a copy of "User Guidelines and Net Etiquette," **http://www.fau.edu/rinaldi/netiquette.html**, by Arlene Rinaldi. Go to the section "The Net: User Guidelines and Netiquette-Index." You'll see it contains guidelines for working with several types of Internet services. Pick one service you've worked with and compare the guidelines in that document with your behavior and experience.

Organizations

4. Use your Web browser to look at the online resources available from the Electronic Frontier Foundation.

   a. Describe the home page for the EFF, **http://www .eff.org**.

b. The home page has a hyperlink, **Major Archive Topics**, under the heading More Info, which takes you to a list of other resources. Follow the hyperlinks **Computers and Academic Freedom** and **Net Culture & Online Community**. Write a synopsis of what's available by following those hyperlinks.

c. Follow the hyperlink **Groups & Organizations** and see what you can find out about two organizations, ones that aren't affiliated with the EFF. Determine the mission and aims of those organizations.

5. Use the URL for the EFF's FTP archives, **http://www.eff .org/pub**. You'll see several subdirectories listed. Pick a topic in the area of privacy, civil liberties, or legislation. Using the Internet resources available through that site, write a short paper or create a Web page about any of those topics.

6. Take a look at the home page for the Electronic Privacy Information Center (EPIC), **http://www.epic.org**.

a. What are some of the latest items listed on the home page? Follow a couple of hyperlinks and describe what you find.

b. Follow the hyperlink to the **EPIC Online Guide to Privacy Resources** List the names of five international privacy sites. Follow a hyperlink to one of the sites and describe what's available at that site.

7. The EFF and Computer Professionals for Social Responsibility (CPSR) both have resources available on the World Wide Web. The URL for the CPSR home page is **http:// www.cpsr.org**.

a. Retrieve or browse statements for each organization that give its mission and aims. Write a brief summary, at most one page, comparing the two organizations and giving differences between the two.

b. If you were to join one, which would it be? Explain.

Privacy and Security

8. Retrieve "Identity, Privacy, and Anonymity on the Internet" by L. Detweiler, from the site mentioned in the text. Using the information in that document, answer the following.
   a. What was the Steve Jackson Games case?
   b. What are cypherpunks?

9. List at least five antivirus rules or guidelines for users. Be sure to state your resource(s) for the rules. *Hint:* Some places to look are:
   - "Anti-Virus Information"
     http://www-tec.open.ac.uk/casg/avone.html
   - "Frequently Asked Questions on Virus-L/ comp.virus"
     http://www.ezweb.net/dmuth/virus/ vlfaq200.html
   - "Only YOU can prevent computer virus infections"
     http://www.av.ibm.com/3-1/CoverStory/

10. One of the more popular antivirus programs is F-PROT, and there's a free version available from Data Fellows at **http://www.datafellows.com**. Follow the link **Virus & Security Info** from the home page and then the link **Other sources of computer virus information in the net (FAQs, links, etc)**. What FAQs are available? Several of the entries represent information in different parts of the world. Which countries are represented? Follow one of the links to a country different from the one you're living in. Write a brief description of what you find at that site.

11. The Web site for The Coalition Against Unsolicited Commercial Email (CAUCE), **http://www.cauce.org**, includes a discussion of the issues of dealing with junk email or spam. Take a look at the Web site and write a two- or three-page paper that states the major issues and proposed remedies to the situation.

12. The Web page "Email Privacy," **http://www2.ncsu.edu/ eos/info/computer_ethics/www/privacy** has a number of links to information about email privacy. It's very well organized and is part of a Web site put together by students at North Carolina State University under the direction of Professor Edward Gehringer. Write a two- or three-page paper that identifies the major issues associated with email privacy and lists some ways of ensuring privacy. Use at least two sources from the Web page "Email Privacy."

GLOSSARY

acceptable use policy

A policy statement from a network or organization giving the acceptable uses of the network for local use and accessing the Internet.

Advanced Research Projects Agency (ARPA)

A U.S. Department of Defense agency that is now called the Defense Advanced Research Projects Agency (DARPA). ARPA funded the development of the Internet's predecessor, ARPANET, and the protocols that made the global infrastructure of the Internet possible.

agent

A program that gathers information or accomplishes tasks without your immediate presence. Agents are usually given very small and well-defined tasks. They are also called intelligent agents, personal agents, or bots.

all-in-one search tool

A tool that provides search forms for several search engines and directories all in one site. The tool also provides hyperlinks that allow you to go to the services directly.

American Standard Code for Information Interchange (ASCII)

A code for representing characters in a numeric form. An ASCII file is usually one that contains characters that can be displayed on a screen or printed without formatting.

anonymous FTP

A means of using file transfer protocol (FTP) in which a user starts a session with a remote host, gives the user name "anonymous," and uses her or his email address as a password.

attachment

A file that is sent as part of an email message but that is not part of the main message. Images, programs, or word-processing files are usually sent as attachments, because most email programs allow only plain text in the body of messages.

binary file

A file containing information such as a compressed archive, an image, a program, a spreadsheet, or a word-processing document. The items in the file usually cannot be displayed on a screen or printed without using some program.

BinHex

An encoding scheme that converts binary data into ASCII (American Standard Code for Information Interchange) characters.

bookmark list

A list of links to items on the Web. It is usually created by an individual as she or he uses a Web browser. The list is a good way to keep track of favorite or important sites; they are saved and can be used at any time.

Boolean searching

Searching that uses Boolean operators (AND, OR, and NOT) in the search expression. Especially helpful with multifaceted or precise topics, Boolean operators help expand or narrow the scope of a search. A search for **rivers OR lakes** returns documents with either word in them. A search for **rivers AND lakes** returns documents with both words in them. A search for **rivers AND lakes NOT swamps** returns documents that mention both rivers and lakes but omits those that also mention swamps.

bot

See *agent*.

cache

A portion of memory (either in RAM or on a disk) set aside to hold the items retrieved most recently. In Netscape Navigator, it refers to recent Web pages and images. It's used because retrieving items from the cache is faster than downloading from the Internet. Netscape can be set so that if an item hasn't changed, it will be retrieved automatically from the cache.

case sensitivity

The ability of a search engine to distinguish between upper- and lowercase letters. Some search engines aren't case sensitive; no matter what you type the search engine picks up lowercase matches only. Search engines that are case sensitive will strictly follow the search request and return documents that contain the search expression in the case in which it was typed in.

civil liberties

The rights or freedoms of an individual in a society. In the U.S. these include the rights of free expression, freedom of movement and association, freedom from unwarranted search and seizure, and freedom of religion.

client/server

Describes the way most Internet services operate. A client program sends commands to and receives information from a corresponding program at a remote site called a server. Telnet, for example, works this way. A user starts a client program on a computer which contacts a Telnet server.

concept searching

The ability of a search engine's indexing program to determine synonyms of the words in its database; when you type in a word or phrase the engine automatically adds the synonyms to the search. For example, if the word **teenage** were in your search expression, the search engine would also look for the word **adolescent**.

content area

The part of a Web browser window that contains the current Web page; it can contain images, text, or hyperlinks.

cookie

A mechanism for transmitting the name of a server and data about a client between a Web server and a Web client or browser. Netscape invented the term and developed the method for working with cookies. The collection of cookies on a computer is kept in a file named **cookies.txt**. A Web server writes a cookie to your computer only if you access a Web page that commands it to do that.

cracker

An individual who gains unauthorized access to a computer system.

decode

To recreate a file in binary format that has been encoded or translated from binary to ASCII or text format. Binary files that are sent as attachments to emails have to be encoded (translated from binary to ASCII) before they can be sent and have to be decoded (translated from ASCII to binary) before they can be received and used.

directory

Topical lists of Internet resources, arranged hierarchically. Directories are meant to be browsed, but they can also be searched. Directories differ from search engines in one major way—the human element involved in collecting and updating the information.

domain name

The Internet name for a network or computer system. The name consists of a sequence of characters separated by periods such as **www.mwc.edu**.

download

To transfer a file from a remote computer to a local computer.

duplicate detection

An output feature of some search engines and meta-search tools that automatically filters out duplicate URLs from a list of search results.

Electronic Communications Privacy Act (ECPA)

The U.S. law that prevents U.S. agencies from intercepting or reading email messages without first obtaining a warrant.

email

Electronic mail. A basic Internet service that allows users to exchange messages electronically.

encode

To translate a file from binary to ASCII (American Standard Code for Information Interchange) format. This is done so the file can be sent via email.

encryption

A procedure to convert a file from its original form to one that can only be read by the intended recipient.

field

A field is a part of a Web page or bibliographic record that is designated for a particular kind of data or text.

field searching

The ability to limit a search to a particular field. For example, in some search engines, you can search only the URL field, title field, or any other data element that was designated as a field. Field searching helps to reduce the retrieval of irrelevant information by narrowing the scope of searchable items.

file compression

The use of an algorithm or scheme to compress or shrink a file. A file in compressed form must first be uncompressed or transformed before it can be read, displayed, or used. Files available through anonymous FTP are often stored in compressed form and must be treated as binary files.

file transfer protocol (FTP)

A means of transferring or sharing files across the Internet from one computer system to another.

firewall

A security device or system, usually a combination of hardware and software, meant to protect a local network from intruders from the Internet.

frames

Some Web pages are divided into rectangular regions called frames. Each frame has its own scroll bars, and in fact, each frame represents an individual Web page.

freeware

A software program that's available for use without any charge attached. This doesn't mean the program isn't copyrighted; the originator generally retains the copyright. Anyone can use the program, but it can't be legally sold or distributed without permission.

frequently asked questions (FAQ)

A list, often associated with Usenet newsgroups, of commonly asked questions and answers on a specific topic. This is usually the first place users should look to find answers to questions or to get information on a topic.

FTP archive

A collection of files available by anonymous FTP.

FTP client

A program that sends or retrieves files from an FTP server.

full-text searching

A feature of most search engines that indexes every word, significant or not, in Web pages.

Gopher

A menu-oriented system that gives access to documents, files, and other Internet services, regardless of where they are on the Internet. The software for Gopher was created and developed at the University of Minnesota to allow users to browse and retrieve documents in a campus environment.

helper application

A program used with a Web browser to display, view, or work with files that the browser cannot display. For example, graphic or image files in GIF or JPEG format can be displayed by Netscape Navigator. If an image file of another type were accessed through a hyperlink, then a helper application would be necessary to display it. As another example, Web browsers can work with several protocols but not with Telnet, so a Telnet client, separate from the Web browser, has to be used. Web browsers include ways of being configured to recognize when to use specific helper applications.

hierarchy

A list of subjects in a directory organized into successive ranks with the broadest subject listed first, with more specific aspects or subdivisions of the subject listed beneath it.

high precision/high recall

The optimum search result: all the relevant documents in a database are retrieved, and every document retrieved is relevant.

high precision/low recall

This results in a very small set of hits from a search, and while each one may be very relevant to the search topic, some relevant documents will be missed.

history list

A list of Internet sites, services, and resources which have been accessed through a WWW browser to arrive at the current item.

home page

The screen or page that displays when a Web browser is opened.

HTML editor

A program that's used to create or modify the source for a Web page using only text and HTML tags. An editor often has items you can select from a menu or toolbar to insert or modify HTML tags.

HTML tag

A code used in HTML that identifies an element so that a Web browser will know how to display it.

hyperlink

Words, phrases, images, or regions of an image that often are highlighted or appear in a different color and can be selected as part of a WWW page. Each hyperlink represents another Web page; a location in the current Web page; an image, audio, video, or multimedia file; or some other resource on the World Wide Web. When selected, the resource represented by the hyperlink is activated.

hypermedia

An extension of hypertext to include graphics and audio.

hypertext

A way of viewing or working with documents in text format that allows a user to follow cross-references and return to previously viewed documents. This presents a nonlinear means of dealing with text and is accomplished through a computer interface to text.

hypertext markup language (HTML)

The format used for writing documents to be viewed with a Web browser. Items in the document can be text, images, sounds, or links to other HTML documents, sites, services, and resources on the Internet.

hypertext transfer protocol (HTTP)

The protocol used by Web servers and clients to communicate.

implied Boolean operators

The characters + and - used to require or prohibit a word or phrase as part of a search expression. The + acts like AND and the - acts like NOT. For example, the Boolean expression **rivers AND lakes NOT swamps** may be expressed as **+rivers +lakes -swamps**.

Internet

A collection of worldwide networks that agree to communicate using specific telecommunication protocols, the most basic being Internet protocol (IP) and transmission control protocol (TCP). It also refers to the services supplied by those networks.

Internet message access protocol (IMAP)

A protocol used to retrieve email from a mail server. It is similar to POP3, but has more features.

Internet Network Information Center (InterNIC)

Established by NSFNET in 1993 to handle domain name registration, information services, and directory services. InterNIC now handles domain name registration only.

Internet protocol (IP)

The basic protocol used for the Internet. IP puts information (including the sender's and recipient's addresses) in a single packet and then sends it. The receiving system removes the information from the packet.

keyword indexing

A feature of some search engines that indexes significant words in a document or record.

limiting by date

The ability of a search tool to limit search results to pages that were indexed after, before, or between certain dates.

low precision/high recall

This is a phenomenon that occurs when you retrieve a large set of results from a search request with many unwanted documents included.

mail user agent

The software used to access and manage a user's electronic mail. Examples are Pine and Eudora.

menu bar

The series of pull-down menus across the top of the Web browser window. All commands are accessible through the menu bar.

meta-search tool

A tool that either allows you to search more than one search engine or directory simultaneously, or lists search tools that can be accessed from that site. These two major types of meta-search tools are called parallel search tools and all-in-one search tools.

meta-tag

A keyword that is inserted in the meta-tag portion of an HTML source document by its author. Meta-tags help a Web page that doesn't have much text come up in a keyword search.

modification of search results

The process of changing an initial search expression to get more relevant results. This can involve searching the results by field, limiting by date, adding keywords, subtracting keywords, and more.

Multipurpose Internet Mail Extensions (MIME)

Extensions to standard email programs that make it easy to send, receive, and include nontext files.

nested Boolean logic

The use of parentheses in search expressions using Boolean operators. For example, the nested expression ((**rivers AND lakes**) **OR canoeing**) **NOT camping** will first find resources that contain both of the terms **rivers** and **lakes**, then add those that contain the term **canoeing**, and then omit resources that contain the term **camping**.

NSFNET

A network established by the National Science Foundation in 1986 to connect five supercomputer centers in the U.S. and provide connectivity to the Internet primarily for colleges and universities. The main traffic on the Internet was turned over to interconnected network providers in 1995.

parallel search tool

A search tool or service that takes one search expression, submits it to several search services, and returns selected results from each. This is an example of a meta-search tool.

personal home page

A Web page used by an individual to give personal and/or professional information.

phrase searching
The search feature supported by most search engines that allows you to search for words that appear next to each other. It may be the most useful search feature.

plug-in
An application that's used along with a Web browser to view or display certain types of files as part of a Web page. Shockwave from Macromedia is a plug-in that allows a browser to display interactive multimedia.

point-to-point protocol (PPP)
A protocol that allows a computer with a modem to communicate using TCP/IP.

post office protocol (POP)
The way many email programs retrieve messages from a mail server. Email is delivered on the Internet to the mail server, and the email program running on a personal computer retrieves that email through POP.

privacy
The notion of personal information such as email being hidden from the view of people other than intended recipients.

protocol
A set of rules or procedures for exchanging information between networks or computer systems.

proximity searching
A search feature that makes it possible for you to search for words that are near each other in a page.

reference work
A resource used to find quick answers to questions. Traditionally thought of as being in the form of books (such as dictionaries, encyclopedias, quotation directories, manuals, guides, atlases, bibliographies, and indexes), a reference source on the World Wide Web closely resembles its print counterpart. A reference book doesn't necessarily contain hyperlinks to other resources, although it will often have hyperlinks to places within the document itself.

relevance
A measure of how closely a database entry matches a search request. Most search tools on the Web return results based on relevance. The specific algorithm for computing relevance varies from one service to another, but it's often based on the number of times the terms in the search expression appear in the document and whether they appear in appropriate fields.

relevancy ranking
A ranking of results (items retrieved from a database) based on the relevance score assigned by a search engine.

results per page
A search output feature of some search engines that allows you to choose how many results are listed per page. Search engines usually list 10 results per page.

robot
See *spider*.

search engine
In the context of the Web, a program that seeks out, visits, and indexes URLs. The resulting index is searched for keywords or phrases entered by a user. The engine returns hyperlinks to pages whose description, title, or content match the search words.

search expression
The keywords and syntax that you enter into a search form. With an expression, you can ask a search tool to seek relevant documents in a particular way.

search form
The rectangular pane or oblong box that appears on the home pages of most search tools. In this space, you enter a search expression.

serial line Internet protocol (SLIP)
Software allowing the use of Internet protocol (IP) over a serial line or through a serial port. It is commonly used with a modem connection to an Internet service provider.

server
A computer that shares resources with other computers on the Internet. In the context of

Internet services, a server is a computer system or program that provides information to other programs called clients. When a user starts a Web browser she starts a client program, which contacts a Web server program.

shareware

Software that you are allowed to download and try for a specified period free of charge. If you want to legally use the program after that time, you are expected to pay a usually modest fee.

signature

An optional portion of an email message often consisting of information about the sender such as full name, mailing address, phone number, etc. A signature is stored in a file and is automatically included with each message.

simple mail transfer protocol (SMTP)

The Internet standard protocol used to transfer email from one computer system to another.

sorting

An option in some search engines that allows you to determine how you'd like your search results listed: by URL, relevance, domain or location, date, etc.

spam

Unwanted and unsolicited email. The electronic equivalent of paper junk mail.

specialized database

A self-contained index that is searchable and available on the Web. Items in specialized databases are often not accessible through a keyword search in a search engine.

spider

A computer program locates such resources as Web documents, FTP archives, and Gopher documents on the Internet. It indexes the documents in a database, which is then searched using a search engine (such as AltaVista or Excite). A spider can also be referred to as a robot or wanderer. Each search engine uses a spider to build its database.

status bar

The bar or rectangular region at the bottom of the browser window that shows several items of information regarding the transfer of a Web document to the browser. When the mouse is moved over a hyperlink it shows the URL for the hyperlink; when a Web page is requested it gives information about contacting and receiving information from a server; during transmission it tells, in terms of a percentage, how much of the document has been transferred and indicates whether transmissions are being carried on in a secure manner.

stop words

These are words that an indexing program doesn't index.

Usually stop words include articles (a, an, the) and other common words that appear often.

subject category

A division in a hierarchical subject classification system in a Web directory. You click on the subject category that is likely to contain either the Web pages you want or other subject categories that are more specific.

subject guide

A collection of URLs on a particular topic. Most easily found in virtual libraries, they are also referred to as meta-pages.

syntax

The rules governing the construction of search expressions in search engines and directories.

Telnet

Allows for remote login capabilities on the Internet. It is one of the three basic Internet services. A user on one computer on the Internet can access and log in to another computer.

text editor

A program that's used to create or modify a file that contains only plain text. This may be used to create or modify the source file for a Web page.

text file

A file containing characters in a plain format. There are no formatting commands such as underlining or displaying characters in boldface or different fonts. It is also called an ASCII file.

toolbar
The sequence of icons below the menu bar. Clicking on an icon executes a command.

top-level category
One of several main subjects that occurs in the top of a hierarchy in a directory's list of subjects.

transmission control protocol (TCP)
A protocol used as the basis of most Internet services. It is used in conjunction with Internet protocol to allow for reliable process-to-process communication.

transmission control protocol/Internet protocol (TCP/IP)
A collection of protocols used to provide the basis for Internet and World Wide Web services.

Trojan horse
A program that appears to be legitimate but contains in its code instructions that cause damage to the systems on which it runs.

unified search interfaces
Meta-search tools that allow you to use several search engines simultaneously.

Uniform Resource Locator (URL)
A way of describing the location of an item (document, service, or resource) on the Internet and also specifying the means by which to access that item.

upload
To transfer a file from the computer system being used to a remote system.

uudecode
A program to recreate binary files from the ASCII or text formto which they were converted by uuencode. Used by someone who has received a file or email in uuencode form.

uuencode
A program to convert binary data into ASCII form. It is necessary for sending binary files on some email systems. Uuencode is used to send binary files on email systems without MIME.

virtual library
A directory that contains collections of resources that librarians or "cybrarians" have carefully chosen and organized in a logical way.

virus
A program or executable code, which must be part of another executing program, that changes the configuration or causes havoc with a computer system. Viruses are usually hidden within some useful or standard program.

visual Web page editor
A program that's used to edit or create Web pages. It's visual in the sense that the software makes changes that you see immediately. Some examples of visual Web page editors are Microsoft Word (a word-processing program) and Netscape Composer.

Web browser
A program (software) used to access the Internet services and resources available through the World Wide Web.

Web page
The information available and displayed by a Web browser as the result of opening a local file or a URL. The contents and format of a Web page are specified with HTML.

Web page source
The text file that contains the HTML tags for a Web page. A browser reads the source for a Web page from this file and then, using the HTML tags, displays the Web page.

wildcard
A character that stands in for another character or group of characters. In most search tools, it is an asterisk. While a wildcard is most often used with truncation, it can also be used in the middle of words (e.g., **wom*n**).

World Wide Web (WWW)
The collection of different services and resources available on the Internet and accessible through a Web browser.

INDEX

403 forbidden, 47
404 not found, 47

A

acceptable use policies, 26
Advanced Research Projects
  Agency (ARPA), 25
.aiff, 186
all-in-one search tool, 128
AltaVista, 147–51
  advanced search mode,
    147–51
  Boolean searching, 148–50
American Standard Code for
  Information Interchange
  (ASCII), 84, 169, 194
Andreesson, Marc, 27
anonymous FTP, 223–29
  downloading a file, 225
antivirus software, 232
ARPANET, 26
.au, 186
author's comments (HTML
  tags), 175

B

background (HTML tags),
  188–90
basic search strategy, 145–48
  formulating, 148–49
Berners-Lee, Tim, 27
Bina, Eric, 27
BinHex, 84
body (HTML tags), 174
bookmark, 43, 60–66
  adding, 60, 62
  deleting, 61,63
  folders, 64–66
bookmark list, 47, 60–66
  jumping to an item in, 61
  searching, 61

Boolean operators, 141–42
  implied, 142
Boolean searching, 127–28
  nested, 148–50
browser, 2–3, 9, 37–38
  configuring for Telnet, 217
  home page, 36
  preferences, 40, 48, 66
  starting, 37
  stopping, 38
  viewing a local file, 59

C

case sensitivity, 144
character formatting (HTML
  tags), 176–77
civil liberties, 256
  unwarranted search and
    seizure, 260–61
client/server, 10, 21
Coalition Against Unsolicited
  Commercial Email
  (CAUCE), 263–64
component bar, 44
compression, 230–31
computer crime, 260–61
concept searching, 144
content area, 44
cookie, 259–60
copying and pasting, 40
copyright, 25, 264–65
cracker, 266

D

decoding, 84
default setting, 127, 141
descriptive list (HTML tags),
  179–80
directory, 111–20
  Infoseek, 156–59
  strengths, 114–15

Other Titles from Franklin, Beedle & Associates

INTERNET

Searching & Researching on the Internet & the World Wide Web
Ernest Ackermann and Karen Hartman

Web Essentials
Ernest Ackermann and Karen Hartman

Learning to Use the World Wide Web: Academic Edition
Ernest Ackermann

The Web Page Workbook: Academic Edition
Dawn Groves

OPERATING SYSTEMS

Windows 95: Concepts & Examples
Carolyn Z. Gillay

Windows 98: Concepts & Examples
Carolyn Z. Gillay

Windows User's Guide to DOS: Using the Command Line in Windows 95/98
Carolyn Z. Gillay and Bette A. Peat

DOS 6 Fundamentals
Carolyn Z. Gillay

DOS 6 Principles with Practice
Carolyn Z. Gillay

SOFTWARE

Microsoft Office 97 Professional: A Mastery Approach
Patricia L. Sullivan

Access 97 for Windows: Concepts & Examples
Patricia L. Sullivan

Excel 97 for Windows: Concepts & Examples
Karen Jolly

COMPUTER SCIENCE

Computing Fundamentals with C++: Object-Oriented Programming and Design 2nd edition
Rick Mercer

EDUCATION & REFERENCE

The Dictionary of Computing and Digital Media: Terms and Acronyms
Brad Hansen

Technology Tools in the Social Studies Curriculum
Joseph A. Braun, Jr., Phyllis Fernlund, and Charles S. White